In Morocco

Faith Mellen Willcox

IN MOROCCO

Harcourt Brace Jovanovich, Inc., New York

First edition

ISBN 0–15–144410–2

Library of Congress Catalog Card Number: 74-142101

Printed in the United States of America

A B C D E

For my husband,
whom I am happy to owe so much

Contents

Illustrations

Preface

This book grows out of three visits to Morocco in 1965 and 1966. My purpose is to introduce the general reader to a country long outside the stream of European civilization but now closely involved with the West, and what I offer here is one individual set of perceptions and the questions they raised in my mind. Recognizing that even scholars and specialists are at times confounded by the contradictions and information gaps common to developing countries and so are slow to speak of "hard facts," I have tried to avoid flat statements. I hope any errors I may have made will not obscure the broader truths I have tried to present.

My thanks are due to many people both in and outside of Morocco who helped us establish contacts there. If some in the higher echelons of government stuck rather closely to the official view while speaking with us, all were willing to pass us on to those responsible at the local level. It was here that we met the greatest openness. We were surprised by how few people bothered to inquire why we were poking about in their country; perhaps a healthy egoism convinced them that nothing was more natural than for us to find their problems absorbing. I hope our interest may have afforded them a momentary lightening of their burdens.

Men of the opposition, in talking freely with us, have put me under the obligation to disguise them beyond any possibility of identification. None of them, I think, would recognize himself, since most of my characters are composites. Those within the regime who are positively identified—the Cherifa of Ouezzane, the Governor of Fez, Messrs. Bennouna and Messaoudi, etc.—I have tried to quote faithfully.

I am grateful to many who are in no way responsible for what I have written, in particular to Professors Rémy Leveau, Richard Mitchell, William Schorger, and John Waterbury; to Robert Lapham and Mohammed Guessous, who were generous with ideas and with their time; and to Jim and Sue Bernstein for their lively contribution. I would especially thank my daughter, Molly Willcox, for a careful and sensitive reading of the manuscript.

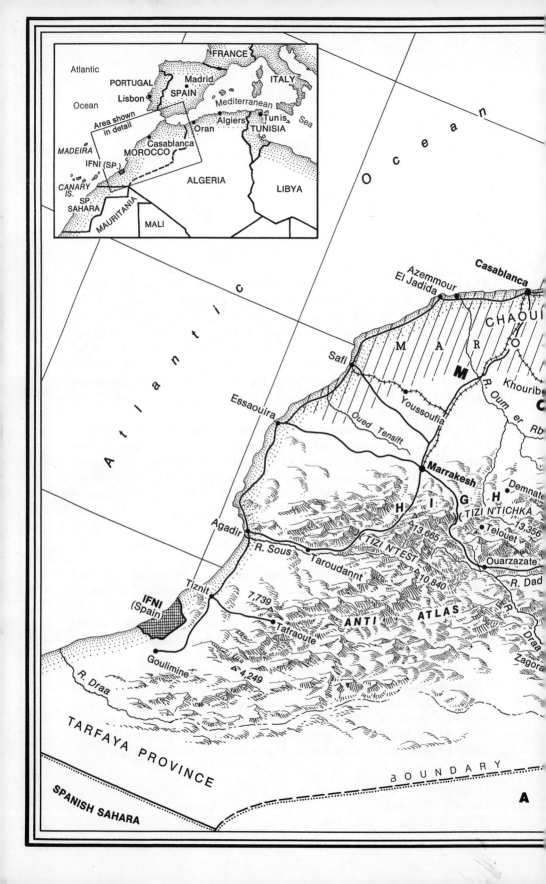

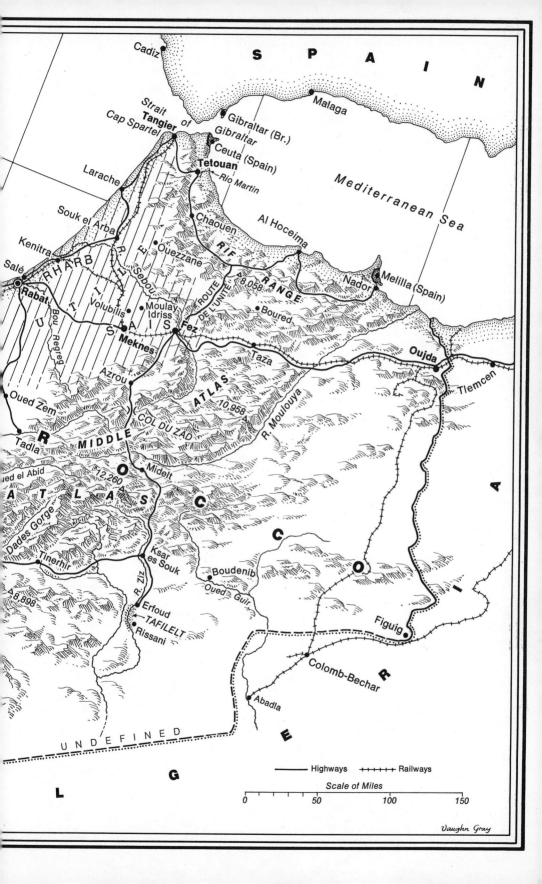

In Morocco

THE TRAVELERS

*He who knows only his own country is like a man who reads
but the first chapter of a book.*—SAINT AUGUSTINE

It is not often that a saint can enjoin upon the rest of us something so compatible with our desires as travel. But he would require of us an exacting kind of travel—an exercise in seeing the familiar and the foreign illumined by each other. Even if the whole book is now too large for the span of our lives, we can but read while we may. I feel quite sure that in studying Morocco, I have been learning about my own country; and that in listening to Moroccan voices, I have also been hearing voices of men and women everywhere, facing the new occasions and new perplexities of our time.

My taste for travel was formed early. As a child growing up in Manhattan, I ogled the world from the wonderful, lost-forever Third Avenue Elevated Railway. It was an enthralling way to learn. I saw scenes unfold, almost at my fingertips as the train rattled slowly by, that opened vistas to me: a huge, deep-bosomed woman lighting a candle before an ikon on her wall . . . a child of my own age, deftly rifling the pockets of men peering at a peep show . . . a couple screaming at each other in a frenzy that must surely lead to murder, then breaking off to fall passionately into each other's arms. I would come home, moody and preoccupied, wanting to be left alone to ruminate. I was finding travel broadening.

The history book deemed suitable for children posed more questions. It was pompous about Charles Martel's "heroic stand against the Moors," but did not explain why everyone was so down on the Moors—unless it was because they invaded Europe and were not Christians. My imagination now invested the "savage hordes" with the darkling colors of valor and poetry. At about the same time, the strange name of Abd el Krim was much on adults' lips. Here was another Moor, I gathered, and his successes made people frown. Was he a modern Othello, then? My mind conjured up the towering black figure of Paul Robeson as the Great Moor, and I thought I heard again that organ voice.

There followed for me a long period divided between this country and Europe, and this at a time when the two worlds were far more disjoined than they are now. Passing often from one to the other, I became used to being a stranger in both, and learned to solace the pangs of not-belonging with the secret pleasures of observing and wondering. The world, I discovered, affords more than one way of being and behaving.

Luckily for me, the man I married is another committed wanderer and wonderer. At the time of my present account, Bill was a professor of English history at the University of Michigan. When, in 1963, a sabbatic leave was in sight but still at that delectable distance when any possibility is food for day-dreams, we were also confronting a brand-new family circumstance: two of our children were married, and the youngest was in college and sailing a tight breeze on her own. We were savoring for the first time that bittersweet flavor of shrunken family obligations. Bill had just completed two books, was temporarily free of research commitments, and felt the need of new stimuli and new perspectives. It looked like the right time to satisfy his lifelong hankering to visit the Near East.

If I have not already betrayed it, I will admit to a bias in favor of the "free-wheeling" style of travel—unsupervised, loosely scheduled, limited in range, and open to the greatest possible number of one-to-one encounters. There are, I know, places and times when a guided tour is the safest, most convenient, and perhaps the only practical way to travel. There are occasions when a professional guide is a necessity. But whenever it is at all possible (as in Morocco), I ardently prefer to explore unchaperoned. Knowing, of course, that I will make mistakes, sometimes be diddled, often act clumsily and appear in an unflattering light, still I would much rather try it, risking "Montezuma's revenge" or the "North African Quickstep," and many another vicissitude, just on the chance of meeting, really meeting, some members of a new branch of the family. It is much easier to make a friend when you are vulnerable. Too many of us fear the shaking-up and all those shocks of strangeness that are among the great values of travel. I think we might be wiser to fear the Hiltonizing or homogenizing of our experience through being too protected. I am afraid of group tours, afraid of the passivity they encourage, and fear that their tight scheduling and rapid sweeps are making inroads on a precious birthright of us all—lively and persistent curiosity.

The language barrier deters people more than it should, especially Americans. Gesture is an effective language, and is apt to elicit good will. Contrary to the usual belief, freewheelers do not require money or even time in abundance. We met a Kansas insurance man and his wife in Marrakesh. They had three weeks' vacation in all, and had allotted one week apiece to three Moroccan cities. They had read some books before the journey, and carried a French dictionary. Their eyes were keen and their comments perceptive. Later, on the banks of the Jordan River, we ran into two middle-aged couples from

Birmingham, England. They had parked their home-built campers in a willow grove, and a tumult of dogs and children boiled about the camping area. One of the women told us that this was their second overland trip to India; this time they were to cross the great salt desert of Persia, in company with the second vehicle for safety's sake. This woman, with her skirt still hiked up from wading in the Jordan, stood with us and followed our gaze out over the fearful landscape at the head of the Dead Sea, where the caves of Qumran had yielded up the Scrolls. She laid a hand on my arm and said: "It fair gives you to think, luv, don't it?"

I would be foolish to imply that freewheelers automatically acquire deep insight into the country where they travel. And it would be the height of arrogance to suggest that a westerner can readily comprehend an exotic culture. Those who know most about the Muslims are the first to recognize how much more there is to know. I learned this when I began to study. For a year and a half before our projected trip I cashed in on one of the greatest blessings of an academic wife's lot and followed courses on the Michigan campus. I haunted the libraries, with guidance from the staff of our Center for Near Eastern and North African Studies. There was not time enough to get even a little Arabic—it is not a language one can pick up in a few months. Lack of it would be a handicap. But fortunately, Bill and I have serviceable French, the second language of North Africa and most of the Levant.

As I studied, it was Morocco that drew me more and more, until I found myself urging that we begin our journey there. "The Near East is chill and rainy in winter, but Morocco's climate is delicious," I argued disingenuously, and Bill was not hard to persuade. As a child, he had developed a grudge against North Africa. His family, seized by an urge to explore the antique ruins and oases of Algeria, left the baby behind in the care of a loving spinster aunt. So he was condemned to grow up hearing tales of the camel race to Biskra and the white camel foal his sister nearly succeeded in bringing home, of Timgad, the Roman city, and Trajan's arch still standing in a wilderness of sand. All Bill could show for the period were the scars on three fingertips, which he nearly lost in the hinge of his baby carriage. While his brothers told their stories, he would finger the scars and vow someday to even his score with North Africa.

So there were many things that drew us to Morocco. Not the least of them was its multicolored history, shaped in large measure by its position: the point where two continents face each other across nine miles of water. Morocco is almost a land bridge between Europe and Africa. For twenty-two centuries it has belonged to two worlds at once: the African world, whose sub-Saharan riches have been brought to Morocco by caravans snaking their way across the Atlas Mountains; and the Mediterranean world, with its successive conquerors and their dream of an empire encircling Mare Nostrum.

Its mountains have shaped its history in a different way, for they almost create two Moroccos. The first is "Atlantic Morocco," spreading from the feet of the Atlas to the ocean, and sealed off on the north by another mountain range, the Rif. Atlantic Morocco is a rough parallelogram in shape, since the Atlas are inclined on the same axis as the coastline. The climate is tempered by winds from the west, which deposit fair amounts of rain and snow on the western mountain slopes, and there are two major rivers. Though it constitutes only about one-third of the country, Atlantic Morocco has often been the only part the central government could control. The mountains have served as a refuge area for dissidents, too inaccessible to subjugate. While the French occupied the country, from 1912 to 1956, they called the accessible part "Useful Morocco"—thereby implying their opinion of the other two-thirds. Behind the Atlas, the rest of the country lies in a perpetual rain shadow, dependent for irrigation on the seasonal streams that carry down some of the melting snow. These *oueds* can become roaring torrents within a few hours, tearing out bridges, sweeping over roads and carrying away whatever is moving on them. But from May to October, the oueds are dry, rocky channels; the crops planted beside them are reduced to stubble. Near the border with Algeria, the Sahara intrudes a long tongue of desert right up to the Mediterranean.

It is a country of many and abrupt contrasts. Where a dependable river flows, it can create a belt of fertility, heavy with grain and vineyards; only a few miles from the water, the steppe takes over. From the parched, lunar landscape of the eastern Rif you can look across to the forests of the Middle Atlas, where cedars of Lebanon grow to immense heights. Perpetual snow lies on the High Atlas peaks, while, beyond their southern flanks, palm oases can appear with the suddenness of a mirage and just as suddenly yield to the stony desert around them.

Morocco's history is just as full of abrupt changes. Its Mediterranean neighbors have never been able to leave it alone. Carthage implanted trading colonies; Rome swept westward to the Pillars of Hercules; Rome declined, and Morocco felt the heels of Vandals pouring eastward. Byzantine emperors and then Turkish sultans won control of its neighbors but never conquered the Moors. Perhaps there is some truth in the popular saying: "The Tunisians are women; the Algerians are men; but the Moroccans are lions."

In the seventh century came the Arabs. That astonishing irruption out of the Arabian Desert was one of the fastest and farthest-ranging conquests of all history. Within fifty years of the Prophet's death, his servant, Sidi Oqba ben Nafi, drove through Egypt and Libya to establish a base in Tunisia, then continued westward to the shores of Morocco. The story goes that he spurred his mare into the Atlantic and, raising his voice to the sky, called Allah to witness that His realm now extended "to the ends of the earth." A century later, the Arabs had overwhelmed Spain and were pounding on the gates of Tours.

Soon the overextended empire split apart into a number of rival caliphates. In the tenth and eleventh centuries, North Africa was overrun by terrible waves of horsemen fresh from the Arabian peninsula. The great historian Ibn Khaldoun compared the invaders to famished wolves and devouring locusts. Though himself an Arab, he wrote that "any country conquered by Arabs is a ruined country." But in a remarkably short time there arose in Morocco the first of a succession of strong native dynasties which ruled over most of Northwest Africa and Spain, and fostered the brilliance of the Hispano-Moorish empire. From the twelfth century to the end of the fifteenth, the gifts of Arabs, Jews, Moors, and Spaniards were mingled in a great civilization.

This empire brought Europe, among other things, the orange, cane sugar, rice, and cotton. It taught Europe irrigation, the concept of zero, and advanced astronomy. Then Ferdinand and Isabella, having reconquered Spain, expelled 150,000 Sephardic Jews and all the Muslims who would not convert. These refugees crossed the Straits and enriched Morocco with their skills and learning. But the cutting of the ties to Europe began that long isolation of Morocco that came to an end only in the French protectorate of 1912.

There were a few brief periods during that long isolation when Moorish civilization revived. But none of the great movements of Europe spanned the Straits. No humanism born of the Renaissance came in to modify the rigid scholasticism of religion and learning. No Reformation or Age of Enlightenment eroded the theocratic power of the sultan, who was pope and emperor in one. The absolute authority believed to reside in him was not contested; nor did men entertain even the idea of the consent of the governed. When a lax sultan too greatly abused his power, he was simply assassinated, and a new sultan was raised to the throne. While modern states were being born in Europe, along with the institutions that could support stable governments, in Morocco great feudal barons, called *caïds,* continued to war with one another and exercise the power of life and death over serfs and slaves. Insurgency and separatism prolonged the feudal pattern for four hundred years after it had disappeared in Europe. No Industrial Revolution came to bury the Middle Ages.

The towns were small—congeries of twisted lanes and densely packed houses clustered about palaces and marketplaces. You can see them almost unchanged today in the ancient *medinas.* (*Medina* means simply "city.") The French did not disturb the old towns; they just built their *villes nouvelles* adjacent to them. The people were largely rural, as three-quarters of them still are today; and only now are the bonds of tribal organization breaking up. In the cities, Arab merchants built great fortunes from the caravan trade and from the wide market that Morocco enjoyed during her periods of greatness. Manchester, for instance, regularly had its colony of Moroccan agents.

An expanding mercantile Europe was not likely to ignore the wealth to be wrested from Morocco. With guile and with acumen, the great maritime powers of the West began their penetration. From the sixteenth century to the beginning of the twentieth, the economic infiltration gradually undermined both the sultans' wealth and their power to maintain order. (It must be added that the wealth was usually extorted and the power despotic.) The West was glad to make loans—sometimes the rate of usury was 100 per cent—and when the restless caïds didn't overturn a sultan, bankruptcy often did. In 1912, the Sultan was not only bankrupt but besieged in his palace at Fez by furious armies of tribesmen. He called on the French to rescue him, and the curtain rose on the forty-four-year Protectorate and that shadowy subprotectorate called the Spanish Zone.

And the people over whom all these centuries and invasions have flowed? The natives of Northwest Africa are Berbers, about whom ethnologists argue warmly. The incidence of blond hair and blue eyes among Berbers suggests that they may have come from Europe, but now they are more typically brown-skinned, and their language shows no affinity with any European one. Wherever they originated, Africa has probably been their home for more than thirty centuries. They seem in many ways to be members of the Mediterranean family, in looks often very like Spaniards or Greeks. Yet, though their art and folkways are closely related to the Mediterranean culture, they have never been Europeanized. They have accepted alien religions, but have never quite cut off their pagan roots. There was, for example, a young Berber citizen of Carthage in whom the old mysticism and the sturdy, ineradicable sensuality combined; he came under the spell of Rome, converted to Christianity, and described the subsequent struggle in his *Confessions*. We know him as Saint Augustine, Bishop of Hippo.

When the Arabs first reached Morocco, they must have found a still fairly pure Berber type: oval head, almond eyes, delicate features, and light, slender build. But interbreeding must have begun immediately, once Berbers had accepted the Islamic faith, for the conquering Arabs were few and could not have held the natives long in subjection. Both peoples profited. Surely, no other faith could better have suited the Berber warrior soul. Nor could the Arabs have carried Islam into Spain without the convert legions. It was a Berber general, Tariq, who invaded Spain at the head of an army of 12,000. He gave his name to the first mountain he held—Djebel Tariq, or Gibraltar —and plunged on to capture Toledo from the Visigoths.

Though there were both Arab and Berber dynasties in the history of the Moors, the general population was a blend of both races. And both were continually receiving generous admixtures of Black African blood. The caravans brought not only gold from below the desert but also slaves and concubines in great numbers. The black women were highly valued for their "cool skins," especially during the torrid months. So the black contribution to the gene pool was considerable.

The Arabs, in melding with the Berbers, provided them with two unifying factors: the Islamic faith and a common language, Arabic. (There has never been a written Berber language; and then, as now, Berbers spoke different regional dialects.) The Moorish empire provided a political and cultural unity for the whole *Maghreb*—the land now divided into Tunisia, Algeria, and Morocco. But today, this unity has been lost. Though all three countries fell under French rule, and all wrenched free at about the same time, they seem quite unable to make common cause in their joint struggle toward development. Monarchic and conservative Morocco and socialist Algeria eye each other with suspicion, and, a few years ago, went to war over their common boundary. Moderate and republican Tunisia irritates them both. Despite the bitterness of their fight for independence, all three have close economic and cultural ties with France. Algeria alone purports to align itself with the U.S.S.R. and with Egypt. The United States is therefore very busy in the other two. We have a large stake in Morocco—larger every year. Its strategic situation is of great relevance to our concern with the Middle East; we have satellite-communications bases and radar stations scattered throughout the country. Some measure of our interest in Morocco is reflected in our economic assistance: between 1963 and 1965 alone, we contributed over $147 million. More than a hundred Peace Corps Volunteers work there each year.

And so, in 1965, we found in Morocco an ancient country that was only ten years old. We found a people whom the French Protectorate wrenched out of the Middle Ages and left abruptly, unprepared for the modern world. Moroccans drove out the French so that they might recover their Muslim heritage and become once more a nation. Free now, they find that that heritage throws them into uncertainty. They carry their past on their backs, and falter under it as they try to discover who they are today.

After so many months of anticipation, when the time came for our departure, I found myself besieged by doubts. It was January. All at once, home seemed safe, comfortable, and ineffably dear. But it was too late for second thoughts. There in my hands lay thirty pages of plane tickets, promising to take us as far as Persia and back. But it was right here on American soil that vicissitudes lay in wait for us. The weekly through flight from New York to Rabat stops once in Boston, where we went to board it. While we were enjoying a farewell dinner party, a blizzard closed down Logan Airport. We sat among the crumpled napkins while our plane headed straight out to sea from Kennedy.

The next day, we boarded a plane for New York, to connect with a flight to Paris and another to Casablanca. The jet gathered speed down the Boston runway, tipped its nose upward, and then the brakes threw us forward in our seats as we came to a sickeningly sudden halt. Engine trouble. An hour later, the plane was ready again, and the line wired New York to hold our connection and transfer us and our baggage at top speed. We landed in New York and sprang into the aisle, first in line at the exit. The door opened two inches, then jammed. The crew wrestled with it for several minutes before it could be opened. When finally we stood shivering on the airstrip, we found that no one had heard of us or had the least interest in our transfer. I fled in one taxi across the expanses of Kennedy Airport, to hold onto the Paris plane, by force if need be, while Bill stayed to seize our luggage from the belly of this plane and race with it to another taxi. Agonized minutes followed. When I reached the Paris plane they were rolling away the ramp. I waved my ticket at them and pleaded and cajoled until they replaced the ramp. Only then did I tell them that I must find my husband before boarding; whereupon I disappeared before they could protest.

Bill, white from his exertions at the other end, was scrambling out of a taxi when I found him. With a frail-looking, elderly porter in our wake, we began to run again. Panting up the long concourse, I looked over my shoulder to see if the old man was still with us. And then I tripped and fell. Everything burst out of my handbag. The porter's churning legs went by while I re-assembled air tickets, traveler's checks, keys, and passports. When at last I rounded the corner of that nightmare concourse, I saw that the plane was still there.

And that was the way we left home. If it had happened abroad, we might well have said to each other, "This kind of thing could never happen at home."

I sometimes wonder if the romance of long-distance air travel is not for those who are left wistfully behind. Whenever I see someone off from an international airport, I find the atmosphere painfully thrilling. I hear the calls to "Rome, Beirut, Teheran, Bombay," and my feet strain to lift off the ground. A minute later, I watch the great jet gather speed and slant power-fully upward. Like a steeplechaser, it seems to lengthen its neck and gather its forelegs for the climb into the air. In my heart, I pay homage to the wonder of flight, and of speed that contracts distance like a released rubber band. But when I watch the incoming travelers, I find no sign of tingling amazement; they only look numbly at the airport clock and reset their watches.

And when I was myself a passenger, the monotony of that womb existence brought only stupefaction. I tried to reawaken excitement—"I am 30,000 feet above the Atlantic, on my way to Rabat!" It did not work. The plane droned on through a vague cloudland, negligently ripping time and space to shreds. Again I roused momentarily to examine a thought that had come into my head: flies, I have been told, become immune to DDT after repeated ex-posure; had I, too, become shockproof? And wonder-fast? . . . Then I lapsed into the groggy sleep of the helpless airborne.

Only next morning, in Orly Airport, did some zest begin to return as we drank cup after tiny cup of *café exprès,* hot, black, and sweet as sin itself. In a few hours a neat little Caravelle was carrying us over snow-covered Pyrenees. Two swarthy, ill-kempt men in seats directly ahead of us hunched together in their flimsy European suits and spoke to each other in harsh, hawking sounds, as if they had fishbones caught in their throats. One turned and, with a smile that displayed a row of gold teeth, passed back to me his passport. His horny finger stabbed at the red, five-pointed star embossed upon the front, the seal of the Cherifian Empire of Morocco. I handled the passport gingerly, not sure what I was meant to do with it. Getting a nod of encouragement from him I turned the pages and discovered that he had been only a short time in France. I studied the Arabic script, comparing it with the French stamped above it, and guessed that he was part of the labor force that comes seasonally into France to help with one crop or another. I handed the passport back, feeling a little constrained. He was so very swarthy. Only a few minutes later did I realize, with a sudden flush, how I had failed in courtesy. I should have reciprocated his wordless cordiality by giving him my passport to examine. I was disappointed in myself.

Far below us, a crescent of water flashed like a scimitar where the Straits of Gibraltar sliced between the Pillars of Hercules. The men in front were pointing excitedly downward now, eager for the first sight of their country. Bill and I craned our necks to gaze down on the vivid tapestry of greens that was our first glimpse of the Tangier peninsula. We looked at each other in wonder. After the snow and icy winds of yesterday, those tropical greens seemed hardly possible. The men in front watched us, enjoying the pleasure in our eyes. "Maroc!" they exclaimed proudly, and the brilliant teeth gleamed again.

During the flight, I had glanced now and then, and somewhat apprehensively, at an immense shrouded figure sitting at the very front of the plane. He was wrapped in a dark homespun wool garment, with a peaked hood drawn up over his head. He looked from behind rather like a Franciscan monk, except for something very un-Franciscan about his posture. Just now, he rose suddenly and strode down the aisle toward us. The robe was not belted like a monk's; it was the *djellaba,* the Moroccan's traditional outer garment. It was wide and full, and fell free from his shoulders to his feet, accentuating the impressiveness of his burly figure. His stride down the narrow aisle was that of a man who disdains crowded places and lives much of his life outdoors. Involuntarily, I shrank back into my seat, and again was annoyed with myself. Had I come to Morocco to shrink from Moroccans?

In a few more minutes the plane was descending, swinging out over the Atlantic in a wide tilting arc to come in on Casablanca. All was restlessness in the cabin while we taxied in between much larger planes. One was an Aeroflot en route from Accra to Moscow, another a Czechoslovak airliner. So this *is* the Third World we are entering, I said to myself. Our pilot addressed us first in Arabic, then in French, requesting us to remain seated, etc., etc. A moment later, I stepped down out of the plane and into African sunshine, shaking out the raincoat I had not unfolded since we left New York. Now, from its waterproof creases, all that remained of a January blizzard dropped quietly onto Moroccan soil.

CHAPTER TWO

RABAT

There is something different about the Casablanca airport. It is not just the row of veiled women on the roof watching your arrival, nor just the stream of bandy-legged porters released upon you from the low white building ahead. (One of them falls upon you, grabbing the small things you are carrying and assaulting you with the gutturals of Arabic and pidgin French.) Neither is it just the crackling gibberish pouring over the public address system. (The second announcement seems to be in French but is quite as unintelligible as the first.) The real difference is in the impromptu spirit of the arrangements.

It was just past noon when we arrived. Standing in line before a booth labeled "Bureau de Change," I could see out a window. Under a row of date palms, several black-skinned workmen lay prone on the grass, their long white shirts thrown over their faces. When a taxi passed within inches of their outstretched legs clad in loose Moorish trousers, the legs did not even twitch. The line I stood in was making no progress. I saw that there was no one in the booth, but because I was a westerner and believed in signs, I continued to stand patiently, never dreaming that the immutable law of the three- or four-hour siesta would apply now, when several flights had just come in. Through another window I could see the airstrip; a military band seemed to be awaiting the arrival of some state visitor. When a plane taxied into view, the band stepped out bravely, all pipes and thin wailing horns and thumping drums. Soldiers in baggy red trousers marched behind it, and behind them some dignitaries with stiff ceremonial faces. When the plane's door opened and a regal African stood there at the top of the steps, the dignitaries were lost among the ranks of the band, trying to shoulder their way through.

Ahead of me, a handsome young Arab in a snow-white djellaba admonished his tour group to be patient. I caught snatches of their conversation: ". . .

not really a nightshirt, is it?" ". . . like from a Bible picture book!" Throughout the waiting room, the impromptu air persisted. Though many figures hurried past, it seemed to me they always returned soon, hurrying in the opposite direction. There was a long, unintelligible burst on the loudspeaker. A crowd surged off toward the gates and halted. In response to another burst, they swayed, turned, and stampeded back. Bill appeared with a small brown sparrow of a porter, incredibly nimble under our luggage strapped to his back. I said I was still waiting to get some dirhams.

"Let it go, then," Bill said, and fished up some American money, to which the sparrow's response was ardent.

Grande Auto Route

Acres of dreary housing projects; a big oil refinery at the sea's edge; then rows of beach cabins—all this could as well have been France. Indeed, this stretch of beach was popular with the French, and now prosperous Moroccans enjoy what they left behind. Then the coast became a line of cliffs, the road turned a little inland, and Morocco rushed at us—red earth, thinly etched with wiry grass, Barbary fig cactus five feet tall, a low stone wall surrounding a group of conical thatched huts in the shape of beehives. Off to one side of the enclosure was a domed mud bake oven. A few roosters pecked about, and a blackened pot sat on a charcoal fire. Ahead of us a *fellah* (peasant) plodded behind his wooden plow, himself as thin as the strange team he drove: a sad, disdainful camel harnessed with a mule. More huts, and beside them a well sweep and a small, blindfolded donkey trudging in a circle.

Our horn blared suddenly. Men sitting sideways on their donkeys drummed with their heels on the moth-eaten flanks, and the beasts trotted off the highway. Another blast on the horn, and a man driving some sheep flapped his arms to hurry the stragglers off the road. With his shirt hiked up about his waist and all the fullness of his baggy trousers gathered between the legs, he looked from behind quite a bit like the fat-tailed sheep he drove. Our driver, bent low over the wheel, had a piratical profile. Suddenly he turned full around and told us in English how he had fought with the American army in 1942. I complimented him on his English but urgently wished he would turn around and face the road; a motorcycle was cutting in from the left. He followed my glance, put one hand back on the wheel, and aimed the car straight at the cyclist. At the last instant, both swerved slightly, and both dignities were preserved.

All at once, the U.S. intruded. A familiar Flying Red Horse ramped on a sign above a filling station. A few yards away, several truck drivers stood together under the sign of a huge Coca-Cola bottle. Coca-colonization must have spawned the widest empire in history. I remembered an American friend who had done much for the cottage industries in Southeast Asia. She created an American market for table mats and napkins, and sent her orders across the Pacific. Someone asked her, "How on earth do you cope with the lack of standard sizes in those underdeveloped countries?" "That's easy," she replied breezily. "All my orders go out in terms of how many Coca-Cola bottle tops wide, and how many high. Complete standardization!"

With almost no transition, the countryside gave way to the outskirts of Rabat. Our taxi raced through the streets with homicidal speed; each intersection provided a chance to see who could outbluff whom. Our pirate rarely lost a bout. Then he swung onto a wide avenue lined with double rows of palm trees; an esplanade ran down the middle. Here he drove with decorum, for at each main intersection, a policeman stood on a podium directing traffic with operatic gestures. I saw a man with his djellaba hiked up above his motorcycle wheels. When he braked for a red light, the veiled woman riding pillion behind him was thrown off balance and clutched him around the waist.

Then the pirate was pulling up beside a broad café with a solid roof of trees. Behind rose a stately old building, tall for Rabat. "The Balima!" the driver cried. Our legs swayed under us as we approached the desk. Quite suddenly, the time of reckoning had come, and our inner clocks were protesting this endless day that had known no night. Through a fog, I heard someone say that our room was on the top floor, with a terrace, and Ahmet would take us there directly. Ahmet looked about twelve, shy and very beautiful in Moorish trousers, with a tasseled fez on his head. His long pointed slippers slapped the floor as he led us down the corridor. And then at last we were alone, and could create an artificial night.

Hours later, we stepped out onto our terrace. Rabat, the white and silver city, lay at our feet. It was a panorama of flat rooftops, interrupted here and there by splendidly tall trees. The straight avenues of the *ville nouvelle* led away to the medina in the distance, where roofs were smaller, tightly massed together, and punctuated by slender minarets. A blue arc of sea swept behind the medina and only disappeared where a massive, earth-brown citadel rose against the horizon. The mild air held a hint of salt and the scent of orange trees in flower. Gently, the sea paled and dusk gathered. Floodlights bathed an impressive façade across the street, white pillars against brown stucco; "*Cour d'Appel*" was carved on the façade. A faint hum of voices rose from the café below us, where little colored lights now hung in the trees.

All at once a lighthouse sprang to life on the far cliffs and winked out across the graying sea. One by one, lights blossomed on the tips of the minarets, and on each a white flag fluttered out from a mast. I had always thought of minarets as cylindrical, but in Morocco, which knows no Turkish influence, they are rectangular and end in a small domed cupola. Now the call to prayer rang out—an eerie, hoarse, ascending wail. But it was a recorded voice, amplified through a loudspeaker on the rim of the cupola. As the call was repeated from one after another of the scattered minarets, I realized that mechanization does not necessarily mean a consensus on the moment of sunset. Standardization like that would violate something essential to the Moroccan spirit. Instead, each muezzin decides for himself the precise moment when the sun has sunk below the horizon and, I suppose, rests happy in the belief that the faithful of his quarter will heed his call alone. From our vantage point on a distant rooftop the result was a desynchronized caterwauling.

Boulevard Mohammed V

The Balima is very central, a natural and easy place for government personages to meet visiting foreign officials for off-the-record conversations. From the less conspicuous café tables, solitary and rather somber gentlemen watch these discreet discussions and try to guess at their import. In times of crisis, it is here that the men of the press come to sniff the wind and try to guess what the King will do—who is on his way out, and whose star is rising. Shoeshine boys haunt the tables; four minutes is a good respite between solicitations. A troupe of youngsters in scarlet costumes sometimes puts on an acrobatic show in the narrow aisles. I used to gasp that they could cartwheel so freely or build their pyramids so quickly, before a waiter bore down on them.

Beggars are discreet about pushing in here, though the sight of so much pay dirt must be hard to resist. There was one striking old habitué with a plaster cast on his arm. (This, in itself, is a novelty in a country where fractures are normally left to set themselves.) He was tall and emaciated, and sometimes used to bar my way with the outthrust cast, which was, I felt sure, retained as an asset to his trade. The arm within had probably long since withered to uselessness. I noticed that the waiters who swooped down on him with flapping arms, as if they were driving away goats, reached into their pockets at the last moment for coins before they herded him off the territory.

Boulevard Mohammed V, the main axis of the *ville nouvelle* on which the Balima fronts, was once called the Cour Lyautey, after the great marshal who was the first résident général of the Protectorate. He ordered the new city designed with this main avenue to run from his palatial residence straight to the gate of the medina, wholly bypassing the royal *Mechaouar* (the palace complex)—a metaphor clear enough for all to understand. Rabat had only recently achieved a Mechaouar and become an Imperial City, on a par with

Fez and Marrakesh.[1] Before that, it had been merely a prosperous carpet-manufacturing city, and before that a tiny pirate principality. Lyautey made it *the* capital; let the sultans visit their several Mechaouars in rotation, as they had always done—Rabat would now be the seat of government. Today the Cour Lyautey has been renamed after the first sovereign of the new Morocco, the father of the present King. (Every city in the land now has its Boulevard Mohammed V and its Avenue Hassan II.) The Boulevard is always thronged, the esplanade down the center often bright with the skirts of country women on their way to the medina from the railway station.

There are more European suits than djellabas on the Boulevard. Some men wear the robe open, showing the business suit beneath. But even then they cling to the red fez. Headgear is an index of status: the working classes, lately come to the city, are apt to wear the countryman's little round, tight-knit cap with a geometric pattern in a band around it. No Muslim will wear a brimmed hat, for the brim would prevent the wearer from touching his forehead to the ground as required in the prayer prostrations. Men who haven't prayed in a dozen years still will refrain from wearing a brimmed hat. (Kemal Ataturk, who modernized Turkey at a breathless pace, ran into real trouble when he tried to persuade his countrymen to wear western hats.) Modernists will go clean-shaven or wear a mustache; the traditionalist wears a full beard, wraps himself in a fine djellaba, and winds a turban about his head.

Our first morning, I saw two stately figures deep in conversation on the steps of the Court of Appeals. Their faces were bronze and patrician under white turbans; their djellabas fell in Giottesque folds to their feet. One man held a loop of turquoise beads in one hand and lightly fingered them as he talked. When they were about to part, I saw the traditional gesture of farewell: after a handclasp, each carried his right hand to his breast. One stood with head slightly inclined until the other, presumably of higher degree, had turned to go.

Bill and I set out along the Boulevard. On either side rose those pompous, no-style buildings the French loved to build in the 1920s. In the ground-floor shops, imported cameras, watches, and household articles were displayed at fearful prices. There were few customers in any shop. Bill bought some pipe cleaners and discovered that one packet was worth forty cents—two dirhams. Each street corner we came to boasted at least one bank, decorated with a profusion of Islamic motifs and stucco arabesques. One such building I could not pass without an incredulous glance upward. It began at ground level with the rusticated sandstone of the Italian Renaissance, rose upward through successive stages of blind arches intended to recall the Alhambra, and culminated four stories above in a frieze of fake Arabic calligraphy.

---

1. Meknes is sometimes also classed among the Imperial Cities, though it had only a brief period of greatness.

I stopped at a news vendor's kiosk and bought a paper, then lingered to investigate the Arabic comic books. I was curious about them, for Islam forbids representation of the human figure in art. I soon saw that these are not classed as art. Then I wondered by what argument Moroccans rationalize the very prevalent photographs of Mohammed V, which are as venerated as any paintings of popes or saints could be. Mohammed's benevolent, smiling face, or his son's gloomy one, looks down on every shop, every restaurant, public building, and marketplace.

As we stood there, Bill felt someone touch his elbow—a very tattered old man with a raw sheepskin over his arm. It gave off a rank smell. We shook our heads, but the old man murmured in Arabic—some plea, some blessing on our heads if we would buy. An old fellow "selling from the arm" like this in the *ville nouvelle* must be working on consignment for some sleek merchant, and chances were the merchant would absorb all but a coin or two of the man's daily take. Bill thrust a half dirham into his hand, and he shuffled off.

We separated in front of a bookstore, agreeing to meet later at a café up the Boulevard. I studied the titles in the window with some surprise: French translations of Gorki, Kierkegaard, Hemingway, and—stranger still where anti-Semitism flourishes—I. B. Singer. An Arab had written *La Sociologie du Jazz,* another a book entitled *Du Bon Usage d'Alcool.* At that time, I was unaware that there was any usage, good or bad, of alcohol in a Muslim country. Inside the store, the people poring over the bookshelves were not tourists or French businessmen, but young Moroccans. Not a book was bought while I was there, but quite a number were being read standing up. There were books in French on every conceivable line of inquiry, including several works of Marx. Then it struck me all at once: Why were good Moroccans reading in French? Where were the Arabic shelves? They were in the back, a few of them; the titles of course were indecipherable to me. But not a soul approached them while I was there.

I almost forgot I had to collect a parcel at the customs office before meeting Bill. My daughter had phoned as we were leaving the States to say that even in Rabat she would find me with a birthday present. Warmed by the thought of her, I stood patiently in a long line that hardly seemed to move at all. At last the man ahead of me reached the window. I could not see if the paper he handed in was in French or Arabic, but, whatever the language, the young woman behind the window could not read it. An older clerk came over. He abused the girl with a withering scorn. Perhaps he had winced under the same treatment by the French; it is a style one remembers well and can master quickly, and it must be very sweet to find oneself in a position to use it. As I reached the window, he brushed the girl off the stool and turned a suddenly composed hauteur on me. Delivering my parcel to me, he managed to imply that I had been guilty of a breach of taste in witnessing the girl's ineptness.

I reached the café where I had agreed to meet Bill as shutters came rattling down on all the shopwindows; it was noon. Every Moroccan, be he merchant, clerk, or even Minister, goes home to lunch and rest. The men sitting here over their newspapers were evidently in no hurry. I saw right away I was the only woman there. Few enough Moroccan women ever sit in a sidewalk café; none arrives alone and sits near the front to survey the street. Feeling constrained, I put back my cigarette unlit. A Moroccan woman was crossing the street, her djellaba rippling subtly as she moved. A wisp of veil hid her nose and mouth, and the hood of her djellaba was folded back and pinned smoothly flat on her head. There is nothing like a gauzy triangle of veil to set off dark eyes and a flawless forehead. For a moment, the western style of dress seemed grotesque to me.

Ten years ago, Mohammed publicly unveiled his daughter, announcing a new era for women. Many have followed her example; those who have not may have been forbidden by husbands or fathers, but I suspect that many more retain the veil out of choice. As for the djellaba, wearing it became a symbol of patriotism and nationalist sympathies during the years of the struggle for independence, and it remains popular today. But there is much latitude allowed in women's dress, especially in the large cities. Shopgirls troop out into the noon-hour crowds, bare-armed and bareheaded, clicking along on their spike heels and giggling over the furtive glances of passing young men. One reason women have traditionally been required to cover their heads in public is that their hair is beautiful—thick, vibrantly black, lustrous. They love to steep it in henna on the slightest provocation; then it glints even more beautifully. But now that things are changing, the little office girls copy hairdo's from Paris magazines, and would not dream of covering them.

The drone of motor scooters drowned out the muezzin's noon call. Brakes screamed as pedestrians leaped for cover. Bill arrived, quite angry. "A motorcycle drove straight at me. It almost cut me in half." We decided to stay where we were until the noon rush should subside.

A man strode past, heading for the gate into the medina. Three paces behind him came his wife, carrying two suitcases as well as several bundles on her head. They must have been coming from the station. She was an ungainly hulk, flat of breast and gross of hips under the dun-colored djellaba. Why had I thought Moroccan women beautiful? This sweating creature's walk was a ham-shamble.

"Look at her!" I said furiously. "She's not a woman, she's a slave. No, she's a pack mule!"

Bill looked at me quizzically. Even I was surprised at the heat of my reaction. I knew well enough about the position of women in the Muslim world; but no amount of foreknowledge prepares you for the shock.

"But why is *she* the butt of your anger?"

"Because—can't you tell from looking at her?—she expects just what she gets! She doesn't protest. . . ." I had to stop there, having discovered—in the enlightened West—that protest is rarely an effective tool.

But any inequity western women have suffered pales beside the situation of the Muslim woman. A desperate choice confronts the young Moroccan girl as marriage looms ahead of her: Shall she defy her parents, refuse to accept an arranged marriage, and fight against everything her society has sanctioned? Can she know in advance how she will fare if she does so? Or shall she settle for the known way of security and hope for slow amelioration of her lot? What *can* it be like to be a Moroccan, and to stand with one foot in the late twentieth century and the other in the Middle Ages? How natural that Moroccans should ask impossible things of change—first, that it should be sweeping and radical and brook no delay; and in the next breath, that it be gentle, lest the whole social fabric be torn apart. Many Moroccans, especially the young and the half-educated, race to catch up with the West and model themselves upon all its outward appearance. Others entrench themselves against change, seeing it as subversion of religion and all that Muslim society rests on. The soberest and wisest know change must come but insist it must come gradually, in response to wider education and a slow and delicate reshaping of attitudes.

Clothes along the Boulevard show many responses to this dilemma. One youth wears the skintight jeans and long hair he has seen in the movies. The next wears pointed Italian shoes, a flashy suit, and his djellaba overall. But he unbuttons it, pulls the hem up around his neck, and lets the rest hang down his back like a cloak, swinging at every step and enhancing his bravura. The conservative declares in his demeanor his divine right to rule—over family, over parvenus, and over subversive ideas. And he cuts a formidable figure. His impeccably wound turban is magnificent above hawk nose and deep-set eyes. The djellaba hood lies upon his shoulders, framing the elegant beard, and the heavy robe hangs in sculptural folds. His feet shod in bright yellow slippers, he treads the stage with perfect composure, perfect assurance.

We used to wonder why these traditional slippers are worn with the heel turned in under the foot. Then Bill bought a pair and found that the heel was not made wide enough to be pulled up in place; yet, with the heels trodden under in native style, the slippers flew off one after the other when he walked. We concluded there was deliberate artifice here: to walk confidently in spite of such a precarious grip served to declare once more the masterfulness of the wearer.

For the conservative, the Koran is the source of all truth. All relations between the sexes are subject to its rigid regulations. It speaks clearly to the obligations of marriage but recognizes no intermingling of the sexes before then. A relationship not defined in the Koran would seem to such a man both irreligious and disruptive to society, for the truth revealed to the Prophet is total and final; there can be no revisionism. Nor should there be any contesting a man's authority over the lives of his family, vested in him by the Book.

The son of this man, however, may be secretly much opposed to the King's regime, may feel that religion is on the wane and its restrictions repressive and archaic. He will be likely to take alcoholic drinks when the setting is discreet, and think fasting in the month of Ramadan ridiculous. In all probability he has not set foot in a mosque for years. He may be among the crowds of students who demonstrate on the street for a westernized education or for more scholarships. He may resist the thought of a marriage arranged for him by his parents and serve as the confidant of his younger sisters, who shrink from the same prospect. With them, his authority is beginning to supplant that of their father, though all may try to disguise the shift.

One such young man said to us, "How can we hope for a relationship of *persons* in marriage, if we follow our parents' hope that we will meet for the first time after the bride price has been paid? How can any man love and respect a wife he has been forced to pay heavily for? My father has three sons and little money; why should I have to pour all my savings into the pocket of some greedy old man?" His voice was shaky with anger—and fear that he might not be able to resist his parents.

Cultures in collision. So many, so frighteningly many readjustments to be made if Muslim society is to keep its equilibrium while old values are replaced with more adaptive forms.

All Arabs love their language to the point of obsession, and I am told it is one of the most flexible and precise languages in the world. Though to my ear the Arabic sounds were harsh, I recognized something compelling in the rushing delivery and the intensity of the outpouring. Luckily for us, who couldn't understand it, Moroccans indulge also, while speaking, in a finely developed language of facial expressions and gestures. We often watched a street-corner conversation escalate into a dramatic production. Fingers stab for emphasis, men smite their palms or fling them wide apart in exclamation. They turn on a heel and look back derisively over one shoulder. They tap each other on the breast to underline significance, and emphasize the reply by knocking with the knuckles on the other's clavicle. So much vivacity goes into some of these exchanges that a listener must sometimes move a step or two backward to recover his balance. Then there is a way of answering a question silently: a man cocks one eyebrow, jerks his chin up and over his shoulder, and rolls his eyes. The innuendo can be so telling that I sometimes found myself smiling when I had not understood one word.

Greetings between equals are effusive. Time can always be found for them —lots of time. Some men embrace warmly and kiss on both cheeks. This habit was despised by a friend of ours. "They learned it from the French. Let them unlearn it!" Certainly, the older style of greeting, the handclasp and salaam, is more impressive. If there is a great difference of rank when two men meet, the man of lower degree will make as if to kiss the hand of the other, but etiquette requires the hand to be withdrawn before the lips touch it.

I came into the lobby of the Balima once to find a tall, princely figure standing alone, slender and straight as a lance, surveying the people drinking coffee. The pure white of his gossamer wool djellaba accentuated the ebony of his face. Just as I approached, he was recognized by one of the hotel porters, who rushed forward and dipped as if to kneel. He seized the princely hand and carried it almost to his lips. The hand was withdrawn, the tall man smiled very slightly and moved off to the doorway. Later, I asked the porter who it was that he had greeted so warmly. He drew himself up very straight at the recollection and answered, "He is of the Alaoui, Madame." The Alaoui are the King's family. The dynasty originated in the far south, in an oasis on the edge of the desert where the slave caravans came regularly. Though the King is very light-skinned himself (he is the child of a beautiful Berber wife of Mohammed V), the African strain still prevails in at least one of the many branches of the enormous clan of the Alaouites.

I used to sit in a corner of that same lobby, reading the local newspapers that appeared in French. They were bland, adhering pretty carefully to the official line; they had to, unless they wanted to find padlocks on their doors. But they sometimes slipped in a comment, such as: "His Majesty's government has declared new restrictions on the importation of goods from France, to be in effect until the trade balance reaches a more favorable position. Yesterday, one heard the question expressed, 'How long shall we continue to enjoy investment of French capital in the face of such restrictions?' God forbid that any more French francs should flee Casablanca industries." I would look up from my paper to gaze discreetly at the people bent over neighboring newspapers, and find some of the faces somber with anxiety. Or I would see a young man who bore the stamp of the new bureaucrat: tense, nervous about his job tenure, irritable after a morning of grappling with regulations in triplicate.

Men often came to the Balima lobby to make telephone calls when they couldn't get a free line or re-establish a broken connection in their office. The telephone is a true mania with thousands of the new Moroccans; the result is that the lines are overstrained, and almost any number is busy almost all the time. Then there is the telephone directory: one book, one only, for the whole of Morocco. It is half an inch thick, and was compiled in 1962. Only a tiny fraction of its listings are now relevant, and thousands of new numbers have to be obtained through an information service that would make the most placid man paranoid.

Oudaïas Kasbah

One of the joys our terrace afforded was watching the life on those flat roofs that provide a natural extension of indoor living space. Quite the most useful thing I had brought with me, after doubts about cluttering our baggage, was a pair of very small binoculars. They proved to be a joy. Leaning on the terrace wall and cupping the glasses in my hands, I could scan the city. If the woman laundering on a nearby roof looked up, she would only see me leaning on my elbows, looking about from a decent distance. She was a servant and wore a long white garment called a *haïk* wrapped around her. I never ceased to wonder that a woman so swathed could pound and wring and shake and ultimately hang that laundry, and still keep her haïk about her. Like most countrywomen, she did not wear the veil, but kept her head covered. Each time the head shawl slipped down, she replaced it, for she was outdoors, even if presumably unobserved. The gesture of hand to head and the repeated motions of snugging a loose fold into her waistband were so habitual that they never interrupted the rhythm of her work.

Sooner or later, I always shifted my glasses to the crenelated citadel high above the sea at the edge of the medina. It was the Oudaïas Kasbah, and we were awaiting word from a man who lived there. Before we left the States, a Moroccan friend had given us an introduction to a relative lately come to the Kasbah. Bill had written a note. In the reply, formally polite in French, the writer set a date and an afternoon hour for our call, and gave the Arabic street name in the western alphabet. "Ask anyone in the street," he wrote, "and you will be directed to my home."

It was raining on the appointed afternoon—one of those brief, warm rains quite common in Rabat in January. The overcast sky is almost a relief. The white city turns a gentle silver, and all the many greens deepen. Drops glide softly down the big magnolia leaves, and the birds of the city rejoice. So we took a *petit taxi* to the gateway. There is a fleet of these sugar-lump-size little cars licensed to carry two passengers behind and one beside the driver. If the *petit taxi* starts out with less than its full complement, it will stop along the way for anyone who hails it; the extra passenger is taken aboard when the destination is roughly the same. It is a cheap and sociable way to travel, if rather circuitous.

No car enters the arched portal of the Oudaïas, so we got out before the massive brown gateway. Originally, a high city wall swung along the cliff from the citadel and then turned south to embrace the medina and connect eventually with the Mechaouar. Long stretches of this red-brown wall survive in the midst of what is now the *ville nouvelle*. Several of its triple-arched gateways straddle the main arteries of the city, their narrow horseshoe arches slowing the passage of traffic.

The Kasbah was once impregnable. The land falls away steeply on two sides to marshes bordering the sea and the estuary of a slow, shallow stream, the Oued Bou Regreg. Very early in Moroccan history a tribe called the Oudaïas had settled on this rocky promontory. When in the twelfth century a sultan in faraway Marrakesh was trying to unify the country, the Oudaïas refused to recognize his suzerainty; so warrior monks came north and built here a fortified monastery or *ribat* (from which the city's name derives). This portal before us was its main gateway. The high horseshoe arch is decorated with a tracery of interlacing arches carved in low relief; each corner above the arch is accented by a scallop shell. It is this pleasing contrast of delicacy woven upon strength, grace upon massiveness, that is the surprise and the art of traditional Moroccan architecture.

We walked toward the gateway up a broad cobbled ramp. Facing us was a line of old bronze cannons which were captured from the Portuguese originally, then used against restless citizens of Rabat; today their muzzles are stuffed untidily with trash. Inside the portal, the Kasbah is a tangled skein of steep, narrow lanes and cobbled alleys opening off each other at random angles. The whitewashed walls that line the streets are blank, the strong wooden doors solidly closed. The doorframes are so softened with successive layers of lime wash that they often look to be covered in blue or white velvet. An Arab house does not give onto the street but, rather, turns its back upon it, preserving the life within from any uninvited gaze. The only windows are small, high up, and blue-shuttered or closely barred. Women may look down through the bars, but no one below may look in. Many of these houses in the Kasbah are very poor, the people living there densely crowded in with new arrivals of their kin from the country.

The house we were looking for was somewhere in this indecipherable tangle of streets. The few street signs were in Arabic script, and no one we consulted could decipher the western alphabet our friend had used for his address. One after another, they turned away from us, shaking their heads and muttering. Suddenly we were surrounded by little children, all offering to guide us where they thought we wanted to go. They spoke a few words of French, most of them, but each pointed in a different direction and tried to tug us along. This situation, which repeated itself a hundred times or more in our experience of Morocco, takes getting used to. The boys peered up into our faces, repeating, *"Guide? J'suis bon guide!" "Argent? cigarette?" "Je ti guide!"* They pushed and shoved each other good-temperedly, their eyes shining like polished teak in their handsome, dirt-streaked faces. At first I thought it rather engaging to be "thee'd" and "thou'd" by eager, raisin-brown urchins bobbing in our path. The little girls jigged, in their short dresses and long flowered trousers, gold rings glittering in their small ears and tendrils of lustrous hair escaping from their bandannas. They circled us with a singsong dance: *"Bonjour Madame!* Bye-bye! *B'jour M'sieur!* . . . Cigarette, bye-bye, *b'jour!"* The women in the street drew themselves into their doorways, pulling their white shawls across their faces, only to turn and stare after us when we passed. The whole thing was getting less engaging as the minutes wore on.

An older boy appeared, wearing tight blue jeans and old, tattered Keds, his greasy hair combed back into a ducktail. He scowled, and the children fell back a few yards. Then, in rapid French, he offered to guide us "to the Andalusian houses of this famous quarter, and the mosques, *ti sais?*" And did we wish to get rid of any French money? He had an excellent contact. Bill sighed, pulled out the slip of paper once more, and with it a coin. The boy looked at the paper, asked for double the amount Bill offered, and then guided us to the house we wanted.

The walls were as blank as all the others. The nail-studded door bespoke a degree of prosperity at the time the house was built, and there was a bronze Hand of Fatma for a knocker. An old crone came to open to us, her hair a lurid henna, dark tattoo marks on her chin and sunken cheeks. With her only three teeth she was chewing sunflower seeds. Ushered into the courtyard, we stood under an old fig tree, adjusting our eyes to the sudden shade. Round the court on the ground and on all ledges were flowerpots, gasoline cans with the tops ripped off, and large earthen tubs. All overflowed with pink and scarlet geraniums, mint, artichoke plants, and tomato vines. In and out of the trailing geraniums hens scuttled, pecking, and several children squatted on the ground.

We were led to the open door of a sitting room, where we paused to remove our shoes. (This is another reason why heelless slippers are popular.) Then we went in and took our places on one of the low divans placed along the walls; it was rigidly hard, stuffed, I suppose, with cane or corn shucks. The long bolsters against the wall were hard, too. In our first glance around the room we could identify the customary seat of the master of the house: a sheepskin, flattened with much sitting, was thrown over it. The other furnishings were several leather poufs and a big walnut radio, vintage perhaps 1945. A low table was covered by an oilcloth stamped in bright colors with game birds and rifles. Imported oilcloth enjoys a hideous prestige and costs more than a native-woven cover would.

Our host entered. His dark eyes swept over our faces as he came to greet us; his plump, full-lipped face was quite expressionless, except for a faint smile of formal courtesy. He was short, clean-shaven, and wore western clothing and leather slippers. While we spoke of our friend in the States who had brought about this introduction, I think we were all wishing we had never acted upon it. Awkwardness hung palpably in the air. We thanked him for his kindness in inviting us, and in my heart I devoutly wished myself back sitting in a café on the Boulevard, just an onlooker. He gestured us back to the seats we had risen from, and himself skirted the sheepskin-covered place of honor, and sat down beside it.

We knew nothing about this man except that he had come recently to live with an uncle in the Kasbah. He told us that his wife, knowing no French, was shy about joining us. Would I be good enough to do the honors when she brought the tea tray—that is, if we cared for mint tea? I assured him we did, but that I should need instruction in the preparation of it. Bill, sitting beside the oilcloth game birds, asked if he was fond of hunting and where he went for his sport.

"I find little opportunity to hunt nowadays. All the game have long ago left this part of the country; it is not like the slopes of the Atlas, where I was born. But life there offers few opportunities today; so I came with my family to join my uncle, a rug merchant with a good shop here." He sat more erect as he spoke of the uncle, and glanced at the sheepskin seat. I wondered about the crone who had admitted us; was she some other rescued relative?

A handsome woman came in with the tea tray and set its short legs down on the floor before me. When I offered her my hand in greeting she looked startled but took it. She was younger than her husband, barely thirty, I thought. A Berber face: small, delicate features and very large eyes. A flowered skirt fell to her ankles. She was light-boned and still lithe, but under her embroidered blouse and many necklaces her breast was flattened from much nursing of infants. I asked her husband to congratulate her upon the beauty of the children we had seen in the courtyard. I gestured toward them and turned back to the young wife, smiling. Her skin was the color of toasted almonds, light enough to show the flush that spread across it as her husband translated. Then she sped out to the courtyard.

The brewing of mint tea is a ritual. The tea service provides a display of the family's wealth—silver for the prosperous, nickel for the modest. Even in nickel, this tray laid before me, and the kettle on its stand, must have represented a good part of the wife's dowry. Sprigs of mint were tightly packed into one canister, tea and rocks of crude sugar were in two more. Following instructions, I scalded the pot, spooned in tea, added mint and sugar, then more mint and more sugar until there seemed scarcely room for water. "Now the other herbs, please," said M. Hamid, indicating a dish on which verbena leaves were laid out, and sprigs of what I think was marjoram. When at length I proffered the first glass to my host, he looked surprised and bade me fill all the glasses first. "Otherwise," he said, "someone might think himself the last to be served."

His wife returned with almond cakes. But the crocheted doily thrown over them became tangled in the ornamental legs of the tray, and several cakes dropped off as she struggled with it. M. Hamid, embarrassed, jumped up and switched on the radio. Against the blaring of the news in Arabic, he began a conversation with Bill. Moroccans prefer to talk against noise. I gathered from looking at the two men that our host now felt at ease, and that Bill was having an extremely difficult time keeping up his end of the conversation. I sipped my tea, thankful to be at a little distance and at liberty to gaze out into the courtyard.

There, the little girl I had noticed earlier was binding twigs together into a broom. From time to time, she brushed back her thick curling hair and, with each interruption, crept a few feet forward, the better to look into the sitting room. Called back with a crisp command, she finished twisting the twigs into a tight clump; when it was bound with cord, she thrust in a sturdy handle of wood, twisted another length of cord around it with her small, deft fingers, and tied a firm knot. Mme. Hamid was pounding bread dough and aerating it with each hearty thump; the flat loaves were set in a row on a board, for carrying to the neighboring bake oven. A toddler was lurching around the courtyard, stuffing everything it could find into its mouth. The mother gestured with her head to the little girl, who took off briskly to mind the baby. There were no slaps or cries, but a good quantity of stuff was disgorged.

I came to myself and served second glasses of tea all around. The fresh-tasting, pungent brew was thoroughly refreshing in spite of its sweetness. The almond cakes were even sweeter. I thought of all the gold teeth I had seen; perhaps here lay the answer—a people so addicted to sweets could not long avoid the dentist. The men were leaning together; Bill somehow was managing to satisfy his host with suitable responses. The news on the radio had given way to songs: they wailed hoarsely upward, were punctured by gasps, and then slid downward by quarter tones. I remembered how Bill hated the outpourings of the small transistor radio we turned on regularly in our room, and I grieved for him. Until it was time for the final, third glass of tea required by etiquette, I was free to watch the courtyard.

As we came in, we had seen an older girl there, of twelve or so, but she had escaped into the house at our approach. She reappeared now, her hair pulled back under a bandanna, a shawl over her arms: the privacy of the home had been breached; she had gone indoors to cover herself suitably. Now she sat down and resumed her scouring of a large copper pot, her skirt neatly pulled down to her ankles, and her eyes averted from the sitting room; after every few motions of her firm young arms she readjusted the shawl. She did her scouring with a wad of straw dipped in sand. At length she tossed away the wad and looked with approval at the pot; then she thwacked it roundly on its bottom and set it upside down upon the ground. The mother had now disappeared indoors, and the five-year-old answered the invitation and came over to sit upon the pot. The girls' heads leaned together; the younger one was, I think, relaying to the older all that she had seen going forward in the sitting room. They laughed together as they tore apart and chewed a sticky honey cake.

The men had emptied their glasses, and I hastened to refill them. That third glass was somewhat harder to dispose of. The radio burst forth with new wails of anguish, torn from hoarse throats. When Bill had drained his final glass, he rose. As he came near, he turned on me the blandest of faces and enunciated very distinctly, and in English, "Hyenas!" Arab music is, indeed, hard for western ears to accept. The melody is punctuated with gasps, as if the singer had been winded by a blow. The Andalusian music that Moroccans love is a variant, softened with flamenco slurs; but there are no harmonies, only a plaintive melodic line, always in a minor key, that wanders chromatically in wistful curlicues. A flute utters a soft complaint, then reedy pipes repeat it poignantly. The music is full of nostalgia, haunting. You hear it drifting from windows in the evenings, when the men pick up their lutes and thin pipes and the women sing—sad songs, deriving from the long-ago past when Spain was part of the Moorish empire.

A sardonic view of this nostalgia would see it as sentimentality, a flight into the past to escape current realities. And so, undoubtedly, it is. But as we bade M. Hamid good-by, I wondered if some form of escapism from current uncertainties might not be very healthy.

The Kasbah wall has many small projecting turrets with musket slits and conical roofs. From one of these, we looked down on the Oued Bou Regreg. The "Stream of the Father of Reflections" winds slowly through shallows to the sea. Across the marshes, the white houses of Salé are set upon the cliff like a tumble of sugar cubes. Rabat's Kasbah and Salé's citadel, on their opposing promontories, effectively command the estuary, and the two cities once vied with each other as corsair bases. Ships from both terrorized the eastern Atlantic from the sixteenth century onward. Once Spain had thrust out her Moors, many of the refugee "moriscos" joined their talents to those of the native pirates and thereby found at least a measure of revenge.

Salé and Rabat won evil reputations among the navies of Spain, Portugal, and Britain. The sultans must have shrugged when these powers protested, for not only were they helpless to control the corsairs, but they cannot much have wished to restrain them. Relations with a sultan in far-off Fez or Marrakesh were loose at best; there was even a period when the two pirate cities were known as the Republic of the Two Shores. What could the rulers of Morocco do—or wish to do—about their operations? They amounted to guerrilla warfare by sea, the Moors' only weapon against the Christian dogs they could not engage in naval battle. (Morocco has never had a navy; it has been difficult enough to assemble a sufficient army to keep order on land.)

Standing in a gun embrasure on the wall, I could see well enough how cannon could rake the estuary, but why should a foreign vessel ever come in so far? Bill dug from his capacious memory some information: in the eighteenth century, British and Dutch renegades used to join the "Sallee Rovers." They taught the moriscos to build larger, faster vessels with heavy armament, which nevertheless drew little water. Far out at sea, these three-masters would engage the merchantmen sailing past with wealth from West

Africa and Spanish America, and then, by breaking off the engagement and appearing to flee, would lure them in toward the coast. While the corsairs raced in across a hidden sand bar, the pursuing vessels would drive hard aground, right under the guns of Salé.

"Once," Bill told me, "in the midst of a manuscript about the Rhode Island colony, I came on the story of some seamen who fell into the hands of the Rovers—they had been seized from a British sloop that had pressed them into duty. I always wondered if they fared any worse here than if they had continued to serve in the British navy of the period. Not much to choose between one captivity and the other."

Though the enraged powers frequently sent in warships on punitive forays, somehow there were always new corsairs, and fortress walls were rebuilt and furnished with newly captured cannon. Even in 1854, Salé must have been a substantial nuisance, for the Portuguese thought it worthwhile to bombard her once more. Now we two westerners stood on the citadel wall and cast a last look across the sun-gilded marshes. The evening tide of bicycles flowed across the bridge; swallows dipped and soared in the still evening air. The shallow estuary of the Father of Reflections was dotted with small blue and green rowboats, striped red along the water line. When one boat made a catch, others rowed near to watch the haul-in. The progeny of corsairs bent their bronze backs low over the shimmering water to pull up ten-inch fish for supper.

Wards of God

It is like climbing over a high threshold to come back to the *ville nouvelle* from the Kasbah. You are reminded that Rabat is not so much one city as an aggregate of quarters: the Oudaïas, the medina, the Mechaouar, the university quarter, the sector of government ministries, and the cosmopolitan area around the hotels.

But the poor penetrate everywhere. In those little back streets behind the Balima lined with *boulangeries* and *épiceries,* where you can buy imported food and drink, a news vendor sits on the pavement. Not only has he no legs; his trunk ends at the hip socket. I asked several people about his deformity, and was told he was not unique: "Malnutrition of the mother during pregnancy." Once, as we stood staring in the window of a boutique where a cocktail dress was displayed for an astronomical price, I heard a rusty creaking behind us. The cripple whose beat this was propelled himself toward us in his ancient handle-bar wheelchair. That shopwindow was his target area, and anyone who looked at that price card was fair game. He defended that street of his against all other beggars with a flow of language that we could admire without understanding a word.

We had American friends living in Rabat that winter—Josh, an anthropologist with a long experience of Morocco and the Levant, and his wife, Mary, both generous of their time and invaluable for guidance. They gave us practical advice, and were a comforting presence when we turned to them. (Josh alternated between encouraging us to rent a car and start touring the country, and tossing off ghoulish remarks like "Saw another corpse in the street today—.") One afternoon as we left the Balima and walked toward his car, a lounging figure detached itself from a wall and bore down upon us, obviously expecting a tip. Bill asked Josh what the lounger expected to be paid for.

"For minding my car for five minutes."

"But you've parked at a meter—why did it need minding?"

"How would a parking meter see that no one broke into my car? When you ask why I should tip this character for minding my car, the best answer is: because he has no other employment. He and several hundred thousand like him. And a job is anything that nets you a few dirhams a day. The trick is to see the makings of a job no one else has seen yet."

He handed the man a coin and unlocked his car.

"You have to lock it even when you know he's going to be tipped for watching it for you?"

"Of course. If I didn't, he'd think I was such a rare fool that I *needed* to have something stolen from my car. . . . You're going to have to revise a lot of ideas if you want to understand these people. They have a perfectly good view of things, but it's a different one, that's all. One of the things you'll need to revise is any western idea about one job to one man. If a fellow like this is lucky enough to find a job somewhere in Rabat, he'll feel obligated to send for his uncle or his wife's brother, and maybe a couple of nephews, too, to share the work and any food that's going. The employer will generally be shamed into a little extra pay for all those extra hands. A man's honor binds him to look after his family, and family is a big category here."

I questioned him about industrial jobs, citing the factories ringing Casa and Rabat. He answered that the big cities were but a tiny fringe of industrialization that did not touch most of the country, and that anyway all the cities were flooded with twenty times more people than there were jobs. Then he drove us to the outskirts to see for ourselves.

Military barracks always dominate the approach to any industrial section. Here the raw young soldiers stood at the gates, wearing their red berets at rakish angles and holding their carbines at the ready. The Cherifian flag, with its green star in the center, hung languidly in the smoky air. Near the barracks was a cement factory, all the buildings filmed with white dust. Before the gates stood about a hundred men in the uniform of the poor— thin black trousers and denim overalls. Josh thought most of them were probably job applicants, hoping against hope. They were leaning on bicycles or shuffling around on feet bound in bits of burlap. Almost all were smoking, for cigarettes, like tea, are a luxury even the poorest will sacrifice anything for. ("It was the French who brought in tobacco," Josh said, "while at the same time, they denounced kif—marijuana—which Moroccans have smoked since time out of mind. This was a nice deal from the French point of view, since they had a monopoly tax on cigarettes.")

The factory gates swung open and disgorged a stream of scooters and motorized bicycles. "The new blue-collar elite," Josh called them. "It's quite imperative that they ride something that makes a noise, to distinguish them from the bicyclists. Then there are some further distinctions between those who ride 'motos' and 'vélos'; I can't tell one from the other, but I'm told there is a real caste distinction in the making there. The nastier the snore the motor makes, the higher your status."

Trucks were pouring through the gates now, loaded with men packed in like upright cattle. A white film caked their faces, their knitted caps, and their crisp hair. As the trucks roared away, the sea of figures who had been waiting ouside washed through the gates and up to the factory door.

We followed the trucks along the belt road ouside the city limits. "They'll unload their cargo at the edge of the *bidonville* and pick up a new consign-ment there for the next shift," Josh told us. "This way, the factory can get workers who have just arrived, and who can't yet afford the price of a bicycle —the lowest wage bracket."

The belt road swung around the shoulder of a hill. Before us, the huts and tin-roofed shanties spread down the hillside and into the marshland bor-dering the Oued Bou Regreg; it is unhealthy land, worthless for any other use. A *bidonville,* or city of oil-drum shacks, looks from a distance like a pale mold creeping over the earth.

"Can you see, far over to the side, a few neat housing units?" Josh asked. We could. "Government-built, to stop the proliferation of the *bidonville*. But look how the game goes: before a man can afford the government unit, he will have had to rent his tin-can shack to a newcomer; then, cash in hand, he'll go and buy a few more bidons and throw together another shack for a second newcomer. So our friend is a landlord before he ever moves into his government quarters."

We sat in the car in silence for some minutes, just looking. "Josh, what on earth is the answer? How do you cope with your own feelings about poverty like this?"

There was nothing of his usual sardonic manner in his slow reply. "I've got no answer; nobody can pretend he has. The best I can do is remember there has always been poverty of the meanest sort in Morocco. Western intrusion hasn't created it, any more than it promises to end it. Nothing will end it, with the birth rate what it is. As far as protecting my own sensibilities goes, I just regard handouts as a sort of tax on living here."

"But it never stops! If you give to one beggar, three more spring up. I feel myself growing resentful, guilty at the same time. . . ."

"You haven't seen begging in the Near East yet—the hired babies, the careful training of deformed children to put their worst stump forward."

"But I've seen a perfectly healthy-looking boy change his gait and contort his face into a grimace of suffering as he sees me coming!"

"Do you perhaps approach begging with a moral bias? Most of us do—the old Protestant ethic! You know as well as I how hard we're finding it in our own country to swallow the idea of a guaranteed annual wage—most of us can't reconcile it with our inherited prejudice about getting something for nothing. This Muslim culture has a certain advantage: almsgiving has always been a religious obligation, and the poor have the dignity of 'wards of God.' Maybe they have something there. Someday you may see a fine gentleman step outside his door to meet the line of indigents waiting for him. You may not like the sight, but don't make the mistake of thinking that Sidi Idriss, or whoever he may be, is gratifying his exhibitionism; there you'd be importing your own cultural values quite inappropriately."

"But a ward of God shouldn't have to screw up his face in a phony grimace!" I said with distaste.

"That comes about because the government is trying to stamp out begging, and the young fellow you saw is up against a newfangled policy; so he thinks he'd better play on your human feelings. Not that I blame you for refusing him. I probably would have done the same. . . . I guess the gist of it is that each one of us must find his own cutoff point. I make an arbitrary rule that I'll give something to the blind ones. It's only a rule of thumb, but it's better than laboring under an unreasonable sense of guilt."

The Medina

Like the Oudaïas Kasbah, the medina is a quarter that has changed relatively little. Pass under the arch at the foot of Boulevard Mohammed V, and immediately you are in the midst of life still organized on a medieval pattern. The rabbit warren of lanes is full of ceaseless activity; it is well to let yourself be carried with the crowd, for it is an organism, not easily resisted. Life is in the streets. The congestion is at once the business and the entertainment of the people, and there is no great pressure of time. The streets are the marketplace, and the marketplace is life itself.

Each narrow lane, or *souk,* is the home of one of the crafts. The tailors' souk consists of twenty or thirty almost identical booths, each about ten feet by twelve. A little way along, the grocers' souk cuts across it, and the next lane is the spice souk. In this manner the medieval guilds clustered together, so that the vigilant eye of the warden might keep tabs on the hierarchy of apprentices and craftsmen, and on the standards of work being produced. The tailors' street is about ten feet wide, the booths on both sides as close as teeth in a jaw. Counters project out into the lane, and wares piled on the ground narrow the passage still further. In each booth, a tailor sits cross-legged upon the floor, which is raised a little above ground level. Behind him, on a rush mat, sit the apprentices and journeymen, cutting and stitching patterns or embroidering. Out in the street stand two young boys switching bobbins rapidly from hand to hand. The line of braid they are making stretches taut from their fingers to the tailor, who stitches it onto the garment across his knees. The boys could stand in closer to the booth, and when the crowd forces them to, they reel in their lines; but they prefer to stand well out in the street so that they can watch all that is taking place in both directions.

Do the handicrafts persist, Bill and I were asking each other, because there isn't yet enough machinery to replace them? Or are they encouraged by the Bureau de l'Artisanat chiefly to give as many people as possible a pittance? "Isn't there probably also a stabilizing factor," Bill wondered, "in keeping illiterate people close to the system they know? I suspect keeping all hands busy is even more important than industrializing."

Sounds of a hubbub came from the intersection behind us. Some urchins had managed to topple a hamper of tomatoes, and the tiny red globes were rolling about the cobbles. In the melee, while the grocer cursed and flapped his arms at the dodging children, who could see how many tomatoes were escaping? Bill would focus his camera quickly to catch scenes like this, for to him wandering the medina was a precious excursion into the Middle Ages. (Taken for his own purposes—to add body to his lectures on town life in fifteenth-century Europe—those slides have let me relive scenes whose details would otherwise have faded in memory. Now, as I write, the tailor cranes his neck to peer down the crowded street, his needle momentarily stilled; his apprentices have let the line of braid fall slack, and their eyes are alight with admiration for the swift-footed boys fleeing the grocer.)

Bill would lament that he couldn't also capture the sounds and smells— the voices chaffering over a purchase, the wheedling and soliciting addressed to passers-by ("Just step inside, M'sieu, M'dame! A *coup d'oeil* costs you nothing!"—with a jab of the finger toward the eye). The sounds are compounded of talk and the braying of donkeys, the hawking of wares, the plashing of fountains, and the jingling of the water-seller's cups. The smells derive partly from the spice souk ahead—pepper, cinnamon, cardamon, and fresh-cut mint and coriander—and partly from the scarcity of indoor sanitation, and from the great density of people and of donkeys.

We stopped by a group around a public fountain. The water seller was filling his goatskin sack from the spout; then he buckled on his shoulder harness, fastening a small cup to each of its hooks. He was a villainous-looking fellow, his matted hair straggling from a rag of a turban, his short tunic patched together with many colors—a fine match for the bloated, hairy, oozing water bag, from which grotesque goat legs protruded stiffly. He loved to stand with his feet planted firmly in the basin below the waterspout. The women coming to fetch water in their pitchers shrank from him, prepared to wait until he moved off. Some brought vegetables to wash in the basin, and scowled after him; but no sour looks could penetrate his braggadocio.

All at once a whiff of incense pricked our noses. (Incense has no orthodox place in Islam, but it is dearly loved and often bought at considerable price to honor some venerated member of the family or the saint of some quarter. Saint-worship is equally unorthodox, but almost every Muslim population has found its own way to temper the austerity of the faith to match the needs of people as they are. It is especially hard to suppress men's desire to place some intermediary between themselves and the awful purity of Allah. The Moors have long since found ways to satisfy their emotional warmth, their sense of racial continuity, and the value they set upon the sensual.) A man pushed past us, cradling a small incense burner in his hands; three women followed him closely, their figures wrapped from head to foot in long white haïks, and entered the mosque door behind him.

Morocco, alone of all the Muslim countries of North Africa and the Near East, keeps all her mosques rigorously closed to unbelievers. So we never lingered long by a mosque doorway, and thus would catch only glimpses of the courtyard, over the backs of men stooping at the threshold to remove their shoes. At the center of the court there is always a fountain sending a bright shower of water into the basin below. Men crowd around it, splashing their heads and arms and turning up trouser legs to wash their feet. Outside in the street, beggars sit against the mosque wall chanting their pleas or silently waiting, hands cupped before them. Few cross the threshold without distributing alms.

Carried forward by the crowd, we heard a car horn blaring insistently somewhere ahead. Here and there in the medina the government has widened a street, tearing out some old buildings to bring in more light and air. We came to one such widened street and found it solid now with human beings. At first I thought there must be some crisis, but as I watched I saw that nothing unusual had occurred. Where there is a limitless number of people, a wide street will be engulfed by them, as the tide invades a beach. Here a small car had become impacted. The driver, a plump man with dark jowls, had run down the car window, the better to shout scurrilities between bursts of his horn; but he could do no more than inch forward. Pedestrians slapped the car as if it were a donkey, or leaned on it as they passed. From the opposite direction came a Vespa, scattering people like chaff. Children stepped out of its path only at the last possible moment and then raced behind it, posturing in imitation of the lordly rider. With lips and blown-out cheeks, they made ribald noises very like the Vespa's blatting.

As we stood waiting to cross—for we could not share the unconcern of Moroccans about the mingling of soft flesh with motorized steel—I said,

"There is probably a better reason than just hygiene for widening some streets in the medina. The King no doubt remembers that insurrections starting in the countryside have more than once drawn strength from kinsmen and malcontents in the city. It might be very practical to be able to send in some truckloads of troops if the occasion should arise."

A medina is not a slum. It is simply an old city, with poor quarters and more prosperous ones. Before the French built the *villes nouvelles,* the medinas *were* the cities. And since only great palaces had parks and reflecting pools and vast orange groves, the people found their recreation either within their own courtyards or in the streets. This is still true today—for all but those who have migrated to the *villes nouvelles.* The people of the medina gather beside the oven of their quarter to wait while their loaves are baking, or line up at the fountains to draw water. In any angle between two walls, a storyteller may squat and draw a crowd around him. The public baths are social clubs—for men in the mornings, women in the afternoons. There is a hierarchy, of course; no one would challenge the right of the most respected in the quarter to bathe together on Thursdays, the eve of the holy day.

In the prosperous streets are fine old houses with green-tiled porticoes above their doors, and windows framed by arches on slender columns. Silver knockers—the Hand of Fatma, with a jeweled bracelet—gleam against the dark cedar doors. Some have a second, higher knocker, at the level of a horseman in the saddle. Wooden balconies—blue-painted and closely shuttered—extend out from upper stories, enabling women to scan the street through crescent peepholes.

The poorest quarter is always the *mellah,* where Jews have traditionally been segregated. Now that most of Morocco's Jews have emigrated to Israel, the Rabat mellah houses the poorest Muslims. On its streets you will still see a few black Jewish skullcaps, but ragged turbans are far more numerous. The old men spread out their wares between their thin shanks on the cobblestones—twists of string, combed and knotted together to sell for a sou, empty bottles, and the precious motor-oil cans with their lids ripped off. A sad listlessness pervades the mellah. I thought of our black ghettos, and wondered.

"These people must be cruelly disappointed," I said to Bill. "They migrated to the city in response to word of a new world awaiting them—and now they find themselves hemmed up in a pocket of medievalism. What *we* enjoy about the medina is hardly the life of their expectations. Yet I have seen no surliness."

"Who knows the time lag between the 'revolution of rising expectations' and the 'revolution of rising resentments'?" he answered. "Our ghettos were apathetic for years, remember." Ahead of us loomed the gateway that separates the mellah from the *ville nouvelle.* The throng that carried us along spilled through it and out into the traffic of an arterial road. Standing under the horseshoe arch, I could hear the sounds of two worlds commingled. Behind us looms banged, a water seller cried hoarsely, an anvil clanged.

From the road ahead came the hiss of air brakes, sharp as the crack of a whip, as a giant Diesel-engined truck churned through the sea of people.

Ramadan

One evening, after much wandering, we came back to our roof terrace, kicked off our shoes, and sat back to watch the sunset; a reflective peace settled on us. Suddenly a cannon shot crashed. Down the narrow streets its echoes roared, diminishing, and dwindled into silence. When no second shot followed, our spines relaxed, and our frozen stares at each other gave way slowly to surmise: Could it be the Ramadan gun, signaling the beginning of the month of fasting? Lights sprang out at the peaks of the minarets, the prayer flags fluttered out, and the muezzins' calls wailed upward in the violet dusk.

Sounds from the street below were entirely as usual. It must have been the Ramadan gun, we concluded, and went down to where we had parked our newly rented little Simca. We were going to dine with Josh and Mary that night, and were also inaugurating the adventure of driving ourselves. Everyone in Rabat seemed to be out walking in the middle of the streets—a sea of men, and youths holding hands as they strolled—a custom startling to the foreigner at first. Tonight there was a general air of animation about the crowds, but it was the animation of carnival, not of revolution. It took forever to make our way across the city.

We arrived at the new apartment house where Josh lived, and panted up the four long flights of stairs. His first words to us were "How did you like that cannon blast a while ago? You seem to be breathless; have you been imagining bands of Bedouin circling Rabat with their rifles held high for the charge?"

We made some succinct remarks about his stairway, and said of course we had had no such ludicrous imaginings.

"If this is the beginning of Ramadan," I said, "it certainly doesn't have a Lenten appearance."

"No, the Fast begins at sunup tomorrow. The days will be hard to get through, all right, but the nights will be something like a prolonged Mardi gras—several meals packed in between lots of visiting, the radios going all night, very little sleep. So, naturally, much of each day will be spent sleeping, to make sundown come quicker."

"What an inappropriate routine for a country trying to modernize!"

"So both Colonel Nasser and President Bourghiba of Tunisia thought. But whenever they said anything about it publicly there was a strong popular backlash."

Another guest that night was an American Arabist and historian doing archival research in Rabat. Ralph was also an old friend. "Is it true," I asked him, "that there's a lot of brawling in the streets during Ramadan?"

"Brawling is more common when Ramadan falls in summer. The Muslim year, remember, has thirteen months, and rotates through our western calendar. So, for several years in succession, Ramadan comes at the hottest time of year. The sun can be merciless then, and since the Fast applies to water as well as food, tempers can get pretty short."

"Maybe it's the ban on smoking during the day that makes tempers short," Josh put in. "You know Moroccans and their cigarettes."

"What time does the Fast begin?" Bill asked.

"At the moment when 'a black thread can be distinguished from a white.' "

"Are children expected to fast?"

"Not young children. Or pregnant women, or the sick, or travelers on a necessary journey (you can see the possibility of some loopholes there). All but the children are supposed to make it up later. Nowadays, it's becoming fashionable for the young radicals to break the Fast as a protest against the religious and political conservatism of the *Ulema*.[2] Other people break it, too, but more discreetly. Watch the papers; you'll see announcements about youths being sent to jail for 'public disrespect of the Fast.' "

Mary remarked that Berbers were quite casual about fasting. "Yes," Josh agreed, "they are casual about a great many aspects of Islam. But since they don't break the Fast flagrantly or for political reasons, they aren't apt to be sent to jail."

Having seen the great bulk of the people going ahead with their business while the Friday service was going on, and having so far seen no one stop what he was doing when the prayer flag went out on its mast, I observed that it seemed arbitrary to punish anyone in particular for laxity. "You're right," Ralph said. "The government is quite arbitrary, or the jails would be overcrowded. In practice, it's the political motivation that's punished; the police have more urgent things on their minds than supporting the 'Five Pillars.' "

"The Five Pillars of Islam" are Prayer, the Fast, Almsgiving, the *Hajj*, or pilgrimage to Mecca, and the Profession of Faith. The last, the act of embracing Islam, is performed only once. This crucial declaration is surrounded by no ritual. It is boldly simple: in the presence of three Muslim witnesses, the individual affirms that he takes Allah to be his God and believes Mohammed to be His prophet. Those words are binding for life.

Prayer is required five times a day: at dawn, noon, midafternoon, sundown, and in the middle of the night. Nowadays, only the professionally pious and the exceptionally devout adhere to the full schedule. The prayer exercises are rigorous and impressive. They are also functional; a man's mind is not

---

2. The Ulema are the ruling elders of the religious community.

prone to wander when he must coordinate his recitation with deep breathing, wide arm movements, and repeated kneeling and prostrations, all strictly timed.

The hardest requirement to satisfy is, of course, the pilgrimage. Bill asked how many men could achieve it. "Mecca is too far for any but the wealthy," Josh told him, "and the politically ambitious conservatives for whom the title '*Hajji*' still carries much weight. Most of the devout make pilgrimages to famous saints' tombs, which they believe will afford a sort of aggregate credit, instead of the true Hajj."

"A few minutes ago, Josh," I said, "you remarked that the Berbers are casual about religious practice. Who *are* these Berbers in the Morocco of today—after twelve centuries of mingled bloodlines?"

"You may as well forget true ethnic distinctions," he replied. "A *sense of race* remains strong, more a consciousness than an ethnic reality. The urban elite consider themselves Arab, just because historically the Arabs have preferred city life, and the Berber culture is stronger in the country. In point of fact, however, there may be more Berbers than Arabs in the medinas today."

"You just said to forget ethnic distinctions—!"

"There very definitely is a Berber culture that governs the attitudes of almost half the population. Language, folkways, and tradition are what count. The basic distinction is this: the Arab mentality has always been authoritarian, and the Berber has been distrustful of authority since time out of mind. Berbers lived originally in small autonomous communities, rotated power regularly among elected elders, and recognized only a customary law based on precedent. The Arab reveres a Sacred Law that hasn't changed an iota in centuries. As I see it, the ethnic amalgam has not bred out the stresses between a republican outlook and the Arab insistence on a hierarchy of power under the sultan, whose authority is absolute in both temporal and religious matters. Remember, the very word *Islam* means 'submitted.' That's why I say no Berber can ever be a thoroughly orthodox Muslim."

"And is it possible to keep a republican outlook alive today in the medina?"

"The government would very much like to believe it impossible! Perhaps we shall know before long."

Thinking of the ghetto-like aspect of parts of the medina led me to ask about black-skinned Moroccans. Were they yet another division and another distinctive culture?

"Much less so," Josh said. "Oh, there are dances no one but the Black Africans would try to perform, and bands of African drummers who tour the country; but these are too few to be significant. The main reason there is no black culture is that there has been free interbreeding with slaves from the beginning. By Muslim law, the child of a black woman, slave or concubine, is accorded the status of the father, and lineages are traced only through the male side—hence the princely black clan of the Alaoui. In principle, any black who is a Muslim is the equal of any man. Islam, they say, is entirely color-blind."

Ralph interpolated quietly, "Yet there is only one Arabic word for both 'black' and 'slave.' In spite of doctrine, the Moorish empire rested on a base of slavery; in fact, wherever there are blacks among Arabs, you'll find the status of the blacks ambiguous at best." (How deep and sad an irony, I thought, in the light of what our Black Muslims believe.)

Ralph went on, as if thinking aloud, "Maybe there is as little color bar in Morocco as you could find in any mixed society. But still you'll find the black-skinned pretty much at the bottom of the economic heap."

Josh reminded him that there is a tomb in the necropolis outside Rabat that is said to belong to the "Black Sultan." Ralph shook his head. "He wasn't pure black, I'm sure of that, though his mother probably was. Even a freed slave—and manumission is recommended by the Koran—would never become sultan."

"How long has slavery been dead?" Bill asked.

"That's a very delicate question. On the books, the Protectorate terminated it; but there is evidence of a clandestine trade persisting as late as 1961. Perhaps it could better have been called merely the importing of cheap labor, with the guarantee of a job and a home, and always with the possibility of manumission. The record is a little more benign, I'd say, than ours in the United States. I know a man in one of the ministries who says quite frankly, 'My grandmother was a slave; she lives quite comfortably in Salé today, in her own little house near the mosque.' Lots of old family retainers pensioned off by wealthy people probably came in originally as slaves. But I'm afraid it's only just to say that, in general, Arabs haven't dealt much better with questions of race and color than the Christian West."

No private conversation between foreigners in Morocco goes on for long without coming to the subject of the King. Everyone agrees that he is both intelligent and astute. But, in that case, why does he repress the Left and withhold any real power from all the political parties? Holder of a French degree in law, he himself gave his country the constitution that created a parliamentary system. Is he right in saying now that the country is not ready to be governed as a constitutional monarchy? Is he autocratic because he believes that he alone can balance the stresses on the frail economic and social structure, or because he cares only for power? Is his fear for his throne realistic, or merely phobic?

Ralph told that night of an episode he had witnessed the day before: "I was crossing the Boulevard up near the Grand Mosque when soldiers began spilling out of trucks and lining the street. I heard somebody say the King was coming back to the Mechaouar from a meeting with some ministers. It was only a matter of minutes before the road was cordoned off; the small crowd stood still to see him pass. His car came along quite slowly. Just as he came abreast of where I stood, a man burst through the line of soldiers and ran at the moving car. He was a ragged old fellow and looked as if he were just in from the country. My first thought was that he was trying to carry some private grievance to the King's ear. (Every Muslim subject has the traditional right to throw himself on the mercy of his sovereign.) I guess Hassan thought so, too, for he started to roll down the window of his car. At that instant soldiers pounced on the old man and dragged him back; guns were unslung quickly, and the King's car spurted forward. In the crowd there were murmurs of confusion and inquiry. The man was pouring out a story of having been passed over for some job he thought he'd been promised; he was roughed up a bit and then released."

How can anyone tell, I wondered, whether some ragged fellow like this is an assassin or just a loyal subject bringing his plea to the Imam of All the Faithful, whose hand alone can dispense justice in an imperfect world?

At the end of the evening, Mary said to us, "Would you like to go with me Friday to the Mechaouar? The King will go to the mosque for noon prayer; it's quite a show. You'll have a chance to see some of the things the monarchy means."

On Friday, well before noon, we passed through the high wall enclosing the palace compound. The Mechaouar is really a large village. There are palaces for the King's wives and his sisters and brother, and establishments for high-ranking Alaoui guests. Companies of the Royal Guard live in barracks with their families; nearby is a ring for training and exercising horses. In a hilly quarter known as the Commune of the Tuareg Guard, very dark, heavily veiled women in blue carry earthen water pitchers on their shoulders. On a large playground, black-skinned youths play soccer tirelessly. Crowning the compound, the palace buildings are undistinguished in style and quite modern; they are a jumble of green-tiled pyramidal roofs, grandiose gateways, and blank walls.

When Mohammed V returned from exile as king of a newly independent Morocco, it was here in the Mechaouar that he gave his first Speech from the Throne. At that time of great rejoicing, nomads camped for weeks along the wide esplanade running up to the palace gates. Sheep were slaughtered, and there was feasting every night; the drumming and dancing continued until dawn. Only reluctantly were the tribesmen persuaded to return to their home territory and get their seed in before the winter rains. Sidi Mohammed[3] was not only a very able man; he was also the adored Hero of Independence. In his short reign after exile—only five years—he began with flair, with firmness, and with astute compromise to build unity in Morocco. Even if he had lived, the task would have become increasingly difficult as the first ecstasy

3. A sultan named Mohammed may not be known by the usual title, "Moulay" ("Lord"), for there is only one Lord Mohammed. He is therefore given the lesser title "Sidi."

waned; but he died in 1961, leaving his son Moulay Hassan to complete his work.

On this first Friday of Ramadan, nine years after Independence, there were no nomad encampments, but the grassy spaces on either side of the esplanade were thronged with people. City and country folk alike, rich and poor, stood shoulder to shoulder: women wrapped in white haïks, men from the mountains in heavy burnouses so wide that they seemed to be wearing a tent on their shoulders, Berber women in bright embroidered skirts and blouses almost lost behind necklaces of shells and coins. Soldiers kept the esplanade clear for dignitaries arriving by car and on foot to pay their homage within the palace. We threaded our way toward the fountain opposite the palace gates; there we could see another avenue leading between rows of palms to the mosque where the King, as Imam, prays in the name of his people every Friday. The water seller passed among us, jingling his brass cups. Children scuttled between legs and out into the open space cleared for the procession; no one shouted at them or jerked them back, and in due course they found their way back to their parents.

A troop of mounted guardsmen trotted down the avenue, scattering the crowd. Then they backed their prancing horses into a solid line along the procession route. Their pleated scarlet trousers ballooned against white saddle blankets, and their white gauntlets held their lances upright, pennants flickering. The horses were matched companies of bays and chestnuts, blacks and dappled grays; all the harness gleamed with gold, and the horses' heads were decked with tassels.

We found room to stand near the fountain, where we could watch the palace gate open again and again to admit the arriving dignitaries, who swept on foot up the esplanade in shimmering white djellabas. Now and then, one of these would step out of procession and warmly embrace a friend among the onlookers, kissing him on both cheeks. (During any such public ceremonial as this, the pace of pomp may alter abruptly to allow for individual improvisation; dignity does not rest upon conformism here.) The greeting enhanced the joy of the occasion and nothing was lost, for the dignitary could jog smartly ahead to regain his place in line. Once more the palace gate opened, and a company of blue-turbaned Tuareg halberdiers marched out to stand on either side of the portal. Their cloaks fell splendidly in folds of orange and green over their scarlet trousers.

Another procession of officials swept up the esplanade, this time in gossamer blue djellabas. Behind us on the grass slope was a vivid knot of young tribeswomen with headdresses built up of coiled hair, woven bands, and silver bangles. From time to time, they clapped out Berber rhythms and sang snatches of song; there was no room to dance.

In another moment, a band comes marching out around the fountain with a flourishing of drumsticks and the shrilling of fifes and cornets. Intervals of drumming punctuate the music. The cornetists fling their gleaming instruments high in the air and, without pausing in their march, neatly catch them just in time to resume the music. More horse guards appear in the open palace gates—the Black Guards, who always surround the royal person. Now the top of the golden coach appears behind their ranks. The Tuareg present arms with a sweep of their brilliant cloaks. The guards lining the procession route rise in their stirrups and stand rigidly in salute. Their horses are as motionless as if cast in bronze; only the pennants on the lance points flutter and the fountain whispers. The golden coach rolls by, hemmed in by the Black Guards; within the coach, the lone white-robed and white-turbaned figure gazes directly before him. A somber melancholy seems to lurk behind his fixed expression. In the wake of his coach, grooms lead seven riderless stallions, dancing lightly on their gilded hoofs and jingling their jeweled harness; across each high-cruppered Arab saddle is thrown a rich blanket of crimson or green or yellow.

The band music is stilled as the King approaches the mosque. Through the open doors, chanting can be heard as the carriage stops. The King enters, the coach rolls back, and the officials and dignitaries follow him into the mosque.

For half an hour the crowds waited almost silently. There was little movement except for the arches of crystal thrown up by the fountain, and the nervous darting of a corps of street sweepers, in and out among the ranks of horse guards. The long-handled dustpans and the twig brooms were in great demand, as excitement told on the tensely waiting horses. Then came a stiffening, a prickling attentiveness, and the indrawn breath of hundreds. There appeared in the distance the figure of the King, now mounted on a white stallion; six curvetting, riderless horses and the empty coach followed him. He approached slowly, smiling now and turning to this side and to the other in stately greeting. His head was shaded from the sun by a crimson umbrella held up on a tall stalk high above him. As his shadow passed over the people, there came from hundreds of throats, "Hassan . . . Hassan . . . Hassan." The long-drawn-out sibilants were like a great sigh, like a wave receding over sand. The tribeswomen around the fountain behind us broke into ululation.

CHAPTER THREE

THE NORTH

The Bled

Every time we left Rabat for the *Bled*—the countryside—we were struck afresh by the immeasurable distance, not in miles but in mentality, between the sophisticated capital and the hinterland. City people in general, and the Rabati more than most, use the word *Bled* as we use "boondocks." With some justice, they view its people as primitive, suspicious, and stubbornly averse to change. It is not hard to understand the traditional opposition between city folk, with commercial interests, and a pastoral and tribal people. In spite of the rural exodus of recent decades, better than three-quarters of the population lives in the Bled—by stock raising and agriculture, most of it marginal.

Originally, the Bled consisted of many loosely designated tribal territories, each tribe holding its land collectively. The sedentaries had a highly developed system: the rain-watered land was allocated to pasturage; the rest was irrigated ingeniously and parceled out in plots for cultivation. The migrant tribes had their winter and their summer settlements, and bartered or fought for their rights of passage between the sedentaries. And preying upon both groups were the camel nomads, with their lightning raids out of the steppe or desert.

But various forms of private ownership intruded. There were the very extensive crown lands that could be leased out as patronage in return for support of an often shaky throne. Thus there evolved a class of feudal landlords who grew fat on a sharecropping system amounting to serfdom. One can easily see how a feudal politics developed: the historic opposition between the *Dar el Mahkzen*—"House of [Central] Government"—and the *Bled es Siba* —"Land of Insolence"—the often insurgent countryside, manipulated by ambitious overlords.

There was another category of lands, whose ownership not even the sultans dared tamper with: *habous* lands. A habous is a religious foundation or trust; it may be as innocuous as one I knew of that set aside a fund in perpetuity to provide for a middle-of-the-night prayer to be chanted from a minaret to allay the distress of insomniacs; or as ingenious as another, located in Fez, which was able to create scholarships to a religious school through the sale of pigeon droppings, which make good fertilizer. But more often a habous consists of a large tract of land that a man does not wish to subject to the parceling out among heirs required by Muslim law. By deeding his land to a foundation, he can keep it whole, stipulate how it shall be managed, and indirectly retain a profitable interest in it.

With the coming of the Protectorate, a new group of owners intruded—the French colons. Many of them bought their land legitimately. But many others acquired their *domaines* by guile, because few land titles had ever been registered. Even when a sum was paid, it was often absurdly small, since the ignorant fellah could not see beyond the immediate allure of cash in hand. So, one way and another, the French acquired a very large share of the richest and most promising land. With their historic talent for cultivation, they made the best of it, very often improving their holdings beyond recognition by modern methods and hard toil.

All the tribes suffered from these various encroachments of private ownership. The Berber tribes, without a written language, suffered most severely, since their lands were only orally described. Because of loss of territory, and for other reasons, tribalism has been on the decline during this century. And today the government does all it discreetly can to loosen tribal ties, because of the separatism they give rise to.

One summer, we drove north from Rabat into the western Rif range, and saw men's tireless efforts to wring concessions from nature. Here, in the northern Bled, they have built their stone huts on ground too rocky for any other use; the better ground they terrace into miniature hanging gardens. They hew irrigation channels and coax water down from every mountain spring. If they are fortunate, their fruit and nut trees will survive the winter and spread summer shade over the vegetables planted at their feet. For this is not temperate country. The rainfall is meagre at best, with fearful drought about every fifth year; blazing heat in summer, but, in the mountains, frost for eight months. The terrain is sliced into compartments by mountain ridges and steep valleys running northward toward the Mediterranean. That so many can live here is due to the pertinacity of the fellah, and the willingness of barley to grow in the least auspicious places.

Knowing very well their survival is at the mercy of Allah, these people do all they can to wrest a supernatural blessing. Every hamlet has its mosque, the doorway and the tip of its minaret freshly whitewashed each season. And they leave no route to Allah untried. Let the learned men of the mosques inveigh as they will against saint-worship; the country people fasten their hopes on every possible intermediary between their humble lives and the ineffable Allah. Stories of healing or of other supernatural powers have sprung up around a local personage, and he becomes forthwith a holy man, a *marabout*. Even in death he continues to dispense blessing; wonders come to pass at his tomb, which itself is referred to as a marabout. The countryside is dotted with these tombs—small mud-brick cubes crowned with a dome, the whole lovingly whitewashed so that it gleams with comfort and hope.

The animism never entirely stamped out by the pure faith lives on in these beliefs and in many ideas about the evil eye, about springs and other orifices in the earth's surface, and about the potions, amulets, and rites that bring protection. Many a deranged person is thought to be a marabout and is allowed to roam the country, receiving food and shelter as he goes, in return for the prophecies that rise to his lips.

We drove cautiously, for a tight curve could bring us upon a road-mending team clearing away an earth slide. In this country, the melting snow creates spring torrents. Only the sheltered slopes, with forest cover above to hold the water, make good growing ground. Here the grain rippled like the play of good muscle under tawny skin. This sown land alternated with *maquis*— brushy growth of scrub oak, juniper hunched low against the wind, and that spreading pest of degraded land, palmetto, whose roots are not to be dislodged by a single-blade wooden plow and are punishing work to get out by hand.

On all the sown land, men and women wearing great cartwheel straw hats were out reaping with sickles. (I don't think I ever saw a scythe in Morocco—stones are too abundant.) The women wore red-and-white-striped homespun skirts and often straightened up to wave when they heard us coming. Youngsters high above the road with their goats would leap downhill ahead of the car to clamor for cigarettes, or tips, or just a ride with us. One persistent child managed to run beside the car long enough for me to identify what he thrust out—a long string of locusts threaded closely together and still wriggling. Enough locusts make, I suppose, a few grams of nourishment. (The first time we passed through an airborne army of them, raining like bird shot against the car, I couldn't guess what they were, and tried to get out and investigate. I was immediately so peppered I couldn't scramble back in fast enough. From then on, I rejoiced to feel our tiny Simca playing the juggernaut.) In the Bled, if it is not drought, it is locusts—unless it is both.

The fellah of the North is still, in his own mind, a sedentary tribesman. He and his blood kin (all the members of a tribe believe themselves to be descended from a common ancestor) populate the small hamlets strung out along the road we followed. Each hamlet, or *douar,* surrounded by its croplands and common pasture, comprised a cluster of perhaps twenty stone huts around the mosque and marketplace; dirt tracks converged upon it from still smaller settlements in the hills. For the market is the hub of life. Each day of the week, except Friday, is market day for some douar. In fact, many of them are named simply "Monday Market," or "Thursday Market," or sometimes, to avoid confusion, "Thursday Market of the Tribe of Hassan."

Early in the morning on market day, dust rises along the dirt tracks, as donkey and mule trains wind steeply down the mountain slopes. By full morning, the open square is ringed with stalls, and all the beasts are either tethered or patiently waiting their turn at the water trough. Much of the trading is by barter—figs and raisins, lentils, chickens, and barley in exchange for wool, cheese, or animals brought in to be butchered from the mountain farms. Money must change hands for the city items—sugar and tobacco, and perhaps some cotton cloth—all of which come in by truck. So, of course, does the most important item of all—the indispensable tea. In such a douar as this, "foreigner" still means someone from another region. As for a European —the few they ever see are still designated as *Roumi,* Arabic for "Roman," or *Nasrani,* for "Nazarene," *i.e.,* Christian.

Two or more neighboring douars make up a tribal "fraction," which, for all practical purposes, is any one man's total community. The fractions are semi-independent and tend to ignore one another in normal times. One fraction may even have migrated a considerable distance and live quite apart from the rest of its tribe. But, in principle, its members can call for support from the whole if they become embroiled with a neighboring tribe. Feuds are apt to break out over water rights when your crops must depend on your tapping the same stream as your neighbor, or when an adjacent tribe has encroached upon your grazing land or violated one of your women. These are occasions when the whole tribe gathers to cooperate, with an enthusiasm only fighting can arouse. Tribal wars used to be frequent, and were vengefully pursued until one or another population was decimated. Now, because of an intrusive central government, only quieter feuds can be waged, with as little notoriety as possible.

Not only does the royal army—small, but effective—move quickly to suppress tribal feuds; to the tribesman, it seems that today's Mahkzen puts its nose into every man's business. Roads and telephone lines cut across the grazing land; tribal boundaries have been erased from government maps, and in their place outlines have been drawn of Regions, Provinces, and Communes. Fractions of different tribes may be lumped together into one commune, for the sake of rational geographic boundaries, and administered by a caïd sent from Rabat.[1] He tries, with varying success, to align the thinking of his people with new realities. But not all his people agree that tribalism is a thing of the past, that ways of life can be erased from men's minds as easily as boundaries from a map. There is room for wonder about the "reality" of these five hundred and one new communes, especially to men of the steppes

---

1. The title "caïd" means simply "agent of the government." Today the caïd is no more than a middle-rank civil servant. But in the feudal days just gone by, a caïd's loyalty had to be politicked for, and his willingness to raise taxes and provide troops for the Mahkzen was in direct proportion to his distance from the arm of the sultan. His independent power often grew too great to challenge.

and the mountains, where change is very slowly felt, and to the men of this poor, magnificent mountainous North.

The North has never been part of what the French designated as Useful Morocco—*Maroc Utile*. Because the North had always been inaccessible and generally hostile to the Mahkzen, and because there were ancient ties with Spain, the French never tried to administer it. Instead, they sublet it to Spain as an ill-defined sub-protectorate whose boundaries with the French Zone were none too clear. The Spaniards were never recognized in the treaty that the Sultan signed with the French at the start of the Protectorate. In sum, the Spaniards were never fully masters here, as became clear when Abd el Krim's rebellion was more than a match for them. But that story must wait.

The road we had been traveling led to Tetouan. Before we reached it, I wanted to taste the flavor of this northern Bled. So, well short of the city, we began to watch for a spot where we could thankfully stretch our legs and eat a picnic lunch. Leaving the road, we bumped down a track until it got too narrow even for the Simca. We locked the car and started walking toward a douar perched on the lip of a ravine.

The vibrating color of the Bled in June struck us like a physical onslaught. As it descends to the horizon, the Moroccan sky does not gently mute its color as our skies do; the blazing blue of the zenith continues down to the clear sharp line where sky meets earth. Its intensity heightens the color of everything seen against it—white parapets, a tawny boulder in silhouette, a black cypress throwing a long ellipse of shadow. No wonder North Africa has driven painters mad with desire to capture it on canvas. From Reubens to Delacroix, Matisse, Klee, they have tried to convey that unbelievable brilliance—the lacquer crispness of the magentas, oranges, pinks, scarlets . . . the spear of a century plant stabbing the sky, its low, sharp leaves curling back to earth . . . a turquoise jay flashing on tan wings. All colors are sharp-edged, unambiguous, in air which seems to have been polished to a sheen. Only the shadows are subtle—in them lurks every tone the eye can register.

We veered away from the huts when we found a path overhung by some shrub with hibiscus-like flowers and two-inch thorns. It led us past the last hut, and I heard hens and the rasp of a spade on rock. Then the track corkscrewed steeply downward, skirting caves in the side of the ravine, some of them thickly masked with shrubbery. One had a great flat boulder before its mouth and a tossing overhang of oleanders. We settled here because it was cool and free of dung. The pink blossoms hung down in rivulets, filling our shelter with their scent, which fought with a strong, gamy smell of goats. From the crackling in the underbrush, we judged the animals to be not far below us. Two children shouted to each other as they herded, and now and then a brown arm or a round, shaven head would surface through the brush for an instant. They seemed to be working their way uphill, which would mean discovery of us and very probably an invasion of our picnic site. We inched backward on our boulder toward the mouth of the cave. The shade was dense, the tossing oleanders dappled our figures with an effective camouflage.

The first child appeared, trundling a goat as one propels a wheelbarrow: he held the creature's hind legs at his waist and forced it up the path before him. The effort took all his strength and agility, and he did not look up. Several more animals followed, leaping from rock to rock along the track. They had just been shorn, and their tight muscles bunched under gleaming black and brown hides. Then came the second boy. One of his animals jumped out of the path, heading in our direction. The boy aimed a sharp pebble at it instantly, nicking it lightly on the belly, and the goat jumped back into line. The child had looked directly at us, but his sharp black eyes did not detect us, so completely were we camouflaged. As he swiveled his shaved pate to see that the other goats were following, we saw his long scalp lock, golden brown and curly. Such a lock is often spared when the scalp is shorn in order to allow the child's good djinn to reach down and grasp it, and so rescue him from a tight pinch.

Glad as we were to have been left unnoticed, our flesh prickled a little because we had been utterly invisible at a distance of only a few feet. We felt a need to leave this place. We stood up and began gathering our things together. Then a new commotion broke out nearby—the voices of women shouting in altercation, and more thrashing in the brush. Suddenly a red bandanna appeared, the face below it sweat-streaked and angry. A woman stumbled out onto the path and tugged sharply on a rope she held. The underbrush parted again on a young calf balking at every step. Wisps of grain dangled from its mouth, very likely the cause of the quarrel. Calf and owner struggled up the path until, just below our rock, the woman suddenly looked up and saw us. The black eyes narrowed in that first instant of surprise, then an expressionless mask fell upon her face. She uttered one short sharp word to the unseen woman, and the tirade stopped abruptly. In the uncomfortable silence, Bill and I nodded gravely to her. Stiffly, she bent her head a little, then quickly turned her eyes away. She might have been any age between thirty and fifty, weather-beaten, slightly bent with rheumatism—or from bending over the earth to reap for days on end. Her bright striped skirt caught on the thorns as she hurried away from us. Rawhide leggings showed below the skirt, and her feet were wrapped in burlap and laced with thongs. She manhandled the calf up to a dense growth of cane, and there dealt the animal so smart a blow on the rump that it crashed through the cane, dragging her along. As the grasses parted for a moment, we saw the eaves of a hut almost completely hidden by the high screen.

She needs to be strong and tough, I thought, to survive the life of a woman of the Bled—caring for the cattle, milking the goats, pounding her laundry on a flat stone beside the stream and then carrying it up this hill on her head, collecting the dung from her beasts and spreading it to dry for fuel or daubing it on the leaks in her thatched roof, carrying water on her shoulder from the nearest spring, very likely a distance of several miles every day. If she has not borne enough children, or if not enough have survived to share this burden of work, her husband has probably taken a younger wife. More hands to work, but more mouths to feed—it is a difficult equation a poor man must work out for himself. The Koran allows him to divorce a wife if she has failed in her duty to him; or he can keep her and take up to three more wives, provided he can care for them all equally. Polygamy is common today only at the top and at the very bottom of the scale. Among the hard-pressed of the Bled, "equally" can mean an equal share in a very meagre life.

An inaccessible region, a terrain of dense scrub and many caves, a people predisposed to separatism and secretiveness—these were the ingredients for the Land of Insolence. The distant city, the occasional appearance of the Mahkzen's soldiery with a demand for taxes—these were unreal, and to be resisted. But real enough were the local brigands who preyed upon these tribes of the North. One of these was the notorious Raïsuli, who, less than fifty years ago, was the despot of this region. He was not just a tribal sheik, he was also a Cherif, that is, directly descended from the Prophet. A Cherif enjoys a genetic holiness, transmitted from the holiest of men, an inborn quality called *baraka,* a combination of sacredness and supernatural power. Ahmed er Raïsuli was called Moulay—Lord—from boyhood to the end of his remarkably lawless career.[2] He terrorized the countryside and ambushed the Mahkzen troops sent against him. The terrain was in his favor, for in any of these caves men could lie hidden, listening to the feet of their pursuers overhead, or stalk their prey through the matted scrub.

He kidnaped Europeans from their homes in Tangier; then the complaints reached the Sultan with such force he sent a message to the Bey of Tangier: "Raïsuli's head or your own!" The Bey planned to trap the Cherif, but the first messenger he sent was never seen again until his head at the bottom of a basket of fruit was returned to the Bey. The next messenger brought Raïsuli a new type of rifle and guaranteed his safe conduct to the Bey, who wished to treat with him, and promised these new rifles for his men. Raïsuli, no doubt believing in his own baraka for protection, walked into the trap. It cost him five years in a dungeon, chained by his neck to the wall. (Not even the Sultan liked to hang a Cherif.) Few men could have survived this; Raïsuli not only survived but managed to escape.

From this time on, he was single-mindedly dedicated to one purpose: to drive the Mahkzen from the North. Moved by the power of his reputation for both courage and brutality, and by the superstitious fear his baraka inspired,

2. In what follows I have drawn freely (but not exclusively) on Rosita Forbes's *El Raisuli, Sultan of the Mountains* (London: T. Butterworth, 1924). This Englishwoman was so attracted by his mystique that she took down his story from his own lips.

men flocked to him. The Sultan sent army after army against him. On one occasion, Raïsuli's men lay hidden on the mountainside and watched the troops below advance. At the right moment, each man released a large boulder and sent it bounding down the slope, precipitating a landslide that killed most of the troops. Those who survived came over to Raïsuli, saying, "How can we fight a man whom even the mountains obey?"

This was around 1900, and by now the western powers were meddling in Morocco in earnest. The Sultan was almost an imbecile, sinking every year into deeper debt to the powers, and relying on them to bail him out of each new crisis. It was quite clear to Raïsuli that the Mahkzen was being bought by the Christians. As a Cherif, he appealed to all the tribes of the northwest to join him in the fight against "this new thing the Christians would do to us." They came to him. Once again, his army lay hidden on the mountainside. The Sultan's army camped on the plain below, a perfect target for the rebel guns. The fire the soldiers returned tore into the rocks and did little harm. In the thick of the battle, Raïsuli stood up, clearly outlined in his white djellaba, and shook a quantity of spent bullets out of his robe. He stood there, in the midst of withering fire from the plain, untouched. This was sufficient evidence of the baraka; the Mahkzen troops began immediately to desert to the Cherif.

He grew bolder—and richer. Some of his captives brought enormous ransoms. A Scottish officer had been seconded to the Sultan's service to renovate the demoralized royal army. Maclean must have made a striking figure in a djellaba woven of his own clan tartan; conspicuous enough, at any rate, for Raïsuli. The Cherif ambushed him, treated him most hospitably, and held him for ransom. They hunted together in amity. To make the Scot's sojourn more enjoyable, the Cherif "sent to the city for those curious pipes like cushions full of air, which his people play . . . even the Blacks can not sing against them." The ransom demanded was £25,000. The Scot demurred, refusing to write the ransom letter. Raïsuli then threatened to add a further demand: the protection of Britain for his own operations against the Mahkzen. Maclean still hesitated, and Raïsuli played his trump card: saying he must provide music for his guest, he stationed corps of drummers and cymbalists outside Maclean's tent, in relays through the days and nights. After five days of it, Maclean wrote the letter—and went to sleep. He was ransomed.

Then the Cherif pounced on his most notorious captive: the American Perdicaris, for whom he demanded an even larger ransom. Theodore Roosevelt's slogan "Perdicaris alive or Raïsuli dead!" was on the front page of every newspaper in the West. But something in the obscure diplomacy of this period of fishing in Moorish waters changed Roosevelt's mind, and he began to see in the Cherif "not a bandit nor a murderer, but a patriot forced into acts of brigandage to save . . . his people from the yoke of tyranny." The U.S. sent seven warships to lie off the coast of Morocco and back up Raïsuli's demands on the Sultan, which now included autonomy of his region. The hapless Sultan gave in, Perdicaris went free, and the Cherif reached the peak of his career.

But from this point on, his path was downhill. For the whole course of Moroccan history was now changed by that very "invasion by the infidel" he had so feared. The sultanate collapsed, the French installed their Protectorate, and Spaniards came to administer the North. Raïsuli intrigued, and betrayed, and intrigued again. Finally he fell—not to the Spaniards, but to a wilier fighter than himself, Abd el Krim.

Tetouan

Morocco's northernmost tip—a finger thrust toward Spain—has had everything to do with the fortunes of both countries in many periods. Power reached across the Straits from first one direction, then the other. The northern Moroccans have been shaped by that flow—their history is in their faces, faces that recall a Velasquez painting: long and narrow, with high foreheads and beards trimmed to a point on their chin. For the blood of Spain is still here; and so, since the Protectorate, is the language. The avenues are avenidas, the squares are plazas, and Ahmed has become Ahmedo.

The Christian *reconquista* of Muslim Spain, beginning in the twelfth century, was a three-hundred-year struggle, with intervals when strong Moorish sultans managed to reassert their dominion. But gradually Andalusia shrank under Christian pressure until all the remaining Muslims were penned up in Granada. There they continued until 1492, effete perhaps, but not without the genius to build the Alhambra and make it the most dazzling court in Europe. Finally, the last languid Prince was dislodged by Isabella, *La Católica*. The people of Granada still look up and point to the "Hill of the last Sigh of the Last Moorish Prince." With little more than sighs, he fled. And then *La Católica*'s crusade entered a new phase. Expulsion was not enough—the infidel's territory was invaded, trading colonies were implanted on the Moroccan coast, and Spain was embarked on that mystique of spreading the True Faith in Africa that jibed so neatly with dreams of empire.

Though she held onto these enclaves, Spain soon focused her attention on her New World colonies, and the Moroccan dream dwindled. But it was never forgotten. What Spain did not realize was that, by expelling her Moors and Jews, she had made her old enemy a gift of renewed vigor. It was the early Andalusian refugees who stimulated the fourteenth- and fifteenth-century renaissance of Moorish culture. The last to flee brought with them not only their refined skills but the new Spanish concepts in military architecture, new expertise to turn against their former home. Their influence can still be seen all over Morocco today—those citadels so like the fortifications the conquistadors built in the Americas. (You could transpose the little domed turrets on the walls of San Juan's El Morro with those on the Oudaïas Kasbah in Rabat, and no one would be any the wiser.)

The refugees went mainly to the North, many to Tetouan, the city Spain had razed, which they rebuilt in the Andalusian style, with gardens and arcades, exquisite wrought-ironwork galleries, and grilles throwing black filigree shadows over white walls.

We first came into the Plaza di Spagna, the hub of the town, in time for that honorable Spanish custom of the late afternoon, the *paseo*. There were, of course, no ladies to be seen, for Tetouan is still Morocco. But men walked arm in arm, with their djellabas thrown back and swinging behind like bullfighters' cloaks. In the center of the square was a graceful little loggia open on all sides between pairs of delicate columns; beside its bright green roof tiles, the tapering cypresses looked black. (I have sometimes wondered if the art of wrought-ironwork was perhaps born when a man was gazing at such a cypress—at its lean, rigid branches, the intricate pattern of its fronds, its stately immobility when all other trees are stirring in a light breeze.) Behind the Plaza, the minaret of the Mosque of the Pasha gleamed clean and white. The sound of many fountains refreshed the air, and each transistor the young blades carried poured out Andalusian music. At little tables under the plane trees, men were playing checkers while their tea cooled beside them.

As I watched, a bizarre figure slipped along the rows of tables. A filthy green felt cap sat askew on his unkempt curly hair; his tunic was mostly burlap, with bright odds and ends patched in; below, his thin legs were the color and texture of a hank of tobacco. His eyes glinted with the pleasure of what he was doing: surreptitiously he tossed back the dregs of tea from each unwatched glass. I believe he must have been seen, but was disregarded as a familiar institution. He saluted each glass as he set it down with all the appearance of a thoroughly happy man. A year later, I saw him again—same place, same game, same enjoyable blend of stealth and bravura.

Tetouan, one of the few cities of the North and long its capital, is small and elegant. It is overlooked by mountains, yet high enough itself to look down on a narrow plain where the serpentine Rio Martin glides to the Mediterranean. Mountains and harbor between them tell Tetouan's story. The river mouth was a favorite corsair base, and so the target of continual avenging raids. There was no century when Spain did not invade at least once, to scour the harbor and then march on the city. Tetouan would be seized and looted. Then soon, the mountains would release their wrath of tribesmen, and the occupiers in their turn would be butchered. While it was no great matter for Spain to take the city, to hold it was something else again. For the Berbers of these mountains never ceased to watch for their chance.

The name "Tetouan" comes from a Berber word, *tittawen,* which means both "eyes" and "springs." (For what are springs but eyes opening out of the earth's mysterious body?) There is the story in one word. The springs have always made the city glad with fountains; but not so those other eyes of the mountains—the eyes of rapacious tribesmen, always waiting for a weak spot, an unguarded moment. Neither Spain nor the native Mahkzen ever long controlled the city. Yet always, between wars, the citizens rebuilt their city— rebuilt their embracing wall, repaired their homes and their seventeen minarets gleaming with the soft colors of Andalusian tile, and resumed their exquisitely refined life. The North—zone of dissidence—and its often ravaged, always civilized little capital, seldom came within the grasp of the Mahkzen, until at last the Infidel took over the government.

We made a friend in Tetouan, a man of one of the old families who have directed the city's troubled destiny. He had just returned from serving as am- bassador to Iran, and told us we could identify his house in a new suburban villa beside the sea by the Persian-blue tiles around his doorway. Without them, we could never have found him, for suburbia in Morocco is as repetitive as elsewhere, except that instead of neo-Neo-Georgian touches, here the past is recaptured by a neo-fourteenth-century crowstepped gable in fresh stucco, or a portico of freshly minted green tiles.

But there was nothing dull about the man who greeted us. Mr. Bennouna was delicate in build, not tall, and his face was stamped with a rather sad reflectiveness. The dark eyes searched ours without making us uncomfortable; his voice was very quiet, his English supple and easy. As he led the way to a sitting room, I felt that here was a man effortlessly in command of himself. New cedar rafters filled the room with their scent, and as we settled ourselves, our eyes returned again and again to a splendid Persian carpet. We fell naturally to talking about Iran, where we had recently visited and been deeply impressed both by the art of her great periods and by her backwardness today. While our host talked sympathetically of her current problems, I reflected that, despite all its evils, the Protectorate had unquestionably brought gains to Morocco—the network of roads and bridges, the great industrial city and modern port of Casablanca, the brisk *villes nouvelles*.

I heard Bill say, "In the West, the Shah is often mentioned as one of the radical reformers of our time. What did you think of his plan for redistribution of lands?"

It was a bold question. In every developing country, land reform is one of the touchiest of political subjects. Many people supposed that reform on a wide scale would follow promptly after Moroccan independence. But no such thing has occurred. For the sake of good relations with France and her con- tinued help, those colons who could show legal title to their lands were allowed to remain or to sell their properties at will. The other, illegally ac- quired *domaines* reverted to the crown and then passed along the patronage route to powerful Moroccans whose support is vital to the throne. Thus most of the best land is still in the hands of a wealthy few. Many of these large holdings are run on modern, efficient, and highly productive lines. But the vast majority of the fellahin work small, unproductive tracts by the traditional methods and just manage to subsist. For this reason, the Moroccan Left makes land reform a cardinal principle and, charging that government studies are no more than delaying tactics, clamors for redistribution.

I watched Mr. Bennouna, interested to see how a diplomat would handle Bill's question.

"The Shah—what an extraordinary man!" he said. "I admire him greatly. But perhaps it is his fate to miscalculate, because he is too far in advance of the intelligence of his people. . . . In principle, a man will work the land more effectively when it is his own. But in Iran, there have been too many cases of mismanagement by peasants who lacked both the capital and the willingness to try new methods."

I understood that he was telling us, in effect, what he thought would happen in his own country. We had heard the same thing, I said, but because the allegations came from dispossessed landowners, we had wondered where the whole truth lay. Mr. Bennouna's reflective pause—unusual among Moroccans, whose defensiveness toward the West often leads to harangues—indicated that he was still considering an intricate subject.

I ventured, "I've heard it said Morocco has two agricultures, and the trouble is that there is no spin-off from the successful modern sector to the improvement of the traditional. Do you think this is true?"

"I believe we must find ways to change the fellah's shiftless agriculture, yes. But it cannot be done by abrupt moves. You must know habits are harder to change than boundaries! What we need to overcome is the apathy, the *deadened humanity* of the Bled . . . these men with little sense of their value and little hope. . . . It is the fellah's mentality we must change, for he has grown too dependent; he does not look ahead and make sacrifices for the future."

He paused again. I wondered if he would bring in the tragic losses of productivity that Syria suffered during her brief, unhappy union with the U.A.R., when her modern farms were broken up and parceled out to fellahin on Cairo's order. He must have been thinking on similar lines, for he resumed: "Of one thing I am quite certain: there must be no interference with our great modern *domaines,* where the French long ago introduced mechanized farming. These provide much of our export revenue; but even more important, they are our own breadbasket in a bad year. Only disaster would ensue if they were broken up and their productivity lowered!"

He was referring to those lovely and fertile regions often called the Verdant Three—a triangle around Rabat, the great plain west of Fez, and a big coastal region south of Casa. I could not doubt that he was right about these areas that together make up almost all the profitable agriculture. But where, then, lay any hope, in this largely agrarian society, for the "deadened humanity" he spoke of? His eyes were fixed on some pattern in the carpet, as if he were searching there for some alternative to the fellah's exhausting and unprofitable pursuit of inefficiency. For some time there was no sound in the room except the sigh of a light breeze against heavy draperies. Above our heads, a bronze lantern twisted gently on its chain.

Our host's voice broke in quietly, "I would like to ask you—what do you think of the North?" He addressed it to both of us, and we both hesitated, neither one wanting to tackle such a question. We were not only nonplused, since no Moroccan had ever before asked us for an opinion, but we were sensing for the first time what a difficult position we put people in with *our* questions. It was a neat turning of the tables, and a salutary one.

Bill tried an answer. "I think my strongest feeling about the North is, how far it seems from Rabat. . . . Though it is actually no more remote than other regions, I feel here a different quality of isolation." Groping for words, he looked to his host for help.

Mr. Bennouna's melancholy seemed to deepen. "Sometimes," he said, "we of the North feel Rabat sees us as *foreigners*. We have fewer schools, we are under-invested, short on technical advice. In brief, we are low priority. Yet we have mines waiting for development—mines the Spaniards knew well enough how to exploit!" He stopped quite suddenly to recover his composure and turned his gaze out the window, while his long delicate fingers traced the brocade pattern on a cushion beside him.

As the men talked, I had been remembering how Rabat describes Northerners—"Indolent people . . . keep Spanish hours. . . . They'll never modernize the country on a five-hour workday!" What was strangest was that fellow Moroccans should say "they" and speak of "them" so distantly. I asked, "Is it that Rabat *thinks* in French? Can't get over the idea that people whose second language is Spanish must be stepchildren?"

"Stepchildren!" said Mr. Bennouna. "Ah, stepchildren indeed! You will have noticed that all the modern experts either *are* French or *use* French? But Spain does not send us technical experts!"

"Don't your promising students go to Spanish universities?"

"A few. A few. Spanish universities today cannot offer all a student finds in France. There is not the same breadth. . . . Nor does Spain offer many scholarships. For most of our young people, no education is possible beyond high school. Of all our forms of poverty, the intellectual starvation is the most serious."

How slow and difficult is the task of erasing a partition line, I thought, and rose to take our leave. But Mr. Bennouna surprised us. "We have dwelt too long on hardships. If you will allow me, I will show you a little of Tetouan's greatness."

Much as I admired this man, my heart sank rapidly. I guessed that we were about to visit another arts and crafts school. The state operates many studios and schools and controls their standards through the Bureau de l'Artisanat. The ones I had already seen had depressed me—passive, docile children and young adults perpetuating outworn modes; sterile repetitions and a make-work atmosphere. The rationale is not hard to understand—such training is a life line for the unemployed, the only way to keep the artisan class afloat, at least for the present. Since cheap labor is Morocco's most plentiful resource, the handcrafts are a plausible way of exploiting it. But it had seemed to me the artisans had little faith in the skills they were being taught. They could see well enough that cheaper manufactured goods coming in from France will soon be the undoing of the *artisanat*. But as of now, having no alternative, they go on making the traditional and usually beautiful things in leather and brass and wool. Only once had I seen curios that were a travesty of the old tradition. I remembered that school with horror—grown men, very likely illiterate but intelligent enough for all that, laboriously making Disney characters out of wrought iron. If I were to see such things in Mr. Bennouna's company, what would my face betray?

We followed him back to town and stopped before a doorway: a high, rounded arch carried on low columns. Above the entrance hung a balcony corbeled out on supports as delicate as squares of embroidery—fantasies worked in threads of iron. As we stepped through the little door within a door, we were met by Andalusia. Three wings of the building, arcaded below and galleried above, ran around a patio. In the garden, espaliered trees spread out their arms in rows like a waiting *corps de ballet*. Fountains tossed their arcs of water high, then caught them with a whisper in marble basins. The secret of such a garden is to stop artifice just short of stiltedness. The rose trees were trimmed, but not so stiffly that their branches couldn't droop when drenched with spray. Flower beds were edged with box, but the flowers laughed at the restraint and spilled over. Behind all their colors ran the cool, pale plaster walls of the arcade and the robust contrast of heavy cedar doors, thrown open now to the courtyard.

There was no question that the work here was keeping alive the proverbial refinement of Tetouan. "Where else could this saddle have been embroidered?" the director asked, displaying an old one kept as a model. I looked with disbelief at a gossamer design of silk flowers stitched (with what kind of needle?) on the tough leather. And, "Where but in Tetouan could a desk like this be made?" It was worked in cedar inlaid with thuya (one of the hardest woods on earth), lemonwood, and mother-of-pearl, and beside it stood an armoire with tortoise-shell inlay. Both were new. I began to feel oppressed by a sense of inappropriateness. What troubled me still more was the obedient passivity of the students, some in their twenties and thirties. One worked a plaster frieze from a paper pattern, all curlicues and tendrils around a grapevine motif. "A meter of such carving takes three weeks," the director said proudly.

When I asked what market there could be today for such work, I was told:

"Our products are all of museum and palace standard!" Fretfully, I wondered why the explanation stopped there, when the museums were already full enough, and relatively few Moroccans are building palaces these days. In a studio where our feet were silenced in cedar shavings, I saw a shock of the red hair that the Berber strain still occasionally produces. This carrot-head was working on that most bizarre of all Islamic art forms—the domed roof, carved into stalactites. This exercise has always seemed to me like working a jig saw through a honeycomb to see how many planes can be created. It is hard to imagine a more elaborately unnecessary treatment of the inside of a dome. In a mosque or palace it comes into its own, the ultimate in intricacy for art's sake.

I found myself thinking ruefully about the Berber spontaneity in all art forms. What could not be done, I thought, if someone could encourage that splendid primitivism to flower again today in contemporary style? Whatever the link is between artisan and artist, it must have to do with the freedom—given or withheld—to create fresh forms, to state enduring themes in a new vocabulary. The Berber lyricism in verse and dance, the bold improvisation of their weaving, their jewelry and pottery—what might not happen if these forms found a modern expression?

My eyes dilated as we were led into a dark studio. There was the sound of thin hammering; a spark glittered now and then where a workman bent over his bench. Pistols, daggers, and muskets, inlaid and chased with silver, gleamed from the walls. The craftsman raised his head only briefly when we entered, and resumed peering closely at his work. His eyes were watering from the strain. He payed out the silver wire in his fingers until it disappeared under the chisel and hammer—swiftly, incredibly, accurately, the silver lay down into the hard glossy wood, in a pattern of arabesques that grew under our eyes. Then I saw that the piece receiving the inlay was the stock of a flintlock musket.

That triggered a memory, and now I felt I knew where a good many of these faithful reproductions were bound. I remembered leafing through one of those unsolicited catalogs that flood our mails at home, hypnotized by its dreary vulgarities: "Indispensable for Collector! Flintlock Muskets Imported from Exotic Morocco! Use these handsome desert warriors to bring rich ornamentation to your foyer." Now I felt more than ever oppressed.

After only a few more uncomfortable minutes, we parted from Mr. Bennouna outside the Ecole des Arts Marocains. Some other school had just let out. We stood engulfed in a tide of little girls—blue smocks, black braids swinging like pendulums, and gay, inquisitive faces staring up at us. I let out a long sigh; the vitality was like a fresh sea wind. Some of the children pelted across to a pushcart selling *glacias,* drawn up beside a gate in the city wall. Under the arch, several women crouched gossiping, shapeless within their robes. A man came by in a patched djellaba, rummaged in the old sugar sack he carried, and drew out the items he had scavenged that day. Pleased, he stretched, leaned back against the wall, and settled down comfortably to doing nothing, in the oldest Moroccan tradition of all. I looked down at the children again. Their eyes peered back, hot with life and hope.

A few days later, we are climbing the wide shallow steps that are the streets of Tetouan medina, in company with Mr. Bennouna, who is taking us to his family home. "You see why I find it more convenient to live in a suburb?" he asks. "I have not always time to walk a kilometer from my car to my doorway." Most of the kilometer seems to be uphill, between tall houses built out over the lane. Sometimes we pass through a brief tunnel, often go single file around a staircase from an upper floor. A man swings past in a burnous, the rugged circular cape still preferred to the djellaba in country regions. He looks no hotter than I feel, which makes me ponder again the universal belief here that the body fares better when insulated against the sun. A woman's voice calls down from a high window, and a swathed figure in front of us sets down her water pitcher, wipes her face with her fringed shawl, and calls back a reply. In the market square, a Tetouani lady in white from veil to toe looks ephemeral among the swarthy unveiled countrywomen, as does the crowstepped minaret floating above the rooftops.

We stop before brassbound doors. Mr. Bennouna applies his great key and then pushes hard against a chiseled knob the size of a dinner plate. A little girl runs across the court to seize his hand. He smooths her hair, saying to us, "This little one was born here, to a servant of the house." Apologizing that all is in disorder while repairs are under way, he leads us along the upstairs gallery, past rooms all shrouded in cambric, until we come to the *pièce de résistance*. Here he switches on an immense chandelier, and glare spurts at us—the whole room is paneled in mirrors. It is like being inside a flashbulb in action. As if reading our feelings, he smiles a little and goes on to a smaller room with walls of red damask.

This house he grew up in has aroused his memories of the Spanish occupation—the repressions, the corruption, the secret planning for revolt and freedom: "You don't hear about it today, but the nationalist movement was born in the North—the *first* Independence Party was formed here in Tetouan in 1936, long before the Istiqlal was formed in Fez. Down by the door of the Grand Mosque, I heard Mohammed el Torres deliver the first public de-nunciation of the French. My family, like all the educated, was deeply in-volved in the secret movement."

I followed his glance to a portrait above our divan, the proud and dis-ciplined face of an aristocrat. "My father saw that Spain wanted only military adventure here," he said, "to assuage the shame of an empire lost in the Americas. She never meant to colonize, for France was her landlord. And how obtuse those Spaniards were! They could have driven a better bargain with the French—might even have won Fez for their Zone. Instead, they let the partition line be drawn just south of these mountains of ours. Spain was here for prestige, and to rob us. But her armies were so riddled with incompetence and graft that they could not keep order. The police posts were many miles apart—those wretched Spanish soldiers, with their pay in arrears and their supplies dangerously low, went in constant fear for their lives, while their officers engaged in seductions and extortion. My father felt these abuses keenly; and he never forgot that this occupation had not even the legality of a treaty. It was a point of honor to conspire for freedom."

"Perhaps he knew Abd el Krim?" I asked. "Was that revolt not the seedbed of nationalism?"

He nodded gravely. "That was more than a revolt—it rapidly became a war of cleansing and liberation . . . which might have brought our freedom thirty years earlier. . . . Yes, when Abd el Krim was advancing westward in 1924, my father made contact with him and became his liaison with Tetouan. When all had been prepared, and the Riffi cannon opened fire from the mountains above us, only the Spaniards were surprised. They fled the capital, and for a time Tetouan was free. . . . To the end of his life, my father was proud to have been a friend of Abd el Krim."

Long after we had taken our final leave of Mr. Bennouna, I continued to think of the strange role history forced upon that man whose portrait hung on the wall—a Tetouani of high birth who put his life and the fortunes of his city at the service of a Berber tribesman of the Rif, that primitive region despised by all men of refinement.[3]

Mohand Abd el Krim was no ordinary Riffi. He had studied at the great Qarawiyin University of Fez, and had been given an administrative post by the Spaniards, whose ways and weaknesses he observed acutely. His brother Mohammed had studied engineering in Madrid, and proved to be something of a military genius. In their hands, a purely local uprising gained irresistible momentum throughout the Rif. In a matter of a few months—by July, 1921— a force of between 1,000 and 2,000 guerrilla fighters had ejected Spain from the eastern half of her Zone, 19,000 Spaniards were dead or captured and their transport, arms, and stores in Riffi hands. The garrison of 20,000 men at Melilla, on the coast, was isolated and under bombardment.[4]

For two more years, Spain remained impotent before the rebels. Then France began cautiously committing her own forces, for she would be in serious trouble in her own zone if the revolt in the North swelled into a *jihad,*

3. The Riffi tribes have given their name to the mountain range that runs all across northern Morocco, but they themselves live only in the eastern part of these mountains. Their territory is the only area correctly called "the Rif." I have tried to allay the confusion by referring to the long mountain chain as "the Rif range," and the smaller area belonging to this specific group of tribes as "the Rif."

4. My account of the rebellion is largely based on Walter Harris's *France, Spain, and the Rif* (New York: Longmans Green, 1927). Because he was respected by both belligerents, Mr. Harris was asked by the French to undertake the peace negotiations.

a holy war of liberation. There seemed no limit to the subtlety of the Riffi armies. They moved by night on trails no foreigner knew, and ambushed at daybreak. The world looked on in amazement at the steady retreat of the Europeans. Meanwhile, the Cherif Raïsuli, profiting from Spain's demoralization, was steadily enlarging his territory around Tangier. Intriguing between the many jealous Spanish factions, he made the high commissioners dance to his tune. But there was mutual loathing between the Cherif and the "Riffi dog"; Raïsuli believed he could ride the wave of insurgency to become sultan. However, Krim was entertaining the same ambition by this time, and the North was too small for two pretenders. The Cherif's tribes deserted him in favor of the man to whom Tetouan had fallen. The monstrous old brigand, now too bloated with dropsy to mount a horse, was carried by litter into exile in the Rif, where, refusing food and water from upstarts, he came soon to his death.

France could no longer afford half measures and peace feelers. Krim had laughed at the offer of "undisputed command of the Rif" and prepared to attack the French Zone. During the five-year war, he had compelled two European powers to muster against him three marshals, forty generals, and nearly half a million troops; he had bled Spain white and precipitated the fall of her monarchy. So now France struck with all-out determination. And one morning in May of 1926, Abd el Krim rode alone on a white mule through the French lines to surrender.

He had failed. But he restored to Moroccans their belief in native leadership. This was his bequest to nationalism. He died in exile, but not before Mohammed V had been recognized as king of an independent country.

Tangier

At Cap Spartel, the vast African continent yields to the western ocean. Something as amazing as the wonder of land's end troubles the mind. Our classical forefathers accordingly had the wisdom to clothe it in myth. Lured by the sea, but fearful, they discovered a demigod, Hercules, and ascribed heroic labors to him: he bestrode the Straits, the opposing peaks his stepping-stones, and went on to do battle with Anteus, son of Earth. He lifted Anteus only for the brief instant necessary to break his contact with his mother and hurled him into the waves, a tribute to Poseidon. Then by his widow Hercules sired Tingit, founder of Tangier. Thus was a truce arranged between land and water.

Between Cap Spartel and the African Pillar of Hercules, a shallow bay indents the coast, and here ferries and freighters ply out to Europe and cruise ships swing languidly at anchor in one of the prettiest of harbors. Above the bay, a small city lies back upon her hills—pillowed, smiling, and seductive. Tangier has attracted greedy eyes for centuries. Spaniards and Portuguese traded blows over her; she came in Catherine of Braganza's dowry to Charles II of England. "My God! They've brought me a monkey!" he said, at first sight of his bride, and wondered at the price he had paid for Tangier. But he could not hold it long; neither could the Moors, for the Europeans would not leave the strategic site alone. At length, like a courtesan fought over by many so that no one alone might possess her, Tangier became by informal agreement an international enclave.

During the nineteenth century, the consuls of all the powers lived and did business there, making it, in effect, the diplomatic capital of Morocco. With more and more profits being reaped in the country, large loans were extended to the sultans in exchange for commercial concessions to the West, which would in their turn necessitate still more loans. The consuls' protégés—native agents to facilitate business—bought the protection of the power they served, acquired its nationality, and so escaped the predations of the sultans. In this way, the shrewdest business minds of Morocco, many of them Jews, became tools of the West's penetration.

Any qualms felt by the West were supposed to be assuaged by the sending of missionaries to Morocco. But the obdurate British conscience was not stilled. "It is the fashion," Walter Harris wrote in 1889, "to try and christianize the Moors, and introduce drink, in fact by every means in our power to overthrow the social system. . . . If a strong check were to be given to the liquor traffic, and if the Christians in the country would learn that Moors are men and not beasts, then and only then we might have some reason for expending money and philanthropy in Morocco."[5] But by this time corruption and disorder were so rife that the sale of protection could be justified on humane grounds. Harris admits it was now the only means to safeguard property and lives until "the Sultan can be trusted to rule in such a way as renders it unnecessary."[6]

But life in Tangier offered too many quick profits and too many pleasures to be sacrificed to a scolding voice. Villas and legations staffed by armies of native servants, tropical gardens, a sparkling harbor, fine hunting, and polo—it was better to recognize that a man's private business was his own affair. Tangier was a key port in the opium traffic and supplied many of the brothels of Europe. So, of course, it attracted international rascals and cutthroats. When too many Europeans had been found garroted in side alleys, the foreigners set up their own Committee of Public Safety. Next, they checked the inroads of dysentery by creating their own sanitation system. By such small steps, Tangier became international property in all but letter.

5. Walter B. Harris, *Land of an African Sultan* (London: S. Low, Marston, Seale and Rivington, 1889), pp. 97–98.
6. *Ibid.*

Evidently, *fin de siècle* Europe needed a spot off the beaten track where exoticism, profit, and pleasure met.

Everyone knew the Cherifian Empire was ripe for takeover.[7] All that remained to settle was which power would move in. France, Britain, and Germany for years had been jockeying for position in Africa when, in 1904, the secret Entente Cordiale between the first two gave France a free hand in Morocco in exchange for a guarantee that she would leave Egypt to Britain. The flouted German Kaiser provoked three "Moroccan crises" in the space of a few years, each one bringing Europe near to war. The last occurred when chaos engulfed Morocco in 1911, and the Sultan, besieged in Fez, appealed to France for troops. As the French armies moved to relieve Fez, the Kaiser's gunboat appeared in Agadir harbor. This time, France ceded to Germany her interests in Equatorial Africa, and the crisis abated. Within a year, the Treaty of Fez was signed and the Protectorate in effect. The Mahkzen France had rescued would now dance to the jerk of French strings.

But Britain's cordiality in the Entente had not extended to seeing France installed across the Straits from Gibraltar. Not only had she insisted that Spain's interest in the North be honored, she also required that Tangier be recognized as an International Zone. Specifics could not be worked out until after the vast interruption of the World War; but then, in 1923, the Convention of Tangier stipulated that five European powers should administer the city and two hundred square miles around it. Another partition, and a third Zone. But Tangier proved to be more than a happy hunting ground for Europeans of all kinds—it now became a base for plots against both occupiers, and an asylum for rebels who saw to it that money and supplies flowed through to the nationalists. It was here in 1947 that the young Sultan Mohammed V, in a bold appeal to the world for independence, thoroughly disabused the French of their idea that they had secured in him a pliable puppet. France and Spain had many an occasion to rue the Third Zone.

With Independence, Tangier was reunited with the rest of the country. But a pen stroke has not been enough to re-create her Moroccan identity. Wandering her streets today, you hear the church bells more often than the muezzin's call. Foreigners live here now, not because it is a busy center of commerce —for it is no longer that—but because there is a great deal of languorous charm and no income tax. The artists' and writers' colony keeps to itself, little troubled by convention, for this is a tolerant city still. Almost any banned book, in almost any language, can be bought, its dust jacket neatly turned inside out.

Though most of the Spanish baroque façades are moldering, and abandoned legations are frowzy amid gardens gone to seed, you cannot feel

7. The designation "Moorish empire" gave way to "Cherifian empire" when the Alaouites, Cherifs by descent, became the ruling dynasty in the seventeenth century.

sorry—the place is too beautiful. All the important transactions take place elsewhere now, and even Tangier's strategic position has been outmoded by inland air bases and tracking stations. (Even that prime example of a strategic site, Gibraltar, was the subject of negotiations in 1966. Moroccan newspapers took a pointed interest in the talks, we noticed, and were dropping hints that if Spain were to repossess herself of Gibraltar, she could expect to hear forthwith about those three Spanish thorns still embedded in Moroccan flesh—Ceuta, Melilla, and Ifni.)

The city lost its free port status in 1960, and with it the international bargain shoppers. Now, if at three o'clock a merchant gives you the customary ploy that he is dropping his price "only for good luck, you understand—because you are my first customer of the day," he may just possibly be speaking the truth. Sometimes when I woke in the morning, I thought I was in some village; for instead of city sounds I heard only the raucous sunrise chorus of donkeys and roosters—countryfolk have acquired squatters' rights in many a crumbling villa. Once in the boulevard traffic of high noon, I saw a sheep trotting on a leash.

The medina is listless. Little girls explore the rubbish in the streets, and cats stalking on the roofs drop suddenly from sight through one of the many holes. In the market, the sad, Oriental eyes of Jews gaze out above their little piles of vegetables. Each time we emerged from the medina, leaving the last beggars and pestilential urchins behind as we strode up the hill, Bill would shake himself like a bird dog and tell me that begging is a business like any other, except that it has the advantage of requiring no capital and no training. And if I got angry as we came among the lovely villas of rich Tangierines, he would remind me of the salty truth that social responsibility in any organized sense only takes root in advanced economies. Certainly, Islam's emphasis on almsgiving has been anything but a spur in this direction. The conservative, construing the status quo as the will of Allah, feels under no obligation to question His plan for the unfortunate. This is one of the reasons for the cleavage between the devout conservative and the "irreligious" modernist who believes in intervention.

When the evening breeze begins to loosen lavender petals from the crepe myrtle trees, and white yachts swinging at anchor in the harbor turn copper in the sunset, Tangier can only seem benign. Pendulous datura blossoms overhanging garden walls begin to loose their evening scent, and the sky is stitched in black with the evening flight of swallows. It is time for the *paseo* —time for all comfortable Tangierines to stroll along the boulevard, drop in at a curio shop, or sit down over an *espresso* and stare appraisingly at the European women. Youths congregate at street corners to lallygag over the cruise parties coming ashore for the evening. Uphill from the boulevard along the harbor, steep side streets lead to a quarter of night clubs, small *boîtes,* and shuttered houses. It was here that we fell in with an acquaintance who owned much city property and gave off an aura of many delicate business affairs. Whenever we ran into him, he was both suavely cordial and quick to state that he was on his way, alas, to an appointment and could not linger long in our company.

A recurrent theme in all his discourse was "the April calamity"—that April of 1960 when Tangier's free port status was wiped away and with it the thriving black-market currency exchanges and a brisk export trade in narcotics. The brothels were closed. Prices rose and rents fell, between them demolishing a good deal of our friend's income. He nearly emigrated then, having had an offer of $450,000 for his house—a property on which he paid $20 a year in taxes. But, having investigated the scale of European taxes, he decided to stay where he was. He never ceased, though, to lament "that officious meddling by Rabat in 1960" and to lampoon the bureaucrats, calling them humorless and self-righteous, and picturing for us the typical pursy official panting up one of these steep side streets, with the dancing water of the harbor behind him.

"You know perhaps what the result was?" he asked us on one occasion. "No? Why, the 'cleanup' of Tangier sent every kind of lucrative business over to Gibraltar! Worst of all, when normal operations were resumed, only more discreetly—for you know, I presume, that nature abhors a vacuum? —they were in the hands of foreigners . . . your own good people, in large measure." He looked at us sardonically, settling his fez more firmly on one side of his head. "Well, at least they have saved us from the sad fate of a Gomorrha *passé*."

A young American friend had told us, I remarked, that he had been cautioned when he came here never to walk alone at night in the streets. The Tangierine looked really surprised. "I find it hard to understand why a young man should *wish* to walk alone at night—? There is still room in Tangier for all tastes . . . but hardly for no taste at all." I decided to leave it at that.

He stopped to look carefully at some of the posters outside a night club. The gorgeous women's bodies were laden with bands of beads and glitter, and a few wisps of veiling. "It is still the best dancing west of Cairo," he said. "The *pièce de résistance* is an attractive girl, and she knows her work. Have you seen the dancing yet?"

"No," I said. "I've been hoping you would recommend to us the best place." I kept my eyes away from Bill, who had heard no inkling of this.

"Wait one moment," the Tangierine said, "and I will step in—I am well known here—and can have the best table reserved for you. What night will be convenient?"

"Tonight, I believe," I said as quickly as possible. I dared not give Bill time to enter a protest or to dream up a conflicting plan. While we were alone, I apologized for my ruse: "I think you'll like it, even if you do have to take me with you—?" He eyed me and finally broke into a smile, muttering something about "all phases of Moroccan culture."

Our friend came back. "The table is yours—in the front. Don't come before midnight. They make certain adaptions in the early show, for cruise parties —to the detriment of the art." He pleaded an engagement, and made us a very Continental bow.

The Club Koutoubia was crowded at midnight, and a good many of the cruise party had stayed for a second round, their faces wearing elaborately casual expressions. The Moroccan men, on the other hand, looked taut, as if they had waited long enough for their fare.

There is a world of difference between our burlesque girls and an authentic belly dancer on her home ground, a difference arising from the way each is regarded. The Moroccan girl inherits an old tradition. Great caïds kept gifted dancers in their harems as a sign of wealth and prestige, and, when there was much to be gained, a caïd could make a gift to the sultan of one of his finest dancers. Even today, the belly dancers believe in their performance as a high form of erotic art, its function being to titillate and stimulate, so that life may go forward at its richest. They do not wear surly expressions, like the glassy-eyed girls of New Orleans or San Francisco, who chew gum while they swing their tassels. (Once on Bourbon Street, I saw a girl who reminded me of Will Rogers: just as he used to stand, dead-pan and almost motionless, before the footlights—only his jaw working, and the wrist that swung the lariat—just so, this girl stood on her platform, expressionless. Every part of her ripe anatomy remained still while she rotated one platinum-tipped, silicone-injected breast, and then reversed its direction.)

The girls of Koutoubia appeared to like their work. They carried themselves like some special caste—of Vestal concubines perhaps. When the first dancer burst onto the floor in a swirl of veils and a glittering of anklets and necklaces and a few patches of sequins, she had our utter and complete attention. The body was one of the most beautiful you could possibly imagine. As she began to undulate, the guitars and drums started to throb, and a sinuous flute melody twined through the plucked strings. She swayed and arched and drooped, then electrically arched again. It is a misnomer to call it a belly dance, for each bit of that glistening, perfect flesh has its moment to perform. The art lies in focusing attention on one area at a time. The head and neck and hips are motionless while the shoulders and breasts undulate; or, while the breasts and knees are as still as marble, the hips and belly rotate as if no bones lay beneath the silky skin.

It is so utterly and candidly erotic that it bypasses vulgarity. As the dancer tears off her diaphanous veils one after another and draws her fingers tenderly across her body, the music quickens and deepens in timbre. She arches and bends backward to the ground until her hair sweeps the floor. Then, with a slippery grace, she is erect, her hips thrust forward, her head thrown back, and her teeth bared. Suddenly her head droops on her breast; her body is entirely still, all except for the small perfect navel, which rotates as if detached from the pelvis. She throws her head up as the tempo quickens, her face taking on a sultry expression and her lips curling in a frank challenge. The tension has built to a climax. (I snatch a glance around me. Bill is sitting forward on the edge of his chair, attentive in every pore. Several women giggle. I believe I see panic in one young man's Nordic face. Moroccan eyes blaze.) With a clash of cymbals, the body falls limp to the floor in orgastic climax. There is a second of dead silence, then the applause. With a single fluid movement, the girl gathers herself up from the floor and gives us a brief inclination of her head, then swirls out of sight.

There is not much scope for variation in belly dancing. One woman executed her movements while carrying a lighted candelabrum on her head. After three or four dancers had repeated the same theme, it began to pall on me a little, and I found myself speculating on a surprising idea: Did the flamenco dance derive from the belly dance? Is this another line of inheritance from Moorish to European culture? For all her elaborate costume, her castanets and crisp stamping, the flamenco girl is executing just the same steps—repetitious, unsubtle, designed to emphasize only one thing: the sinuous body. Both performances are aimed at erotic arousal. For the dry heat and crackle of flamenco, the belly dancer substitutes a steamy languor. The one evokes an image of a lithe cat in good fighting trim, the other brings to mind an indulged house pet who, finally tiring of tameness, un-sheathes her claws in earnest. The great difference is in the music, the flamenco being magnificent by itself, while the belly dancer's is no more than a vapid accompaniment. It was intriguing to compare the two forms, and to consider how skillfully the European avoids stating anything too explicitly. As long as he's not obliged to call a spade a spade, all is well.

The night air outside was cool and welcome. "The only thing that put me off," said Bill, "was that seductive little lad in the pink silk trousers. Even allowing for all tastes, I did find him hard to take." In the midst of all the exquisite girls, a youth had appeared for one number. His costume was completely ambiguous—above the Moorish trousers he wore a breastband ornamented with sequins and glittering braid. He spun to the dance floor with a large brass tray on his head, on the tray a circle of tiny cups full of coffee. He performed his bumps and grinds and spun in tight circles, never raising a hand to his head, then slid to the floor and rolled across it, tilting his head at inconceivable angles. When he slithered again to his feet, not a drop of the dark liquid had spilled.

"You know," I said to Bill, "queer though it may seem to us, it is not considered so here. Lots of slender boys put in a year or two at this kind of dancing and resume what we think of as more normal life later. Why? Because the conventional woman doesn't dance for men; in the privacy of the home, women dance for each other only, and would think that what we've watched tonight was depraved. So men have to go out for their titillation."

✿

One day a note lay in our mailbox: "The Cherifa of Ouezzane will receive you for coffee tomorrow at eleven." This lady, wife of the Governor of Tangier, I had been eager to meet on several counts. Her reputation was for modernity of outlook; yet the title she bore evoked all that is most traditional, and I had long wondered about her. John Magagna, young headmaster of the American School in Tangier, was to go with us—she was on his board of directors and wanted to talk with him.

To be Cherif of Ouezzane has meant through the centuries to be head of the religious Brotherhood of Ouezzane. The brotherhoods are sects with secret rites, usually ecstatic in nature, which have supplied the color and drama lacking in the formal mosque service. Each brotherhood has its own "Way," or rule, which demands strict adherence; when a man receives his rosary of prayer beads, he pledges financial support and regular attendance at the local chapter, or Zaouia, and takes an oath of lifelong obedience to the head of his order. The size of any membership being secret, no one on the outside could tell when one of these sects would emerge overnight as a potent political force. The oath of obedience has meant responding without demur to a call to arms against the Mahkzen, against the Christian, or against another brotherhood. (One powerful order first backed Abd el Krim, then turned against him and helped the French; twenty years later, another sect declared first for the Vichy regime, then, as the Allies landed, flocked to Casablanca asking American citizenship in exchange for aid to the Allied cause.)

Ouezzane today is a little ghost town, except when a pilgrimage converges on it. Though the political power of the brotherhoods seems to be in abeyance today, a Zaouia as old and honored as Ouezzane's still draws immense crowds of pilgrims. I suppose no one can measure the potential of such a pious army or predict with certainty whether the piety will remain orderly and passive. The Zaouia was deserted when we saw it, the cells opening onto the court-yard all empty. But something potent lingers in the name, for no sultan would dare to lay hand on its rich coffers, and none, including the present King, has failed to visit the holy precinct as soon as possible after mounting the throne. At the Zaouia's gate, the new monarch waits to receive the Cherif's Kiss upon the Stirrup, which signifies the fealty of Ouezzane.

So when we stood before the Governor's mansion, high on a bluff above Tangier, I half expected to be received by a lady shrouded like the ladies of Ouezzane, with only one eye exposed above a tightly drawn shawl. The soldiers who, after inspecting us, swung wide the gates emblazoned with the provincial coat of arms, studied the proletarian little Simca, which we parked under a huge old magnolia in full blossom. Delphinium grew shoulder-high beside our path, and the roses were so perfectly formed that they looked like embroidery on the tapestry of leaves. I caught a glimpse of a terrace beyond the garden, and of the milky haze of morning lifting from the sea far below.

The door of the mansion opened, and the Cherifa came down the steps to meet us with a complete lack of ceremony. She wore a trim tailored suit, and her bearing was at once fully composed and brisk. The sunlight gleamed on black hair smoothed back from a bland forehead, and black brows arched like wings above the agate eyes. Her strong Arab features—she is Lebanese by birth—softened in a warm smile. She led us to a drawing room furnished in European style, and sat down opposite us. A broad window at her back framed her in the royal blue of the Straits.

John was full of a very grand wedding he had lately attended—that of a former student—and asked if the Cherifa had gone. "Yes, we attended for a short time on the last night. What a *kermesse!*" Turning to us, she asked: "Perhaps you know about the old-style Moroccan weddings? Feasting every night for a week, singing and dancing and visiting the homes of relatives all through the nights . . . everyone completely exhausted and out of pocket at the end of it."

John was a little taken aback. "But you surely like to see the ancient customs observed like this?" The Cherifa cocked one eyebrow but said nothing. He went on, "We, too, could only go the last evening. I heard the festivities had continued until dawn both the nights before. There must have been hundreds of guests. . . . By four o'clock in the morning we were still waiting at the bride's house for the groom to come and fetch her. When he finally appeared, poor young Driss looked tired."

"I'm sure with good reason!" said the Cherifa. "Oh, yes, weddings are the affair of the women. Between bouts of jokes and raillery at the groom's expense, they usually forget all about him."

"At last the bride was ready to be claimed," John continued. "She set out, carried on the shoulders of five or six men, and so stiffly encased in jeweled and brocaded kaftans that she looked like a wax doll. Under all the rouge and the kohl, her face seemed quite expressionless."

"But what would you expect?" the Cherifa responded. "She was tired out—she had probably been standing in those kaftans for hours and hours, sagging under their weight. And all the tumult and the fussing over her, and her mother-in-law always there, looking and looking at her as if weighing her worth! Besides, I am very sure the girl was frightened—she had never seen the groom. . . ." The Cherifa raised her shoulders in an eloquent shrug. "The ancient customs are very picturesque, yes. But I am not much in sympathy with these displays. And how wise is it to expect young people who know nothing of each other to be able to build a strong family life? I think Madame must be of my persuasion?"

Nodding, I asked if many young people were not now pressing for the freedom, if not to choose their partners, at least to have a strong voice. "The young men, yes," she answered, "but the girls are not yet showing enough inclination to take this responsibility. Though a girl may not now be married below the age of sixteen, much earlier betrothals are still common. She is not mature enough to examine what marriage means! And here the coquette tradition is still very strong—girls spend their time shopping and preening, and think marriage an end in itself."

I said I was afraid that the western concept of "romantic love" as the basis for choice did not work out too well either, and perhaps we had lost something in sacrificing the sobriety of arranged marriages. "What," asked the Cherifa crisply, "leads you to think arranged marriages are well thought out? I will name no names, but I will tell you of one case I know about where the girl followed her own counsel. She admired a certain young man and agreed to meet him secretly. They fell in love. But they were very discreet and avoided notice. In due course, the young man's father approached the girl's family in the usual way. It would be a very suitable and agreeable marriage to both families, so the contract was arranged. The betrothal was announced, and plans were laid for the marriage. Then, somehow, it was discovered that they had met in secret, many times. The girl's family felt disgraced. They canceled all the arrangements, returned all the gifts—and I hate to think what they said to their daughter. At any rate, after a suitable interval, another marriage was arranged and carried out with all the proper formalities."

"And has it worked out happily?" I asked.

The Cherifa looked full at me. "It has not. . . . I believe a divorce will soon be made known."

A servant appeared with a large tray, which he set down before her. She looked at the four glasses, the teapot, and the mint still sparkling with dew, then glanced up quizzically at the man and spoke to him in Arabic. His shoulders sagged with disappointment as he left the room.

"I hope you will forgive me. I have invited you to coffee, and now I have only tea to serve you. It is that way these days. . . . I hope you will not mind Moroccan tea?" Smiling, she filled the glasses.

"But surely," I said, "there are also a good many girls with more advanced ideas and habits?" I was thinking of many couples I had seen together in Rabat—and, yes, in Tangier also. She responded quickly—a little too quickly, I thought.

"Oh, after Independence there was a time when all the young had lost track of themselves for a while . . . tried out European habits, wore nothing but European clothes. They discarded the veil—a very good thing, too—after our late King unveiled his daughter, the Lalla Aïsha. Now *there* is a fine model for the young Moroccan woman—she combines progressive ideas and a career with a most circumspect demeanor. [The Princess is married and serves also as ambassadress to Great Britain. It did not seem to bother the Cherifa that, to the average young girl, the Princess is far too exalted and remote to be a meaningful model.] And how beautifully she wears her kaftan! You notice more and more of our girls following her example."

I did not understand the abrupt shift in the Cherifa's attitude—from sympathy for more freedom of choice to sudden emphasis on "losing track of themselves" and the wearing of kaftans. But the Cherifa was not a person to be pinned down when she did not wish to be. She now directed our attention to a plate of *cornes de gazelle*—horn-shaped, filled with almond paste, and extravagantly sweet.

"And what about the girls I've seen in shops and offices—is it acceptable for middle-class girls like those to live independently of their families?" I asked.

The answer was instantaneous: "No reputable girl would think of living outside her parental home! There is only one type of woman who does that." She paused; then, less tartly: "The shopgirls you have seen are undoubtedly very decent young women, and take their earnings home or use them to buy kaftans for their dowries."

"And upper-class girls would not work at all?"

"Very few. The time spent in training for a career would jeopardize their chances of marriage. It is difficult for a woman over twenty to find a husband, and to remain a spinster is a reproach and an encumbrance to her family. I think of one young woman who chose a career instead—she studied nursing abroad. But, on her return home, she could find no work suitable to her station in life. A few married ladies—I am thinking especially of the princesses and some who have married into the royal house—set a public example by devoting themselves to welfare activities."

"Does the general ignorance of French mean that fewer girls of the North can aim for a higher education, to equip themselves for a fuller life?"

"Now *there* you are touching a vital issue. But there will be no problem as soon as we have Arabization of our schools." Her glance swung directly to John.

A little girl of four or so spun into the room and, seeing us sitting around the coffee table, stopped so abruptly that her shoes skidded across the tile floor. Recovering herself, she came and bobbed the most demure of curtsies, then stood in the circle of her mother's arm and went eagerly to work on a pastry. The Cherifa spoke to her—*in French*—stroking her long curls and straightening her pinafore.

John recognized that his time had come, and set down his glass. "Cherifa, I know how important Arabic is. But how are we to allot more time to it?"

"Wherever there are Moroccan students, they must learn Arabic culture thoroughly! How shall we train them to lead their country if they do not know who they are?" She looked at the small head beside her intently, and there was silence for a moment. "Would you be content for your own children if English were scanted in school? Our children will grow up *déracinés* if they are not familiar with their ancient heritage, and with Arabic, the only language that can express it. Of course, we must look to the West for help in developing, but not as a child looks to a parent. Moroccans are not, after all, a primitive people just emerging from darkness."

Since all her mother's attention was now given to John, the little girl drifted over to us, staring with round eyes at Bill's pipe, then at his American sports shoes. Suddenly, she asked how he had come there. Bill inquired whether she meant to her house, or to Morocco in the first place—for it was quite clear she felt he had come from some improbable distance. But she only gazed at him silently. So he tried again, "If you look out your front window, you will see that we drove here in a very ordinary, small car." Now she shook her head slowly, obviously rejecting the possibility.

It was true enough, I thought, what the Cherifa had said: Morocco is not a new country. Twelve centuries ago, Spain was her colony; six centuries ago, she led the western world in the sciences, mathematics, and philosophy, and brought much of the lost Hellenistic heritage back to Europe through Arabic translations. Yet today, her modernists, with the usual ambivalence of postcolonial peoples, seem bent on aping the French, dismissing as regressive whatever has no parallel in Paris. This attitude has been enough to drive the traditionalists to equal extremes. "Only Arabic in our government," they cry, "and only Arabic in our schools." The resulting controversy has led to much backing and filling, and to some reversals of policy that the state can ill afford.

Having concluded her discussion with John, the Cherifa became once more a warm and feminine hostess. She urged more tea on us, and when we refused and said we must leave, she spoke to her daughter—this time in crisp Arabic. The child ran out, and I heard the front door slam. As we walked across the atrium, the Cherifa asked if we would be in Tangier for a forthcoming festival. "I would be pleased to receive you here. . . . It is a great time for visiting and feasting." I explained that we were leaving soon. She chatted about the preparations already in train. "I have arranged for two extra cooks to come in for the duration . . . and I will have four or five women come to the house each day for a fortnight to do all the necessary baking." She opened the door for us. "Times have changed, you see. We no longer keep the permanent retinue a governor used to employ. The young women are all taking secretarial courses!"

We stood under the portico shaking hands. Around the corner from the terrace darted the little girl, in her hand a long red rose, which she held out to me. I thought I had never seen a crimson so nearly black. As I took it, her mother cried, "Be careful of the thorns!" and I saw the enormous spines. "Yes," she said a little sadly, as she raised her hand in a gesture of farewell to us, "in Morocco, even the roses come with many big thorns!" We passed through the gates, and she stood looking after us, her arm thrown protectively around the little girl's shoulders.

✿

Close by our hotel was an Anglican churchyard where I sometimes strolled. It was a place in which to ruminate. Some of the headstones compelled attention—I remember one angel whose robe was hemmed with arabesques, and who seemed (unless it was only the weathering of the stone) to wear a Muslim beard. The garden had gone rank in a way no English garden would—calla lilies choked the aisles between the graves and the lich gate was overhung with lanky poinsettias. But the place was nonetheless very English. It evoked the era when the British flocked to Tangier, drawn by that combination so dear to their hearts: a seductive climate, a scandalous native regime, an exoticism that thrills and chills successively . . . and best of all, ample scope for hard-nosed business ventures. Walter Harris is buried in one corner. "A friend of Morocco," the inscription reads. Few Britons have known and respected Moroccans as he did, and the respect was returned.

The evening before we left Tangier, I was lingering there, thinking how infallibly the British have left behind, wherever they have been, traces of their interesting mixture of egoism, sentimentality, and humaneness. Suddenly I thought I caught a breath of Kent in the air—it was a yew tree, and beneath it were three maiden ladies' graves: Henrietta, Maud, and Editha. Sisters, it appeared. And did they keep house, in the Tangier of the 1900s, for an adored brother, whose business here they never fully understood? Perhaps they talked together in whispers of the scandals of Moorish depravity, and the need to introduce Christian morals. Probably they led wistful lives; almost surely they did what they could to introduce small humanitarian changes in the native lives they touched.

I became aware, as I stood before all that remains of Henrietta, Maud, and Editha, of strangled sounds in the road that winds uphill past the church. There were apparently several drums, a bugle or two in uncertain hands, and the scuffle of many feet. The band was having a sticky time of it, but I detected in the confused sounds the strains of "Britannia." I ran to the wall and looked over. The drums ruffled: "Britons never . . . never . . . NEVER"—then a series of off-key blasts on the bugles—"Shall . . . be . . . slaves." Ten small Moroccan boys trudged behind their band, in Boy Scout uniforms.

Chaouen

In the mountains south of Tetouan, so high and so concealed that its presence would never be detected from below, a little town hangs in a cleft between peaks. Chaouen is the market town for douars still higher up; but its site was originally chosen for other reasons: seclusion and defensibility. Chaouen was a "holy city"—a fifteenth-century saint founded it as a base for jihad, holy war against the Christian colonies on the Mediterranean coast. Every European who came within range was strung up by the ears until he died, and not even a Jew might cross the market square where the Grand Mosque stands beside the fortress. By 1920, only four Europeans had managed to make their way into the city—and live to tell of it. (The mysterious Charles de Foucauld, soldier turned wandering priest in the 1880s, wrote the first such account to reach European eyes. His disguise as a Bedouin was successful.)

Now, like other holy cities, Chaouen turns its reputation to good account in attracting visitors. A delicious little inn faces on the central plaza; across from it, brightly painted houses climb the hillside in tiers, and the zigzag alleys abruptly become mountain trails. The "discovery" of Chaouen is making its impact on the villagers—the little shops on the plaza are beginning to feature kaftans for tourists and *maroquineries* of doubtful value; a sign points upstairs to a bar, where a nice-looking youth dances with a coffee tray on his head.

Inevitably, the boys of the town swarm upon new arrivals. We stood among them, knowing that we must make terms with one if we were to be rid of the others, and saw an older boy shouldering his way to us. One of his eyes was badly infected, and Bill drew back as the boy, in French of a sort, offered to guide us, "Abd el Krim's castle . . . *kif den, ti sais?*" Bill shook his elbow free, and the youth pulled himself up and stared at us with an ugly smile spreading across his face. A hard ring came into his voice. "I know what you mean—shall I tell you? You mean you *just don't—like—Moroccans!*" At that moment, he was dead right. With a mocking smile, he raised his hand to his suppurating eye, as if to confirm his unpleasantness, and flung away disdainfully. For a moment, an unspoken question hung in the air: If I disgust you, what are you doing in my town?

The other boys, uncertain, melted away. We crossed the plaza uncomfortably. A six-sided minaret, red-brown like the earth and rock, ended in an immaculate little whitewashed dome topped by a crescent. At its base, old men with Spanish faces drowsed on benches, their burnouses drawn about them. We began to climb a steep alley between the blue and pink and apricot houses. From one of them came the gabble of very young voices. Through an open door, waist-high at one corner because of the pitch of the lane, laughing faces gazed at us out of the dark. The chirping stopped suddenly as an austere old man with a grizzled beard pushed past and scrambled up the high steps. Folding his legs under him on a rush mat, he faced the children and barked an order. Singsong voices replied in unison. We drew away.

It was then that we acquired Abdul, who had been following us from the plaza. Blue jeans, much too big for him and patched at knees and seat, hung on his hips from a braided grass belt. He would be a good guide for us, he said, because he knew French well. We liked the self-respect in his face and offered terms: a dirham-fifty[8] a day. We would expect him to be with us for only a couple of hours a day, provided he told the others to leave us alone the rest of the time. We knew this was a large sum in the streets; the question was always how far we could go without setting a precedent that would lead to wheedling with later foreigners. It is a fair conjecture that much of the sycophancy you meet in the world of Have-Nots being invaded by Haves began with the discovery that tourists have tender sensibilities.

Bill asked the boy if he had attended the Koranic school we had just seen. "Not here, but in Ouezzane, where I passed my childhood," he replied. He looked barely ten.

"So it was in Ouezzane you learned such good French?"

He was very pleased. "Yes, but not in Koranic school. There, I had to sit twice a week, all morning. . . . My back ached, for we were not allowed to lean against the wall."

"Did you understand the words you learned?"

"Some of them, a little. But the Arabic we speak is not the Arabic of the Koran. . . . However, we are all very good Muslims, and can recite many verses by heart!"

Outside another open door, higher up the alley, a man sat on the cobblestones beside several earthen jars. Each held a clump of kif pipes, long-stemmed and with clay bowls no bigger than thimbles. Some little girls who had been gaping in the doorway fled, giggling, as we came up. Inside, men sat side by side on benches and leaned against the wall, or lay on the floor, clearly impervious to any discomfort. The room was dark and quiet, filled with haze. Some men were still smoking, and passed the little pipes lovingly from hand to hand; others lay back and let peace invade their bodies. They looked straight ahead of them, their eyes unfocused, oblivious of us in the doorway.

I was a little surprised at the openness of it all, for the state has been trying to suppress kif. It grows freely in several regions of Morocco, and smoking it used to be a perfectly acceptable pleasure. I think it would be hard to establish that the customary moderate usage has proved either injurious or addictive. Certainly, it is far less so than the alcohol and tobacco introduced by Europeans. Probably 90 per cent of Moroccan men now smoke cigarettes feverishly.

Abdul was looking up at us, uncertain whether he should be embarrassed. "Have you ever tried it?" I asked.

"Where would I get that much money!" he retorted quickly; then, more carefully, he added, "Of course, I take home all that I earn, so that we may

8. Any unit smaller than a dirham is referred to in centimes for the foreigner; in fact, we were usually quoted prices in French francs rather than dirhams, a hundred old francs being exactly the equivalent of one dirham.

eat. We are eight children." He was not a wheedler; though he looked longingly at our cigarettes, he never asked for one.

"Is there any work for you in Chaouen, Abdul?"

"From time to time. Lately, I worked for the baker in our quarter, carrying loaves to his oven from all the houses, and then back again when they were baked. But this is what happens: a board with twenty loaves on it is balanced on my head, I am coming down the hill and meet somebody who wants my job, and so wants to make trouble for me. He trips me, and the loaves start rolling down the street. I chase them all, and since they are already baked, it is easy to wipe them off and reload them. But the other boy tells the baker, and even though I've done the work, the baker refuses to pay me."

"What did you say to the baker?"

"I said, 'Bism'illah—God wills it. But will you pay me next week?' But he only cuffed me for impudence. Men are the way God makes them: there are good men and bad men."

One day, he led us up a mountain path to a sacred spring, where white rags fluttered on the overhanging branches. Again, he looked uncertainly at us: "The old women say there is a djinn. . . . Wherever the earth is open, that is where a spirit comes out."

"A good djinn or a bad one?"

"Who can tell? It is safer to pray, and tie a rag, and leave a bit of candle burning . . . or so the women say!" With his bare toe he scraped some wax off the rock.

Across the valley another path ran zigzag up the opposite hill. A man was trudging along it, a winnowing fork on his shoulder, and behind him a woman led a panniered mule. They climbed slowly, and paused for a moment before the gleaming white of a marabout's little tomb. The man wiped his face with a loose end of his turban; the woman pressed her palms to the tomb's wall; then they climbed again. The very top of the hill had been flattened to make a circular threshing floor, piled now with grain in glittering mounds. After resting only a moment to drink from a jar tied to the mule's neck, the man began to thrust his narrow wooden fork into the grain and throw golden sprays of it up into the air. The chaff streamed away in the wind. The fork rose and fell, rose and fell, with a steady, indomitable rhythm. Skirt tucked up into her waistband, the woman bent low to gather the grain into her shallow scoop, which she emptied into the panniers. They worked without pause, and the midday sun blazed. It looked as though they would be there for the rest of the day before the sacks were full. And even then, I wondered, how much of the grain would be theirs to keep, and how much would they owe the owner of the land on which it had ripened?

Abdul's view of market day was that it made the week worthwhile. The night before the weekly event, he pulled us to a break in the fortress wall, where we overlooked the plain far below and the ribbon of the Tetouan road. (Spanish soldiers had been besieged in this citadel in 1922, thirsting to death and scanning the supply road below, which came to be known as "the graveyard of the youth of Spain.") Abdul pointed to mountain paths converging on the village. Down each came a procession of figures under cartwheel hats and mules laden high with bales. "Those who come tonight and sleep beside their beasts will be the first to sell in the morning," he said. The caravansary for the night was a court with little roofed bays opening off it, for shelter in winter. Goods were stacked along the walls; close by, women squatted near their charcoal fires, on which rested the little blue enamel teapot no Maghrebi family can be without—import from France, of course, but more durable than the earthenware it replaces. Men were unloading the animals and carrying hay into the little bays. Beside me in a circle on the ground lay five hens, their legs tied together at the center. I thought them dead until a thin croak escaped one long yellow beak. Slaughtering, all according to strict Muslim rules, was being done in a bloody clearing behind the caravansary. Several men of city demeanor were circulating through the crowd in the courtyard—Tetouani buyers, or landlords come to collect their due in kind.

When a donkey winds up for a bray, he begins with thin creaks, which, I suppose, serve to limber his throat. I woke to those creaks on market day, and finally could pin down what it was that the sound had always dimly recalled: the creaks of an old hand-pump handle, just before the spate. When I reached the market and first saw the line of women on the bottom step below the mosque, I thought they were all deformed; but nothing of the sort—they had just arrived and were beginning to unsling from waist and shoulder and back one bundle after another. One opened a shawl and loosed a stream of chickpeas into her large upturned hat; then, with care, she pulled a grass pannier free from her waist and opened it out into a tray, disclosing dozens of little rounds of butter still miraculously intact and glistening with moisture. She broke off a sprig of mint and with its stalk quickly etched a five-pointed star in the center of each pat.

Even divested of their bundles, the women were strangely lumpy about the hips. One red-striped skirt was torn, and I saw what they wore—a hoop of braid, wound round and round to a thickness of two or three inches. (I never learned whether it served any other purpose than to accentuate the pelvis, which is worth accenting, since it keeps the tribe alive.) Mounds of lentils filled other hats, and pyramids of eggs and soft fresh figs, green and black and yellow. A pile of unpromising-looking, hard little pears was decorated with clumps of Moroccan parsley, wide-leafed and very aromatic.

A burro stood in the middle of the plaza, invisible under a load of earthen jars; a lad lifted them down, careful not to dislodge the sprig of oleander that stoppered the long neck of each jar. While customers lined up with jugs for the milk, a withered old man behind the boy's back tipped a jar to his mouth and swallowed twice before he was seen. I watched him drift about the market, stealthily reaching for a plum or trying to snatch an egg under the women's sharp black eyes. He succeeded only about half the time. Some of the squatting women pulled their skirts over their wares as he approached, and stared balefully up at him. Flushed with the excitement of market, their faces showed dark tattoos on forehead and chin. The women shouted to passers-by and cackled to each other what I supposed were ribaldries; they spread their rawhide leggings wide—this was the day they would recall for entertainment all through the coming week.

A handsome man bent over the tray of butter displayed beside me. One sleeve of his shaggy djellaba hung loose; his left hand was holding his purse inside. With one deft motion, he twitched aside the cheesecloth, ran his finger over a creamy pat and licked it, while the woman screamed at him. He raised heavy-lidded eyes to her face and stared impassively back at her. Then his purse appeared in the neckhole of the djellaba. He flung a small coin at her feet, swept up the pat of butter, and dropped it in his basket. Her stream of abuse didn't change his expression; he merely tossed her another twenty-centime coin. She threw them both back at him and pointed a gnarled finger at his face, shouting, her earrings dancing with her anger. But both were enjoying this. The man had the butter, the coins lay at his feet, he could have walked away. Instead, he negligently swept up the coins, added a third, and dropped them on the hem of her skirt. (Butter comes high, in a country of lean cattle.)

Toward midafternoon, people began to prepare for the trip home. A badly loaded mule, slithering on cobbles slick with discarded fruit, was clouted and dragged by the tail until he kicked, and everyone scattered, shouting. A man beside me, still holding up to his ear the egg he had been shaking, turned to look, and the vendor snatched it from the man's hand before he could forget and drop it in his basket. Out under the archway that led to the other plaza, treadle sewing machines whirred; men who had bought lengths of homespun now sat under the acacia by the fountain, sipping tea and waiting while the garments they had ordered were run up for them. Prices were falling now, as the day neared its end, and children danced around the watermelon stall, cadging free slivers. A cripple approached the stall, inching his way over the cobbles on his seat, a leather apron tied under him to ease his bones; he propelled himself forward with his hands, on which were strapped a pair of shoes.

I had earlier watched a lad cutting the melons into sections to be eaten on the spot: he eyed each piece like a sculptor, pared back the flesh until the neat pattern of black seeds lay exposed on the crimson, then fretted the green rim with quick strokes of his knife. I had bought one, a perfect little Moorish rosette. It had almost no taste. Now the rosettes were going for a song. The crowd parted for the cripple, who ate three in quick succession. Four youths were reloading the unsold melons into their wagon. They tossed them from hand to hand, and sometimes held one a moment to strum on it. A Moroccan sees a drum in any taut-skinned object with some air inside it.

Clots of bees hung on each bit of crushed fruit on the cobbles. The pitch of sound began to lower. Tired, people were thinking of the long way home. One man dismantling his stall stowed all his unsold wares and all he had bought or bartered in the panniers of his waiting mule, and in hampers and burlap rolls, which he strapped onto the animal's back. He hung his pails to the beast's neck and about its rump, and lashed more bales on top of the load. When the mule began to shift his feet uneasily, the owner turned and began to load his wife. He rolled up the blankets and stakes with which he had built his stall and strapped them to her. She bent her broad back. Her fingers went to the straps and loops, settling them so they would not gall her shoulders. The husband then piled on his stack of unsold homespun blankets. She spread her feet and bent lower, took the last cords from him, looped them around her elbows, and closed her fists on them. The mule and the woman waited stolidly; the man stepped up to a neighbor's stall and bought a shallow clay basin. Returning to his wife, he looked her over thoughtfully, then set the basin upside down on her head. It just cleared her eyes. He took up a bundle in each hand and went to the mule's head. The three moved forward in unison, heading for the mountain trail.

The Rif

Driving eastward from Chaouen, we entered what remains of the magnificent forest that once clothed the entire Rif range—Atlas cedars, whose multiple spires the clouds seemed to be stirring as they passed, and towering cedars of Lebanon in greater numbers than survive in that little country whose name they bear. Since we were crossing the grain of mountains running northward, we were always either climbing or spiraling down. As soon as we would get below the frost line, cedars and umbrella pines mingled with ancient thujas, in whose dense shade a hundred chittering birds took shelter, and cork oaks, whose harvest was stacked beside the road. Then downward still more and we would find terraced orchards and steep grainfields—or else *maquis,* dwarf oaks, and goats. Then uphill again. This is the only road across the North; there can be no coastal road because mountains pitch to their knees at the Mediterranean's edge. (If only there were a Moroccan Riviera, what revenues the Bureau of Tourism would now be turning over to a grateful state!)

Midway across the mountains, a single bold road comes in from Fez and *Maroc Utile.* We turned onto it. This is a famous road, proudly called the

Route de l'Unité. Building it was a heroic undertaking of the first summer after Independence; it was to be a tangible symbol of reunion with the ex-Spanish Zone, and an attempt to bring the North into full partnership. The project was born in the mind of a brilliant young nationalist, Mehdi ben Barka. (If his name is familiar, it may be because of the international scandal surrounding his kidnaping and presumed murder in Paris in 1965—a scandal that involved Moroccan army officers and French police.) He had a further vision, beyond the physical need for the road: building it would bring together youths from all regions and all classes—it would be a melting-pot experience. Ben Barka proposed to set teams of volunteers to work in shifts of a month apiece; he promised that the road could be built in this way for just a tenth of normal cost.

Twelve thousand recruits were sought, to work in the full heat of midsummer; 30,000 volunteered. The road was built up those awesome gradients almost entirely by hand, with shovel and pickax. The French writers Jean and Simonne Lacouture visited the road-builders' camps that summer and reported what they found.[9] Young volunteers were discovering for the first time a community larger than the oasis or mountainside where they were born, and learning that the Mahkzen was not some form of calamity that devours the crops, but the central government of a new nation. After six grueling hours of road breaking, the volunteers would gather at midday under some tall cork oak to listen to explanations of the new nationalism and take a fresh look, with their instructors, at their Muslim traditions and how they could be adapted to a new era—a sort of impromptu people's university.

But there was one great disappointment. Even in the euphoria of that first summer of freedom, there were few volunteers from the middle and upper classes. All but a handful of each month's crew were fellahin. Caste was not banished overnight; nor was the traditional disdain of the educated for any form of physical labor. The road was built, but no thanks to the privileged classes.

The *Route* runs like a lizard along narrow ledges, where one hopes not to meet one of *Les Cars,* the huge autobuses that travel the road regularly, Diesel monsters panting and grinding their gears. I saw hemp growing profusely; however earnestly the young nationalists had urged the local tribe to tear it out and forswear the kif traffic, the plant was back again. To the east of us lay the region called the Rif, and as soon as a passable road offered, we turned off the *Route* onto it.

Within a few miles, the forest ceased, victim of that terrible ecological change triggered centuries ago. The devastation began when the invading Arabs lighted forest fires (for the same tactical reasons we have defoliated Vietnam's jungle); succeeding generations pillaged the trees to make roof

9. J. and S. Lacouture, *Le Maroc à l'Épreuve* (Paris: Editions du Seuil, 1958), pp. 51–52.

beams for mosques and palaces; and pastoralists completed the ruin by taking their flocks into the forest to graze while civil wars ravaged the plains. Now the deterioration is hard to reverse. The battle against it is still in progress.

The Rif is primitive, magnificent, and rather frightening country— cathedral rocks against a cobalt sky, ravines as raw as claw marks gouged in the red earth, and sudden streams with the pink froth of tamarisk growing in the scree. Wherever there was water and vegetation, we were on our guard for sheep, for in summer they must come as high as this for fodder. And sheep do not leap from your path as goats do. You slam on your brakes, and then wait while they dither. One young shepherd with carrot hair and freckles—for we were among the Riffi now—recovered sufficiently from his astonishment to snap us a smart military salute before he ran at his herd with flapping arms. Then we climbed again into an awesome Dead Sea landscape—ashen gray hills across which cloud shadows drifted like somber thoughts.

It is not entirely true that the North is a forgotten stepchild. In fact, signs beside the road succeeded each other with a bewildering variety of acronyms that I tired of trying to decode—Bureaux of Waters and Forests . . . of Irrigation . . . for Restoration of the Soil . . . Rehabilitation of Riffian Vineyards. Often I felt we were driving across a battleground where the opposing forces were lined up in full sight of each other: on one side, a single file of goats silhouetted along the crest of a wan hill, their rapacious mouths groping low; on the other side, a hill pocked and scalloped with little saucer-like depressions, and protruding from each saucer the feathery tip of a young eucalyptus. Or again, women bending with sickles over soil so thin my eye could trace the rock skeleton. Some had no sickle; they snatched the grass out by the roots, and a puff of powdery soil blew away from each wound in the earth. Then, around the next corner, a new vineyard. Thousands more of the careful saucers, each holding a small, bare, black shape—a new vine lifting its stumpy arms to the sun.

The outcome of the battle was indeed still at issue. This was a summer of drought. Even when I had no reason to be thirsty, my throat seemed painfully dry. I said to Bill, in sudden fear, "I've almost forgotten what rain sounds like! Can you call up the sound of it, falling softly on a retentive soil? And can you remember how the thrushes sing in the silence afterward—those notes like the ring of a glass bell?"

He couldn't spare attention from the road, for we were spiraling down into a village. We stopped in front of gates with a coat of arms and crossed Cherifian flags—the headquarters of the caïdat into which we had come. (A caïdat is a caïd's administrative unit, and usually embraces two or three communes, the smallest governmental units.) In 1961, a new state project was born—the *Promotion Nationale*. It somewhat resembles our PWA of the 1930s. In the Bled, its emphasis is on pick-and-shovel self-help, its object being to stop the rural exodus, anchor the fellah to his soil, and raise his productivity above subsistence level. It is the state's answer to that "deadened humanity" Mr. Bennouna had lamented. His parting words to us had been, "If you would see our effort to change the fellah, go to the local caïdats and search out the *Promotion*."

With most of the state's budget and supply of technicians engaged in the major projects with acronym titles, the *Promotion* gets along with small funds and little expertise. It enlists fellahin in work they can understand and benefits from directly and quickly, such as irrigation works, new housing, and marketplaces—familiar projects, carried out in slightly more sophisticated fashion (with some concrete, for instance). The cost of materials and the salaries of touring technicians are borne by the state until the project affords the basis for repayment; meanwhile, the workers receive two dirhams a day in coin, and an equal amount in U.S. surplus grain.

A soldier was asleep at the caïdat gates, his chair tipped back and his beret over his eyes. He scrambled to attention as we slammed the Simca's door, but looked confused when we reiterated *"Promotion Nationale"* several times. After taking us to an office, he went off muttering about the khalifa (a caïd's deputy). We gazed at a regional map labeled *Grande Hydraulique,* whereon a list of projects and dates and little red flags told a story: the date for each project had been scratched out three and four times and a later date inked in. If the work of the *Grande Hydraulique* was stalled, there would be all the more need for the *Promotion*'s less ambitious *petite hydraulique.*

It was thoughtless of us to have come here during siesta time. When the khalifa appeared, he was tucking back a flannel pajama cuff under each sleeve of his uniform. He immediately ordered bottled drinks brought, and we sat down for some painful moments of groping into his Spanish. When there is no other recourse, I dip into Italian, and charge each word with hope and a plea. I did manage to make him understand that we were not Belgian, though why he thought so took longer to discover. Finally, I grasped that the caïd was today touring his realm with a mission of Belgian agronomists, and that this hot and bewildered man had supposed us to be strays of that party. When we had finished the gaseous fruit drink, we were led to another office. A young man poring over maps on his desk raised eyes of a northern blue and then rose to a surprising six feet of height. I thanked God for a Frenchman.

He was an engineer, and a *militaire*—one of the several thousand young Frenchmen released from military duty to do alternative service in Morocco. (Cultural agreements with France bring in yearly quotas of young technicians and teachers.) The blue eyes lit up when we mentioned the name of another Frenchman, Patrice Blacque-Belair, whom we had known in Rabat. This is the *Promotion*'s guiding genius, a man who knows Morocco almost like a native son. He spends his life flying from one end of the country to the other and reports directly to the King, who presides over the *Promotion* council.

Our *militaire* talked of his own work with an evangelist's ardor. He had been bent over blueprints of a new system of irrigation channels and dikes. "It's nothing new to them—I'm just taking the guesswork out of their labors by calculating the incline necessary for a guaranteed flow of water."

He had no sooner said it than he smiled at himself—at the idea of guaranteeing anything in a climate as capricious as this. "Even the *Promotion* cannot beat all the uncertainties here—when is it safe to sow seed in the spring? Was that torrent the last one? How long can any one plot be irrigated before salinity will begin to creep into the soil? No, the returns from agriculture are never certain here. We can only assume that *sometimes* nature will cooperate —and that moment must be exploited to the fullest. The only thing I know for sure is that the men of Boured are staying here now. There *is* work for them, and there *will be,* as long as our project lasts; crops are growing where there have been none before. After we leave, we can only hope. . . . And there is the other gain as well: we have done something for those *bidonvilles* where otherwise the men of Boured would be rotting."

"But is the fellah changing?" I asked. "Or is he just accepting what the *Promotion* hands out? Is he becoming a *peasant,* with a single-minded passion for the soil, or is he still half pastoralist at heart? Will he, after two bad years in a row, turn his field back to his animals?"

The engineer sighed. "Thank God I do not have to answer for that!" We sighed also and, in the fraternity of the moment, even accepted Gauloise cigarettes.

He went on: "Our caïd here is a fabulous fellow. Tough-minded. He plays these people on a long line. I think he will yet persuade them to sell their flocks—and then it will be too late to turn back! Oh, he is as stubborn as they. Otherwise he would be pulling wires to get himself transferred to an easier berth." (A caïd's is still a patronage post. He is appointed, dismissed, or reassigned at Rabat's will. A caïd "with connections" is apt to play a game of musical chairs.)

"And you, Monsieur—are you hopeful?"

"I am far from discouraged. I have been with the *Promotion* a year and a half, and have seen much that is hopeful. In another six months, my period of service will be done. It has been hard work. But I shall have mixed feelings about leaving Morocco."

Surely there will be mixed feelings on both sides, I thought, as we resumed our journey. Whatever form the French presence takes—whether it is the businessmen and colons still sending profits home to France or, the other side of the coin, the thousands of advisers and experts on whom every phase of Moroccan development depends—this presence always inspires in Moroccans quite understandable fears of dependency, of the intrusion of a new kind of colonialism. But certainly the French participation in the *Promotion* looks disinterested. A Frenchman works under a tough-minded caïd and admires him as a fabulous fellow . . . and the whole agency looks to another French-man, who believes in Moroccans' ability to help themselves.

We came to a sudden stream, its banks a chessboard of terraces, all bright with ripening fruit trees. Then, climbing again, we met a train of mules laden with cut wheat. They were heading for a threshing floor, where four mules, harnessed abreast and hock-deep in golden grain, were churning dog-gedly around a central pole. Fine dust caked on their sweating flanks; their long ears were laid back, and their nostrils strained for air as they circled under the whip. The man who drove them uttered short harsh cries and swayed with each stroke of the whip, as if strength must flow from his own body to keep the animals circling. How many hours under this blazing sun before those hoofs cracked each grain of wheat? And then the winnowing, the backbreaking bend and lift, bend and lift, while the two long wooden tines flashed and the sweat ran down. . . .

The next saddle between austere gray and tan hills was our last. We looked back, toward a tumult of peaks above which clouds were massing with a promise of rain, which would not materialize; and then we swung our gaze to look down upon the plains of Taza and *Maroc Utile*. Several dirt tracks, "*pistes*" in the *Promotion's* terminology, debouched from the lower hills onto the plain. Hundreds of douars owe their new connection with the outer world to a new *piste* achieved by the muscle and sweat and shovels of the *Promotion*. The *militaire* had spoken of them as "precious capillaries of a new circulatory system."

Our own road was severely pitted, and Bill had been driving far too long, I realized with compunction. It was he who did most of the driving so that I could stare out the window or write up my notes, he who computed distances and made sure of a hotel for the night . . . and complained only when the driving became more than merely adventurous. Now water lay over the road ahead of us, more water than we had already crossed several times. I couldn't tell if it was all the same stream, because the hillsides seemed to reel around us as we descended. "Pretty soon we can call it a ford, can't we?" he asked, his voice steady and composed. "And if the Simca hangs up on a boulder, do you think we two can rock it off?"

"The water should be deliciously cool. Probably some boys will pop out of the tamarisks to help."

He swung the car masterfully along wagon tracks disappearing into the water and out onto the other side, where a few shoots of cane held the shale in place. "Aren't you tired by now?" I asked. "Shall I drive for a bit?"

"I'll tell you when I've had enough—go ahead and write your notes."

They looked like Arabic, from all the swaying and jouncing—they would have to be transcribed soon. Oh, splendid Bill! How much I owed him! Never again would I nag—even his gift for procrastination would go unchallenged, I promised myself.

The car hit a pothole, and I pitched against the roof. Bill fought the wheel to regain control.

"For God's sake, can't you give me any warning?" I snapped. The pencil I had been sucking had jabbed me painfully. "You almost drove this through the roof of my mouth!" I glared at the peerless husband.

He delivered himself of a pungent flow of language. "Open your mouth," he concluded, "and let me see what you've done to yourself. Maybe one day you'll stop sucking pencils. . . . Looks perfectly all right to me. Suppose you take the wheel now, will you? Then you can work out all the Early-Warning Systems you like."

Sheepishly, I slid over into the driver's seat for the rest of the day's journey.

CHAPTER FOUR

TAZA

Where the Atlas massif all but meets the Rif range, only a narrow corridor connects Atlantic Morocco (*Maroc Utile*) with the east. This is the "invasion corridor" through which Arabs flowed westward and later Moorish conquerors marched eastward to dominate the Maghreb. On a hill above this crucial gap sits a small city—Taza. In peacetime, it is only a somnolent backwater, the gateway to inner Morocco—that is, to steppe, desert, a long sluggish river that all but disappears in summer, a couple of small mining and industrial cities, and the often troubled border with Algeria. Taza would not enter this account at all except for a chance encounter there.

Through the gap runs a thin black line on the map: the only east-west railroad between Rabat and Tunis, 1300 miles across the Maghreb. Today, a new city, Taza Bas, has grown up astride the railroad, and wears all the self-importance of a provincial capital. Above it, on the hilltop, hangs Taza Haut, tight-packed old houses, mosques, and a citadel within a crenelated wall. We looked down on both from a roadside turnout. Only one other person was there, an important-looking man who glanced sideways several times as we used our binoculars.

I was musing on the French colonial dream of binding all the Maghreb into a fruitful unity—which today seems farther away than ever, since all three countries depend heavily on France and have little to offer each other except a share in the same economic and cultural distress. The gentleman approached us, offering a formal welcome to Taza while his eyes strayed to the glasses in my hand. Since even well-placed Moroccans are delighted with any form of gadget, I offered them to him, expecting him to do as we had done—sweep them first across the looming massif of the Rif, gaunt and pale and wrinkled, in outline like an aged and recumbent lion, and then across to the opposite range, the rain-watered and forested foothills of the

Middle Atlas, with golden grain lapping at their feet. Instead, he focused on the railroad, where I now saw a train panting westward at the head of a long line of boxlike little freight cars.

"Does it carry many passengers?" Bill asked.

"Monsieur, you would not find that train comfortable! It is miserable humanity that travels there. This summer there is terrible drought in many areas, and the nomads who push northward every summer can find no pasturage this year on the burned steppes east of Taza. So they have thrown their sheep onto this train and then jumped in on top of them. Insofar as they think at all, they think they will find room farther west. Some of them climb off the train in Taza—" He stopped speaking and trained the glasses on the station. "They bring us no good. Right away there is friction with those hillside tribes." He pointed with his chin in the direction of the Middle Atlas. "They try to drive a bargain with our sedentary Ghiatta—the right to graze among them in exchange for meat and milk. But trouble always flares up...."

"The tribes hereabouts are all sedentaries?"

"We who represent the state are offering them inducements to settle—they are becoming cultivators. If you are interested, I advise you to go up into those hills—you will see the Ghiatta in the process of becoming settled." He saluted us rather abruptly and left. He must have been a *fonctionnaire* of some kind, I thought, for there was something about him that suggested the exile. I suspected his assignment here was the result of having displeased some superior, for Taza serves as a useful cooling-off spot for those who have not shown the proper tact.

Because Taza Bas and our hotel would be hot until nightfall, we did drive up into the Middle Atlas foothills, a world of overarching, centuries-old wild olive trees and springs gushing from the hillside. The Oued Taza, gathering up the waters of the springs, poured down a rocky ravine in a spectacular series of cascades. There were many caves, some of them clearly inhabited, and some fields of blue-green barley. We saw no human beings, but young animals ran from the sound of a car. Kids stood on their hind legs, and small donkey foals raced for their mares in an explosion of heels. There were horses, too, and cattle, and both tents and stone huts at the edge of every clearing—it looked as though the Ghiatta, in the process of settling, must leave a few of their number up here, shivering in their huts through the winter, while the others strapped their tents on their horses' backs and descended with all the herds and flocks to roam the steppe for eight months. Now, in summer, they were reunited; but why should any of them remain here to brave the snow? Then I saw the school: a little one-room stone hut with a flag and the seal of the Ministry of Education. "We offer inducements," the *fonctionnaire* had said. Though one might think of tribesmen as indifferent to school-ing, the fact is that the Moroccan tribes have shown themselves mad for education for the children—and the children of ceaselessly moving nomads cannot attend school.

The midday siesta hours were just coming to an end as we returned to Taza Bas. Shop-front shutters ran up with a clatter, and people were already waiting in line outside the door of the principal pharmacy. Bill and I stood in line, too, and discussed what, if anything, was the French equivalent of calamine lotion. We were both suffering from some itching bites whose genesis we preferred not to dwell on. A country fellow was standing in the middle of the square, thoughtfully rewinding his rather greasy turban and staring at us. A Peugeot's horn blared at him and he jumped out of the way, then edged toward us for a better look. Over his full blue trousers, gathered below the knee, and the usual long white shirt, he wore the khaki jacket of a uniform that could equally well have been of French, Moroccan, or American issue some twenty years ago. It was clearly his best—saved for visits to town— because the brass buttons shone. An empty net of braided hemp hung at his back. Having sold his hay, this countryman was looking for amusement, and my bare head, my height, my strange shoes, and my whole unlikely appearance met his need admirably. When we realized how attentively we were staring at each other, we both broke into a smile of great mutual appreciation.

"I doubt very much this place would have calamine lotion," Bill was saying. "Anyway, the line is hardly moving, and I want some beer, badly."

A clear young voice spoke behind us, "If you'd like some calamine lotion, we have lots. And we also have some beer!" A young woman smiled at us from a motorcycle pillion.

Oh, we said, we must not think of taking their calamine lotion. But a delight was taking possession of us. Americans! Oh, the joy of falling in with one's own kind!

"You're a Peace Corps Volunteer?"

"So is my husband. That's Jim, coming out of the pharmacy now. We both teach English at the local lycée. Come and have supper with us."

"But we couldn't do that! We always like to play host to Volunteers wherever we find them...."

"Jim! Here are some Americans. I want them to come to our apartment for supper tonight."

The young man had brown hair curling crisply back above deep-set blue eyes, and his smile was sudden and complete. "Sue makes a terrific lamb *couscous*. And we could do with some news from home."

These two looked very attractive, and the thought of escaping for once from the routine of hotel meals was powerfully appealing.

"Then it's settled. I'll come back for you here at seven o'clock, to show you the way." The scooter shot off, jack-rabbiting over the cobblestones.

The story of every ex-colonial country's effort to emerge into modern nationhood is at its most troubled where education comes in, and Morocco's story is at once admirable and tragic.[1] France had done nothing in her forty years to train Moroccans for independence. The Cherifian system she found operating had been content to give all children a few years of Koranic rote learning (which of course did not bring literacy); a small number of boys went on to religious high schools called *medersas;* and for a tiny few of these, there was the illustrious Qarawiyin University of Fez, still dispensing "an education for the year 1000." France saw no reason to change this system, except where change could profit the Protectorate. The sons of notables who collaborated well were admitted to the private schools that France had built for her own children in Morocco; these natives she could expect to turn into useful tools.

Even under strong pressure from the nationalists during the final years of her occupation, France yielded little ground. A count in 1954, two years before the moment of freedom, showed 2,700 Moroccan children in secondary schools modeled on the French system. Some few more who had graduated earlier and could afford it had attended universities in France. These, and the young people who had come up through the parallel but inferior system of recently built Muslim schools, would soon have to provide the trained leadership for a population standing at around 9,000,000.

But French exclusionary tactics had not prevented western ideas from seeping in—of democracy and its corollary, universal education. These principles had taken root in the nationalist movement and the Istiqlal Party. Thus a fateful anomaly was there from the start: European concepts were embedded in nationalist goals; most of the men who would have to shape Morocco into a modern Muslim state were French-speaking and *French-thinking*.

Independence came in 1956. King Mohammed V pledged himself to restore the Islamic heritage within a parliamentary democracy; and to realize such a union proclaimed the necessity of universal, free education. Surely, everyone thought, the way to modern nationhood lay through the minds of the young. Only education could forge unity among a grievously divided people —Arabs divided against Berbers, the Bled against the cities, the oasis cultivator against the migrant pastoralist. No one had time to debate what single curriculum could possibly fit all these diverse life styles, for right away the language issue absorbed everyone's attention.

The Arabization controversy quickly became political, pitting the great men against each other. Allal el Fassi, one of the founders of the Istiqlal and the first Minister of Education, though he was himself bilingual and fully recognized the need for French, was pushed into the position of spokesman for the traditionalists. They believed that health would only come to the new state through the language that embodies the culture—subtle, sensuous, flex-

1. I owe many of the following facts and figures to: Charles Gallagher, *The United States and North Africa* (Cambridge: Harvard University Press, 1963); William I. Zartman, *Morocco: Problems of New Power* (New York: Atherton Press, 1964); and to the Moroccan Ministry of Education's copious yearly reports.

ible, the expression of their religion and their philosophy. How could a new Moroccan identity grow out of the use of *French?* So drastic Arabization was ordered, in government and in the schools. And fearful confusion ensued. For Arabic, as the young modernists had been insisting all along, is still largely a medieval language; the vocabulary cannot express the needs of a modern society. And the country could not afford to wait while the language adapted itself. Government floundered. Qualified teachers-in-Arabic were few, and the children were myriad. Finally, everyone could see that compromise was necessary, and once more policy was changed.

But meantime, whatever the stated public policy, whatever Plan or Revised Plan was on the books, the tremendous public clamor for education, in no matter what form, was compounding the confusion.

Schools were built by volunteer labor almost overnight, and a quarter-million children enrolled the first year. The population was spiraling.[2] Each year, 150,000 new pupils surged to the classroom doors. Schools-on-wheels toured the villages, films were used where there were no teachers. A crash program was launched to turn likely pupils just emerging from grade school into teachers in three months. In the acute crisis, Morocco accepted Egypt's offer of teachers. (Only Egypt, of all the Arab nations, had made some progress toward a modernized Arabic.) But the visiting teachers turned out to be evangelists for Nasser's socialism, and were sent home as rapidly as possible. Now Morocco had no choice but to turn to France.

Each year, about 8,500 French teachers have been coming into the Moroccan schools—more than a third of the total teaching force. With this proportion of Frenchmen, who bring with them their French texts and curriculums and examinations, Morocco's fears of "cultural dependency" are not mere paranoia. It is perfectly reasonable to believe that Moroccan children are continuously receiving an injection of western cultural values at variance with the Arab-Muslim view of life. However, it is only those children considered the lucky ones who will be so injected. Uniform though the educational system appears on paper, there are wide disparities between schools. In the one-room school of the steppe, the teacher, ill-trained, underpaid, and overworked with two sessions, will probably know little or no French. What he can offer to pupils who attend half-days for a total of perhaps four years is very different from what the children of a well-to-do city merchant will receive. These are on what amounts to another "track." They have seven years in which to complete the first six grades, with about half the instruction in French. At fourteen, if they pass their exams, they can either attend a collège for a three-year vocational course or, if they are very successful, pass into the "Long Course"—six years at a lycée. Theoretically, either secondary course is open to all classes in all regions. But few children of the Bled or the

2. It is now estimated at around 14,000,000—*more than half of it fourteen years old or under.*

slums are well enough prepared to win a scholarship (and how could there ever be enough of these?) to one of the secondary schools. So the great educational attempt to close the cultural gap has not been able to achieve a system that is either truly uniform or truly universal.

Girls fare considerably less well than boys. When the only available school is overcrowded, both parents and teacher will think twice about giving a place to a girl. Schools drawing on the middle and upper classes are far less crowded (for the same reasons they are so in this country), and here the ratio averages out to about one girl to three boys in the early years, and about one to four or five later.

It is clear enough that what jeopardizes the whole attempt at education is the spiraling number of children. Only by dint of sacrifices in quality has the state been able to school one out of two for any period at all. As I sat by the hotel window listening for Jim, I could not help wondering if the promise of *free* education had been misguided. I recalled Elspeth Huxley's words that a man will not want twelve children if he has to pay for their schooling. Writing of Kenya, she says: "The most reactionary step that could possibly be taken in modern Africa, the step most fatal to progress, would be to abolish school fees."[3]

I was impatient to hear what Jim and Sue had found in the tiny elite at the top of the pyramid. Now the charts and tables of the Ministry of Education might come to life for me. Were there girls in Taza's lycée, and, if so, how did they fare in competition? Were girls and boys alike being subtly converted into minor Frenchmen, or was there some reality to the "Moroccan orientation" that the Ministry's yearly reports dwelt on so fondly and so ambiguously? And how were these adolescents sustaining the collapse of the old value system?

When Jim came back for us that evening, the sun was low enough to work the daily miracle that makes Morocco unforgettable. The light becomes almost incandescent, and every outline is invested with a golden haze. The shadow of a wall becomes a widening triangle of midnight blue, while the old stone flushes to a warm tan. As sunlight slants across the hills, they appear to be gathered into folds, as if a pleated garment had been thrown across them. Even the sharp staccato of speech seems to blur a little, and gestures lose some of their jaggedness. Evening falls with beauty.

As we walked with Jim down the streets of Taza Bas, even the starkness of the new concrete buildings had mellowed. Children playing in the streets paused to wave to him, and he called back to them by name.

"They seem to take you very naturally—is the Peace Corps popular?" (It was the summer the exposure of the CIA's infiltration of American student groups abroad had been headlined everywhere, and even Peace Corpsmen

3. Elspeth Huxley, *Forks and Hope* (London: Chatto and Windus, 1964), p. 173.

were embarrassed and uncomfortable. Once, a Volunteer I was trying to talk with had parried all my questions, and finally asked me: "How much of this conversation is going back to Washington?")

Jim replied, "The kids I know have probably never heard of the Peace Corps. We're just strange teachers to them—individual curiosities they may or may not like." (So this was why many of the young Moroccans we fell in with casually would speak so personally—"Perhaps you know my friend ——? He is a lab technician who lives in *Tchicageau*." A rumpled envelope would come out of a pocket. "We write letters. Someday he will come back.")

We turned in the doorway of one of the bleak buildings and began climbing an iron staircase. Smells of French cooking smote our noses, and scraps of French conversation filtered out.

"Mostly French people living in this building?"

"Yes—businessmen, technical advisers, teachers—a lot of them at our lycée. We have fifty—about twice the number of Moroccan teachers, as a matter of fact."

"Are they better teachers?"

"Not necessarily. They average out about the same. Some of the French are very devoted. We know one couple who stay on year after year. They say in France you don't get a promotion until somebody dies!" (And the fact that Paris pays them a good supplement in addition to their Moroccan salary might have something to do with it, too, I thought.)

Jim went on, "There's one thing about the French, though—they stick pretty closely together, never mix socially with Moroccans. I've been discovering some of the reasons. . . . When I came, nearly two years ago, I found a room in the medina, thinking it would be good to live among the families of my kids. Pretty soon, I began to learn why the French don't fraternize. So, after we got married, we moved down here—"

"You were married in Taza? All alone?" We had emerged onto the top floor, and Sue was there, cold beer in her hands. She smiled at my last remark.

"Hardly 'all alone.' No, we had lots of help getting married!" She led us into a room bright with Berber rugs and magnificent old flintlocks on the walls. "When I first came, they were very suspicious of my morals—a single girl of twenty-two turning up all alone in a foreign country! There was only one family that dared befriend me. 'How could your mother spare you?' they'd ask; and, 'How could your father let you go so far away unattended?' After we'd become really close, there were hints of their trying to arrange a suitable match for me. So it was quite a relief all around when Jim and I decided to get married. They made it their affair and took over all the arrangements."

Jim broke in, "I guess it was the first time the Tazis had had a chance to show some Americans what a wedding feast should be. The night before we were married, they gave me a *mechoui*—three young lambs roasted whole on spits. I had to watch while they skinned the animals—have you ever seen how they insert a hollow reed up the shank and blow a layer of air between the hide and the carcass, so that the hide comes off all in one piece? I was torn between admiration of the technique and queasiness. But the thing that almost did me in was hearing that the brains are always set aside for the guest of honor. Don't ask me how I got through that part. But the rest was the best roast lamb I ever ate. We all squatted on our heels or lay on cushions on the floor, tearing great hunks of sizzling meat from the spits. By that time, I even liked that spicy chick-pea paste, and the flat barley bread, and the curdled yoghurt. . . . Moroccan food takes getting used to, but it's worth it."

"Could it have something to do with why the French don't fraternize—?"

Jim gave a snort. "No, there's a much better reason than that. Discipline! That's the bugbear of most of us Volunteers, who come over thinking we'll win respect by treating the kids in a fair, friendly way. . . . Listen: each night of my first month here, I used to hope I'd die in my sleep! My classes were complete bedlam. I wasn't supposed to use any language but English, and even if I'd tried to I couldn't yet speak Arabic. It took them about two days to take my measure. Then they began: whistling, rolling marbles across the floor, tossing chalk, banging desk lids. Little kid stuff. There was one guy about my own size I'd try to face down, and he'd just stand his ground, smiling insolently. I consulted one of the French teachers, and he showed me an essay that boy had written about me. It began, 'The English teacher I have is a *crétin,* because he thinks to make us his friends.' "

Jim cracked his beer bottle down on the table, his face hardening grimly as the humiliation swept over him once more. Then he went on: "This Frenchman was a hero to his boys; he kept them in line by a mixture of brute force and gruff paternalism. He told me never to come into class without a big stick, and to use my fists freely for the first six weeks. That's not my style, but I tried. And I was shocked to find I enjoyed clobbering them. They sort of folded up as soon as I struck. One guy, who must have been at least twenty, fought back, and I saw I'd better make it to the principal's office with him, fast. I'll never forget what I saw that *directeur* do. He motioned to the thugs he kept posted by his door. They held my big ape down while the director took off his shoes and beat the soles of his feet till the skin came off— the bastinado!"

Sue said quietly, "Don't you leave out the rest of it: that man was fired not long after."

"Yes, but he was fired for queering the account books. His brother was comptroller for the school—they had a nice thing going! But Sue is right— they were both fired, and our new director is straight as a die. There's no bastinado, but he keeps a military discipline. Students jump when they see him coming, and stand with their backs flat against the wall and eyes front."

"They've grown up in submission to their fathers' absolute authority. . . ."

Sue stopped to reconsider. "Or, rather, a show of submissiveness. I guess they do think for themselves nowadays, but in secret. A young man is treated as a *child* as long as he lives at home."

I protested. "Jim says this boy was twenty, yet still in what we call tenth grade?" By my calculation, he should have been no older than eighteen. The government had recently ordered all overage students dismissed; had the decree been ignored? Jim explained that lycées all over the country had had to compromise after violent street demonstrations on behalf of students who were dropped. His director had decided the decree couldn't be applied retroactively. "Besides, the day hasn't yet come to Morocco when an 'arrangement' can't be reached for a man with connections. . . ."

It wasn't the nepotism that shocked me, for I had taught myself to remember that many Moroccans see nothing dishonorable about it; in fact, honor compels a man to do everything in his power for his kin. Nepotism has acted as the cement of society, and the tradition dies hard. But I was depressed by the picture I was getting of that precious little elite, the lycée students, and now I protested that they sounded like a pretty sad bunch.

"No, they aren't that—when you realize what's going on," Sue said. "I'll admit there are a lot who test well but perform poorly. Perhaps it's laziness, but I'd guess it's more a matter of not knowing where they're heading. And, particularly at this age, health has a lot to do with performance—the languors of puberty can be severe when there's been no medical care throughout childhood. I'd say about a third of the students know where they want to go; and they work to capacity because they know what it takes to get there." She stood up. "I'll have to see to my couscous now—Jim, take them up on the roof for a little, and I'll join you in a few minutes."

The sunset drama was building to its climax. Taza Haut, high on its hilltop, floated like a heavenly city, its minarets gleaming. Even the squat fortress and the harsh medieval wall had been seized and invested by the sun, and the air of the middle distance seemed to be a shower of gold dust. Taza Bas, at our feet, looked as though a golden scrim had been pulled over it. The railway station was asleep. One discordant, raw spot of color stood out: a turquoise-lined swimming pool on the edge of town. A brown body flashed through the air, evidently from a high diving board, and was succeeded by another. "The French who built it for themselves must be turning in their graves," Jim said, "but *there's* one legacy from the Protectorate that nobody is complaining about."

A motorcycle roared through the canyon of the street below us, backfiring. Jim's eyes followed it. "One of our *yé-yés*. Whenever we're holding an exam at school, that crowd makes a point of backfiring their engines under our windows."

The French *yé-yés* of this period—I suppose distant cousins of our hippies —were all young, gay, and sad in the same breath, irresponsible from every point of view but their own, seeing themselves as a living rebuke to a sclerotic French society. They dispensed with bourgeois morality, and "celebrated life." Françoise Hardy sang, *"J'ai jeté mon coeur à tout vent,"* and her voice swung from happiness to pain and back again, with the suddenness only the disengaged can achieve, in the refrain: *"Ah! Yé, yé, yé! . . . Oh, yé . . . yé . . . yé."* (You can read anything you like into the syllables.) Their hedonism, however, was without whimpers; they acknowledged the cost of hanging loose. They were ironic, disoriented, and irrepressibly feckless. They fascinated young Moroccans.

"So the *yé-yés* have come to Morocco!"

"Yes, but the Moroccan goes *yé-yé* with a difference. Here they don't dwell on the emptiness of bourgeois goals—I guess it takes a degree of sophistication to see things that way. Few of these Moroccan kids have that much poise; by nature they lean rather to a grievance against the world. . . . But they don't *do* much in Taza. Our kids don't dare go as far as they do in Casa and Rabat."

"Well, what *do* they do here?"

"Get drunk. Break Ramadan furtively. Whore it up in Fez. A lot of the older guys are doing their *service à l'état* by teaching grade school, which they loathe. Now and then you get a spoiled kid with a father who has managed to stash some money away in a French bank, and who feels better about about his boy's not getting into the lycée if he can stake him to a vacation abroad. Then the boy buys his motorcycle in Paris and spend the summer touring Europe. When he gets home, he'll have an earful to tell about all the Scandinavian lovelies who fell into his arms."

"And his father?"

"Hears a different story. Or, if he did overhear some of the gamy bragging, he might be secretly pleased. Sons of families like that are apt to be indulged right up to the moment when they're married off. Then—wham! they have to shape up rigidly. It's an old pattern."

"These fathers who stash away money in France and send their sons abroad—who are they?"

"Oh, they are the new Establishment—the bankers and merchants who have muscled in on the power structure the French left. The dignified graybeards, strolling now before dinner in Taza Haut, represent the *old* power. They're the conservatives—the cadis [judges under the Sacred Law], the pasha, the mayor and the clique around him, the khalifa. . . . Some of them are less prosperous than others, but they are all related by marriage. I can't help liking them—they're good, sound old fellows who mean to keep Taza in their hands for its own good. They all speak Berber together; it places them as the native aristocracy. Of course, they know it is looked down on elsewhere as the language of women and of the plow, but here they speak it proudly. Naturally, they use Arabic for all their business affairs and their contacts with the outside world—they wouldn't dream of speaking Berber in Fez. Take my friend Sidi Brahim ben Salah, for example. He used to be chief of police, a job that he has now passed on to his son; his brother is Imam of the chief mosque; he himself owns a lot of farm property on the outskirts. He has a couple of grandsons in the lycée; they're good kids—I used to coach them in soccer after school."

"Is that perhaps why he has been friendly to you?"

"Maybe, but I don't think that's the only reason. I think he loves to show a foreigner how good the native life really is. It was he who let me rent a room in his house. Even though he'd just added an indoor bathroom—and painted the whole thing peacock blue!—he still patronized the hammam [the public bath] regularly. Your day at the hammam is according to your social position, and he naturally goes on the best day. He invited me to go with him once. We stood around in the outer room for a few minutes, getting into the right mood of sociability and relaxation with all the others. Then we moved into a room so dense with steam I couldn't see. Sidi Brahim took off his djellaba; so I went ahead and stripped. All of a sudden he was hissing in my ear, 'No, no, NO!' Please observe!' He pointed to the underdrawers he was still wearing; so I hastily put mine back on again. Then we proceeded into the next room, and sat on the bench while an attendant sluiced us. The men were all mulling over business deals, this time—out of courtesy to me—in Arabic. They were passing tips and blackening their rivals' reputations, and calling on Allah to witness the iniquities of the tax collector. But I spent the whole time worrying about having to go home on my scooter in mid-winter with soaking-wet undershorts!"

Sue had appeared, to cool off before dinner. "The women aren't such prudes!" she said. "They use their hammam afternoon to much better advantage. The bath's their club, their spree for the week. They line up on the benches, naked as jaybirds, and lampoon their husbands. While they rub each other's backs, they rip off all the ribald stories they've saved up. Every story is sure to be at some man's expense—the war between the sexes goes on a guerrilla footing in the Muslim world."

A shaft from the sinking sun spotlighted the rows of *bidon* shacks not far from where we stood. The corrugated tin roofs were studded with rocks to hold them down in a wind. Women with water jars passed through the narrow aisles between the huts, trailing their bright skirts in the dust. A little girl was fetching fuel for the evening fire from the brush pile on the roof, and a smaller child climbed up to get the rush sleeping mats that had been airing all day. On another roof was a heap of grain, and beside it, a woman was bending over her grindstone while her two babies rolled about the roof, as unheeded as if they had been safely on the ground. One was bare-bottomed, with a little shirt stretched across the top of his belly. He lay down and rolled deliciously in the bright grain. Along a path on the edge of the *bidonville*, a man walked beside his donkey. The panniers were piled high with charcoal.

He didn't bother to lead his beast—a Moroccan donkey is the most docile and reliable of creatures. Both were grizzled with age. Behind them came a woman, sitting sideways on her donkey and wrapped closely in a pale blue haïk, her face muffled against the dust. There was something strangely familiar about the picture—the title could well have been "The Flight into Egypt." A little boy leaned back against the woman's chest, his face peering out of the folds that swaddled him. Little puffs of dust rose from the donkey's small, deliberate hooves, and his shadow danced, elongated and delicate, on the stony track behind him.

Off in the northern distance, the bare, dun-colored mountains were being magically transformed in this ultimate moment of the day. All the city and the surrounding lowlands lay in shadow now. The sun, lying on the horizon, flung out its last power and touched the whole Rif bastion into burnished bronze. We went slowly downstairs.

Sue brought in the couscous on a large platter: a steaming mound of semolina and gobbets of crisp lamb surrounded by vegetables, and a ring of coriander and mint leaves around the edges. We watched the two of them mold balls of the semolina and wad them around the meat, but we kept burning our fingers and had to descend to tucking the hot hunks into envelopes of flat bread. It was incredibly good.

"There is something wrong with this picture," Jim said suddenly. "The women should not be eating with us, they should be waiting for us to finish— standing in the doorway, watching for signs of approval."

"Clasping our hands across ample stomachs," Sue added, "we'd hang on your every word and beam every time you licked your fingers noisily."

"Well, your wall, at least, is as it should be," Bill said, nodding at the photograph that presides over almost every Moroccan home. Flanked by two little red Cherifian flags, Mohammed V gazed out across the room with his benign half-smile. He wore on his head the white cap, almost like a fez in shape, that only he habitually wore. The face was clean-shaven, the eyes both kindly and compelling. Pure white folds of his robe lay softly on his shoulders. Saint, hero, father of the country—he is all of these still, perhaps the more so because he died only five years after freedom had been won, while joy still blurred some of the harsh realities.

Jim wiped his hands on the hot wet towel that must accompany eating in Moroccan style. "It will feel strange, when we're back in the United States, to sit down to a meal without that presence on the wall . . . almost profane."

"Where are you going to be when you get home?"

"We're hoping to do graduate work at the University of Michigan. Do you happen to know the place?"

That was how it came about that the conversation in Taza that night was only the first of many. Again and again during the following year in Ann Arbor, I listened to Jim and Sue talk of the young Tazis they had worked with, until I seemed myself to have known the people they described, and to have watched Taza reacting to all the stresses of Moroccan life today.

Aïsha

The girls in Lycée Hassan el Mansour were a minority of one in four, a hard-working group garnered from all over the province. Most of the out-of-town girls were on scholarship—for what man could afford to pay room and board for a *daughter*? But even so, they were a drain on their families, for western clothes were required in school, there were textbooks to be rented, and now and then an incidental expense. It was hardly to be wondered at that the girls were well-behaved in class; they were there on sufferance. They were taught, of course, in segregated groups, except for one solitary girl who—unprecedented occurrence—qualified to prepare for the Baccalauréat. There was consternation. Only Aïsha herself appeared unruffled as she slipped into class among twenty-odd boys who had been classified into the top group. Most people blamed Sue for Aïsha's being there.

Aïsha's father, a prosperous local merchant, brought her every day to the lycée gates in an old Peugeot—she apparently suffered from some kind of liver complaint. Though she was very bright indeed, she seemed to have to push herself all the time. Her face was doughy. When Sue began to urge her to go to the city clinic, she demurred; she was already receiving the ministrations of a local midwife, who was treating her with herb concoctions and poultices of goat giblets and urine. Aïsha's family was unwilling to consult the clinic lest word get around she was unhealthy, which would jeopardize a favorable marriage. When eventually Sue persuaded the girl's father to take her to the clinic, the trouble turned out to be nothing worse than severe anemia, which a course of injections promptly began to clear up. But by then, just what the father had feared happened: the marriage he had been arranging broke down because of a rumor she would never bear children. The humiliated merchant appeared at Sue's side as she walked home one day and hissed in her ear that she was entirely responsible for what had happened.

"But why aren't you pleased, Sidi Jacoub? Now that she looks so much better, you'll surely be able to arrange an even better marriage?"

But no, he said. It was too late. "The girl is set against marriage—you and the school have filled her up with wrong ideas!" Aïsha, released from the apathy she had so long combatted, was now quietly and completely determined to become a doctor. The first class ever to be graduated from the new medical school in Rabat would receive their degrees that spring—and there was no woman among them. If Aïsha had not been uncommonly precious to her father, he would have found some way to block her. As it was, he grieved on and on, and made Taza understand Sue alone was at fault—a young woman who dared to go abroad unmarried would be sure to twist young girl's minds.

Mahmoud

While Jim was fighting for disciplinary control of his classes, it dawned on him that what eluded him as an English teacher he might win on the soccer field, where the boys he coached were giving him a grudging respect. If he could win them over outdoors, perhaps he would not have to carry a stick into class. The enthusiasm over soccer surprised him, for Moroccans are supposed to be too individualistic for any kind of cooperation; yet here they were, playing soccer with frenzy. It was the only place they could submerge themselves in a team effort. Even more surprising, they would turn on any boy who relapsed into horseplay.

There was a good-looking young fellow who had neither the narrow shoulders nor the weak physique that handicapped many of the boys, but he was slight, and easily overborne by the best players. He would flush whenever he fell, and lapse into sullenness. Jim began coaching Mahmoud after hours, and found he had good coordination and was fast on his feet. He was also—disconcertingly—studying Jim. He seemed to have guessed at the American's strategy. Without ever putting it into words, he delicately made it plain that he could advance Jim's cause—whomever he talked up, the boys respected—in exchange for the coaching. When Jim realized the arrangement was in force without his meaning to enter into it, he was embarrassed, and wondered uneasily if he himself were becoming a little Moroccanized. But it was true that he needed to win his battle for the boys' acceptance; and it was equally true that Mahmoud was becoming a fine soccer player. A born leader, the boy could make any team perform better than its best. And so began an odd friendship that often threatened to founder.

Mahmoud's father was a cadi, a judge trained to interpret the Sacred Law as it bears on many things the West thinks of as secular, such as inheritance laws, divorce, and property rights. A cadi is therefore apt to be a strong conservative. One day during Ramadan, Mahmoud came to Jim's apartment in the middle of the afternoon and asked for a sandwich. Not just any sandwich, but a *ham* sandwich, as taboo for a Muslim as for a Jew. Jim lit into him.

"If you're going to rebel, why be furtive about it? Why not have the courage to get arrested like the other students who break the Fast on principle?"

Mahmoud's eyes blazed. But, instead of the angry argument Jim expected, the boy turned sullen and prepared to leave. He opened the door a crack and squinted elaborately up and down the street, like a criminal making his getaway. Disgusted, Jim tugged him back and tried again to provoke an argument. This time, the boy burst out:

"What do you think it's like, being the son of a cadi? When everybody knows my father and the Ulema stand in the way of any kind of progress? And when nobody believes in religion any more? I love my father, but I can't talk to him—he thinks all young people are atheists, because we don't go to the mosque, or stop what we're doing three times a day to face Mecca and rattle off prayers. Because we say, 'I'm going to do so-and-so,' and forget to add, 'if Allah wills it—'nch Allah'! Because we listen to the French broadcasts and line up to see the foreign films! You don't know what it's like to feel that all the people you ought to look up to are only hypocrites. . . ."

Jim tried to stem the flow of angry grievance. He couldn't help agreeing that religious conformity seemed far more prevalent than real piety. But what Mahmoud didn't want to see was that his self-pity was an indulgence, and that he was wasting his time in petty defiances. The boy's nineteenth-birthday party strained their relations to the breaking point. Jim accepted the invitation and then wished he hadn't when Mahmoud added, "You'll bring your camera, won't you?" Jim thought to himself that everything the boy did was disingenuous—he paraded friendship when all he wanted was pictures of his party.

It was, of course, an all-male party. The women of the family carried in the food on trays and were dismissed. Mahmoud then poured the tea into the geraniums and served cheap Spanish brandy, while the boys danced together. They showed their liquor quickly, probably more out of excitement than because of the alcoholic content of the awful stuff they drank. Jim was angry and uncomfortable when a young fellow came up and told him his eyes were beautiful and asked him to Twist. He refused, backing away. Struggling against revulsion, he tried to remember that the Arab attaches no social or moral censure to homosexuality. It is not a problem for him, merely an alternative way of life. Or simply a phase in his development, made necessary by the traditional segregation of the sexes before marriage—a phase that will in no way interfere with his later heterosexual adjustment. All well and good, Jim thought—perhaps even very sensible; but he still winced away from every invitation to dance. As the evening wore on, he began to see that the eroticism was never carried far; it was just a gloss on the occasion, a conventional way of livening up a stag party.

The boys seemed to have forgotten all fear of detection, while Jim worried lest the cadi arrive home unexpectedly, or lest the women, who must have known pretty well what was going on behind the locked door, tell him tomorrow about the liquor that had been smuggled in (disguised in fruit-syrup bottles and paid for through the nose because of the risk to the seller), and about the noise the boys made as they threw themselves into the Twist. Jim watched them, wryly acknowledging how beautifully they took to what was, after all, originally a tribal dance. These were Berbers, not West Indians. But dance was in their blood.

Mahmoud kept on seeking him out after school. Jim saw that there was more going on in his mind than was apparent. When they talked about his future, he looked ironically at Jim. "Do you suppose I would work so hard preparing for the Baccalauréat if my ambitions were like the others'?"

He was, in fact, one of the few students who seemed really determined to sit for the much-dreaded exam and to win the degree coveted by all and achieved by only three or four from this lycée each year. And even those three or four would have to meet fierce competition across the country for the few available places in Rabat's Mohammed V University. Mahmoud, Jim thought, might very possibly make it, through a combination of grades and influence. He might not be a true scholar, but he had an uncanny knack for doing well in exams—he gauged each teacher's mentality carefully and then directed his cramming accordingly; he was already keeping track of all the Baccalauréat questions over the past few years.

"And what," Jim asked the boy, "do you suppose the ambitions of all 'the others' to be?"

"At least 95 per cent want to become *fonctionnaires*—even when they know the bureacracy is already a huge apparatus with very few further openings. They'd be delighted to start in the office of the pasha and dictate memos to other bureaucrats, and hang on the phone, and make deals, and inch their way up the ladder, until they end up as *chef de cabinet* to some governor in a remote province . . . the kind of career my father has mapped out for me. Well, my ideas are different. But I keep quiet about them, for I need all my father's influence." He saw the quick disgust on Jim's face and flushed. Then, forcing a light laugh, he went on:

"You Americans label all Moroccans venal, don't you? You don't bother to understand our ways—everything we do differently from your way is 'corruption.' So easily dismissed! But—let me think—don't I remember something about a 'Kennedy machine'? Yet has that prevented your knowing how great a President he was? Every politics must have its own machine, I think. Perhaps our countries are not so very different—in each there is a great outcry, from time to time, when something is exposed. Then there is a scapegoat. But we do not forfeit the really able. Do you? I do not see why Americans feel so superior morally! Does it upset you that frequently one arm of your government plays a secret game with another group? You follow me?"

That really hit the mark—a thinly veiled reference to the CIA. Once again, Jim wanted to take Mahmoud by the scruff of the neck and throw him out. Controlling himself with an effort, he asked Mahmoud what he meant to do once he had maneuvered himself into a position of power. The boy was vague and evasive, saying only, "I mean to get to the top fast, or I shall get lost in the bureaucracy. My generation does not like my father's world.

We want to change it. But change is only safe if it is guaranteed by people at the top—don't you see that? Maneuver is necessary, if one is to grasp power; and power is necessary if there is to be change. Is it not the same the world over?"

That proved to be their last private talk. Mahmoud did well on the Baccalauréat and suddenly was gone from Taza. Jim could not discover more; he wished the young man well, and only wondered how tenacious he would be in his fight toward the top. Each time he met a setback would he relapse into the sullen sense of grievance so common among young Moroccans? It must have something to do with their upbringing—indulged one minute like young princelings, and the next minute disciplined like naughty children. They got little encouragement to test their own ideas; all around them, there was too much emphasis on preserving face. Young men are loath to run risks if any mistake means conspicuousness and failure means disgrace. Is this why the whole Arab world is so self-conscious? Jim often wondered. And so defensive, and so eager to cast blame? Would Mahmoud only be comfortable with himself when and if he reached the top?

Omar and Ali

Omar, with his rural background discernible in his accent, his freeswinging gait, and the old burnous he still wore in winter, was regarded by his classmates as a rube. He who had supposed that winning a scholarship would open the whole world to him was disgusted to find that class distinctions were quite palpable even among the elite of the Lycée Hassan. The sons of the well-born chose the prestige courses—the humanities and modern sciences. But Omar was directed into the commercial course, to train for a good position in industry. He decided to make the only career open to him appear a matter of free choice, and pronounced himself a rebel. He despised the others for their "Frenchiness" and sought Jim out as much as possible so that he could improve his English. His ambition then became exactly opposite to that of most young men in the lycée, in whom the need to push westward into *Maroc Utile* was an obsession like the blind drive of the lemmings for the sea. Omar used to say he didn't care a fig for the west. "Let the rest of them fight each other for position in *Maroc Utile,* where there are openings for no more than one in ten! Omar will go east, not west! You know what is promised for Oujda?"

Jim knew that the United States had promised to complete by 1975 a system of dams and reservoirs on the Moulouya River, east of Taza, that would bring millions of acres of steppe under cultivation. But this wasn't what attracted Omar. "It is the electric power we shall have that counts!

Then, for the first time, we shall have the beginning of industry, real industry—steel!" He jabbed excitedly at a newspaper announcement that General Electric was considering moving into the Oujda area, the only place in Morocco where both coal and iron are found in proximity to each other.

Jim held his peace but was skeptical. The main factors that deter foreign investments are the fragility of the political situation and the dearth of skilled labor. Foreign firms are willing to maintain small businesses that can exploit the endless supply of cheap, unskilled labor; but they are prudent about risking any move toward heavy industry. Furthermore, Jim thought, even if General Electric does come in, it will bring in its own managers and skilled cadres. Americans regard educated Moroccans as dilettantes in industry, and with a great deal of justice; one of the strongest upper-class traditions requires its members to wear only the whitest of white collars from the beginning. If you should once soil your hands, the stains will remain. Industry means grease, and grease clings to the hands. Was Omar really ready to risk his new lycée prestige and challenge Moroccan mores? And if he were willing to start at the bottom—the greasy level—would he be able to win American recognition?

One night while they were talking, another student arrived. Jim felt Omar bristle as soon as he recognized the other. For Ali Saïdi was everything Omar could never be and detested: Tazi of prominent family, conspicuous even among the *lettres modernes* group for his facility in languages. He, too, was a candidate for "the Bacc." and stood the best chance of any of that small group of winning a place at the University in Rabat; yet—and this was hard for Omar to understand—he remained in very close touch with his parents and their values. The Saïdis seemed able to preserve respect, as few other families could, for much that was traditional while they embraced much that was modern. To make all this harder for Omar, Ali was well built and a success on the soccer field.

Omar began needling him almost before he was seated, and seemed set upon proving him a hypocrite, who, as soon as he was ensconced at University Mohammed V, would forget his liberal ideas. Ali intended to be a journalist.

"And, under this regime, how can a journalist afford to be bold?" demanded Omar.

Ali took up the challenge quietly: "We must find ways to loosen the controls on the press. One does not begin by attacking the regime; one looks for ways to expose graft and corruption, which the regime cannot then fail to punish."

"Do you imagine you can expose graft effectively without naming names? And whose names do you think they will be but of those close to the palace?"

"The King is not averse to seeing corruption close to himself exposed—he has often initiated it himself."

"Yes, indeed—so that he can thereby remove someone who has grown too powerful!" retorted Omar. "Yes, he is surely a great believer in diversifying his supporters!"

Jim attempted to mediate by pointing out that press controls were not uniformly imposed, and scandals were not infrequently reported in the papers, shortly followed by the announcement of a reshuffle of power.

"It is our way, the only possible way for Moroccans—we proceed forward only inch by inch," Ali conceded. He had a distressing habit of cracking his knuckles when thinking. "If I refuse to practice journalism because of the restraints we now suffer under, how should we ever achieve more freedom to write? And what will become of the men of courage amongst us?"

Omar shot out his underlip and remained silent, probably thinking that Ali would cultivate every bit of influence he could muster to shore up his career; or else he would settle for being mealymouthed like all the rest. Jim watched them, thinking it a pity their antagonism should prevent each from seeing the other's value. And they were much alike in some ways; they were, in fact, about the only students Jim could think of who had really original minds. Where most of the young men leaned heavily on rote learning and were never so pleased as when he assigned them a drill that meant hours of memorizing, both of these boys came into their own when a problem required abstract thought and analysis—just where most Moroccan students broke down.

Ali's quiet manner didn't preclude a relentless persistence: "You hold, I think, that the key to everything is in economic progress? You see Morocco's future in bright colors, once industry is well established?" He smoothly brushed aside Omar's attempt to interrupt. "But why do you not see that no changes in the economy, none at all, will mean anything until we have seen changes in people and in their attitudes? Until we learn to dispense with nepotism? Until we discover that there are other ways than graft to gain our ends, what good will factories do us? They will be in the hands of the same profiteers!"

Omar lunged out of his chair. "And what about the attitude that makes every lycée graduate clutch his French Bacc. to his breast and run to Rabat to your precious university? What about the attitude that nothing but a desk job befits an educated man? What about the *fonctionnaire* mentality that the French are nurturing amongst us?" No one spoke. Then Omar advanced toward Ali and, standing over him, thrust a finger in his face.

"Who are you to talk to me about changes of attitude! Why do you suppose I am going to Oujda instead of to Fez or Rabat? Why am I going to risk starting out among the boilers? Because of *your* attitude that needs changing! Because you and everyone like you is so sure manual work is beneath you!" And he flung out of the room.

A week or two later, he was back. No apologies, but he brought Jim a book by Driss Chaïbi, the gifted young Moroccan writer of social protest.

"What he writes is true—I think you should read it." And then he added, as he tossed the book onto the table, "Just tell me—why need he write it *in French?*" Then he asked to listen to Jim's records, which, he averred, helped him with his English. Jim sometimes asked himself how much worse Omar's pronunciation *could* have been; but had to admit the boy made up for it in fluency.

They talked little. Omar played an Elvis Presley record over and over, until Jim was sorrier than ever that he owned it. When it came to an end for the third or fourth time, the boy remarked, "Do you know which two Americans I most admire?"

"No," said Jim cautiously.

"Elvis Presley and John Kennedy."

Shocked speechless by the juxtaposition, Jim turned his head away and heard the needle drop into place and the throaty voice begin again. Damn, damn, damn! he thought, and regretted every word he had ever said to Sue about Omar's surprising maturity in the encounter with Ali. He's just about as mature as my baby brother, he said to himself, and all that the other night was probably out of some book. He wondered about Presley's attraction for young Moroccans, and thought sourly of what he called their "virility syndrome." He supposed it was not just Moroccans but Arabs generally who were fixated on virility; and he wondered whether it was the fixation that was responsible for polygamy—or was it the other way around? Had polygamy led to an emphasis on potency, which, in turn, had created a deep anxiety that a man must spend his life trying to allay? Jim's annoyance with Omar began to ebb as he saw why Presley was bound to appeal so strongly—the bold, bad, handsome rebel against taboos, furnished with an aggressive sexuality and no compunctions. Elvis is a natural, Jim went on inwardly, for their fantasies about themselves. He reassures this young guy because he so blatantly lacks self-doubt.

When the remorseless record came finally to an end, Jim asked quickly—in order to forestall another playing of it—"But why John Kennedy?"

"Because he showed no fear!"

Jim shuddered, remembering "eyeball to eyeball" and the Cuban crisis. Did Omar suppose JFK had *felt* no fear? "And because he was young . . . and because he was magnificent. All through the developing world, we heard his cry, 'Let us *begin!*' He was not afraid to try something new, to take risks." Had anyone, Jim wondered, listened to this young fellow at home and encouraged him? Or was he just born different, and strong enough to go it alone? The trouble with Moroccan upbringing was that a boy never had a chance to air his most egregious ideas for fear of being disciplined. But Omar did not, like most, take care to avoid risks. All at once, Jim hoped vividly that Omar *would* go to Oujda; and he hoped General Electric and Allah in conjunction would give him a fair try.

As if he had read the last thought in Jim's mind, the boy crossed to the door. After saying good night, Omar added, "As for me—I am not going to to say 'nch Allah—if God wills it. *I* am not a fatalist. I shall take my risks, relying only on my own will." He squared his rather narrow shoulders and, perhaps seeing himself as the JFK of the Maghreb, went down the hall with a much longer stride than usual.

Zobeida

Sue sometimes felt the girls' physical-education classes were a farce. Though she was glad enough to teach them anything, even physical jerks, that might promote their health and poise, she chafed under the distractions that beset her efforts. The first half of each hour was interrupted by late arrivals, because many of the girls shared the expense of a gym suit with someone roughly the same size, and thus had to change between classes; and they giggled during the rest of the hour about the boys playing on an adjacent field.

Zobeida, too, was self-conscious, but with a difference: she had no trouble with her hands and feet, but she seemed overly preoccupied with her beauty. For it was of that sort that is bound to take a young woman far—the only question was, in what direction? Sue learned only gradually that the girl played a key role in the struggle between her parents. Her mother, a dark little Berber from the mountains, had adopted the veil when she married into Taza society—but not out of modesty. She veiled because the other city women did, and thereby disavowed her country of origin. Her husband, much older, was prominent, conservative, and a disappointed man because neither of two young wives in succession had provided him with a son. This little Berber wife wrung one concession after another from him—by what means was a subject people often speculated about. She first won his acquiescence in having Zobeida enter the lycée, then wrung his permission for her to walk home after school in a mixed group of boys and girls, all of them respectable enough, and the girls sworn not to loiter en route.

One hot afternoon, Sue went to the ex-French swimming club during the women's hour, and was hailed by a girl in a bikini, the first Sue had seen in Taza. "Madame Dj'mms! Don't you recognize me?" (Like all the others, she couldn't pronounce James.) She stood there smiling, in her ripe beauty. Sue glanced at the proud little mother beside her, a few dark tribal tattoo marks showing above her veil, and wondered.

When she told Jim about it that night he related what had happened a few days earlier. Zobeida had sought him out and, frankly seductive, asked him to "see if he could arrange private English classes for her." Now Sue was angry, as well as worried for the girl. A day or two later, a drastic change was apparent in Zobeida. She sat through English class sullen and stormy, and afterward burst into furious tears when Sue questioned her. "Everything is closing in on me! My father threatens to take me out of school and lock my door until the day of my marriage! Nothing is the way it used to be—my mother can no longer prevail on him. Oh, Madame Dj'mms, I know you are angry with me—but tell me—what shall I do now?"

Her father answered the question for her by withdrawing her from school. Sue heard nothing for a while, and then a spate of rumors: Zobeida had escaped from home . . . had eloped with the Frenchman who presided over the local insurance company . . . the man turned out to be married and left Zobeida stranded in Meknès. Then Sue saw her one day, clicking along the street in spike heels and a miniskirt. They had only a brief exchange, for Zobeida did not like to remember the last time she had seen Sue. It appeared that the Saïdi family had taken her in, her father having publicly disowned her, and Mr. Saïdi was arranging a business course for her in Casa.

The Establishment

The Saïdis were a large family, widely respected; how could it be otherwise, when Youssef Saïdi had done so well in business? From time to time, the Establishment was constrained to wonder why Sidi Youssef allowed his wife so much latitude. She was the largest and widest woman in Taza, if not in the province; built like a monument, she had not been worn out by childbearing. After raising three sons and three daughters, she had returned to teaching school. By the time Ali, the youngest son, was preparing for the Bacc. in Jim's class, she had risen beyond teaching to become the first woman principal in Taza. Not without frequent setbacks, of course. Time and again, she was passed over while a less-qualified man was promoted. In spite of her breadth of beam, she managed to appear unaggressive, always veiled, and she usually accomplished what was necessary by persuading a number of men that it was their favorite idea. Thus she was able to introduce in her school all the innovations that the system permitted. Sue had greatly depended on her friendship when Taza still looked askance on a young unmarried American teacher; at Sue's wedding, Mrs. Saïdi stood in as mother of the bride.

Usually she avoided taking a conspicuous position. When Zobeida became for the moment a *cause célèbre,* Mrs. Saïdi took her in only because no one else was willing to; even so, she knew she could count on some concealed support. For the Establishment was not truly a bloc; it was many individuals, who would respond variously to each social crisis in turn. Each episode involved the whole community, because, at bottom, the real conflict was between tradition and change. But it wasn't safe to predict the line-up over any given issue—the centers of power were ever-changing coalitions, depending on the particular issue at hand. There would never be a uniform reaction to anything; that would have brought too many individualists into one camp. *L'Affaire Zobeida,* like a magnet placed under a lot of dispersed steel filings, drew people into temporary alignment. Every prominent citizen consulted afresh his private interests and his conscience, and sought to rank order his loyalties.

So sheltering Zobeida and arranging a home for her in Casa was a victory that would have to be challenged. It was a Jew who offered the occasion for the challenge. Ramadan came; people were sluggish until nightfall, then overate, and were tired and irritable the next day. It was a time for every Moroccan Jew to feel doubly sensitive. For the Jew who taught at the Lycée Hassan, the month was an exasperation. He slept badly, since people were laughing and feasting next door. One morning he lost his temper at a pupil who dozed off in class. Taking the boy by the shoulder, the Jew marched out into the courtyard and, in full sight of the director's office, forced the boy to take a drink of water to wake him up.

Nothing happened immediately, though all Taza soon knew of the incident. The steel filings were regrouping. Then the skirmish broke. The Jew was suspended from the faculty. Mahmoud's father, the cadi, was visited by many men in turn. He conferred at length with the Imam, who would preach at the mosque on Friday. Word went out that the Jew would be run out of town. This was quickly followed by another rumor: he had often called at the Saïdi house, where there was a daughter who was both marriageable and dreadfully plain. Mr. Saïdi was accused of a truly serious offense against racial segregation: he was said to be considering the Jew as a son-in-law.

Friday came, and for once the mosque was packed. After the prayer and the reading from the Koran, the Imam climbed the stair to the pulpit to preach. Men sat cross-legged on their rugs, their backs stiff, and all eyes were on the venerable Imam. The women behind their screen squatted motionless. The old man announced the cadi's ruling: a Jew could not be expected to obey the Sacred Law of Islam. Indeed, that very Law guaranteed the safety of all Jews, recognizing them as People of the Book, who, though non-believers, at least shared common scripture with believers. But a Muslim boy who took water into his mouth during the Fast must be punished. Then the Imam launched into a diatribe against men who could not instill respect for the Law into their sons, against young men who never darkened the mosque door. . . . By the time he began to inveigh against the use of alcohol, he had lost his audience. Men had relaxed and were leaning back against the pillars, composing their features into expressions of piety while they digested the import of this new incident. The Jew would almost certainly find it more convenient to leave Taza anyway—no worry there. The wonder was: what part had the Saïdis played in this?

Among all the shifting forces in Taza, there was at least one constant: the enduring hatred between the pasha and the governor. Every skirmish was sure to affect the equilibrium between them. Jim began to perceive this during his first year, as his daily existence became subtly embroiled in the grand feud. While he was still living in ben Salah's house in the medina—the house with the new peacock blue bathroom—he knew the pasha was a frequent guest. Sidi Brahim, his brother the Imam, his son the new chief of police—these were all valuable friends of the pasha.

The day came for the lycée to be used for a province-wide exam. Rural children would come in to take it, in the hope of qualifying for the certificate of primary studies. Jim was expected to serve as one of the monitors. Before dawn that morning, families began trooping in from mountain douars and from the one-room schools for newly settled nomads. Many had had to travel all night. Jim woke before it was light, hearing unaccustomed traffic in the lane below his window. Old cars, older motorbikes, bicycles with pillions, and files of mules were converging on Taza by every road and dirt track. Jim hurried to the lycée, where women were squatting before the gate, brewing tea for their doleful youngsters. While they coaxed the charcoal fires to life, their men went off on errands in the town and to visit any old friend they thought might put in a good word for their children. Even if they had been aware that the exams were graded in Paris, it would have meant nothing to them. Each father was sure there was someone in Taza who could secure his child's success.

While the desks filled up at the appointed hour, Jim's fellow monitor pointed out to him which boys were sons of this or that caïd or large landholder. Jim hated this teacher, and thought him all but illiterate. But he stood well with the director; indeed, he had witnessed the bastinado Jim could not forget. Now, a child before them asked some question about one section of the exam, and this fellow gave a wrong explanation.

"No, wait a minute—that's not right," Jim interrupted, and proceeded to correct the misinformation. Several minutes had been lost by the time the children bent again over their papers, and time was of the essence in this test. So the older man walked between the rows and murmured a few words in the ears of the boys he had pointed out to Jim. Sickened, Jim went as soon as he could to the director, who looked stonily back at him through slitted eyes and, after a long silence, suggested Jim would be well advised to learn to carry out *his own responsibilities* as soon as possible.

From then on, Jim began to put together a number of things he had noticed. The comptroller of the school system was the director's brother. They both drove very large black cars. Both maintained summer villas up in the hills and kept notably comfortable houses in town as well. The comptroller was a frequent guest at the governor's dinner parties. The governor was known to be a very accomplished distributor of favors. Whenever a new list was published of young men called up to do their *service à l'état,* the governor was busy for days thereafter according half-hour interviews in his office. On one of these lists there appeared one day the name of a student Jim knew to be very slow-witted and also over lycée age. By the following day, his name had been stricken off. Soon afterward, Jim noticed the colonel in charge of the army base outside Taza driving a new Alfa-Romeo.

Hardly a month later, word was being passed that the governor had dismissed one of his secretaries, and that a new post had promptly been created for the man in the pasha's office, where "he would be found very useful." Now the tempo quickened, and there was a sense of threat and of promise in the air. Ben Salah was frequently closeted after dinner with his son and the pasha. One early morning, the pasha left for Rabat on urgent business; driving the car was the young chief of police. Taza held its breath the rest of that week. Men met at street corners and talked trivialities, but almost everything that was said carried an innuendo that made half of the citizenry smile and the other half flush angrily. Soon after the pasha's return, the local paper carried the news that His Excellency the Governor had accepted a transfer to the Rif—one of the least attractive assignments in all Morocco. Featured in the same paper was a eulogy of the comptroller and his brother, the director. These faithful servants of Taza would leave forever their imprint on the young people and their families. The editor grieved to think of these affectionate brothers suffering a separation: the director had been co-opted into the army, and his brother would continue to serve his country—but in a new school for illiterates, in the steppe.

It was almost a clean sweep for the pasha. Many people breathed more freely than they had for months; as many others began quickly to consolidate new alliances. That one particular feud had been settled did not signify that it would not be followed by another. But for a time, life went on uneventfully, that is to say, rather pallidly.

No sooner had the new director arrived the next fall than the lycée became the center of a new excitement, this time over the Girls from Fez. They were not, as one might think from the title Taza assigned them, some song-and-dance team of ill repute. They were, in fact, merely a number of young basketball players recruited from several schools in Fez. It was all planned to stimulate health-through-sport and to raise competitive games for girls to the level of respectability. The Ministry of Youth has a difficult responsibility: to ease the old social patterns without putting the young at odds with their parents. Working with the schools, it encourages all manner of clubs where girls and boys can learn to meet naturally in interest groups. This is a delicate assignment for the *Ministère de la Jeunesse, du Sport et des Beaux Arts,* for of course the issue of greater freedom for youth is fraught with fear and suspicion on the one side and with overeagerness on the other.

These particular young girls were touring several provinces and, as they went, playing off a tournament with each local team. Every school they visited was expected to organize a community reception for them, and a dance after the final game. The poor new lycée director was almost out of his mind. None of it was his idea in the first place, but now he had to push arrangements upon a hostile city. For once, Taza closed ranks—to oppose this innovation forced upon it from the outside.

The Girls arrived. No matter how nicely they comported themselves, Taza tongues clacked. It didn't help matters that the outsiders won all their games handily. At the dance, they mixed naturally and freely with all the boys, and Twisted with them with unfeigned enthusiasm. It was really a thoroughly enjoyable occasion. But what the elders of Taza were enjoying was the novel experience of town solidarity in a wholly unanimous disapproval. In their hearts, they knew such unanimity could not last long. In the meantime, everyone joined in heaping blame upon Fez for thrusting this indignity upon them—Fez of the austere image, Fez the home of tradition and piety, their long-resented, supercilious neighbor city.

CHAPTER FIVE

FEZ

Old Fez

THE FASSIS

Fez has been, ever since the ninth century, the home of a very special breed of men: the Fassis. Like the Florentines and the Bostonians, they have been both very pious and very talented at commerce—and, on the basis of these two essential qualities, very well satisfied with themselves. Generations of Fassi scholars have dominated the intellectual life of the country. They, and the proverbially astute Fassi businessmen, have always figured largely in government. That they recognize no peers is not, in their eyes, pretension; for to what could they pretend, since they are already Fassis? Rural folk have always been beneath their consideration. The only men they hold in awe are the sacred, inner-circle of Cherifs who have lived among them from the beginning. Venerated, the members of this special caste settle all disputes brought before them, and it is their prayers that ensure the welfare of the city. Even to this day, they do no work of any kind, pay no taxes, and are supported by the community.

Fez was founded on baraka, sacredness and supernatural power combined. A certain Cherif Idriss, fleeing the Caliph of Baghdad, the fabled Harun al-Rashid, came at last to the plain of central Morocco and found refuge in the ruins of the Roman city Volubilis. The neighboring Berbers converted readily to the faith preached by the Cherif, and gave him their fealty. The arm of Harun al-Rashid was long, however, and Idriss died of poison. But not before he had begotten a son by a Berber wife. It was this Idriss II who began to build Fez in 811. The site was not far from his father's tomb, and was protected by encircling hills and watered by the Oued Fas, which no summer heat ever quenches. Idriss sent out a welcome to refugees from all over Islam, refugees from wars and schisms everywhere, from Cordoba to Baghdad. Scholars and savants came and almost at once founded a university—the Qarawiyin.

Merchants and craftsmen followed them. Thus Fez was blessed from the start by the prestige of baraka and by a gathering of men who knew how to turn it to practical advantage. Sitting astride two important commercial routes from the east and south, the city prospered and soon became the key to political power in Morocco. Although after the line of Idriss died out the next several dynasties sprang from Berbers of the south, all rulers in turn made haste to push northward and claim Fez. Time after time, it was before her walls that power was tested; while the old ruler was besieged from within, the new claimant hammered on the gates to depose him.

Fourteenth- and fifteenth-century Fez had few commercial rivals in Europe, and the fame of the Qarawiyin drew men not only from Islam but also from the Christian world. Even while Spain was expelling her Muslims, the sons of noble Spanish families sat among young Moors to study astronomy, mathematics, philosophy, and medicine. "An intelligent and informed observer of the fifteenth century," writes one historian, "could hardly have avoided the conclusion that Islam, rather than the remote and comparatively crude society of the European Far West, was destined to dominate the world in the following centuries."[1] The Merinids were the ruling dynasty of this period. Perhaps because they were not successful fighters—they saw the loss of Muslim Spain and of all the Maghrebi lands that earlier Moors had annexed to the empire —they put all their energies into building hundreds of mosques and medersas (religious schools) in all the cities. They welcomed tens of thousands of refugees from Andalusia, and through their talents brought Moorish culture to its peak of artistry and scholarship.

But one shrewd native mind had already seen that brilliant urban life could not survive without the Bled. Writing in the fourteenth century, the great historian and father of modern sociology, Ibn Khaldoun, warned that the culture was doomed to decline if deprived of regular transfusions from country stock. Even while exquisite medersas multiplied in Fez, incursions of nomads had ravaged the provinces; abandoning orchards, farms, and vineyards, the villagers had themselves been driven back to nomadism. Ibn Khaldoun's warning went unheeded, but within a hundred years his fears were realized. Intellectual creativity had centered too long in the cities and the Bled had slipped away from the Mahkzen, which now had lost the vigor to redeem it. Institutions became static, no new forms evolved, and Morocco, cut off from Europe and committed to despising all that "the Christian dog"

1. William H. McNeill, *The Rise of the West* (Chicago: University of Chicago Press, 1963), p. 485.

was experimenting with, had nowhere to look but backward. Her society became fixed in medieval amber.

Herein lies the dilemma for modern Morocco. But herein, too, is the great fascination for the traveler. The manner of life in Old Fez has changed very little since the time of the Merinids.

A broad hillside overlooking the city is dotted with tombs, white among the silver green of olive trees—the Merinid necropolis. Gray-green and silver leaves, and tombs roofed in green tile; armies of clouds passing overhead; spread out below, the soft limestone grays and tans of the city—a cubist drawing of flat roofs, pale walls, and high, narrow keyhole arches. Vertical lines of scores of minarets, glinting with the soft colors of faïence tile, and below each the green pyramid of its mosque roof. Above, around and between the slender minarets, storks planing on all but motionless wings. The distant sound of rushing water—the Oued Fas tumbling zigzag through the city, separating the quarter of one guild from another. The stream comes milky white from the limestone hills, turns a few paddle wheels, slides under little humpback bridges, and emerges murky and stained below the dyers' and tanners' vats. On one bank are the potteries, on another the tileworks of the Andalusian Quarter, where most of the green roof tiles of mosques and palaces throughout the kingdom have been made. Metalworkers and leatherworkers still have their own quarters, and merchants of each commodity cluster together. Their goods still arrive at the souks by muleback from warehouses on the fringe of the city. The biggest change is that trucks, not camels, bring them to the outskirts.

The Fassis' aloofness and reserve is reflected in their medina. Tightly compacted in the congestion of centuries, it faces inward on the swirling life of its steep lanes, where no car has ever penetrated. Above and around it, the city wall swings along the hillsides, reinforced at intervals by great square towers and pierced by many triple-arched gateways.

A vizier came to power at the end of the nineteenth century and, having amassed great wealth, built his palace beside one of these gates. The Palais Jamai lies up close to the wall, hemstitched to it in a series of courts, walled gardens, and tunnels leading downhill into the medina. A forecourt lies behind a second gateway, where the vizier would sit in judgment, cross-legged on a dais of carpets, listening to the stories that rose from the prostrate figures before him. Human heads on pikes decorated the wall at his back—a warning to the populace of the Mahkzen's way with enemies.

Today, the Palais Jamai is a hotel, and at the outer gateway, *Les Cars* disgorge swarthy countrymen come to sell crates of hens or bales of wool to the pale Fassis of the medina. Crowds gather about *Les Cars,* either waiting to depart or simply curious to see what is afoot, and shepherds from the immediate hillsides pause with their flocks to gawk at new arrivals. There is a general cacophony, a swirl of dust, and bleating of sheep—which threaten to drift under the wheels of the unregarding buses. In the forecourt, a country-man pauses to gather his forces for the bargaining session ahead; he counts his hides for the last time, then tightens the rope about the pile, hoists it to his back, and sets forth down a dark tunnel. On the bench where suppliants once sat waiting for the chamberlain to disburse the vizier's alms, a line of beak-nosed official guides now sit, number plates pinned to their djellabas. No suppliants they; as we stepped out of our car, they assessed us, and waited. Everyone knows this most tortuous of medinas requires a guide. Let the strangers come to them.

MEDINA

The room we were assigned had been the vizier's bedchamber. Up a tiled stairway we were led, down long corridors, through portieres and under carved and painted arches. A door was thrown open at last, and we stood in a large, high-ceilinged room of which the focus was a brocade-draped dais for the bed. Tile mosaics covered the lower walls, plaster friezes climbed to the coffered ceiling. I bent my head back to gaze up at the sunbursts carved in cedar between the rafters, then looked down at the dizzying tile lozenges and brilliant carpets on the floor; I wondered if the vizier had ever found peace in this room.

The furniture was all carved and painted, too, and a row of little wooden arches with pegs to hang your clothing on ran along a stretch of wall. At the far end of the room, an intricate black fantasy in wrought iron covered the windows. I pulled the glass panes inward and pressed my face against the iron arabesques, the better to see. Peering between the fronds of a banana palm, I saw terraced gardens dropping in stages down to a central courtyard with pavilions and a fountain. The gardens blazed with flowers and blossom-ing trees, though it was early February. Around a court with a fountain at its center, more pavilions backed up against the looming, gray medina wall.

When I came back from the window, Bill was staring at a pair of brass-bound, nail-studded doors in the side wall, directly opposite the dais. They were fifteen feet high, and securely padlocked. He tried the bolt on a small door cut into one of them. It slid back, and we stepped over the high thresh-old into what must have been an audience chamber. Another pair of cedar doors rose almost to the ceiling. Again the dadoes and friezes carved on the walls, even more elaborate here, and again the high coffered ceiling. Was all this height intended as a metaphor of the vizier's stature? Huge bronze filigree lanterns hung down on long chains, stirring faintly. Strong, hard colors and intricate patterns overwhelmed our eyes. All at once I was reminded of what a sad young Moroccan friend of ours, an architect who had trained in the U.S., had once said. "It is not that Moroccans have bad taste, it is rather that they have no taste at all."

In this chamber, carving, painting, and mosaic inlay seemed to strive against each other for intricacy of detail; textures of divan and cushion and brocade hangings tried to outdo the carpets in richness. Opulent it certainly was, and dazzling. Over every surface there was movement—sunlight glinted off chased brass, and curlicue shadows cast by the wrought-iron grille came and went as palm branches darkened the window. Suddenly, down in the garden, a peacock screamed. That was too much. We fled, bolting the little door behind us.

Decoration and elaboration are at the core of Islamic art, as they are in the art of the fugue. But only talent knows where to draw the fine line between restraint that is beautiful and redundancy that is vulgar. The nineteenth-century Moors knew no such distinction. We must get into the medina. . . . The desk clerk inquired if we would like an English-speaking guide. It sounded like a pleasant relief, so we agreed. At the appointed time, we saw a man move languidly out onto the top terrace, his djellaba buttoned up against the fine rain, and his red fez set at a dapper angle. As we approached and shook hands, he flourished a calling card and announced, "Hajj Youssef Benjelloun!" I took note of the title "Hajj," used only by those who have made the pilgrimage to Mecca. Yet he certainly did not look devout. Even as we addressed him by the title, he was tapping his lips above a yawn.

"Pardon," he said, ". . . is now Ramadan. No sleep night."

Bill told him the things we wished to see—the tomb of Moulay Idriss, the Qarawiyin, a medersa. While he was speaking, I watched the pale-brown face and saw a hard opacity come into the eyes. He will show us just what he means to show us, I thought . . . and pretend not to understand anything we say.

We were in the dark downhill tunnel to the medina when he stopped abruptly and turned to me.

"Caution, Missus! Your satchel must go so . . . and . . . so." He pulled both my hands to my purse, and then pushed them up until I was holding it almost under my chin.

"Why?" I demanded, my hackles rising.

"Thieves!" he muttered darkly. "Only so is safe—like baby at breast." I balked, but slung the shoulder strap around my neck and hugged the bag under one arm.

Emerging from the tunnel, we stood at the top of a lane six feet wide and packed solidly with people. Dark djellabas, red fezzes, intent brown faces, white veils, and women's darting eyes . . . figures straining against the crowd, moving slowly uphill or down, and the sound of countless feet scraping over stone . . . the hum of voices, and the repeated cry, "*Balak!*"—"Make way!" . . . a mule almost lost under a pile of bales, blindly straining forward and slipping on the wet cobbles . . . stalls raised a couple of feet above the level of the lane, the front and sides of each stall hung with clothing, woven fabrics, bolts of material, flowered, loose pantaloons for women . . . a man standing at the front edge of each stall, calling out to the crowd, and behind him, a single light bulb hanging down above the heads of workmen. Sheltering anyone with business to transact, a little portico projected beyond each stall. A woman must do her bargaining from the ground; but a man, once persuaded that a deal is likely, will catch hold of a rope hanging outside and swing up into the booth.

Carried along single-file behind Hajj Youssef's brown-striped shoulders, we turned into the canyon between high whitewashed walls above the porticoes, and here the din of chisels on brass hammered our ears. The tall houses leaned in so dangerously that they had to be braced against each other by beams across the lane. Without warning, the guide swung up into a stall between piled trays and coffeepots with domed lids and long curved snouts, and, seizing my arm, pulled me up after him. As we had suspected, he feigned not to understand our protests that we did not wish to buy and propelled us along to the rear of the souk, where he gestured us to seats on a brassbound chest. Sabers, antique pistols, muskets with intricate, chased silverwork were thrust into our hands; our headshakes only made Hajj Youssef smile the more sleekly and assure the merchant that we were not interested in things such as these, which anyone might buy, but only in his finest things. Out came a beautiful wrought-steel dagger, and then a little silver-inlaid coffer for jewels. These, too, Bill waved away, until the merchant took him to be a really expert bargainer. Down the prices came, and down again, as the oily old man warmed to his task and the hajji's teeth gleamed his approval.

Abruptly, Bill stood up, threw a firm good-bye over his shoulder, and led me to the street.

"I've an idea of the way to bring this guide of ours into line," he said. "First, we'll have no more of his pidgin English and his not understanding us. Second—well, he's coming toward us now. You just keep still while I spin my tale." Beside us, a lovely little fountain gushed out of the wall into a mosaic basin. A mule driver finished roping two great chests to his beast's narrow back, and came to the fountain to douse his head and neck with water. He was careful to keep his lips firmly closed, because of the Fast, but I could guess at the thirst the sound of the water must have provoked.

The hajji had barely opened his lips before Bill cut him off crisply in French. I learned that we were on a cultural mission from the United States in order to view certain artistic monuments of Fez and observe the way of life in the medina. We had only limited time to prepare for our report—and Bill glanced hard at the number plate pinned to the brown homespun djellaba. The guide's eyes narrowed, weighing this new aspect of things. Even if he missed a good commission on a sale or two, there might be some satisfaction in presiding over a cultural mission.

But he could not let us have our way without reminding us of our limitations. We knew, did we not, that the great monuments were sanctuaries of the faith, and thus closed to non-Muslims? That we should not even pause to look in at the great doors of the Qarawiyin mosque? I thought I detected a note of satisfaction in his voice as he continued, "You may not see that grand prayer hall—room for twenty-two thousand to pray there together . . . more than two hundred columns rising like trees to a great height . . . each capital a different marvel from the next one . . . the old and precious prayer rugs covering the floor . . . gold and azure mosaics . . . showers of light thrown by the great chandeliers and caught in their thousands of crystal pendants. . . ." I looked at him suspiciously. Was he just repeating phrases he'd culled from some guidebook? Or was this his way of expressing a real devotion? Was he trying to evoke a picture for us, or was he just maliciously enjoying the restrictions placed upon us? Or all of these at once?

Now he was saying, "Nor may you linger near the tomb of our holy Moulay Idriss, father of our city. But I will lead you past the portals."

"We'll follow you. But please look back often to see that we are still with you."

Down alley after alley we plunged after him, sharp right through a keyhole arch and into another tangle of humanity, two-wheeled barrows, and straining donkeys. We came upon an impasse—two wide loads facing each other from opposite directions, the drivers waving their arms and shouting "*Balak!*" One finally lost face and backed his mule around the next corner. Smells hung in the air: leather, tea, spices, a whiff from the tanneries. Burlap sacks stuck out into the lane, their necks rolled back to display dried beans and chick-peas, and little twisted horns of red and green hot peppers. Sharp left under a garland of artichokes strung across the alley, and we came up short against a pile of yellow leather slippers.

Hajj Youssef pointed across the street to a shop larger than any souk, with glass windows and a closed door. Fabrics were piled on shelves up the walls, and among the stacks of folded rugs out on the floor a single figure stood motionless. There was no sign above the door. Our guide studied his fingernails, enjoying our ignorance. "You would like to know what you see over there? Well, that is one of the great fonduks—the business place of one of our men of importance. He is no little man of the souks, he imports from Cairo and Damascus and has another establishment in Casablanca. . . . *You* may look in and think that nothing is happening—for you would not know that important deals are never arranged out in front, under the stares of the street! No; business here is conducted comfortably, in some quiet back room, over long conversations and—when it is not Ramadan—many glasses of tea."

The traffic sucked at us. No one can long stand against it. A load of hides, red and stiff and rank-smelling, caromed into me; only when it had passed could I see a man's legs lurching under it. The hajji stalked ahead, and we hurried to keep his fez in sight. In this city where fezzes are made, and every man wears one, you can only tell them apart by the angle on the head. We were swept through a tunnel under some house, and came out into a little square where an old sycamore grew, the paving stones raised in a mound by its roots. Bricks, thin and tan like Roman bricks, showed through the houses' worn plaster. I looked up at a finely carved old grille and wondered what Fassi matron with kohl-rimmed eyes might be looking down on *us*. Above the roofs, against a rain-washed sky, rose a plain little brick minaret, cumbered at its tip by an untidy mess of twigs. A stork's head just showed above, the beak resting on the rim of the nest. The effect was of a slight, dowdy woman with an erratic hat clapped on her head.

Across from us was a small café, apparently quite empty except for a table with a samovar on it and rows of glasses, and on the opposite side of the room a number of grass mats rolled up tidily. There were no chairs; customers would sit, in the usual fashion, cross-legged on the floor. A man sleeping quietly under the table, his head pillowed on an old tin cashbox, stirred, shifted his legs, then lapsed into sleep again.

"His business suffers a good deal during Ramadan?" Bill asked. "Or would there not be much doing until evening anyway?"

"On the contrary, you would find five or six men here at almost any time of day—people from this quarter alone, you know, for each neighborhood has its own such club—a place of relaxation and friendship, an escape from business by day and a refuge from the home at night."

"Escape from business?" I was surprised. "I supposed business was the breath of life—the great source of pleasure—?"

"Then you have not understood us, Madame." His heavy-lidded glance swept across my face. "For us there is a rhythm—a time for activity, a time for reflection and repose. Each gains from the other. We say: What need to hurry through a transaction? Where is the pleasure in that? Because we know when to pause, we can savor the enjoyment of each moment. A man comes here to refresh his spirit for an hour or two. He meets a friend, two friends, they have a few games of cards, a glass or two of tea, some conversation. . . . Or else his friend has brought a checkerboard. They play. The silence is good, for it is between companions, and the laughter is good, for it is between friends. . . . We Moroccans do not, like the French, just *pass* our time—we *spend* it! Time is the one coin each man may spend as he thinks well. And no one may complain because another has more than his fair share. In this we are all equal; no man is master of another's time!"

He has put his finger, I thought, on something we of the West cannot understand and therefore find exasperating: the Moroccan's sense of time—or timelessness. He is never "on time" for an appointment. Why would he be, if the appointment were with another Moroccan, who wouldn't be there either? When they do meet, as they surely will in the natural course of things, they will settle what needs to be settled. Pity only the westernized Moroccans. They are frantic, for they have a foreign sense of time, and are abraded by it just as we are.

"Hajj Youssef," Bill said, "you spoke of refuge from the home. This is strange to me—for our homes *are* our refuge."

The guide turned a pitying look on him. "And how would a man find peace, amid the clamor of women, the clacking of their tongues, and the hub-bub and cries of children? For you, then, there is no asylum?" They looked at each other wordlessly for a moment. Then the hajji shrugged eloquently. He moved forward, then stopped again and faced us intently.

"We are coming shortly to the tomb of Moulay Idriss," he said. "I remind you that the area around the portal is sacred. You will not stop, please, or even pass at close range." I looked ahead and upward, and saw the green roof, the color of royalty and sanctity, a glistening pyramid set upon impeccable white walls. The roofs of houses drew back from it, leaving it alone and splendid under the pale sky.

It was not left to our scruples to stay clear of the portal. Wooden barriers projected from the walls on either side, as a reminder. We let our feet slow only slightly as we passed at a respectful distance from the great closed doors. Even from there, my eye caught the glimmer of soft colors in the carved and fretted ceiling of the portico, the gentle sculpture of the marble lintel. The hajji darted forward, rubbed his palm against the worn doorjamb, then pressed his hand to his lips. At that moment, the other door swung wide, and a robed figure came out. Just for an instant, I saw the courtyard and the colonnade of white arches, the tumbling fountain, the quiet, white-hooded figures sitting cross-legged on the ground, in the shadows of the colonnade. The door closed then; my feet were still moving obediently forward when the hajji joined us.

"They are very beautiful, our mosques. . . . Our religion also is beautiful. I am sorry for you." He said it quite simply, and he meant it. It was a strange moment: this man whose arrogance was so annoying most of the time was for an instant free of it; but in that instant, he disclosed to me my own unconscious arrogance—until then, it had never occurred to me that a Muslim might feel pity for an unbeliever, so thoroughly had my own culture persuaded me that any pity should flow in the opposite direction.

"However," he resumed in his more usual manner, "it is possible you might learn something about Islam from our medersas. Since they are not in use, you are permitted to enter these."

In the fourteenth century, secret brotherhoods with their ecstatic rites had a wide following. Orthodoxy was in danger. The Merinids countered the threat by building medersas throughout the country, hoping thereby to catch impressionable young minds in time and instill in them the pure and true faith. The schools, when not attached to a mosque, had their own prayer hall and outer courtyard, and a dormitory above the colonnade. Boys from the age of twelve or even younger received free schooling in Sacred Law and the Traditions. Many of the schools required a vow of silence in the cells. A daily loaf of bread was passed in to each boy through a wicket in his door, and he ate it crouching on his pallet. After years of study, he went forth from the medersa to serve some community as a cadi or as the Imam of its mosque.

The guild of attar merchants made a large contribution to one of the medersas of Fez. Even today, their redolent souk surrounds the Attarine Medersa; each merchant in the narrow street tried to waylay my nose by waving under it a wad of cotton scented with oil of orange flowers, jasmine, sandalwood, and a dozen other essences I could not name. But instead of the lovely little glass vials in which attars used to be sold, I saw ranged on the shelves only small pill bottles, probably retrieved from wastebaskets.

Attar of sandalwood—in pill bottles . . . the shadowy portico of the medersa, where mysteries were carved in cedar above our heads—and a row of guides, gossiping on a bench, pausing only to take our measure with narrowed eyes . . . the anomalies of Fez. Our guide, having noted all who sat there leaning negligently back against the splendid door, now laid a tapering hand to his paunch and told us he suffered from a hernia and would do well to rest. He sat down and leaned close toward his friends.

As soon as we stepped past them into the silent courtyard, all irritation slipped away. The place was drenched in soft daylight from above. The walls rose from a colonnade of low pillars to high blind arches, white and encrusted with carving as delicate as foam. At roof level, a deep band of cedar, black with age, framed the white arches and seemed to float above them. There is nothing organic about this architecture; indeed, its very aim is to deny weight and thrust. The walls could have been lace, white lace and black, enriching each other by their contrast. This art is concerned with airy intricacy laid upon flat surfaces, and with profusion made to appear insubstantial. In more ways than one, it reminds me of the art of ballet—playing upon the idea of weightlessness, making the impossible seem effortless. Like ballet, it follows strict conventions, then disguises them with infinite variations. (Surely it can be no accident that ballet has borrowed the term *arabesque?*)

We stood, dwarf figures rooted to the ground, while all about us soared in weightless fantasy. The soft green of the courtyard tiles washed a faint reflective green onto the pale walls. Otherwise, there was no color but the mellow carved plaster and the vibrant dark cedar. Behind us, the fountain sent a plume of water upward in an arc; falling, it spilled gently from a marble basin into the sunken pool below. Above the colonnade and set low in the blind arches, small, closely screened windows had allowed the boys in their cells to peer out onto the court. The bleakness of their cubicles was meant to spell out for these children the distance between man's mean state and the unimaginable Infinite. All the rich intricacy of these walls, of this hollow airy shell open to the sky, would stir them to adoration. For profusion is linked with majesty in the Oriental mind. And if the princes of Islam proclaim their secular power through elaboration of their palaces, how much more intricate profusion is due the Deity?[2]

There is more to Islamic art than just profusion. Its conventions are strict —for a purpose. Only vegetal and abstract forms are allowed; no animate thing may be represented. The purpose, if I understand it, is to get man and all the other wayward creatures out of the way, and preserve art for the pure forms that lift men above themselves. All geometric figures lend themselves to an *infinity* of variations, and thus afford every possibility of stunning the imagination and lifting it free of earth. But, as graciousness mingles with purity in Allah, so should the pure abstractions be tempered—with vine tendrils, with curling leaves, and the rosette hidden at the heart of a palm tree. Then, to lead the human mind back to its duty of worship, verses of the Koran are embroidered in exquisite calligraphy upon the whole. You peer closely at what first appeared to be just low-relief carving, and you see that, in fact, there are three or even four levels of depth. As in a stately dance, some figures recede while others come forward; then they exchange places. The elegant cursive script is never obscured, but it permits graceful interpolations. Each letter is carved with all the care that a western artist might put into a flower. These are the free forms that prevent one from tiring of the symmetry.

The marvel of this medersa—and of all great Islamic art—is that it does not suffocate. A sure hand restrains the profusion, as in a fine fugue, at the ultimate moment of complexity. At the door to the prayer hall, the mood changes. It seems very dark, after the daylight of the courtyard, and is very quiet, for the sound of the fountain is cut off. There is little ornament, so that all attention can come to a focus in the *mihrab,* the small, arched niche in one wall that gives the direction of Mecca. The mihrab is pure filigree, all white and the shadows of white. Above it hangs a huge bronze chandelier with hundreds of little cups for oil to light the midnight prayer. When the boys were called from their cells and all these wicks were lit, any drifting breeze would have sent a flickering across that ever-empty niche. Even the Imam of the congregation would have stood, like the boys, facing the mihrab, but well back from it. Its emptiness is the symbol of the Prophet's presence, at the head of all congregations of believers.

2. The Alhambra is the only extant monument of the great period of Moorish art that is dedicated to a secular glory, and belongs to the Merinid period. Anyone who has wandered through it, stunned and overwhelmed, would question whether Muslim princes can be counted on to reserve the ultimate in profusion for religious buildings only. (Professor Oleg Grabar, under whom I had the privilege of studying, once called the intricate ceiling of the Alhambra's Hall of the Ambassadors "organized whipped cream.") But then, the princes of Granada were hardly noted for the piety of their outlook.

TOMBS OF THE MERINIDS

We came out and stood before the dozing figure of Hajj Youssef. He was all alone now, and had abandoned himself to sleep, head propped against the bronze door. We scraped our feet noisily on the stones, and with a voluptuous sigh, he opened one basalt eye upon us and reluctantly pulled himself to his feet. We were still under the spell of the medersa and said we had had enough for one day and would like to go home the shortest way, little knowing what a steep and crowded passage this would mean. We struggled uphill against knotted traffic. Children on their way back to school slid by, dodging under people's elbows. Several times someone caromed into me and was gone while I was still recovering my footing. Once Hajj Youssef clutched the rope hanging down beside a souk and swung himself up above the crowd, very nimbly, I thought, for a hernia sufferer.

At last the crowd thinned out. I saw the massive gray wall ahead and knew we were near the Palais Jamai. The guide stopped to catch his breath, and I unslung my bag and groped for my glasses, to read a poster about distributions of flour under the "Food for Peace" program. The glasses were not there. Bill looked, and then Hajj Youssef looked. There was no question about it—they were gone.

"When did you last have them?" Bill asked. I remembered poring over the calligraphy in the medersa. "What did you do with them after that?"

"Oh, I'm sure I put them carefully in my bag again." But, even as I said it, my hand went to my suit pocket—a telltale movement. And now I recalled something else: while I pushed uphill against the crowd and the careening children, there had been a moment when I thought I felt a hand at my pocket. The press was too great for me to be sure, and anyway I was confident then that my pocket was empty. But now my unconscious gesture toward my pocket told the whole story. Helpless rage overcame me. "Some wretched child has done this—some fool who knows nothing of their value and cares less! He'll break out my brand-new bifocal lenses and sell the frames for a few dirhams. I wish I could wring the neck of every urchin in Fez!"

With the energy of fury, I covered the last steep pitch to the Palais Jamai. If I could escape the self-justifications of this odious guide and get to my room quickly enough, perhaps I could also escape the recognition of my own foolishness. His voice trailed behind me into indistinctness: ". . . Don't I tell the Missus? Don't I do my best? . . ."

While I was savaging the contents of a suitcase, looking for an extra pair of glasses, Bill came into the room. "He says he'll distribute some money at various 'listening posts' through the medina, and offer a reward—and that your loss is his loss. . . . He all but wept."

"Crocodile tears!" I had found the spare glasses, and reached for the stack of mail in Bill's hand. It was when I discovered that there was no letter for *me* in all that pile that my anger veered onto Bill. I stood glaring at him, and then caught sight of our two figures in the two enormous gilt mirrors that hung on opposing walls—the images bounced back and forth from wall to wall, shrinking progressively into absurd miniatures. (How long had that vizier kept his wits?) I announced that I must go for a walk, alone. Managing to close the door without slamming it, I clumped down the sepulchral corridors: left turn, up three steps, sharp right through an arch, whose velvet hangings dragged across my shoulders, down another corridor . . . tall brass-banded doors on either side, and a heavy silence, except for my footfall on the carpet and the whisper of draperies. An old Arab proverb came into my mind: "If you are summoned to a prince's palace, remember to take your shroud with you."

I took the first path outside the triple gateway, one that led uphill to the Merinid tombs. Though a fine rain was falling, it was an immense relief to be alone, to stride on an empty path as fast as my long legs would take me, until the rhythm had begun its restorative work. Soon I could see that it wasn't just the loss of my glasses that afflicted me. It was a visitation of that mood of disenchantment all travelers must deal with sooner or later during a long journey. The gusto and the curiosity are suddenly gone; one cannot recall *why* one is so far from home, among people who no longer seem to have any attraction. I had experienced this loss of zest before, and surely would again. It had to be waited out. Some inner rhythm would come to my rescue, and soon I would feel the sap rising again.

A few hobbled cows lurched about between the tombs, and sheep raised long, sad, stupid faces to me as I passed. I was glad of their company. A wisp of smoke curled out of one of the caves—the shepherd, no doubt. Mist hung in the air now, the rain having stopped, and droplets ran down the blades of spiky aloes. Some boys appeared and began thrashing the olive trees with long poles, knocking down the fruit. A pale sunset broke through the clouds, toucing them to opalescence and warming the limestone city to a silvery tan. The crenelated wall ran along from hill to hill, looking like the fretted spine of some long, brown prehistoric lizard.

The old medina was joined by a wasp waist of walls to a second Fez. Here, thousands of Jews from Spain had been assigned a new mellah—not out of altruism, but because they were needed as Fassi trade expanded. Since the Koran forbids usury, Muslims have had to turn to Jews for their banking. Now, as I looked down, the evening army of storks wheeled above Fez Djedid. I could forget for a moment what tireless scavengers they are, and how clumsy at landing and take-off, for in flight they are impressive and full of omen. Fassis, associating them in some dim way with the spirits of the dead, never restrict their freedom. They sailed from the roofs of the mellah up and over the expanse of the Mechaouar, over its palaces and gardens and orchards and its large garrison.

Right in front of the Mechaouar gates runs a businesslike, four-lane arterial road, leading to the third Fez, the *ville nouvelle*. Straight as an arrow it runs, as if pointing a moral. Just as directly, the collapse of the Mahkzen led straight into the arms of the French.

The life within this Mechaouar had become an effete circus by the turn of this century. Too many feeble sultans had immured themselves there with their amusements, oblivious of the country except when revenues ran low. The great tribal caïds had to be paid well to pass on the taxes they collected; they withheld more and more as they saw the sultan totter. Now it was mostly foreign loans that propped up the regime. But instead of being applied to governing, the money never got beyond the Mechaouar. A great marble staircase from Venice would arrive at the palace, or organs that no one could play, or an elevator for which no shaft could be made. The sultan's menagerie of wild beasts was constantly being enlarged. Baroque entertainments went on for days on end. Meanwhile in the ruined Bled, the fellahin hid their flocks from the caïds' pillaging. Robbers preyed on the roads; even in the cities householders needed armed guards. The French by now had too much invested in the country to stand back any longer. When this Mechaouar of Fez lay under siege and the impotent sultan appealed for help, the French marched in—"to restore order and safeguard lives and property," as the Treaty of 1912 read.

With a start, I came out of my reverie when lights appeared at the tips of the minarets, like scores of glowworms hovering above the city. A ghoulish wail broke out from the loudspeaker on the roof of a fortified building close beside me. This was no muezzin's voice; it was the shriek of an air-raid siren—installed during the war and used now to signal the dropping of the sun below the horizon. Twilight had come very abruptly. Belatedly, I realized there would be no afterglow to light my way down the slope, because of the rain clouds still in the sky. Hurrying now, I kept my eyes fastened on the uncertain ground at my feet, and jumped when a shape loomed beside me. It was only a cow, closely followed by her calf. From her lip hung some wisps of grass and a spot of orange—bright even in the dusk—one of the tiny calendulas that star the fields under the winter rains. I touched her warm flank briefly, for reassurance, and moved ahead as fast as I dared. Bats were wheeling low all around me and, as the dark deepened, two owls called softly back and forth from one clump of shadowy cypresses to another. Trying to follow the paths was risky now—once I reached the road I would stick to it, even though its roundabout course made it far longer to the Jamai gateway. But I had trudged only a hundred yards by the side of the road before I was aware of a car following me in low gear. "You have got yourself into a poor situation, you fool!" I muttered as I heard the car door open, and turned about to confront it squarely. The car looked very familiar, and I found myself looking into Bill's quizzical gray eyes.

ENVIRONS OF FEZ

I begged to get away from Fez the next day—to Volubilis, the most extensive Roman ruins in Morocco, and to Moulay Idriss, the mountain village where the first Idriss is buried. So we drove west from Fez, across the Saïs plain that once filled the granaries and supplied the olive presses of Volubilis. It is just as fecund today—one of the "Verdant Three" that Mr. Bennouna had insisted must not be interfered with. Many of these great farms were no doubt still held by some of the 5,000 colons who have remained; the rest have passed to politically correct and wealthy Moroccans. One could see why the French called them *domaines*. Each entrance had its grandiose gateway; some were bizarre to a degree—concrete poured in neo-Moorish forms, with strange cacti planted cunningly in pockets and diverticula. Purely horrid.

The fields seemed immense to us, by contrast with the native division of land into narrow strips parceled out to each heir under Muslim inheritance law. (There was once a good reason behind those laws: since so much of the land is hilly, the good soil tends to wash down to the bottom. The fairest way to divide land between sons was to give each a strip running from top to bottom.) As the generations succeeded each other, the strips were divided again and again. By now, a fellah with any land of his own at all has one strip here, another several miles away; so that much of his energy goes into walking between them. Even worse is the way the narrowness of his strip encourages him to plow straight uphill and down again, with entirely foreseeable consequences in erosion. Someday, these inheritance laws may be changed; there is an effort in that direction, but like everything else it seems to bog down in talk.

But these wide fields of the Saïs, which the original colons had reunited from small strips, and then had fertilized, rotated, and skillfully regenerated, were bearing richly. Orchards were already in blossom—plum and peach and apricot trees foaming with tender color. The vineyards were beautifully kept, screened from the wind like the rich grainfields by walls of cypress or eucalyptus. Mechanized equipment moved between the rows. Off at the edge of the fields, the day laborers' tents huddled together—the long, low, nearly black tents made of woven strips of goathair sewed together and supported on a rectangular frame. How could the agricultural dilemma show up more clearly, I thought, than in one of these extravagantly prosperous fields with the motorized monsters prowling them, and the migrant workers shunted off to one side? I recalled Mr. Bennouna's sad voice, saying: "Our fellah has become too dependent. Even if they had the choice, many would rather be day laborers than assume the risks of ownership."

The Roman city Volubilis can be reconstructed in the mind's eye from stumps of columns, foundation walls, the broad steps up to a roofless temple, and the triumphal arch. Bill prowled about, happily tracing the outline of a Christian basilica. But a skeleton city laid bare by faithful archaeology often induces in me a mood of emptiness and contrivance. I used to keep this heresy to myself until a painter friend one day told me how much the restorations of classical Sicily disappointed him. "The acres of tumbled monuments held nothing for me but historical significance and desolation," he said. Nothing could release in him the desire to paint, until one day his eyes fastened on a pattern of cracks in an old wall and the colors of lichens growing on the stones, and at last he was able to paint—in his own idiom. In somewhat the same way, I have wandered over a vast restoration with only obedient, desultory attention. But then, on another occasion, I have been deeply stirred when my hand turned up random bits of mosaic in the sand of some Mediterranean beach, or pulled up fragments of carved marble from a tangle of seaweed, or seen under the receding waves the outline of a submerged Roman quay with a mosaic of barnacles encrusting the giant blocks of stone.

I cannot *summon* the past. I must wait to be overtaken involuntarily—as when I learned that a good many fellahin still go by the Julian calendar . . . and when I discovered that there are Latin words buried in the Berber dialect: *iger* for "field" and *asnus* for "donkey." The Berber for "chick-pea," *ikiker,* is said to derive from Cicero's name. (Because he was as bald as a pea? Or because his orations were mealy?) So, in Volubilis, what meant most to me was the sudden realization that the domestic architecture of the ancients is alive today in the plan and style of the typical Near Eastern or North African home: the rectangle of sparsely furnished rooms opening onto a court where a fountain splutters over mosaic tile . . . the colonnade lighted by lamps the same shape as the lamps of Pompeii . . . the women's quarters sequestered from the men's . . . the charcoal braziers, and even the same broth of chick-peas.

A few miles from Volubilis, and built on the flanks of a formidable mountain, is the city in which Idriss I lies buried. Moulay Idriss is a pure white city surrounded by a margin of silvery olive groves and dark green fig trees, and uniquely holy, because of the venerated tomb at its core. Until a few years ago, non-Muslims had to be outside the gates by nightfall, and even during the day had to keep to the outer rim of the city and look down only from a distance on the sanctuary.

It is a very small town, climbing the hill so steeply that its streets become staircases. It comes alive only when a *moussem* (pilgrimage) is in progress— when one of the guilds of Fez makes its annual trip, or some other city sends a pilgrim deputation to honor the birthday of its patron saint, pious bands camp at the foot of the mountain and make their obeisance to the tomb. There are moussems for healing and for rain, and moussems to exorcise some evil that has fallen upon a community. But between pilgrimages, not much goes on in Moulay Idriss. It must be rather trying to *live* in a holy of holies, especially for the young, I thought, looking down the nearly empty streets to the gleaming pyramidal roofs of the mosque and sanctuary. Then I saw a legend scrawled on a white wall in an all-white town: "*Vive le Twist!*"

Moussems were the occasion for ecstatic rites and for trance induced by dervish whirling or incantatory recitation. Nina Epton gives an account[3] of some less innocuous practices that are severely forbidden today—of initiation rites in which adepts dance in animal disguise, of paralytics thrown in the path of the dance, and of a Dionysiac ritual climaxed by the dismembering of live sheep. As she points out, there is a very real need for catharsis and intense corporate experience among a people who are forbidden alcohol, whose contacts with women are strictly limited, and who have no such outlets as our team sports provide for release of mass emotion.

People under so many restrictions will resort to wars and raids, or else to some institutionalized version of these. So the traditional powder-play, or fantasia, has been kept alive and encouraged. Even the King attends the one held yearly at Moulay Idriss, or sends a royal person in his place. Each year, on the Prophet's birthday, the plain is stippled with tents, the finest horses are decked out with embroidered breastbands, tassels at their heads, and brilliant saddle blankets. Riders, white-turbaned and white-robed, form a phalanx at one end of an open field. At a signal, they break into a gallop, waving five-foot carbines above their heads and screaming "Allah!" Charging at breakneck speed across the field, they seem to be about to mow down the crowd. At the last instant, they rein in, the horses rear, the riders stand in their stirrups and discharge all their guns in the air at once.

It was the twenty-eighth day of Ramadan that we visited Moulay Idriss. The end of the month of fasting and the coming of the feast of Aïd es Seghir would be proclaimed any day now, as soon as the new moon had been sighted. The quiet streets of Moulay Idriss echoed suddenly with a series of hoarse, long-held notes that made me think of a ram's horn. We followed in the direction of the sounds to a square ringed by houses and a mosque. As the notes sounded nearer, doors opened and all eyes focused up one street. Then I saw the trumpet, eight feet long and held to the lips of a striking young man whom a train of children followed. His burnous was tunic-length, his sandaled feet were bare and strong, and his features were classical under a cap of tight curls. He could have been Juba, the Hellenized Berber king of Volubilis, whose queen was the daughter of Cleopatra.

A mule followed him into the square. While the trumpeter blew his hollow notes, a messenger came from each household and emptied into the mule panniers a stream of grain from a basin or amphora-shaped jar. After each contribution, the young man rested the tip of his horn on the mule's back and spoke the same phrase to each donor in turn. A holy name must have been mentioned, for both speaker and listener carried a hand to their lips. Almost everyone looked up to the sky, where a rack of clouds was gathering, and then quickly away again. It did not seem likely that the crescent moon would be seen that night.

3. *Saints and Sorcerers* (London: Cassell, 1958).

LALLOU

It rained as we drove back to Fez that afternoon, more of that abundant rainfall unique to this part of Morocco. All the streams were full, and every bit of uncultivated ground was a mosaic of violets, dainty dwarf iris, and jack-in-the-pulpits just pushing up out of their shrouds. But for those anxiously awaiting the Feast, the rain was hardly a blessing.

That night, the sky was featureless as we emerged from a restaurant in the medina. The *tajin* of roast mutton had been dry, the prune sauce scorched —tempers were evidently short in the kitchen. The best part of the meal had been the young lad who served us, carefully lifting the conical straw cover from each dish he presented so that we might inspect the food. After serving us with grave solicitude, he stood back against the red damask wall, arms crossed on his breast and eyes lowered but, I noticed, watching us discreetly. While he was pouring scented warm water over my hands at the end of the meal, I caught his eye and asked his name. I had the impression he was new to this job, so weighty was his concentration. He set the pitcher down with great exactitude and presented a towel for my hands before answering, "Lallou is my name. It means 'Sweet' in our language." And he resumed his ceremonial rigidity.

Now, standing in the doorway, I turned back on an impulse. I thought I had heard him follow us softly down the stairs, and there, in fact, he was. After a few words to Bill, I asked, "Lallou, have you a few hours free in the daytime? To accompany us in the medina?" The blue Fassi eyes showed pleasure, and we had a new guide. Before we parted, Bill explained our one condition: he must not attempt to use us to bring off any sales. The boy nodded thoughtfully.

Meeting was easy enough, in the clearing around the little Nejjarine fountain gushing out of the wall. Though the matter went unspoken, we guessed, when he asked if we would like to see the dye works from the roof of a friend, that he meant to avoid any exposure to professional guides, who might pounce on him.

But he led the way straight past a famous medersa. High on the wall opposite the portal, a water clock had been installed long ago: a line of corbels projecting well out over the street, and on each corbel a turquoise basin. Water was once channeled up there by an intricate system of controls whereby all the basins would fill at the same rate. Precisely at the hours for prayer, the overfull basins would tip, drenching anyone below who was not already inside the mosque.

Sounds of a scuffle drew my eye away from it, and I turned to see Lallou dodge a blow from two official guides who held the boy between them. Bill strode into the melee; I heard him declare loudly that he, a professor visiting Fez, had hired the youth to lead him to the home of one of the professors of the Qarawiyin. I hoped to heaven no one would inquire just who it was we sought. But at the magical word professor, the guides drew back. Lallou tucked in the tails of his new shirt, and we moved quickly away.

The boy, mortified, soon found a target for his feelings. When he saw a countryman pause to light a cigarette—and this at midday in Ramadan—he walked past him, staring, and then turned to spit on the ground. "*Sale compagnard!*" he hissed, as another Arab might curse "Dog—and son of a dog!" I looked at Lallou's angry face, thinking of the young *compagnard* with the trumpet in Moulay Idriss, and wondered once more at the scorn of the Fassis.

We came to a potter's souk. The old man wore a turban wrapped above his fez, a superstructure so high it seemed to press his beak nose down to meet his sharp chin. Crouching among his tiers of basins and pitchers, he worked with perfectly calculated speed. One sure hand turned the neck of a jar, while a finger of the other, first dipped into a pot of black paint, swiftly sketched on the geometric pattern. Ten seconds, and the jar joined a line of others on the shelf. He lifted an amphora to his lap, and I leaned forward to take pleasure in its lovely lines. Without turning his head, the craftsman spoke shortly in Arabic.

Lallou said in my ear, "He will let you have if for eight hundred francs, since you are his first client—"

"Lallou!" I interrupted. "You are breaking your agreement with us!" I was greatly annoyed with him.

He lifted his shoulders and his eyebrows at the same time, in that way Moroccans have of expressing their helplessness in the face of commanding circumstances. "But what would you have me do? This man is a friend of my uncle. Would you have me insult him by not telling you what he says?"

We left him to work out with the potter as best he might the delicate matter of loss of face before an old friend, and walked ahead a little before we stopped to wait. (I saw that the glass showcase we stood beside was not full of jewelry, as I had supposed from the iron grille protecting it. It contained row on row of full sets of gold teeth, and an arrow pointed up a stairway to the *Cabinet de Dentiste*.) Walking a little stiffly, Lallou came up. There was silence until we reached a door on which there were two bronze knockers, one at the level of a horseman and another that the boy laid hold of.

It was not until we reached the roof he had promised us that the stiffness between us relaxed. But now, with Fez spread out below us and only the minarets rising like candles above the acres of rectangular roofs, he settled himself seriously to his duties as a guide. The turquoise balls along an upright rod at the tip of each minaret's cupola were for the five hours for prayer, he explained. If we would look down along his finger we would see the Qarawiyin courtyard. The figures of young men, their heads bent, paced singly along the edge of the colonnade. "The examinations must be coming soon,"

Lallou said. "In my country, it is the custom to memorize as we walk—the feet take the cadence of the words, and that way, we do not forget."

He led us across parapets dividing the roofs. Sometimes we passed close to a chasm from which rose a sound like distant surf from the street far below. Once, we looked down into the hollow heart of what must have formerly been a very beautiful house. A gallery ran around four sides of the open shaft, but only one pair of columns remained, carrying a single, slender, carved and fretted arch. Grass and weeds, growing somehow up here in the sky, spilled over the threshold between two tall doors hanging awry on their hinges, ready to plunge any instant down into the courtyard. This house had surely been the pride of some merchant prince; perhaps his fortune had been undermined by the rise of that upstart of commerce, Casablanca.

"When you wish to see the dyers . . ." Lallou was politely bored by the decaying house. We crossed several more parapets, while all the time the sound of rushing water came nearer. At the edge of the last roof, we looked down on the Oued Fas running, dark with dyes, at the foot of a high blank wall. Behind the wall was a dyers' yard—an infernal scene in the strictest sense of the word. Earthen vats were scooped out of the clayey ground, each one a gaping mouth full of some violent color, and each sending up a cloud of steam. Figures moved about the vats, their forearms and their legs below the leather aprons permanently stained. Seen fitfully through the swirling steam, they looked like figures in one of the lowest of Dante's limbos. The dyers stood on narrow catwalks between the vats and stirred with long poles, from time to time lifting out a dripping hide to inspect it. The dye ran down their arms and streaked their sweating faces. Boys bent almost double under a load of hides on their backs passed along the slippery catwalks, dumping a few hides into each empty vat. Sometimes a brief skirmish broke out with the dyer if the boy had jostled him and threatened to pitch him into the fearful brew. The scene was devilish, all wraiths of steam and gleaming dark surfaces of dye, and straining dye-stained flesh. We heard a shout, and saw a fist upraised and shaken at us. Even at that distance, the rage on the youth's face was clear enough—rage that tourists should stand high up there on a roof and look down on their awful labor, and that a native boy should stand there with them in a clean white shirt.

All at once, I felt I must leave the medina; I saw from Bill's face he was more than ready. There comes a time, in any medina, when escape becomes urgent. Leaving the roof hastily, we walked as fast as possible and with few words. Only at the Nejjarine fountain did we stop, for there we were almost home. Lallou had been puzzled by our abruptness; perhaps he had been searching his mind to see how he had failed us. To restore his spirits before we parted, I asked him about the forthcoming Feast.

"For three days, there is celebration—good eating and good music . . . dancing, singing with the gimbri—you know it?" Indeed I did. It is a two-stringed instrument, which may either be plucked like a guitar or sawed with a bow. In the latter case, it emits very sad, long-held notes that waver constantly off pitch—or so it seems to me. "Everyone is happy. We visit friends' houses, with flowers or small gifts, and stay for tea and pastries. Everyone has new clothes to wear—or at least a freshly laundered outfit."

Now I understood why I had lately seen such an access of clothes washing. Even in the public Bou Jeloud gardens, while school children chased each other through the tall stands of bamboo or shouted for joy when drops fell on their heads from the great water wheel turning at its ancient pace, women carried their laundry on their heads to the banks of the stream. After knotting their skirts about their waists, they spread the washing on flat stones in the shallows and drubbed it with their feet, their flowered pantaloons driving up and down like pistons in the clear cold water.

"But what," Bill asked Lallou, "if the nights continue dark and the Feast is delayed after they have finished all their preparations?"

"Naturally, they become impatient. . . . But I believe the end will come tonight. You will surely hear the drumming and singing from your windows at the Jamai . . . unless, of course, you would care to come with me through the medina on the Eve of the Feast and see for yourselves?"

"That would be a splendid idea, if there were any way to tell which night would prove to be the Eve. These rainy nights, who can be sure when the clouds will part for an instant and disclose the moon?"

"Ah, the Ulema are sure to see it one of these nights! They know where to meet—in some high place where, through the merest tear in the clouds, the crescent moon will be seen for certain. It has always been so—what need to doubt?"

"Lallou," Bill laid a hand on his arm to stop him a moment, "tell me something: Why couldn't this be left to the Ulema of some place like the Tafilelt, where it never rains?"

The boy looked shocked. "Do you not see that it *must* be the Ulema of Fez? How could it be otherwise?"

"Well, Lallou, you must be right. . . . As you say, 'It has always been so.' If you get a strong premonition that the Eve has arrived, come to the Jamai and send a message to us. If we haven't gone to bed, we'll join you."

The boy took his guide fee with utmost dignity. "I will see you again," he said, smiling, "I have a premonition!"

But that night, the twenty-ninth of Ramadan, as I sat by our window and listened to the sounds from the medina, the sky was low and dark and featureless. There was no wind, and no promise of a break in the cloud cover. I heard a few interrupted snatches of drumming and the murmur of thousands of voices. Everyone must be out in the streets, gazing upward. Once, I heard shouts and quick cries and running feet, then the shrilling of a police whistle —some minor brawl, born of impatience and frustration.

I thought about Lallou. Where but in Fez would a youth confess to a name that meant "sweet," and without a trace of embarrassment? Arabic place names are often descriptive of some attribute—Place of Wild Olives, Gate of Morning, Mount of Victory—but proper names are usually drawn from ancestors, with a prefix of "ben" or "ibn." But in Fez, where the proper ancestry goes without saying, a man can afford to honor a pleasure of the palate when he names his son.

It seemed to me that Lallou's family moved to some extent with the times, for he had spoken of listening with them to foreign news on the radio. He was what I would call a "half-modern." One day he wore a djellaba, the next a flashy sports shirt. He had complained about the number of school hours he had been required to devote to Arabic, and was as practical about his future as any young Frenchman; just now he was taking a correspondence course he hoped would bring him a job as electrician. But he kept Ramadan strictly, and believed with all his heart in the ineffable rightness of the Ulema of Fez.

The thirtieth day of Ramadan was heavily overcast. But as we put the car in the Jamai garage that evening, a figure detached itself and came toward us from the cobwebby shadows. It was Lallou, greatly excited. "The word has gone out! Tonight is the Eve of the Feast! Shall I accompany you in the medina?"

"But how on earth can you tell? It looks just as much like rain as it did last night."

"No, no, no—it is the end, you will see. Tomorrow, you may be sure, the King will proclaim the Feast."

When we met him later that evening, a light mist filmed the air, but no one seemed to worry about it, Lallou least of all. He wore a fine new djellaba, and his eyes shone gay and clear. The medina lanes were thronged with people, but for once there were no mules and barrows. No question that feasting had begun—little spiced sausages came off the long hot skewers and vanished into laughing mouths. Hawkers cried hard eggs with painted shells, dishes of chick-pea paste, and steaming platters of tripe and brains. We asked Lallou what we could treat him to, and he finally settled on a plate of tiny fried fish, which he ate with grimaces of delight. I seemed to be the only person who worried about whether the moon could be sighted tonight—I kept glancing up at the sky, which hung like a canopy above our heads, reflecting the brilliance of many electric lights. The women's hair glinted with henna, and their hands were tipped with it. Even the littlest girls' heads shone coppery; even the babies' soft round heels were hennaed. Fathers carried their small children on their shoulders, and each man wore something new, a crisp new fez if he could afford nothing more. The kaftans were magnificent. Ordinarily, they are worn mostly in the home; but tonight velvet and rich brocade brushed over the clay-slick cobbles. Over their bright flowered dresses, some of the women wore those filmy overdresses called *mansourias,* tissue-thin and gleaming with silver or gilt threads. I saw the popular heelless leather slippers going to a sodden pulp underfoot, and the yellow dye running on bare ankles. Men stopped every few steps to greet a friend: hands were carried to lips and arms thrown about shoulders.

The volume of sound mounted steadily, to the point of bedlam. Sometimes I heard the hoarse ram's-horn note above the tinkle of the transistors that almost everyone carried beside his ear. From a high window above the crowd came now and then a wisp of song, the throb of small drums, or the anguished scrape of a bow on a gimbri's strings. I had to speak into Lallou's ear to ask about a sign beside several doorposts—the Hand of Fatma, in dull red. "Hen's blood!" he shouted back. "The best there is against the evil eye." And he pulled his lips down at the corners apologetically.

We turned at last into a quiet little street. Above the last roof, the tomb of the second Idriss, outlined in soft lights, hung like a crown against the velvet night. An exquisite smell came from a bake oven beside us. Children who had brought their loaves from home were waiting outside, their long boards piled beside the threshold. Every few minutes the sweating baker appeared with a line of flat loaves on his long wood paddle and slid them onto a board held up for him. I could not conceive how any child would know which were his loaves emerging from the red maw of the oven in the background. Perhaps no one did know—maybe one waited just so many minutes, and then stepped up to the baker and held up one's board. As soon as the crisp rounds were settled in a row, the boy would lift the board to his head and skim up the alley, swift and sure and erect.

By midnight, we were exhausted. Lallou must surely have felt that he had justified his hire and was now ready to join his own family festivities. With the gravest courtesy, he invited us to come to his house, but we sensed that this would embarrass him and probably ourselves as well; and so, instead, we began the long ascent back to the Jamai. Festival specialties filled almost every stall—nougats dyed the most startling colors, small earthen drums with hide stretched taut at one end, stacks of honey cakes, mounds of geometrically arranged figs and almonds and walnuts. We picked out several lengths of nougat for Lallou's family and struggled on. Suddenly there was a prick of incense in the air. We came to a booth hung all about with beeswax candles brightly decorated and studded with wedges of what Lallou said was frankincense. "This tiny piece," he said, lifting a fragment on his fingertip from a saucer, "costs more than I have ever earned in one day!" He set it carefully back. Not at all outraged by its cost, he seemed to congratulate himself that there were people who could buy and burn these candles in honor of Aïd es Seghir.

We swung around a corner and came abruptly into the midst of ten or twelve young men clustered about a pinball machine, joking and backslapping and thrusting more coins into the slot. They seemed to be Moroccan; yet they could hardly have been more alien to the people we had just been among. They wore the international uniform of the rootless young—long hair, leather jackets, tight pants, and jackboots. Very likely, they were waiting until other youths, all alike as peas in a pod, should materialize from France or Germany, and sweep the Moroccans into their train; hours or days later, in response to some inner call heard by all simultaneously, the whole flock would organize for departure.

I asked Lallou if he knew any of them. "One or two, I think. The others . . . " He shrugged. "I know this type. They drift. The game they play is called poing paing." I think he meant Ping-pong. I offered no reply but just watched his face as he swung back to look again. There was no doubt he was fascinated as well as disdainful. What young man wouldn't rather jump on a Vespa and be off to Cairo than stay in Fez and finish an electrician's correspondence course? But of course he was too *sérieux* . . . and yet there was a yearning, a curiosity that made him lean toward them like a candle flame sucked by a draft.

Another person was looking on grimly, a gentleman with deep hawk's eyes and a fine, strong, Semitic face. He came and laid a hand suddenly on Lallou's shoulder. The boy whirled, looked up, and saw who it was. A series of quick expressions crossed his face; then he seized the man's hand and carried it almost to his lips. "Sidi Abderrahman!" he said, and spoke in Arabic. The man looked steadily into his eyes while he replied. Then, resettling his fez, he turned on his heel and left.

When Lallou turned back to us, I had a strong feeling the older man had expressed displeasure at seeing him with foreigners on such a night, and even more displeasure at finding him hovering about youths in jackboots. Lallou was in a hurry now to leave the square.

"That gentleman is a friend of my family," the boy said, still walking briskly. "He is a great man. And also a doctor."

"A medical doctor?"

"I am not sure that he has a medical degree, but he is a healer and saver of lives. When the midwife cannot bring a baby, or when the fever strikes, the people call on Sidi Abderrahman. He will come out in the night, or in the rain, when rich doctors are content to say 'Tomorrow, bring me to the house.' Whether he has a diploma or not, for twenty years he has practiced from his heart amongst us here in the medina."

We arrived at the Nejjarine fountain. Tonight, a bronze lantern shone down on the soft green-and-blue faïence, the exquisite lacy white stucco rosettes and the spurting clear water. "We must say good-bye here," Bill said, "for we are leaving Fez tomorrow." He reached in his pocket for the envelope with Lallou's fee and our note of thanks. Before he would take it, the boy asked us to write our address on the envelope. (And how many times since has he pulled a tattered envelope from his pocket and asked other wandering Americans—"You must know my friends in Michigan?")

"Then you will be soon again in Fez, 'nch Allah?" Oh, yes, we said, and we would look for him. While he dictated his address to Bill, I was suffering from a strong sense of our transience, our excludedness from the Feast and from all the pain and pleasure that makes up Moroccan life. No, I thought, even when we return, we probably will not look for Lallou. We have all three tried to bridge the gaps. . . . We have gone as far as we can. If we saw him again, the little constraints would be more noticeable, the breaks in understanding more apparent. Tonight, I had heard Lallou sigh a couple of times before he attempted to explain something—the strain was making itself felt. We had met as far as it was possible for us to meet.

"You will take our greetings, please, to your family? We shall be thinking of you tomorrow—today, that is!" He smiled in reply and grasped our hands. Now that he was about to go home, I'm sure he felt quite fond of us. We turned to struggle up the last incline; when we looked back, he was just disappearing under the vault of a building that bridged the lane. His hood was pulled up over his curly hair, and his step was jaunty. I looked up and thought I saw one faint star behind the clouds.

It must have been at just the moment of dawn when I was wakened by a muezzin calling high above the city, calling for prayer, calling for the forgiveness of Allah on the rejoicing and heedless people of Fez. I fell asleep again to the sound of drums and women's ululation.

Of course, Lallou turned out to be perfectly right. At eleven-thirty the next morning, while we were in the *ville nouvelle* attending to some business, King Hassan went on the air to proclaim Aïd es Seghir. Shutters promptly began to roll down on every shop front. Sirens wailed about the city. Urchins pounced on tin cans lying in the gutter and began to drum on them with sticks. Every donkey standing patiently beside the outdoor market brayed, and I think every rooster crowed. I'm sure that the *petits taxis* jumped forward like bullets and sped around the corner on two wheels. All the carriages in sight were being hired instantly. Ladies with fresh white veils stepped in, gentlemen, carrying gifts and bouquets of flowers and bunches of fresh dewy mint, jumped up after them, just as the thin horses leaned into their harness and began to trot. I felt very lonely waiting for Bill, and very far from home. I left the car and ran across to the open market and bought three bunches of dark blue violets, just before the man closed down his stall. When Bill came back to the car, I tendered him the violets, saying wistfully, *"Bonne et belle Fête, mon chéri."*

New Fez
GOVERNOR BENBOUCHTA

It was to the *ville nouvelle* that we returned more than a year later. I stood by the window in our very modern hotel watching the little narrow-gauge train huffing off toward Taza. A sudden freakish summer storm was funneling down the valley toward Old Fez in the distance. The wind sucked up dust devils swirling off the hillsides, and swept down like an ocher curtain upon the pale towers of the medina. Out of nowhere, a glider appeared in the sullen sky, the toy of some sportsman captivated by the European fad. The wind seemed savagely intent upon driving it against the minarets—it dipped crazily and was fast losing altitude. Then the old city was erased from sight in the yellow rain, before I could tell whether the rider's baraka would be sufficient for him to lift the little craft clear of the battlements.

Immediately upon our arrival in Fez, Bill had been called to the telephone. "Professor Willcox, this is the Governor of Fez. A letter from Rabat informs me that you and Madame your wife would like to call upon me. It will give me pleasure to see you. May I send my car for you tomorrow morning at ten o'clock?"

It was startling that the governor should make the call himself, instead of a secretary. Governor Benbouchta, we discovered, was a man of singular directness. When we first saw him, he was inspecting the dahlias in his garden, bareheaded, a tall, lean figure bending to retrieve a blossom that had broken off. When he heard the car, he came toward us, one hand outstretched, the other delicately fingering the velvet petals of the flower. The white and silver stripes of his sheer djellaba accentuated his height; his calm eyes surveyed us while he made us welcome and spoke warmly of Bill's profession and his own regret that he now had less time to read history than he would like. His face was clean-shaven, and I noticed a mottling of his complexion, produced, I later learned, by some lifelong disease affecting the pigmentation of the skin. Perhaps it was this affliction that had driven him clear of small vanities and confirmed him in an inner poise.

He pushed open French doors to a reception room where modern paintings hung on cool white walls and echoed the colors of the wonderfully mellow carpet that ran the full forty feet of the room. Geraniums, lilies, and a camellia tree grew in pots along the edge of the floor. A desk divided the room about two-thirds down its length; behind it lurked a young man with the air of a secretary. The governor had him bring the phone and set it at his feet, then waved a dismissal. The cord was exactly the length of the distance from desk to easy chair; I gathered Benbouchta liked to be left unattended with his guests, and liked also to deal personally with whatever business arose.

Though the tenor of our conversation was unhurried, he conveyed a great deal in a short time: that our thanks for this interview were unnecessary since, in his view, tourism could bring Morocco little good unless visitors could be encouraged to take a real interest in his country; that whenever we found ourselves in the province of Fez we were his guests, and must call upon him should any inconvenience arise; that he understood I was particularly interested in the position of women in the new Morocco, which happened to be of special concern to him also. Without ever touching ungracefully on the matter of time, he was somehow able to let us know that he was receiving the British ambassador in forty minutes. Even when interrupted by a phone call that proved to be a wrong number, he remained suave: *"Enfin, Monsieur,* it would appear that you have been connected by mistake with the governor's residence. . . . Not at all, Monsieur."

If he was surprised when I told him it was the work with illiterate women of his province that I most wanted to see, he remarked only that the *Centres Féminins* were of course most interesting, and picked up the phone again to make the necessary arrangements. Then he touched on what was clearly a favorite theme: the power of women in Muslim society. "You are surprised that I use such an expression? Let me assure you, then, that power is very great, perhaps the greater because men have for so long closed many doors to them. The more unsatisfied a woman, the more mean and wretched she can make life for her husband—out of spite, she ruins his hopes and his disposition. It is she who molds the children, she who lays the first plans for a betrothal. What scope she has there for advancing her own interests—alliance with a family that will support her desires, even at the cost of an embittered husband! As for the illiterate woman, until we give her something more respectable to do, she will continue to terrorize an uneducated husband with imbecile superstitions."

But the uneducated, he continued, must not be thought stupid. And here he made an interesting digression into his own background. His parents had been untutored people, his father a *moghasni* assigned to the Mechaouar of Rabat. (The moghasni were a picturesque body of mounted irregulars loosely attached to the royal army. Though not in this case, the attachment was often very loose indeed, and these irregulars lived by what amounted to little short of banditry.) So their son's ambition to study was encouraged. In time he earned a law degree in France, and later served as a judge in several provinces, until he accepted this administrative post. And so, he said, we saw in him the power of education to draw a man up from illiteracy.

"And a woman, too?" I asked.

"There is nothing more important than directing her power into the right channels. If I had, say, a thousand seats in a lycée to fill, I would enter there seven hundred girls, even if many boys had to be excluded. In the education of women, as in so many things, Fez has been the 'nursery garden' of our new Moroccan culture. You will allow me, I hope, to complete your picture of how Fez nurtures her women. A good friend of mine, a certain French lady, is the director of a fine lycée for girls."

And, without waiting for an answer, he picked up his phone again and was soon asking Mme. Martin if she could see us the next day. "Oh, my apologies —I had not realized it was Ascension Day. It will not be possible, then?" (He did not seem to marvel, as I did, that a Muslim government school should close for a French religious holiday.) "Well, if you can arrange it, very good. At nine o'clock tomorrow morning, then, and thank you."

With one eye on my watch, I calculated that there was still time to get an idea where the governor stood on the question of Arabization. "We have heard a great deal about the need to Arabize, both pro and con, Your Excellency—"

"Undoubtedly, you will have heard a great deal of exuberant talk about Arabizing overnight! But in my view, it will be fifty years before a modern technical curriculum can be transposed into Arabic. And we cannot wait that long; the need for young trained cadres is of the highest urgency, *now*."

"And if the higher training continues in French, you do not fear that this will undermine the effort to adapt Arabic and translate the required texts?"

"That effort must continue unabated. Our language—one of the most flexible and accurate in the world, which gave the West the medieval basis of all modern sciences—will one day give us a further opportunity to make our contribution. But in the meantime, we must use the one tool ready to our hands: *French*."

Was this wishful thinking, equivocation, or hard realism, I wondered, or a blend of all three? Then I heard the crunch of tires on gravel and rose quickly. The governor, still unhurried, moved with us out into the strong sunlight and the scent of Persian lilac, and walked toward his car that would take us back. Just as the Daimler, with small union jacks fluttering on its fenders, came to a stop, he halted at a diplomatic midpoint between the two cars and bade us good-by. Then, with a smile, he added, "You will, I am sure, observe a certain discretion with Mme. Martin on the subject of Arabization!"

Perhaps it was my preconceived picture of Mme. Martin—icy, correct, devout headmistress—that made me want to get my hair done before the next morning. After a reluctant hairdresser had agreed on the phone to reopen her shop a little early that afternoon to fit me in, I walked slowly down a wide avenue, keeping to the shade of plane trees.

So clearly is the *ville nouvelle* laid out to the French taste—dozens of *bureaux* housed in pseudo-Renaissance buildings, and the inevitable, portentous, ugly banks—that you half expect to find pert French nursemaids in the stilted little public garden, rather than veiled women pushing strollers fresh from French factories. The shoving and short tempers in the Monoprix, the women crowding before the *consigne* to turn in their empty bottles, the young men lining up to see a torrid film starring Jean-Paul Belmondo—all these could be France. But then down the middle of the avenue comes a thin horse drawing a sledge, an oil drum mounted on runners that scrape and hiss on the stones. While you stand waiting to cross, a woman whose fringed head shawl hangs down to her hips in back is trying to thumb a ride. A scooter stops; they haggle over her fare. Finally, she bestrides the pillion, clutching the unknown man about the waist. . . . So goes the contest in the *ville nouvelle,* between the old and new, the native and the foreign.

When I came just on time to the hairdresser's shop, the door was still locked. I stood half an hour before she arrived, with two little apprentices in tow. She could hardly have been twenty, handsome, heavily made up, and dressed in the latest *Paris-Match* style. With the curtest of nods to me while she fitted her key in the door, she went on chattering in Arabic to the younger girls. I could only suppose she had summoned them because it was her right to have them in attendance whenever the shop was open, for no other customer appeared. Half the time, she lapsed into French—for my benefit, perhaps—while she described a recent party, the dancing, the boys who were there, the shortness of the skirt she wore. The girls hung on every word. All the while my head was being doused, wrung, pummeled, and bounced against the edge of the basin. The toweling was turned over to one of the assistants, who handled me considerately and even ventured a little deprecatory smile at me in the mirror. Then the older girl returned and began to tear at me with a razor. Now I protested.

She dropped her hands and eyed me in the mirror. "More gently? You are troubled with a tender scalp perhaps? You would like me to stop—?"

"Yes—please let your assistant proceed with the cutting."

"It is only I who have the diploma. She is not yet permitted to cut, you understand?"

We looked at each other in the mirror. She knew she had me. One half my head was short and wet, the other half shaggy and wet. And the rest of the shops were closed. I had no idea whom I could threaten to report her to; and an empty threat might simply make her more brutal. Leaving me to think it over, she turned to the apprentices and went on with her anecdotes. Pretty soon, the comedy of my situation began to get the better of my anger. I called her back and asked her to finish, letting myself dwell wryly on some stirring words of the governor about "the benefit to society of drawing the proletariat up into the bourgeoisie and equipping lower-class girls for the modern world." This saucy little product of the Monoprix and the fashion magazines that littered the shop was bound for the bourgeoisie, all right. She managed to reproduce quite faithfully the insolent hauteur of the lacquered magazine mannequins, who in their turn felt they were reproducing the habitual expression of the *haut monde.*

MME. MARTIN

Mme. Martin was a handsome woman, and very erect behind her desk. We—who are seldom at our best at nine in the morning, and had been woefully lost en route and became more lost each time we got a new set of directions, so that we arrived out of breath and with scattered wits—we did not impress her favorably. (In general, I don't think the French look very kindly on *any* Americans in Morocco. Unless there is an unusual personal rapport, an unspoken question seems to hang in the air: "Just what is the nature of your concern with Morocco?" Or, in the case of an expert, "the nature of your competence?" Forty-four years have left their mark, and we are seen as johnny-come-latelys with dubious motives.) I got the impression that it was entirely her regard for Governor Benbouchta that tempered her crispness and led her to answer my questions with impeccable correctness. All I really wanted to discover was how different Fez, the "nursery garden," was from little, remote, provincial Taza. I didn't put it that way; I inquired about the aptitude of her pupils, and the difficulties she met. And then, "About how many of your girls sit for the Baccalauréat each year?"

"One in twenty, at best. You understand that the Bacc. is needed only by those girls seeking entry into the professional world—the world reserved by tradition for men. Only a few so far will make that venture—there is deep psychological reluctance to compete with men. Most girls prefer to stay safely within conventional limits—a few years as clerk or schoolteacher, at perhaps 40,000 francs a month; then marriage, while they are still of an acceptable age. Indeed, many of them would rather break off their schooling in midstream and marry at seventeen or eighteen."

Ah! I thought, with all their resentment at being excluded from the freedoms of men, when the way is opened to them, they still do not care to challenge convention. Not unlike many women elsewhere . . .

We must not forget, the *directrice* went on, how fast things had been changing. Twenty years ago, there were in all Morocco only twelve girls attending a lycée; today there were 2,500 in Fez alone. "And I see great changes ahead. In another twenty years, there will be many woman doctors, lawyers, pharmacists—the country's need is so great. It is this generation which suffers such conflicting pressures; they falter because they are deeply confused. If one of my girls today perseveres on a modern course, she will lose all touch with her parents' world—she will be lucky if there is an older brother sufficiently *évolué* to give her guidance and support." She rose, saying we must see for ourselves; some of the students were waiting for us.

The halls smelled faintly of wax, of starch and chalk . . . the odor of bourgeoisie. Cautiously, I asked Mme. Martin how far class distinctions were reflected in the girls who reached her school. But not at all! she replied. *Both* upper and middle classes were well represented, as I would see. It did not seem even to occur to her that there was a lower class. Today, she continued, we could meet only some of the boarders, country girls too far from home to return for the long weekend.

Chattering voices fell silent as Mme. Martin threw open a door. I lost all track of introductions. Someone was a caïd's daughter, someone else came from a *domaine*. . . . Six supporters of the Bled bourgeoisie stood ill at ease regarding us.

Chairs had been placed in a rigid circle. It was going to be heavy weather, I feared, for even after the *directrice* left and we sat down, the faces turned toward us were drained of expression, stiff and attentive, as if for a lecture. Bill settled back in his chair and busied himself with lighting a pipe, his face agreeable but remote, as if to say, "I'm not really here, so forget me and go right ahead." But they were observing him closely—sidelong but intent. Meanwhile, I couldn't get beyond small talk about the long weekend and how sad it was that they could not be at home with their families like the local girls. I'll never get at them, I thought, unless I can take them by surprise.

"Were any of you, by chance, among the basketball tour group we heard about in Taza?"

Glances flew between them. The question disorganized their prepared positions. "Yes," one said at length, "Hassiba and I were in that group. . . . Madame, did you hear something about us?"

"Oh, it can't surprise you to hear you were a sensation in Taza . . . and not only because you won so easily."

There was an unhappy pause. Then the same girl ventured that there might have been jealousy because, after all, a Taza lycée was not quite like theirs. . . . She glanced again at Hassiba, who flushed and decided to speak. "They meant to find us scandalous before they even saw us! When I was getting out of our bus, I heard a loud whisper—'They Frug with boys, you know.' Do you think that was a fair way to receive us, Madame?"

"I'm sure they were on the lookout for things to disapprove. . . . And you can't understand their uneasiness? Were there no shocks for you when you first came to Fez?"

They seemed to look inward, remembering. One smiled. "I still remember how I felt the first time I saw stretch pants!" The smile was erased. "But now the shocks are from the other direction. At home, I feel strange, very strange, in my old haïk." She looked at the others. Their eyes were fixed on her, and they were nodding unhappily.

Did they feel any great differences here at school, I asked, between themselves and the city girls? A girl they called Nadia answered. "Oh, there are some in Fez who speak of themselves as Arabs—so of course that leaves us no choice but to be proud that we are Berbers!"

But it was only older people, someone interrupted, who harped on this theme. I picked up the emphasis on the word *older*. And did they find their parents' generation out of sympathy with them in general? This was the real cleavage, they said, several speaking at once. Older people seemed to *want* to misunderstand them, like the gossips of Taza. "Is it fair to say that I am an atheist, just because I find what the Ulema say ridiculous?" "Last month they said miniskirts were immoral. You say, Madame, is a girl *loose* because she cuts off the hem of her skirt?"

"Or likes to Frug? It does not seem so to me."

"We have few enough dances—most of our mixing with boys is at cultural clubs, film clubs, meetings for book reviews."

"What kinds of films are shown at those clubs?"

"Oh, not James Bond films or anything like that . . . no *yé-yé*'s." A girl next to me opened her mouth, as if she meant to say, What is so wrong with films like that? and then decided not to. "We see the best new serious films—"

"Always French?"

"Naturally, Madame."

"And the books?"

"French also."

"Books about current affairs? Social change?"

"Oh, no, Madame! Only cultural subjects—art, history, the lives of great men." (If, in fact, they did discuss more urgent and personal matters, they were not going to tell me so.)

I turned to Hassiba. "If you could go abroad, where would you wish to go?"

"Oh, to France, Madame—anywhere else I should be at sea. I dream I shall someday visit Paris!" Oh, yes—the other girls sighed—yes . . . perhaps someday.

"And would you stay some time in France? Study perhaps for one of the professions?" I swept a glance all around. The faces had gone blank. Finally, someone answered, "I think I would be homesick; I don't think I could do that." Murmurs of assent and: "Of course study like that would be very admirable, but we . . . Moroccan women . . . it is not expected. . . ."

"Then perhaps, if you are to see Paris, you will have to persuade your husbands to take you?" From their faces I judged this was precisely the solution they meant to work for. Nadia said, "If my husband were to go to Paris without me—oh, *how* sorry I would make him!" Everyone laughed. "Yes, we would be resourceful on a matter of that importance!"

Now that they were talking about husbands, I asked what they thought was a good age for marriage (these girls, I knew, were all between sixteen and eighteen). No reply was forthcoming. I prodded a little. "You, Nadia, won't you tell me if it was a good idea to set the minimum legal age at sixteen?"

"Well, you see," she said, "it depends so much: a poor girl of the Bled loses nothing by marrying at sixteen—she simply works for her own household instead of her mother's. But as for us—*we* are in no great hurry! Only I think that by twenty we should be ready for our responsibilities. And it is risky to wait too long, you understand. Of course, it is the parents who will judge when their daughter is ready...."

"You will not be allowed to choose your husbands?" When there was no answer, I thought I had gone too far. They were exchanging looks and murmuring among themselves. But it turned out that they were only deciding who should answer the question. The girl they ended by designating spoke rather like a union organizer.

"We see three stages; we are now in the first stage—of *consent*. If a girl is married without having consented to the choice, she should at once aim for divorce, which will bring disgrace and worry on the parents, you see. My sister is divorced, at twenty. Now my parents wish they had listened to her."

"But I thought only a man had the right to divorce a woman, not the other way around—?"

"True. But there are always ways to make life so disagreeable that a man is driven to divorce to save his pride!"

"But doesn't the woman suffer? Is there no stigma?"

"Not amongst young women nowadays. My sister is admired—she has shown she is not the submissive type. My parents have learned that it pays to get *consent*. Next, they will learn to *consult*. Someday, they will listen to *choice*. We must all move carefully, since men, too, must be educated in what marriage means; they must do their part. But it will come."

The coolness of it was startling, and I doubt that she really spoke for them all. This group, as they talked, had shown ambivalence on all the big issues facing them: they wanted the best in education, but weren't interested in fitting themselves for a career; they wanted freedom, but feared to be called loose; they criticized the religious establishment, but shrank from being called atheistic; French culture was what they most admired, yet they would be homesick outside Morocco. Like cracks running across plaster, all the conflicts had shown up as they talked.

We were on our feet, about to leave. Bill asked: "All this time, my wife has asked the questions. You might like to ask one yourselves?"

Quick as a flash, there was one: "Yes, Monsieur, if you please. Which of the Beatles is the best singer?"

There are some things Bill just doesn't know *anything* about, and Beatle recordings are one of them. But professors learn to be resourceful. "Without going into invidious comparisons, I will say that Paul is very agreeable to talk with."

There were gasps of astonishment. "You *know* them, then?"

With becoming modesty, Bill replied, "Oh, I wouldn't say that. But we happened in one day at the Cultural Center just outside Tunis when Paul was having a late breakfast all alone. He was very pleasant...."

"Oh!" they breathed. "What did he say?"

"He said: 'Won't you have some orange juice? It's on the house.'"

"But wasn't he *wonderful*?"

Meknes Gateway

An old sycamore grows in a square in Fez medina

At right: Copper craftsman and apprentice

Community life goes forward outside the walls of Marrakesh

EUGENE GORDON

Medersa in Marrakesh

The tailor's braiding boys stand well out
in the lane

At right: Woman and child in a mosque

In Marrakesh medina

City and country women meet

At right: Market square in a country town

Tetouan's ring of mountains

A street in Chaouen

Marketwomen of Chaouen

Basket-weaver's hut

Melon vendor

Marabout's tomb

At right: Glaoui kasbah

Ram for sale

Countrywoman at her bread oven

At left: Kasbah on the Dades
WILLIAM WILLCOX

Buying grain in the South

Women shaking rugs
on a roof

Rest at noon in the Bled

Girl of the Bled

Child carrying baby to market

Gateway to Skoura

Bill considered. Paul McCartney had, in fact, been straightforward and full of questions. "Well, there was one wonderful moment. When he asked what I did for a living and heard I was a professor, his face made me laugh."

It was the right time to leave, while they looked with round eyes at the man who had laughed with a Beatle.

CENTRE FÉMININ

It was quite another Fez and quite different young women that we found at the *Centre Féminin,* hidden away in the heart of thirteenth-century "New Fez." A once splendid old house had been turned into a free clinic, where a long line waited for vaccinations and medicine. Another was a school where the children could not afford paper and so were using wooden slates and chalk.

"But they are the lucky ones!" our escort said. The governor's phone call had resulted in a young official's being assigned to take us to the *Centre.* "They are lucky because they *have* a school. For each one of them, there is another who will grow up illiterate."

In the next street, we came upon a tousled little girl with a baby strapped to her back and a big pail of water bending her over in an arc. Our guide's way with her was very brusque. He had told us earlier that there were three times as many women illiterates as men; and now before him stood one of the reasons: a wisp of a child looking up at him and repeating that she could not be in school . . . there was no one else home to mind the baby.

I knew the course she was on was irreversible: she was past seven, and therefore already out of phase. The schools are overcrowded enough without trying to fit in the children who failed to start on time. To be sure, the government tries to catch them later; but by then the problem has been compounded. I once heard a story about a grandfather who somehow had been dragooned into one of the *Centres* at the same time that his fifteen-year-old grandson was being dropped from school for failing more than one year. "*Me* they try to teach, now that it is too late in my life—" and he shrugged fatalistically—"and the boy they turn away for good." Truly, the ways of the Mahkzen were inscrutable.

Governor Benbouchta saw to it that Fez had a number of *Centres Féminins,* and saw to it also that they caught the women young. And somehow, after a few years, some of the groups were persuaded to run a *Centre* at their own expense, so that the meager state budget could be applied to the next influx from the Bled. The one that we were heading for was a cooperative; they managed even to pay their own rent, and their teachers were all former pupils. When I heard this, I commented to our escort that in the U.S. we were just now experimenting in rather the same way—recognizing in the poor themselves the most effective agents of rehabilitation.

For the first time since we had started out, the Moroccan stopped and looked at us attentively. He was a powerful, tall, very black man with Negroid features. The idea of escorting foreigners had not appealed to him, and he had been taciturn and stiff. I went on to say that our son had been working for several years now in a war on poverty similar in some ways to Morocco's. Then he looked really surprised—surprised to hear Americans mention poverty at home, surprised that people like us should speak proudly of a son doing the sort of work he was doing.

The scene we came upon in the *Centre* was unexpected. As the door of the old, down-at-heels house swung open, we heard rhythmic clapping and a voice that cried out snatches of song. We came in unnoticed and stayed back in the shadow of an archway. Young women stood shoulder to shoulder in a swaying semicircle, bare feet thudding on the tiled courtyard, heads thrown up so that their eyes stared straight ahead, unseeing. The clapping was in a most intricate rhythm, sharp, crisp, and highly syncopated. Then the singer's voice rose again in a short phrase, the words gasped more than sung. The dancers, tightly packed, their bodies undulating as one body, raised their clapping hands up before their eyes and cried out a line of song in reply.

It was the Berber Ahouache, a dance of the Chleuh people of the High Atlas. No wonder the young women danced with half-closed eyes; they were remembering the proper setting—nightfall, a great fire lit at the center of the semicircle, a canopy of cedars above them, and the men of the tribe seated in an opposing semicircle, beating out the rhythm on rawhide tambourines. Instead of their ragged cotton dresses, they should have been wrapped in sheer white homespun, with rows of chains and necklaces to the waist. Their hair should not have been hanging down their backs in braids, it should have been bound high on their heads, interwoven with coins and beads, amber and silver beads as big as walnuts. A *raïss,* or male drummer, who leads the dance, should have stood before them, raising his voice in the hoarse, almost strangled cry of the song, and quickening the rhythm toward its climax.

One of the girls caught sight of us. Her clapping lost the beat, the others woke to look at her, and saw her staring at us under the arch. They faltered and stopped, and began to giggle. The Moroccan beside us sprang forward, took up a tin plate lying on the floor, and went to face the dissolving semicircle. His fingers teased the plate, searching for the beat, the long, intricate rhythm. He said something to the women, and a few of them resumed the clapping for him. When he was sure he had it right, he called out to them again. But they didn't move, only stood and watched him in surprise. What could this big black man know of the Ahouache? He wore a sports shirt and city shoes—he was no raïss. But the rhythm he beat out sucked at them. Their feet stirred, their lips began to move. He shouted a phrase of song, a hoarse, angular phrase that broke off on a questioning note; the women slipped into their tight semicircle and began to sway together, their feet thudding. Each cry of the raïss they answered with their cry. He raised the tin plate above his head and began to accelerate the rhythm, and the women responded. No longer clapping now, but moving shoulder to shoulder in short quick steps almost in place, their bodies rippled as one body, like grass in a wind. The tempo became too fast to bear. At last, with a harsh cry, the raïss struck his plate against the wall, and the dance was ended.

The girls turned their backs on him and on us and bunched together in a far corner, wiping their sweating faces and arms and slowly coming back to reality. The black man called something to them, and one turned and flung a question at him. He answered, laughing, and came toward us. "I will take you upstairs now—they are embarrassed." He kept working his fingers together; they must have been numb from the plate. "They couldn't understand how I knew the Ahouache. I told them it was not for nothing I spent four years in the High Atlas villages!" He mopped his face and cap of kinky hair. "Four years I worked with those tribes, trying to get them to take their sick down to the clinic in the valley, trying to persuade them to trust the clinic midwife instead of the local hag with her magic and her bags of herbs and offal."

"And were you successful?"

He didn't reply. Instead, he bade us mind the loose stair boards. There were posters on all the stained plaster walls. "Public Enemy Number One," they said in French and Arabic, and showed menacing cartoons of the common house fly. In the kitchen, women were learning a little literacy and a little about foods at the same time. A swarthy girl who was their teacher held up flash cards in Arabic and then said a word or two. "She's telling them how to get clean milk from their goats and how to keep the cheese from spoiling."

"*Goats* in the medina—?"

"A goat in every courtyard," he answered succinctly, "and also flies, dysentery, and tuberculosis. . . ."

In the next room, rows of figures bent over treadle sewing machines, and other girls bent stiffly over embroidery frames. "Why should they learn to *embroider?*" I asked stupidly.

"Because the upper classes like embroidery!"

The upper classes seemed a great distance away. But, I told myself, they can be pretty sure of having their embroidery done for them in the predictable future, as long as the slums are full. As long as the proletariat is thoroughly Moroccan and, if literate at all, knows only Arabic, and as long as the upper classes continue to absorb the French language and French thinking, it looks as though there will be two Moroccos for some time to come.

When we passed the courtyard again on our way out, the recreation period was over. An instructor had been lecturing a group of women on infant care and was now showing them how to carry their babies in their arms or up against one shoulder instead of spraddle-legged across their backs. Our guide said, "She is telling them, 'Strap your bundles to your backs, if you will—a *bundle* has no head that lolls when it falls asleep, and no soft bones that long pressure can deform!'" We stood a moment before leaving, watching a demonstration. A pupil went out in front of the class, carrying a swaddled dummy. The stiff way she held it, her look of concentration, and her anxious glances at the instructor reminded me of a high-school girl rehearsing her scene in a Nativity play.

BARRACKS

In the early 1960s, our newspapers carried a frightful story of a large-scale scandal in Morocco. Some person or persons had adulterated a quantity of vegetable cooking oil with a liberal amount of machine oil—used oil at that, recovered from the drain sumps of filling stations. The results were tragic for all who bought and used it—death or almost complete paralysis. The last I saw in the papers was an announcement that a British surgical team was going out to see what could be done for the survivors. Now, years later, I heard of an American girl, a Peace Corps Volunteer, who was doing rehabilitation work with the victims somewhere in Fez. I reached her on the phone and found she would be glad to show us around. "But don't expect a hospital —it's a converted army barracks," she said.

And that was precisely what it looked like. The first person we met was a young English girl working for the Save the Children Federation, who asked if we were the people Jane was expecting. Walking with us toward a building some distance away, she told us she had been only three weeks in Morocco, couldn't understand either French or Arabic, and simply couldn't believe the inefficiency and disorganization of this place. . . . One thing she did know: you practically never saw a doctor around here. The Moroccan authorities gave her the impression of doing everything possible to frustrate the work. . . . I began to get the idea she was suffering from shock.

"But why are these patients all children? I thought whole families had been brought here, paralyzed by the machine oil—?" Then she told us the sequel to the tragedy: while delays in Britain caused the team of doctors to postpone their departure several times, a miracle occurred here in Fez. Six months after the poisoning, most of the survivors were back to normal, for no known medical reason.

"So now," she said, "what we have here instead are crippled children— tuberculosis of the bone, birth deformities, or—most of all—polio. Yes, polio! Brought by you Americans!" I thought I recognized the relish many Britishers feel as Americans inherit their old role—the unpopular, interfering, suspect foreign power.

Jane appeared, small and sturdy as a pony. As she passed each group of children clustered in their wheelchairs under the trees, she flung some remark at them that brought laughter. A small boy sprinted beside her on his crutches for a little while. I noticed she hardly slowed her pace, but looked down at him with approval. She came up with us. "Well, did you expect to find us quite so much like an army post?" She looked back at the uncompromising buildings, all that dispiriting buff of barracks the world over. "But our new school over there"—she nodded toward some blond young men working on a cement block structure under a clump of acacia trees—"is going to be more cheerful. Only progress is so slow! The volunteers come out for a short stint and have to go back almost as soon as they've learned what to do. Oh, we work against difficulties, all right, but we do manage to make the children self-reliant. Isn't that what rehabilitation means?"

"The English girl"—I looked around to make sure she had gone—"is upset about the inefficiency. And the lack of doctors. And the uncooperativeness of the authorities."

"Yes. We've all heard from her. Don't judge the SCF people by her; she's just arrived. Either she's going to pull out of it—people generally do after a few weeks—or she'll turn out to be a casualty, and have to go home. A developing country is no place for people who discourage easily—or set a lot of store by efficiency! It's true the Moroccan authorities aren't always very helpful, but I don't see a plot in it. And as for doctors being scarce, do you know how many orthopedic surgeons there are in Morocco? Two. And how many specialists who can make artificial limbs? Two. So you can see why there are some long waits. Do you see that little kid hopping around on his one leg, and practicing folding and unfolding his wheelchair? Our chairs are light and collapsible, so the children can handle them almost anywhere."

In a matter of seconds, a number of children had surrounded us. Somebody nudged Bill's camera with a crutch tip, and they all grinned and bunched themselves into a group. "You'll have made their day if you'll take their picture," Jane said. While Bill was focusing, the boys composed themselves— stumps or leg braces stuck conspicuously forward, or withered arms displayed to the best advantage. If they had nothing sensational to thrust before the camera, they looked cross-eyed or pulled dreadful faces. I said it seemed a bit macabre the way they featured their infirmities. Jane disagreed: "Learning to clown like this is their surest defense against shame. A kid who was sensitive about his stump would be terribly vulnerable once he left here—you know how street urchins like to make fun of a cripple."

Jane had to go up to one of her wards, and asked if we would go with her. Walking over to the barracks, we learned that she hadn't expected to work here—she'd come to Morocco to be a lab technician, and then found there were more technicians than labs. So, like many of the Peace Corps, she had found out where she could fit in and applied for reassignment. "Now I drive a jeep up to a douar in the Rif two days a week. What I do up there is listed as 'Home Management,' but actually, since their Arabic is even worse than mine—they're Berber-speaking—I'm trying to give them a smattering of literacy. I take up flash cards, and we talk about child care and getting more meat substitutes into their diet. Meat three or four times a year is about normal up there, and the rest is bread and barley stew."

I said from what I'd heard, her Arabic was quite extraordinary. How could she become so fluent in only two years? "I assure you, it's pure 'kitchen Arabic,' but after all, that's what I need. . . . I *love* my days in the Rif. Those women—you can't beat them for vitality. Lately, they've been teaching me their tribal dance. My God! I thought *I* had stamina! It's fantastic what dancing means to them. I've seen a woman fall on the ground, unconscious from exhaustion; and then two minutes later come wading back into the dance again. . . ."

We began to climb a bleak cement stairway, to the fourth-floor ward to see some bedridden older girls. "We call what I'm doing here occupational therapy, but since no materials or instructions are provided, I have to go on horse sense and improvise. Like these crayons and coloring books." She tapped the parcel under her arm. "It doesn't matter that they are for kindergarten— my girls had never seen any. Coloring makes them use their fingers with control; and they have to sit up in bed to do it, instead of lying on their backs. That's the way I have to operate: watch what each girl *can* do, and then wheedle her into doing it oftener, and a little better . . . and give her a lot of praise. Is that what you'd call occupational therapy? I hope so."

There was one touch of color on the dismal stairway—a brilliant poster of children running, skipping, jumping. I saw it and winced. "Oh, no—don't feel that way. I put that poster up myself. It's important for these kids to remember what normal children are like, or the shock when they get home will be too much for them. The one thing we've got to do for them here is make them accept the way they are, without any self-pity. Because when they leave, the going is sure to be a lot rougher. No one is going to treat them as special; very likely their families would resent them if they came home dependent. So while they're here, they'd better learn self-reliance and all the skills we can possibly give them."

We came out at the top of the building onto a long gallery. Some lunch trays had been set down on the floor, and the food was already congealing into grease. "I wonder how those orderlies think my girls are going to get up and serve themselves," Jane said. "They must have dashed up on the roof to catch a smoke." At the door to her ward an appalling smell met us. "Yes, it's pretty bad isn't it? Nobody has much time to bring bedpans or change sheets. You stay out here on the gallery while I give them these things and make them sit up for lunch."

She moved among the beds, chattering, joking, making the girls come to life for her. Jane and I carried the trays in. Each time we came back for more, a clattering in the stair well was louder and closer. "It sounds as if the boys aren't waiting for the orderlies and are coming up by themselves," she said.

I looked at her, horrified. Crippled children crawling up three flights of stairs? "Oh, don't worry, they won't hurt themselves. It's not the first time . . . and they're incredibly agile. I get mad at the orderlies but—"

She broke off as the first child came in sight, easing himself up over the stair on his stomach. His T-shirt and his khaki shorts were dusty, but his teeth gleamed in his shaven bullet-head, and he looked triumphant. Then I saw the source of the clatter: he was dragging his aluminum wheelchair behind him. He emerged on the gallery and briskly opened up the frame and slid up into it; then he stretched out his arms with a grin, and Jane handed him his tray.

One after another, the boys arrived at the top of the stairs. Not all were grinning—some looked exhausted. "Jane—how often—?"

"Not very. I'll report the orderlies, and it won't happen again for a while."

"And if you hadn't been here to hand these boys their trays?"

"They'd have yelled like banshees until the orderlies came down from the roof!"

EVENING

In a villa set among the hillside orchards above Old Fez, I stood by a window watching dusk fall in the garden. Here, outside the Gate of Peaches, the air is always fresh. This evening, the scent of jasmine filled the room where we were gathered before dinner. Standing with me was the young American wife of our host. Ahmet Benaboud had only lately returned to his country with an American degree in sociology and this gentle, fresh-faced girl from Iowa. Ahmet had done his work with an old friend of Bill's, and this had led to our meeting.

"I am trying to recapture a phrase of Colette's," I said to Lynn beside me, "something about 'the base trickery practiced by the evening scents of a garden in Fez.'"

"Ah, Colette!" said a voice behind us. "I believe she was very much in love when she visited Fez! Oh, yes—it is clear from all those nightingales she heard. . . ." The woman who spoke was so opulent in her beauty, I said to myself: she can never have been a child—she must have been born a woman. She stood there smiling, in a Nile-green kaftan, her burnished hair piled high above the old-ivory pallor of her face.

"This is Chedlya," said Lynn, "my sister-in-law, who lives with us—"

"—the burdensome sister-in-law who imposes herself for a few weeks, while the divorce arrangements are completed!" Chedlya added. I thought I understood then why Lynn did not seem quite the mistress of her house. Chedlya was not born with a second fiddle.

We were all speaking English, for the other pair of guests had spent several years in the U.S. Professor Hadidi was as tall and gray and stooped as a philosopher is supposed to be. I couldn't be sure if he was really nearsighted—his wife, a tiny Frenchwoman, made a point of shepherding him around protruding furniture—or if it was merely a marital convention between them that she, so small, should play the protectress. Before they arrived, Ahmet had told us, "She is not nearly so bird-like as she appears. She has, for example, just learned to drive a car. If you have been driving in Fez, you will appreciate she is not without courage."

The professor was explaining to Bill why he was here, instead of at his post at Mohammed V University in Rabat. Students there, we heard, were on strike. (In 1966, this seemed quite extraordinary to us. It must be some Moroccan vagary, we thought, that led students to boycott classes.) "So, as a result, you see me here, enjoying my unexpected leisure. No lectures? *Tant pis!* Then I get on with my book on Plotinus!"

At the dinner table, I asked him if it felt strange to work, in the very shadow of the Qarawiyin, on the life of a pagan and a mystic—shouldn't he be under anathema? In spite of his smile, a certain grimness was in his voice as he spoke of the intellectual bankruptcy of the Mother of Universities. "That citadel of reactionaries," he called it, "where all that is secular is called *profane*. The Ulema would put us all in an Islamic strait jacket—"

"But strait jackets come in all sizes and shapes these days!" Ahmet broke in. "In Rabat, too, the truth can be called profane. I have, as you see, been relieved of my teaching at Mohammed V and reassigned to its new annex in Fez."[4] Whenever his expression darkened, he had a rather simian look, perhaps because his hair grew low on his forehead and his eyes were very deep-set. "And why have I been disciplined? Because a sociologist cannot lecture in a vacuum. If he sees his country on a dangerous course, he must speak the truth! Last winter, they came to tell me that my 'services were needed at the annex'—in this shadowy place, they felt sure I would come to my senses. . . ."

Chedlya had had enough. "What nonsense you talk! It takes our attention from the *bastilla* our little Lynn has provided for us." She turned to Bill and resolutely took over the conversation, listing for him all that went into the great cartwheel pie that was being presented to us: pigeon flesh, eggs, ginger, almonds, a score of subtle herbs, all covered with a crust of cinnamon and sugar.

But Ahmet was not so easily deflected. He cut her off. "It is not that I fear prison—I am too conspicuous for that. Or too highly connected, if you prefer. The Benabouds are still in every phase of government and professional life, as they have been for ten generations. . . . But there are subtler kinds of imprisonment: pressures, 'discipline'—many ways to bend a man. I have wondered if I should not have left the country instead."

4. To ease the overcrowding at Mohammed V, the Ministry of Education was trying to launch two annexes. The other, which existed only on paper, was to be in Casa.

Lynn stirred in her chair; he glanced at her and then away. Professor Hadidi looked deeply shocked, and his wife, who evidently knew Chedlya well, attempted to distract her to the subject of her divorce. But Chedlya glowered down the table at her brother.

"If our father were to have heard a Benaboud speak of deserting Morocco! Was it, then, only a passing whim that you, only a youth at the time, risked your life daily in the nationalist cause? That you organized secret cells of the Istiqlal and called out a thousand students to demonstrate before the guns of the French?" There was silence around the table. Chedlya's heavy rings glinted as she twisted the stem of her wineglass.

Then she spoke again. "There was work for us young women, too. We, who had been so empty-headed, grew up overnight. We always looked so *bien élevées,* the police never noticed us as we relayed messages from cell to cell. It was we who brought food and orders to the men who were being closely watched. If French soldiers stopped us, we would scream we were being assaulted, until an officer arrived. . . . Oh, the young *poilus* learned to leave us strictly alone, though they hated us venomously." She smiled around at the eyes all fixed on her, and did not see that she set her wineglass down at the very edge of the table.

"We became bolder, and often carried weapons and explosives strapped to our bodies in the outline of a pregnant belly. This actually protected us, you understand? If a French policeman so much as looked at a pregnant Muslim, the crowd could be at his throat the next moment. . . . Many a time, I taught men how to wire fuses. When necessary, I carried a pistol in my hand, but under my djellaba, so—" She slipped her arm inside the wide kaftan sleeve, and her bunched fist pushed out the garment at her waist.

"Only once did I have to turn my gun against someone of my own race. I came to the doorway of a lad of fifteen who was to wire a quay in Casa port that night—a terribly exposed job—and I feared the boy might falter at the last minute. His father had been killed only a week before. Just as I turned in the dark doorway, the boy came tumbling down the stairs. He was in a panic and meant to run away from the job. Instead, he ran into me. . . ." She pressed herself closer to the table. "I hemmed him in and nudged him hard with my gun." Illustrating with a gesture of the concealed hand, she struck the wineglass on the table edge. Crimson spurted all over her gown.

It was fortunate that we all managed to suppress the instinctive reaction to the accident—laughter, which would have relieved the tension. For I really believe that Chedlya might have flown at anyone who laughed. She was furious to be robbed of her climax; but she was even more concerned with the spreading wine stain. She fled the room. Little Mme. Hadidi sprang up to follow. In a moment her voice could be heard offering comfort in the next room.

The professor said, "And after a story of such hatred, is it not interesting how it turns out to be a Frenchwoman who now performs for her the office of a friend?"

When we were all once more in the room overlooking the garden, moonlight swam on the reflecting pools, and a glittering thread of water spilled from the lip of one pool into the next. Now that night had fallen, datura blossoms were pouring out their heavy perfume, and crickets were sawing noisily under the windows. My hope of giving in to pleasant languor for the rest of our last evening in Fez was dashed when Bill turned to Ahmet, asking what he meant by "the dangerous course" he saw the country taking. The young man sat forward immediately and began to talk of the changes that had become apparent in the six years he had been away. The danger, he said, was of polarization: the great underclass was drawing to the Left; in reaction, the rest of society might be swept to the Right—into the arms of the Istiqlal, which now, he admitted sadly, had become the party of privilege. All the political parties had forsaken the principles they were supposed to represent. Infected with the virus of power, the politicians would rather let the King manipulate them than lose their posts. He could not see a single man in politics today of the stature of Ben Barka.

Chedlya appeared then in the lighted doorway, lovely as a Muse by Pollaiuolo, in bronze velvet to her toes. "Ben Barka—that absurd Marxist! And he would have liked to have been an assassin to boot!" Her brother contradicted her—the evidence linking him to a plot on Hassan's life had been trumped up, he was certain.

Chedlya cut him off. "Anyone who makes the King responsible for the poor caliber of his politicians does not know him as I do. I have known him since our childhood. While my husband was in his Cabinet, I often frequented the palace. I will tell you what the *real* trouble with this country is: it is the pettiness of the men who serve the King. He picks up the blame for abuses that never come to his ears, for stupid, corrupt officials—"

"—with whom he makes a point of surrounding himself! Yes men, every one of them!" Ahmet managed to interpolate.

She swept on, shaking her head at him. "You shall not interrupt me—I know what I am talking about! All of you know of the commission to draw up a plan for the reintegration of Tangier, appointed in 1956, when the city first came back to us? *Three years later,* they still had not brought in a sensible plan! By chance, I was at the palace just after the commissioners had left. Seeing the King alone, I came unannounced into the room where he sat. He had thrown his head down on his arms, which lay spread out across the sheets of charts and figures, and he was muttering over and over, '*Imbéciles!* . . . *Crétins!*' He saw me, and pushed some papers at me. 'Look—they have labored, and brought forth this MOUSE!' "

I didn't want to hear any more, I wanted to be waylaid by the soft seduction of the night outside. A light breeze had sprung up and flowers tapped against the window, soliciting me. . . . Who could possibly know the whole truth, anyway? It lay buried somewhere, under all this controversy. . . . I looked up into the dark cypresses by the window and saw bright heads of geraniums growing, vinelike, high up in the black trees. But pictures kept passing between them and my eyes—of women bent over embroidery frames, and girls dancing the Ahouache with closed eyes . . . of Mme. Martin's bright little *bourgeoises* being nurtured on French "culture clubs" and "the lives of great men" . . . of Ben Barka murdered . . . of politicians cleverly played off against each other . . . and of the King, distrustful of power in any hands but his alone.

I shook myself. These were not the pictures I intended to see tonight. I would concentrate on the crickets' drowsy song until other images came. And they did come: faces shining in the lamplight, listening to the storyteller . . . the worn, patient, stubborn faces of the Bled . . . the men of the streets, with their gift for laughter. No one knew better than these how to pluck the instant, revive their hearts in small delights—a brawl to watch, a warm spot of sunshine, and a nap. Cool water on the head and a cool breeze on the skin. Sticky sweet tea to drink, an overheard joke, an emotional meeting with a friend. . . . But when a purpose moved them, they could be serious enough— after all, the French had been no match for them. No, surely, Ahmet would not leave Morocco. The returns were not all in yet.

CHAPTER SIX

ATLAS AND OASIS

Azrou

Only a little south of Fez, one is already on the knees of the Middle Atlas. Magnificent forest clothes the hills; snow lingers on the peaks until June, mirrored in dozens of little lakes—one pair called Islit and Tislit: fiancé and fiancée. The steep-roofed chalets and hillside farms would be at home in the Vosges or the Haute-Savoie; the town of Azrou in particular has the air of *un petit coin de France,* with its chestnut trees, its red roof tiles, and its neat middle-class inn, where dinner is served family-style and habitués sit nightly to the right and left of the *patron,* while his wife ladles out the soup. The food and wine are good, the talk local and witty. Skiers or vacation fishermen may join them for a few days, but for the most part the clientele is stable, and French.

But a few miles out of Azrou, mountain trails come down to cross the good macadam road and disappear into the forest on the other side. In spring and fall, Berber tribes cross here, driving their flocks before them on their long seasonal migration. As the snow melts and the skiers leave, this new population moves in; their goathair tents spring up beside the ski tows, and their herds fan out through the lush alpine pastures. So Azrou is much more than *un petit coin de France.* It has always been a marketplace for these tribes, a chance to exchange their hides and wool and surplus animals for city goods. Right in the center of town stands a large school; and a story attaches to it that is closely interwoven with the Protectorate.

The first *résident général* was the great Marshal Lyautey, a brilliantly capable man who combined paternalism, a strict conscience, and a very practical realism. He saw the Protectorate as precisely what the word implies— a temporary responsibility undertaken to "preserve lives and restore order" in a country on the brink of chaos. He had served in Algeria, and hoped to expiate in Morocco the sins of exploitation he had seen there. It was the duty of the *résident,* he felt, to strengthen the Mahkzen and sustain and encourage native culture, while he installed an effective modern administration. The European community should remain apart, in the *villes nouvelles,* in order not to infect native life. This was his romantic idealism. Hand in hand with it went the qualities of a gifted soldier. The tribes must be pacified. Seeing himself as a *grand seigneur,* he dealt with the caïds as a feudal overlord should—with a nice balance of force and respect. The Berbers he romanticized as Noble Savages; by winning their fealty he could impose order in the Bled and simultaneously offset the power of the urban Arabs. He was remarkably successful.

Two things, however, worked against him and were, in the end, his undoing. The first was the rapidly growing power of business interests and the colons. French banks, interlocking commercial directorates, France's need for an overseas market in the years after World War I—all these things came together with the determination of the colons to expand their interests. It was the home government that had encouraged them to settle here; the motherland offered no such opportunities as were to be found in the Maghreb. The Protectorate was on the way to becoming a colony. Lyautey fought this trend and warned against it. In a 1920 memorandum, he argued prophetically that European ideas of self-determination were taking root overseas; that the spirit and rationale of the Protectorate were being subverted, and would soon come into direct conflict with an intelligent people's desire to direct their own destiny: "More and more they will realize their own strength and worth. They are neither barbarians nor apathetic. . . . They are eager for education and very adaptable. . . . Lacking the outlets which our administration provides in such small measure and under such inferior conditions, [their determination] will seek its road elsewhere."[1] He concludes by urging an immediate end to assimilationist tendencies and a program of training for independence. His was a far-seeing mind. But his vision ran counter to strong forces.

The second thing that brought him down was the Rif revolt. By 1924, when the French and their inept Spanish allies were in very serious trouble, Lyautey was cautious, trying to prevent a tribal uprising from becoming a war against the foreign presence—a jihad. But there was clamor in Paris to win the war without compromise. An icy Marshal Pétain was sent to take over the high command; thus publicly humiliated, Lyautey soon resigned as *résident.* He asked that when he died, his body be returned for burial to Morocco. It is an Islamic grave, white stucco with a green-tiled roof, which crowns a little hill behind the royal palace in Rabat. The inscription reads:

1. Quoted by Edmund Stevens, *North African Powder Keg* (New York: Coward-McCann, 1955), p. 46.

> Here lies Louis-Hubert-Gonzalve Lyautey,
> Born a Christian, died a Christian,
> Who wished to rest in this Moroccan earth
> Amongst his Muslim brothers
> That he so loved.

There must have been some who recognized in his 1920 report the soundness of its argument, and probably many Frenchmen who pondered uneasily what fruit the colonial policy in the Maghreb would ultimately bear. But then, as now, foresight was not enough to change policy—especially when it meant forswearing short-term gains. The Protectorate evolved along a now familiar pattern, dictated by powerful private interests—the great shipping companies of Casa, the mining enterprises, the banks and the holding companies that financed them, and the ever more entrenched colons. Charles Gallagher writes: "Morocco was conceived of as an enterprise installed by and for the profit of the European minority, and what was unnecessary to this end could be kept and retouched as a colorful museum."[2]

It took far more time and effort than anyone had expected to "pacify" the tribes—more than twenty years, in fact, or half the duration of the Protectorate. To make the job easier, a *politique berbère* was devised—deformed child of Lyautey's romantic affinity for the colorful tribesmen. The principle was the old one of divide and rule. It was not at all concerned with ethnicity; it was purely a tactic to pit the rural half of the population against the cities, playing upon the separatist tendencies of the tribes in the name of "protecting them from the virus of Arabism"—that is, from the fast-growing nationalism of the cities. To this end, the French opened a College for the Sons of Berber Notables in Azrou. It proved a successful way of creating a Berber elite, which, needless to say, drew on those chieftains who were quickest to learn the value of collaboration. By further manipulation of tribal affairs, the French subverted the traditionally loose tribal structures and promoted the power of a small group of "Great Caïds," who rose to feudal dominion over thousands of lives. Like many another risky game, the *politique berbère* was to end in backlash.

Meanwhile, the French devoted themselves to building and exploiting *Maroc Utile* to the west—the productive farms in the plains, the growing cities, and a small commercial empire built on cheap Moroccan labor. They were not, however, allowed to go at it unmolested. The Istiqlal published its manifesto in 1944, demanding freedom. The Sultan Mohammed was proving quite other than the pliable puppet they had anticipated when they put him on the throne as a boy of seventeen. Though he restrained the independence movement while France was engaged in World War II, and loyally supported the Free French with troops, he let the Istiqlal know of his sympathy.

2. Charles Gallagher, *The United States and North Africa* (Cambridge: Harvard University Press, 1963), p. 82.

When Franklin Roosevelt was in Casablanca for the Conference of 1943, a secret meeting with the Sultan was arranged. If Elliott Roosevelt's account of the conversation is substantially correct,[3] Mohammed had good reason to believe that the United States would back Moroccan independence as soon as the war was over. But, when that time came, neither America nor the Free French nor the United Nations listened to the cry for freedom.

In his Tangier speech of 1947, Mohammed V openly endorsed the Istiqlal, and in the early 1950s the period of terror and counterterror began. It was only slightly less bloody than Tunisia's struggle at the same time, but shorter and less tragic than Algeria's long agony. Paris was losing control of policies in Rabat. Mauriac and Schuman in vain protested the brutal counterterror measures, but a riot in Casablanca in 1952 provoked vicious reprisals and tricks worthy of a nineteenth-century vizier. One of these was "Operation Mousetrap": after giving nationalist and labor leaders permission for a large meeting, the police cordoned off the area and sprang the trap with machine-gun fire. Decapitation of the Istiqlal followed. Across the country, every leader who didn't escape into exile was thrown into a concentration camp. The French newspapers used scare headlines about rape and murder by the natives to panic the French community and drive them to the most savage repressions.

A grim story and, seen through the eyes of a later era, both shameful and stupid. All the western powers have written similar chapters into their history, and almost all today feel that the verdict of history has been returned against them. This is the era of condemnation of the viciousness of colonialism. Without denying these evils, I want also to recall the credit side of the ledger. France entered a Morocco in ruinous condition from every point of view, and left behind her the basis of today's physical unity—a modern infrastructure. The French built the only safe, all-weather port, Casablanca; they improved public health to such a degree that the population trebled in their time—a dangerous gift! They built schools, hospitals and clinics, and technical-training institutes—tragically few, but enough to serve as models. Above all, and quite in spite of themselves, they brought Morocco into contact with modern ideas and goals. For better and for worse, they wrenched the country out of a protracted feudalism and into the twentieth century.

I believe the recognition that their major failure lay in doing nothing to train Moroccans for independence accounts for a considerable part of the French presence today. It seemed to me that many Frenchmen now serving in Morocco were less impelled by what they could get out of it (or, in the case of the *militaires,* what they could get out of) than by a sense of moral responsibility. In addition, I felt something else, especially among the higher echelons of advisers: a kind of mystique about the whole Maghreb. France's dominion there was a measure of her greatness for more than a century and a half (the duration of her power in Algeria). The need to prove she is still a

3. Elliott Roosevelt, *As He Saw It* (New York: Duell, Sloan and Pearce, 1946), p. 109.

first-rate power surely has much to do with her current activity there. The trouble is that that activity sustains the dualism in Moroccan life today. France is the model for the modern sector of society and of the economy; but that sector *parallels* the traditional sector, without penetrating or revitalizing it. The two modes of behaving and earning a living exist side by side in *Maroc Utile* and create a distressing disparity; but at the line of the Atlas the modern sector stops altogether.

Atlas

Southward from Azrou, the road across the Middle Atlas begins to climb in earnest. On either side is more of that original forest—Atlas cedars, regal pines, and cedars of Lebanon, whose lowest branches make a roof fifteen or twenty feet above the ground and plunge the understory into mossy shadow. When you think of all the palaces and all the mosques, the carved cedar screens and porticoes and wall paneling and enormous doors, you marvel that any of the cedars are still standing. Then your nose picks up an unmistakable fragrance, and you come with a sinking heart upon a lumber mill, and trunks six and eight feet in diameter going under the saw. The air is saturated with their scent—a funerary incense.

Up another notch of mountainside, and lush plateaus begin to alternate with forest. When the snows start to melt, these upland meadows are almost drowned in water. In early summer the tribes begin to arrive and peg out their tents, long and low and black against the prevailing green. Within a month of such pasturage, the horses' coats are sleek as silk. Nowhere else in Morocco have I seen cattle standing knee-high in grass. When we passed here once in June, they raised their dripping muzzles at the sound of the car, and looked about for their young. Poppies blazed in the grass. Here and there among the tents were some stone huts, and around the edges of the pasture-land, pens and byres rudely built in the same black stone.

We drove carefully, for young animals often straggled in the road. Once we surprised a small burro with the black ears and shaggy coat of his first year. Without the wit to jump into the fields, he sprang, stiff-legged as a jumping jack, back and forth across the road ahead of us. We drew under a tree and stopped to wait for him to make up his mind.

Just then we heard voices and trampling in the forest bordering the road. Down the cathedral aisle between the vast tree trunks, a horse and rider were approaching us, unseeing. Behind them walked several women in bright skirts and kerchiefs, who shouted now and then to the laden beasts they prodded. A folded tent was strapped on one mule, and on another the stakes, ropes, and long ridgepoles. In the rear came the flocks, with children darting after stragglers, and more animals laden with blankets, cook pots, basins, hampers, and hempen sacks.

The lead horse was black, and decked with red braid and tassels and a brilliant saddle blanket; his ears came forward when he saw the car, and the rider noticed us. But it was too late then to change course. The sheik sat even more erect, and his deep eyes raked our faces. In his arms he cradled a small son, a child of striking beauty even among Moroccan children, who smiled and wriggled in an effort to touch the shiny car. I leaned out a little, and the horse side-stepped briskly at a touch on the rein. The sheik had stiffened, but even he was not proof against the admiration in my face. Though he turned his turbaned head away, at the same time he held out toward us the laughing, kicking, wondrous pride of his life. The women did not veer away, as Arab women probably would have done; on the contrary, they surged around us, fingering, chattering, staring at point-blank range into our faces. The sheik never turned back. Soon the press of animals debouching into the road drove the women forward on their way.

Transhumants, the French call tribes like this—seasonal migrants between lowland winter villages and upland summer pasturages. They are part cultivators and part pastoralists: they grow a few crops in the low country; and in the spring, leaving some of their number to see to the harvest and guard the stored grain, they climb with the herds, advancing ever higher as the snowline recedes. They follow the same route each year, for transit rights through other tribes' territory involves close bargaining, then great care in keeping the migrating herds and flocks together. The uphill trek is tense and exhausting. Many of the animals are with young; melting snow above means roaring oueds across the trail. Only the prospect of those June pastures ahead sustains the migrants.

One of the Middle Atlas passes is over the Col du Zad. Any Atlas pass is an exciting experience, for, quite apart from the dramatic heights and sweep of view, it means the divide between *Maroc Utile* and the trans-Atlean world. There are no cities behind the Atlas, but only villages nailed onto canyon walls, and towns where some gorge opens onto a sheltered valley. There is little or no rain. Men live by their flocks and by irrigation farming, with the Atlas their only reservoir. Except where there is underground water, life depends on melting snows running off the mountains, pouring through the vertiginous gorges, and coming at last, more tamely now, to flow between checkerboard terraces. Sometimes a stream goes underground for miles before it peters out; then you can trace its course by the green zone projecting like a finger into the sandy waste. In this dry, glittering land behind the rain, the line is sharply clear between the Desert and the Sown.

The snow that blankets the Atlas can spell either life or death to the farmers and herdsmen below—life when the water is released slowly, to follow its prescribed path; death when it is released in floods. Then the torrents erase roads and wrench out concrete bridges, leaving only twisted stalks hanging from the pylons. The water tears through cropland and lays the seeds bare to the pitiless sun. But as little as a week later, such power seems unimaginable. By then all that remains of the stream is glittering pools between the boulders—and drought will grip the land that summer.

The mountains and the world behind them have long been refuge areas for tribes seeking to escape the Mahkzen. Better, they felt, to endure the rigors of mountain territory, to suffer the caprice of drought and flood behind the mountains, than to suffer the extortions of the Mahkzen.

Later, the French "pacification" did nothing to increase their affection for Rabat. Like the Riffians (the Rif being another refuge area), the people of the Atlas and trans-Atlas are largely Berber and still loosely tribalized. Even while they profess deep loyalty to the throne, the workings of a central government are alien to them, since any totality larger than the tribe and its region has little meaning for them. Even the Istiqlal had trouble in breaking down the localism of their outlook sufficiently to involve them in the nationalist struggle.

One of the first things Mohammed V did after Independence was to convoke all the tribes and try to explain to them why they should now trust their Mahkzen. They responded at first with enthusiasm, in a surge of loyalty to the person of the King. But, as the promised changes in their lot proved slow in coming, they began to think the King was listening only to the Istiqlal, which had always been the voice of the cities. Tribal revolts broke out—four in the five remaining years of Mohammed's reign. Each time, the prince, Moulay Hassan, was sent at the head of an army. It was not the most encouraging introduction to the heir to the throne.

The first revolt, in the Rif, was very serious, and was put down with efficient ruthlessness and considerable loss of life. Next, it was in the South that rebellion flared, headed by the governor of a large province behind the Middle Atlas. Shouting denunciations of "the cursed Istiqlal" and ignoring all orders from Rabat, the governor insisted that he owed allegiance to no one but *the King in person.* Mohammed sent word that he had invested his son with his own personal authority, and was sending him in his place. While the royal army closed in on the rebel capital, Ksar es Souk, the prince and the governor came face to face. The rebel tendered his honorable submission to *the King,* and the revolt was done.

Below Ksar es Souk lies a twenty-mile string of oases called the Tafilelt. It was here that the present dynasty, the Alaouite, originated in the seventeenth century. Very soon after the revolt, Mohammed himself came to the Tafilelt. He was the first sovereign to make a royal progress through the South in sixty years. Standing in the back of a Jeep, he was driven day after day through crowds hysterical with joy and shouting *"Yahia el Malik!"* ("Homage to the Lord!") The people prostrated themselves, then leaped up to follow, singing and chanting behind the white-robed figure who spread his arms wide above them. He stopped often to address them. Warning that he would require obedience, he promised them a better life and pledged himself to send them good caïds to govern, men who would understand their usages. But there must be no more dissidence. Loyalty to his person meant obeying the state's agents. . . . Perhaps he convinced them; up to the present there has been no more open insurgency.

It was winter the first time we came to the South. We were then very new to Morocco and crossed the Col du Zad with wonder and some anxiety. When we looked due east, we saw an endless steppe, and a few austere sandstone buttes rising out of the emptiness. As the road veered southward and we began to descend, the mountains became a succession of tipped and crumpled walls closing in on us. Then one more saddle of the pass, and the road drove straight downward into a rocky defile. Even in a land of awesome gorges, whose zigzag walls support the sky, the Gorge du Ziz is breathtaking. You come upon it suddenly, emerging from a tunnel blasted through bedrock by the French Foreign Legion. On either side, the stark seamed escarpments contain much amethyst, which lends a glow to the rock walls. Hundreds of feet below, the water rushes whitely over shallows or lingers in amethyst-tinted pools. The Ziz can be a raging river or, after a hundred seasonal oueds have ceased to empty into it, no more than a silver thread that nourishes the oases strung like beads along its bed—the Tafilelt.

As I stood beside the road looking down into the canyon, it seemed impossible that we had waited only a few hours earlier for the snowplow from Azrou to clear the path ahead of us. Here, the sun presided over a glittering dryness. A shadow slid across the rock where I stood, and then was gone. Only a lizard or a snake could move that fast, but there was absolutely no crevice for it to vanish into. Another shadow slipped across my feet. I looked up and saw the bird circling overhead—a kite, hunting low. God love the cony or lizard whose habitat this is, I thought. Then, all at once, I realized what had been growing on me for the past few minutes: I was afraid of the South. Afraid of this searing light—afraid I might dry out—in fact, afraid of the desert.

Oasis

When we drove into Ksar es Souk, the sun was sinking fast, and we knew we must not try to push any farther that day. We had been aiming for Erfoud in the Tafilelt because there was a state hotel there. But it was another fifty miles, and we had little idea what might lie in between. With dismay we learned that the Ksar es Souk hotel was full, but we were directed to a modest little inn whose main door opened onto a room serving as restaurant, tea house, radio lounge, and local gathering place. There were clusters of tables covered in bilious oilcloth, and on the end wall hung the usual benign photograph of Mohammed V, framed in a sort of elaborate lace doily. Everyone stopped talking as we entered, but fortunately the radio blared on. The proprietor led us across the courtyard, where mint grew in little beds between the pebbled walks, gestured toward two doors at the far end labeled "*Hommes*" and "*Dames*," and explained that the evening meal would be served at 8:00 P.M. and the electricity would go off at 10:30 P.M.

If he was surprised to have two westerners drop suddenly into his lap, he covered it with a grave courtesy and pointed to the candle end stuck in a mineral-water bottle and the small basin under a naked light bulb. There were two faucets, but—he begged our pardon—hot water was available only for an hour or two in the morning. Did we wish him to bring a kettle from the stove? We thanked him but declined, for the lounge was full of people, and there seemed to be no one helping him. When he had gone, I lowered myself onto the bed, which sloped ominously toward the center. Whatever was in the mattress gave not at all.

We looked at each other. Our first night in the South was evidently going to teach us to "hang loose." If we could not adapt to what came, we would have to give up the idea of a loose schedule. We went to the car to get a minimum of overnight things, and as I rummaged, my hand slid thoughtfully over a case in which I carried a few drugs we had never had to use and some sleeping pills. Nonsense, I told myself, and went on rummaging until I found what I wanted: one of those inflatable plastic coat hangers for drip-drying one's clothing. Bill looked askance. "Surely you aren't thinking of doing any laundering *tonight*?"

I removed the metal hook and dropped it back into the suitcase.

"Hardly. But have you had a look at that bolster on the bed?" I had, and was sure it was stuffed with cane shucks.

Whatever the limitations of native village cookery, one thing is uniformly good: the *harira*, a heavy broth of vegetables, dried beans, and any meat that might be available. Like the French *marmite*, it sits at the back of the stove, is replenished day by day with whatever is at hand, and is always ready to eat. In Ramadan, at the moment the sun sinks below the horizon, hands reach out for a bowl of harira to stay the stomach until the rest of the meal is ready. We told each other we were fortified for anything as we returned to our room. The electricity was about to be cut off, so I hastened to the outhouse at the end of the court. The door marked "*Dames*" wouldn't fasten, the plumbing consisted of a jug of water set down beside a pair of stepping-stones and a hole in the ground, and the light went off just as I arrived.

As I picked my way back through the court, I saw that someone had thoughtfully set down a candle by the path. Something glittered in the gravel clearing at the center of the mint beds. I held the candle high and saw the outline of a Cherifian star pricked out in bottle caps among the pebbles. The Moroccan's mosaic instinct will not be put down.

Bill had lighted our candle and was sitting up in bed, carefully pouring from a bottle of cheap Spanish brandy we had been carrying in the car "against some sudden emergency." There was only one glass, so we shared it, and gradually the bed began to feel a little less ironclad.

"Better blow out that candle," I said. "There's not much left of it, and it could be we'll need it in the night." The stars hung low outside the window, abnormally bright and large. I had always heard that desert stars shed a light a man could travel by. But I had never realized how cold the South would be once the sun had forsaken it. I shivered and took more of the raw brandy. Very soon it had done its work, and I dozed.

Some little time later, I woke up, itching. I also seemed to have been dreaming about my first and still very new grandchild, born just before we left home. (How long ago was that? How had we come here?) I thought I had snatched her up in my arms to shelter her from a desert wind that was at once searing and icy cold. What I actually found myself cradling was the plastic air pillow. The itching was not part of the dream; it was real and very urgent. Yet I had not been bitten—that was the one thing I could say for the mattress. This was some kind of rash involving my whole body at once. Bill was irritatingly sound asleep. Even if I woke him, what could he do?

I tried to think about the warm, four-day-old Jessica I had left only a few weeks ago. (If I let myself scratch, the itching flamed up far worse. I fingered the rising welts and knew that I would have to concentrate on anything and everything else.) Jessica had not really been so late in coming; it was more my impatience that had made the waiting long, and fear that our departure date would come first. One gray December day in Ann Arbor, I had met an Egyptian friend on his way to the class we both attended.

"Has your grandchild arrived?" he asked.

"Not yet, Daoud. But it is due any time now."

He looked strangely at me, suppressing a rejoinder. It took urging to get him to explain. "Well, it is difficult for a Muslim to understand the way you think here in the West. You speak as though the baby were *on contract*. We could never say, 'A birth is *due*.' We say, 'Any time now, a new life may be born—'nch Allah.' "

'Nch Allah, 'nch Allah . . . Why should we pretend we are not in the hands of fate? Look at my situation now—how could I have avoided this? And what was there now I could do about it?

Well, I could get up and go to the car for that bottle of Seconal. Welts were rising now in my scalp. No, too cold, too far to go. I slammed my fist hard into the bolster, hurting my knuckles, and pushed the air pillow into the hollow. No good. The tender skin between my fingers and toes felt scalded. Lie absolutely still, *force* every muscle to relax. We westerners really don't know the first thing about thought-control. How vunerable that makes us. Well, this is the moment to learn.

After a long time, I knew that I must do something. If I waked Bill, he might not be able to sleep again either, might even begin to itch, too. . . . But I could at least go to the car myself. The candle end cast so little light that I couldn't find my shoes, so stepped into Bill's instead, pulled on my coat, and sloshed my way to the door. But in the court a figure was crouching low, in the middle of one of the beds. After a second I saw the beam of his flashlight; he was picking mint. Mint, at this hour! That meant the lounge would still be full of people drinking tea. I really couldn't brave those glances, with my nightgown hanging below the coat and Bill's shoes over my bare feet, so I shrank back into our room again. At length I located the bottle of brandy and drained it.

The proprietor was very concerned in the morning, and insisted on going with us to the pharmacy. When he rapped on the locked door, a sleepy man looked out through a little wicket, took one glance at my swollen eyes and lips, and slammed it shut in our faces. The proprietor, ashamed, explained to us that he was only an ignorant fellow; he hoped we would not believe him a true Moroccan. Privately, I thought the pharmacist supposed I was a leper; I was beginning to feel like one. Our friend helped us back into the car, urged us to drive as fast as possible to Erfoud, where, he felt certain, the only doctor in the region was due to hold his clinic today. I took a second Seconal and laid my face against the cool window glass.

The fifty miles passed as in a dream. Palm trees swam by, tipped at grotesque angles. Thinking I must be hallucinating now, I said nothing about them. Anyway, my lips were too stiff to move. When Bill pulled up with a jerk, I saw with surprise that we were in front of the Erfoud hotel and that it looked like a kasbah; then I lost interest again. Dim shapes appeared, helped me, spoke gently, led me to a cool, soft bed. A long time later, I became conscious of people talking softly in the corner of the room—Bill and someone who spoke Parisian French. It appeared that we were waiting for the doctor, who did indeed have a clinic that day, but far down the Tafilelt. It appeared also that the Frenchwoman was the hotel manager's wife, and that she did not take me for a leper. She smiled, and when I tried to respond, my lips were not quite so swollen. I slept again.

Then there was a young, red-haired man leaning over the bed, asking questions in thick French . . . wrestling with a dim phone connection, and shouting instructions about sending an *infirmier* and ACTH . . . finally slamming down the receiver and striding to the door, saying he must go himself to get what was needed. After an interval that might, in my timeless state, have been minutes or hours, he was by the bed again, handing a hypodermic to a giant of blackness who wore a white turban coiled high above strong African features. He bent from his height to take the needle from the doctor, then to find the vein in first one of my arms and then the other, each time sinking the needle with beautiful skill. The doctor gave him another, longer needle, saying something about a relaxant, and the Sudanese bent again and spoke for the first time, "*Sur le ventre, Madame.*" I rolled over, wondering if this were all some fantasy of mine, in which a man who looked like a tribal king addressed me in pure, clear French. His work done, he gathered his instruments and withdrew to a far corner of the room, where he folded himself in one fluid motion and sat cross-legged on the floor. The polished teakwood of his face was expressionless, the eyes turned inward. With the three people by the window still conversing softly, I drifted into relief and then into sleep.

The next day, my scourge had vanished as mysteriously as it had come. I explored the hotel—a newly minted kasbah in architecture, with thick, cool walls topped by crowstepped gables, and a square tower over the main gate. The building was faced with adobe the color of the surrounding rock and soil, a warm burnt sienna. There was an inner court built around a fountain, and an arcade onto which the rooms opened. Mme. el Ghali, the French wife, moved about her domain, constantly busy. She couldn't have been more than twenty-five, but was in sole command most of the time. Her husband, it seemed, provisioned the hotel himself, driving his truck once or twice a week across the mountains all the way to Meknes, and then back through the following night. "But why?" I asked her. "Can't he send someone in his place?"

"He cannot otherwise be sure of the quality . . . that things will not be forgotten. You can hardly imagine what it is to work only with illiterates— you must rely always on yourself. No, when a new hotel is opened, there is no trained staff provided. We want to give employment—the local people need it badly. But, ah, the difficulties!" I followed her into the lounge, high-ceilinged and flooded with light from full-length windows. A cantilevered stairway descended from other rooms upstairs. Berber hangings on the walls were rich in primitive color; a gazelle stood, immaculately preserved, above a great plate-glass case in which the flora and fauna of the desert were displayed, with appropriate warnings beside the jars containing a scorpion, a turquoise-spotted lizard, and several vipers.

The doctor appeared, to check up on his patient. From his name, I now understood the reason for his accent: he was Spanish. "This country is not really dangerous," he said, nodding at the jars of formaldehyde, "certainly not now, in winter. In any case, it is not they, the animals, who are evil, but we, who have upset their ecology. Perhaps there is only harmony where there is less civilization. . . ."

Mme. el Ghali looked sidelong at him. "When you speak so, it means you are restless again. But you know you must not leave us—what would become of us?" Silent, he kept his red head bent above the brilliant lizard. The young woman told me that he was the only doctor for 30,000 souls in the region ("Make it 40,000," he murmured), and how could another man be found like him, willing to race each week between four clinics set fifty miles apart?

When she had gone, he told me a little about his work: about trachoma—"The incidence here is close to 100 per cent"—about tuberculosis and the other endemic diseases, most of them owing to nutritional deficiencies, and about unset fractures. "The real work here is education, persuading them to come for help *in time*. It is a test: How much can I teach in an average of one minute per clinic patient?" All but about 5 per cent were indigent, he said. Survival here was due to the incredible vitality of these people. "But," he finished grimly, "they must quickly be induced to limit births, or medicine will have saved too many lives for the land's resources. . . ."

"You get dreadfully discouraged?" I asked. "You feel you have been long enough under these hardships?"

He looked at me, startled. "My wife and I have agreed it is time for us to move, but not for the reasons you mention. Our baby is old enough now, but not yet in need of schooling. We have several free years ahead—to work in the Congo." As he said good-bye, I thought his smile was that of a man who has just confided a lucky secret.

It being mid-winter, the Ziz was still a reliable stream, and could be tapped at every level by channels leading off to the irrigated lands on either side. But I had not been mistaken about crazily tipped palms. Many of the forty- and fifty-foot trees were uprooted, and lay stricken on their sides, high above the present banks. Remembering the depth to which they sink their roots, I wondered at the flood waters that must have raced here the previous spring. The surviving trees were higher on the banks and braced with stone embankments; they stirred their branches dreamily against the sky, their ripening dates hanging down in golden clusters. At their feet spread a mosaic of tiny plots and terraces where barley grew, and vegetables, and even, here and there, some wheat.

We drove along the oasis, a narrow and verdant finger in the desert, past fortified mud-brick kasbahs large enough to house twenty or thirty families, past fields planted in narrow strips, some cracked and gray, others richly black with moisture. We stopped, trying to understand this alternation. A pair of tiny boys and their donkey were proceeding along a narrow dike between the strips. At first they seemed to be just frolicking—rushing the animal and leaping aboard, then sliding down his side to tumble each other. The donkey kept stolidly on, knowing his destination, knowing his restrictions. He never once tried to crop the acid-green shoots peering up below the dike, but only fortified himself calmly with what grass grew at his feet. The children were not just playing, I realized. With a perfect built-in sense of timing, they were regulating the flow of water to several planted strips in turn, removing from the side of the dike one plug of clay and replacing another, watching the water tinge the baked soil to black before they went back to their somersaulting.

"Sijilmassa!" said Bill, and folded up the map. "Let me see how close we can get to it!" When we reached the next signpost, one finger on it read "Timbuctoo," and pointed down a track no Simca need attempt. Though we could go no farther, the oasis went on for some miles ahead; the Ziz, now wholly underground, nourished the date palms marching southward out of sight. Another finger on the signpost read "Sijilmassa," and pointed east across deep-drifting sand to a blank horizon. We sat and stared in disappointment. No access, then, to the ruined city of the Alaouites that stood astride the slave and gold routes and rivaled Fez seven hundred years ago. . . .

So we took a third track, across semidesert, that brought us finally to a kasbah of tall houses built upon a large outcrop of rock, the whole surrounded by high fortifications. It was the sort of changeless tribal village we had come far to see. While we considered it from a little distance, a crowd of children tumbled out through a gate in the curtain wall and approached the car. They swept close, examined us, circled like a flock of starlings, and swept back uphill through the gate. It seemed like a half-invitation; at least they and we had curiosity in common. We walked, stiff-legged and tentative under the blank gaze of the wall and steep houses behind it, until we stood before an inner gateway where a line of old men sat dozing, hunkered down against the wall. Eyes opened as we neared them, but no one stirred. By gesture, we asked if we might enter. No expression changed, but one ancient nodded.

Inside, we found ourselves in something not unlike a large pueblo—three- and four-story adobe houses built over pens and byres. Where the lane we followed had been built over, I could look up through chinks in the floor and see bare feet passing overhead. We saw almost no one—occasionally, a woman jerked her child out of the alley at our approach—but we felt eyes upon us. An old man passed, a load of hay upon his head, his jaws grinding slowly on some wisps of grain. He looked briefly, blankly at us, and trudged on. There must be, somewhere outside the wall, wells and a net of irrigation channels that made life possible in this kasbah. In the fairly recent past, when nomads still raided every settled community, this tribe would have needed its fortifications; relative security could be won only when the elders could reach some barter agreement with those ever-drifting camelmen who sold their protection, served as porters between distant oases, and traded their own hides and young camels for the dates and grain of such a village as this.

At the center of the compound, we found the citadel of last recourse. The walls were two feet thick, of rock and rubble faced with mud brick and the prevailing rich, red-brown adobe. An arched gateway was flanked by square towers, behind whose crowstepped gables musketmen could shelter. The arch itself was framed in beautiful and primitive adobe sculpture, as fresh as if fingers had worked the damp clay yesterday. An old man in a white burnous sat leaning against the wall, his stick propped near him, the sightless, milky eyes of trachoma turned upon us.

I was thankful for the blazing, sterilizing sun as we picked our way across the drainage ditch that ran around the outer kasbah wall. Palms lay beyond, growing beside a major water channel, where women were flailing their laundry, and the thorn bushes bloomed luridly with skirts and head shawls. Mounds of dates, spread on a carpet of palm fronds, lay drying in the sun. Seeing us, children detached themselves from play, bunched into a group, and sidled toward us. I turned to face them, and the group burst into a score of bright fragments—brilliant bits and pieces of clothing, dark arms, and churning legs vanished into a thicket of young palms.

The village seemed distant indeed when we sat that night in the hotel lounge, over coffee and brandy. Sunk in deep chairs, our feet muffled in thick Berber rugs, we watched a young houseboy handling our cups with the greatest concentration and moving proudly between us in his splendid braided jacket and loose Moorish trousers. From a loudspeaker poured an ingenious jazz version of a Bach fugue; Mme. el Ghali, sitting with us, murmured, "My parents sent me the disc for Christmas, to make Paris seem a little less far away. . . ." Suddenly, her husband saw the houseboy's bare feet beneath the splendid uniform and shouted at him so loudly that the lad backed into a great pot full of pampas grass. Stricken, he looked down at his feet and fled. A hopeless look passed between the young manager and his wife.

The other guests with us were an anthropologist and his wife called Voisin. The spare, grizzled Frenchman had been speaking about survivals of a caste system in the Tafilelt: there was a pure black group living as agricultural serfs without a wage, or as itinerant farriers forbidden to settle. Poverty in the region was no new thing, he said, and the reason for it was a one-crop economy—dates. Even today, with a serious blight decimating the groves, the people here resisted efforts from the outside to encourage citrus growing. Only one lone man—and he was a Jew—was willing to break with tradition; and he had done famously with an orange grove.

I quoted the doctor's bleak words about the region's resources and the birth rate, and M. Voisin shook his head glumly. "They will never accept something as alien as direct birth control. But what they could accept is some adaptation of a practice once common among the pastoral peoples—a sagacious practice that linked the number of marriages allowed each year to the number of lambs dropped that spring. And, since the number of ewes bred was reckoned according to the rainfall and the amount of pasturage that could be expected, those tribes arrived at a realistic balance."

(How often some young Moroccan had asked Bill, "At home, sir—how many children have you? What, only three?" Then, with condescension, "We, sir, are eleven at home!")

Mme. Voisin clicked her tongue. "And would they keep the 'realistic balance' *after* marriage? Is that not more important?" She also was a professional, an assistant to a Rabat psychiatrist. "One must not forget the worship of maleness, of potency! The doctor with whom I work says, 'When dealing with the Moroccan personality, one should paraphrase Descartes thus: *Coito, ergo sum.*'"

She had some interesting things to say about the homosexual phase common among young Moroccan men. It interfered with later adjustment only when a youth *habitually* assumed the passive role. This course was sometimes forced on a young fellow who needed money to finish school and could find no employment. "I once treated such a boy. His classmates had turned him out of school and driven him down the street with a hue and cry. He, I fear, was stamped forever. But most of the attachments are loose and temporary. Perhaps some of them are helpful, in a still largely segregated society; or perhaps they only give rise to more stresses than the young already suffer. I have known men who rely greatly on a close friendship, and who will take pains to protect their relationship from any erotic tinge that might, in the end, threaten it."

I asked her about the kinds of problems her work dealt with—did she see them as attributable to cultural shock arising from too sudden contact with the West?

"In work like ours," she replied a little stiffly, "we are dealing generally with those who find reality difficult, for whatever reasons. The only difference here, I sometimes think, is that many have become so infatuated with their *maux d'esprit* that they would prefer to remain victims. . . ."

"Could the enjoyment of being victimized be part of the colonial heritage—of the experience of being at once despised and exploited? Doesn't the habit of servility, once learned for survival's sake, often become imprinted on the personality in the form of *self*-hatred?"

The Frenchwoman's eyes had flown wide open and were fixed on me severely. But I had started, and could not turn back. So I told of an instance that had shocked me deeply: a young Moroccan, after telling us of a particularly brutal crime that the newspapers were featuring, suddenly turned the criminal verdict on himself: "So you see," he concluded on a note of deep hate, "*we Moroccans simply are not civilized!*"

Mme. Voisin told me, firmly, to remember that Moroccans had oppressed and exploited each other long before the French set their hand to it.

Her husband found psychological discussions less than absorbing. The tribes, he thanked God, have little time for neurosis. "Water, water, water is their constant preoccupation. Its use, its regulation, how to find it, how to do without it—did you know that once, in the thirties, no drop of rain fell in the South for four years? Yet somehow people survived! And when it comes to social organization, is it not water rights that hold a fraction together? Far more than territorial claims or belief in common ancestry! If you want to see the meshing of fine gears that makes it possible for tribes to live in peace with their neighbors, you must look at the intricate water regulations"—and he was off on a favorite topic. "Once the rights have been established, the people work out ways to diminish friction. For friction—fighting—is waste of precious energy! Look, for example, at the way neighboring fractions often exchange lactating mothers: the women of one group nurse the babes of the other, thus creating a 'blood bond' that will prevent fighting."

He ended by directing us to a water hole where we could learn about this "meshing of fine gears." It was a spot where an underground oued came briefly to the surface in the midst of unpromising desert. Two villages, set apart from each other by low mud walls, lay close to the water hole, their growing lands fed by ditches that branched minutely like capillaries. The evaporation rate must be tremendous, I thought, for I saw in places a crust of salt on the soil. There were two tipples set up at opposite sides of the small pool. An ox and a donkey worked one, a resentful-looking camel the other. The camel set his splayed feet down as though each step were his last, and behind him a rope slowly drew up a huge bloated skin from the well. As it reached an upright frame, the water bag tipped its load into one of the channels. Each time the camel reached the end of his narrow track, he turned, swaying his long neck as though lamenting his task, and trod sadly back to his tipple. The men attending the two operations did not speak except to their beasts, but a tacit watchfulness bound each to the other. The same amount of water must pour through each of the two channels during the allotted time.

It was a day of overcast that seemed to promise doom of some sort. The *chergui,* the wind off the desert, was blowing, and the sky was heavy and smeared with dust. Small sand devils went whirling here and there. Whenever two or three came together, they formed a small cyclone that sped erratically until it spent itself and sank into a little mound of sand. Gray dust began to cake the vegetables in the mud-walled plots; it began to get between our teeth and into our ears. Walking between the villages, we had picked up a retinue of urchins. Two of them tagged us closely, grimacing, capering around us, more irritating than a swarm of gnats. I swung my handbag at one of the pests, and was rewarded by a pelting of small stones that dropped just short of my feet.

A man cutting bricks nearby straightened up and shouted something at them, but they were back around us a few steps farther on. Then along the path beside the water hole strode a man of authority. His appearance was the signal that both tipple teams must now suspend work. We approached him, hoping he would rid us of our pestilence. With a deft swing, he reached out and collared both children, and boxed their heads together. One ran wailing down the homeward path, the other wrenched himself away and stood glaring defiantly at the man, holding out for him to see some identifying amulet from beneath his shirt. The man's arm dropped. He had exceeded his authority: this child belonged to the other village. Impudently, the urchin swaggered off.

The man's appearance signaled the time for the close-of-day procession to the water hole. A file of donkeys approached, each bearing six great earthen jugs slung in grass nets. Women in charge of the beasts went down by twos and threes and sank their jars into the water, then strapped them with meticulous care to the animals' backs. The man surveyed them all in silence, watching while they moved off in single file, and women from the other village approached and dropped to their knees at the rim of the water. The level seemed dangerously low, murky under the dim sky.

The sun had begun to sink as we drove home, and the cooling of the earth provoked a minor sandstorm. We closed the car windows tightly and turned on our lights, which stabbed only a few feet into the dense air. A sickly saffron color suffused everything, and the sun turned pale as it began to sink. "White as though chidden of God . . ." Bill said, as he wrestled the little car across the wind. Sand was piling up on the road; the palms thrashed and writhed. All the animals, even the slit-eyed camels, turned their rumps to the wind; women pulled their shawls over their eyes, men used their sleeves. All color had left the world except the oppressive yellow pallor. As we neared the hotel, I saw with dismay that there were no welcoming lights—no one had thought it necessary to start the generator, which rested all day until the normal hour of dark. That meant no hot water for our sand-caked skin. In our room, the phone hummed eerily and incessantly, tormented by the wind. I went to the window, where a line of sand lay along the sill, though the sash was tightly closed. Outside, the garden had vanished, except for long gray whiskers of cactus projecting weirdly out of the sand.

The wind dropped as suddenly as it had risen. The lights came on, people gathered for dinner, but a sense of calamity lingered on. Everyone was edgy, most of all the Voisins, who were leaving the next morning in their Land Rover and now wondered what new dunes would confuse their passage across the desert. The anthropologist was setting out to study the habits of those nomads who wander the eastern desert bordering on Algeria. Since it was also our last evening in Erfoud, we converged together on the bar. Just then there came a long sound of sliding, followed by a thunderous crash of splintering glass. Mme. el Ghali ran to where the terrified boy who never remembered his shoes stood in a welter of bottles and glasses on the floor, the hen's-feather duster with which he had touched off the holocaust dangling from his hand. The Frenchwoman's voice rose in a shriek: ". . . *absolument interdit de TOUCHER CELA!*" But it was obviously too late to remind him what he must not touch. While the kitchen staff wordlessly swept up the mess, we rescued a bottle of Armagnac and found chairs facing away from the carnage.

The eastern desert to which the anthropologist was going is a no man's land, a constant source of friction between Morocco and Algeria, since the boundary has never been accurately plotted. The French first set up a commission to chart the border, then suspended it when they felt confident that one day soon the Protectorate would slip unobtrusively into colonial status, and Morocco would be merged with Algeria. When, after the French withdrawal, rich oil strikes occurred in the Sahara—well inside Algeria, to be sure—Morocco began to take the liveliest interest in defining the border. Claims and counterclaims have never been settled; even the border war that broke out in 1963, and which Morocco won handily, led to no agreement. And, were a settlement to be reached tomorrow, the boundary would remain very difficult to patrol; it is several hundred miles of practically featureless desert. Only nomads, who recognize no boundaries in any case, roam at will —and leave no trace.

"What do you expect to see there?" I asked M. Voisin.

"Emptiness!" he said. "At Boudenib, I leave my wife and pick up my companion vehicle. Thereafter, we will have to rely on compass and sextant, but with care, we shall be able to track from one oasis to another—each no more than a few palms against the immensity. There are remains of many kasbahs, too, slowly sinking into the sand . . . and land mines, plenty of them, if we should get into the disputed territory."

"And will the nomads accept your presence, be willing to talk with you?"

"Desert people still rank hospitality highest among their obligations. Especially since—" his eyes twinkled—"since they have discovered that strangers in their midst are likely to come bearing delightful gifts—transistor radios, tobacco, chocolate, medicine for the camel herd. Both our vehicles will be well loaded, I assure you."

"But who are all these 'strangers in their midst'?"

"Madame," he said, "scarcely a month passes but some engineer, complete with desert escort, is to be found amongst them, taking sand scrapings with the greatest care. Even a small oil strike could make quite a difference to Morocco. And do you suppose the nomads do not understand what such a discovery could mean in their lives? I am not optimistic about the likelihood of finding important oil there—but I do know that my time is limited if I wish to study and record the old habits of the nomads."

Tinerhir

Westward from the Tafilelt, a long road skirts the feet of the Middle and High Atlas in turn. The ribs of the mountain barrier are riven with gorges, where waters race in season with appalling force, and the villages are built high on the rock walls. On the other side of the valley that the road follows, the last, broken spurs of the Anti Atlas die out in a succession of escarpments that tell of a day when the whole continent writhed. Rock strata of many colors are frozen into whorls, as in a Chinese painting. Here, on the only east-west road behind the Atlas, are all the features that compose the face of the South—astonishing colors of rock and soil, brick red, ocherous green, and black of basalt; sudden walled kasbahs beside the acid green of their crop-lands; and between the villages, camelthorn, Barbary fig cactus, and stones, stones, stones, the earth's most abundant crop.

So primitive was this emptiness that I fell to wondering as we drove why we could never remember to have all the wise emergency items with us at any one time—a jerry can of water, two of gas, and two spare tires. I groaned every time a rock loomed in the road. On my left hand, a lowering butte rose out of crimson earth; on my right, High Atlas ridges crowded one behind another. Along the nearest ridge I saw a train of camels in single-file silhouette. The only other living things were some goats picking their way across a slope of black shale.

"Almost anything could happen here," I said.

"Apparently, just about anything does." Bill nodded ahead. Several small mountains of brushwood were coming toward us down the road. Only when we were almost upon them could I see the women's legs below their loads. We were in their midst before we could stop. I ran down my window, and immediately five or six arms were thrust in, fingering my clothes, reaching for my handbag. I ran the window up promptly, and Bill kept racing the motor, out of gear. . . . I groped in my purse for small coins, keeping one eye on their faces. Dark blue arrows and stars and rows of dots were tattooed between the kohl-rimmed eyes, along jawbones, and across chins. They were handsome; their skin was a rich cinnamon. Their gaze on my purse was con-centrated and determined. As they straightened up beside the closed window, I saw how muscular they were. Some had scarlet kerchiefs over their heads; others had braided strings of beads and coins into their black hair. Their necklaces were of cowrie shells and amber and silver; one wore a snail shell on a thong—a potent magnet of good fortune—another a string of handsome safety pins on the end of which hung a mother-of-pearl shirt button.

I heard Bill swearing as he tried to focus his camera in a hurry. I said, "Are you ready? I think I have the right six coins in hand." When I opened the window part way, they almost broke their arms reaching in. I closed my fist tightly while Bill pointed to his camera. They understood well enough, but tried to get the money before he was ready. I ran the window up again, squeez-ing some fingers. The women pointed excitedly at a pack of cigarettes on my lap. I pulled out six, held them with the coins, and waved the women back from the window as I opened it once more. I heard the camera click three times rapidly; so did they, and they tried to duck even while reaching out for their tribute. For an instant I looked into several pairs of laughing black eyes, while fingers raked my palm. Bill let in the clutch, and inched the car for-ward. All at once the women opened their mouths, drawing back their lips as singers do, with a flashing of bright teeth. Their tongues flew up to the

roof of their mouths and fluttered there; a high, shrill, nerve-tingling ululation followed us as we drew away.

Among the Berber tribes, women have always enjoyed more rights than
Arab women. Polygamy has never been popular. Women may hold land in
their own right and act with authority. Some of the tribes seem even to have
been matriarchal. Much magical lore surrounds women at all times, but most
especially during pregnancy. Because, to the primitive, all orifices are suspect
(latrines, drains, even mines—hence miners' disease), it is only natural that
a woman in childbed focuses about her both good and evil spirits. In order
that fertility may triumph in this crisis, her thighs and abdomen have been
liberally tattooed at the time of her marriage. If she is so unfortunate as to be
widowed, a special form of social insurance has been devised for her: the
rule of *ragéd,* or "the child of the bier." Any child born to her within five
years after her bereavement is said to have been "asleep in the womb" throughout the interval.

The jewelry a Berber woman wears—clasps for her shawl fashioned in
silver and chased in cabalistic designs, egg-size lumps of amber or cornelian,
any odd-shaped stone, bracelets of heavy studded silver, bangles of coins and
silver balls to lie across her headcloth, earrings with more coins dangling—all
these are given her to wear so that she may attract good fortune. She is, you
might say, the honey pot to which all wandering spirits are drawn. It behooves
men to ensure that favorable djinns will outnumber the others.

Our road continued, mile after mile, through a landscape of frozen turbu-
lence. At last, the sight of a town ahead—Tinerhir, at the mouth of its gorge.
A humpbacked bridge over a stream, the shock of verdure after wilderness,
acres of palm trees and fruit trees, of violently green fields laced with silver
canals. And then the entrance to the town: two structures closing in narrowly
upon the road. On the right, a traditional kasbah tower with gun slits and
a parapet, the side walls handsomely ornamented with geometric figures
etched in the adobe; on the left, a strictly utilitarian concrete bunker, souvenir
of 1935 and the French "pacification." Uphill again, lurching over rocks in
the road, a steep zigzag to what looks like a citadel built upon a smooth, wide
rock plateau—the state hotel. A busload of very Teutonic tourists was alight-
ing before the gate.

"Let's get down to the town as soon as we can . . . give these people the
dining room to themselves." Bill is apt to become irritable in any high concentration of German tourists. As we wandered the narrow streets, the evening light came on as though from cunningly placed floodlights, casting plum-
colored shadows between the mountains, touching to rose the snow on their
shoulders. The light ran down in rivulets into the folds of the lower hills,
celestial fingers laying a soft grasp on the rumpled land. In a circle around the
town, the slopes bloomed into color—topaz, umber, violet, palest olive green.

A young boy had been following us at a discreet distance. He drifted to us
as the sunset drew to its climax. "Would you like me to show you tomorrow

where 'El Laurans' was filmed? It was shot right in those hills. If you have a car, I shall be pleased to guide you."

So many places claim to be the setting for *Lawrence of Arabia* that one is reminded of the beds George Washington slept in. I believe that this boy was right, as a matter of fact. The spoor of Peter O'Toole can be picked up quite regularly in this region where High and Middle Atlas merge and desert laps at their feet.

But we asked the boy, instead, to walk with us a little through the town. It was Ramadan, and the first cooking fires were being lit. Soon the spicy odors of the harira would fill the streets. The boy said his name was M'Barek, and that he was keeping his third Fast. "But you must have started very young!" I exclaimed, for he looked barely twelve. He was a lightly boned lad, with precise and delicate features.

"I am fourteen," he said. "My conscience told me to begin the Fast three years ago."

"The age to begin is left altogether to the individual, then?"

"Entirely a matter between the believer and his God! When one is no longer a child, one naturally wishes to assume responsibilities." He was charmingly pleased with himself.

The lanes were slick with moisture; down the center of each ran a small drainage tunnel. House doors were faced with a crazy quilt of hammered-out oil cans, bright with legends. One announced, upside down, "Shell Is Good for Your Motor." M'Barek said they were nailed to the doors to prevent fires; but the gnawed edge of unprotected doors suggested another reason.

M'Barek produced a snapshot from under his djellaba. "This is my friend, M. Harold of *Tchicageau*. He comes to us every year. You will know him, I think?" We peered obligingly and then asked for further identification. "Well, he is tall; and he is learning Berber. That is where he lives." Smoke was rising through the cane roof of the house he pointed to. The Hand of Fatma was painted brightly a number of times on the door, and a Barbary fig grew in the wall, its roots an integrated part of the structure.

"Well, is he here now?"

"No. It is the family he lives with who are cooking. He will come soon. He finds our marriage customs very interesting. When he is here, he has an arrangement with a young boy about my age and also with a young girl. They come daily to visit him."

An arresting description, indeed. "Do you know what his business is here?"

"Yes. To ask questions. To write down the answers in many notebooks. He also measures our heads, from time to time. Even the arms, on occasion." He looked obliquely at us, to see if we too thought this a bizarre gratification. "But he pays very well. He is a good man, I think—?" We decided not to try to explain to M'Barek what makes a working anthropologist do all that he does.

All at once, the town's electricity came on; the street lamps made us blink.

A radio wailed the news that the sun had set. "You must go to your meal, M'Barek." He took the dirham absent-mindedly, with dignity.

"You will see, as you pass by the market square, the tents being set up in preparation for tomorrow. Perhaps I shall look for you there."

Back at the hotel, the Germans were still singing and calling for more wine. I watched a waiter, very Moorish in white pleated trousers and a white turban, refill the glasses. His face as he gazed down on the moist eyes and loosened lips showed nothing but a great reserve.

We turned aside to wait. In the bar was an astonishing sight: a television set. I still have no idea how reception was possible so far from a big city. A French voice announced, "In a few moments, we shall bring you a broadcast from London," and the lurid square of light danced and flickered, until at last black specks resolved themselves into figures marching four abreast to the sound of slow drums. Berber eyes around us watched the oldest tribal act of all, as the casket of Winston Churchill moved slowly along Whitehall.

This intrusion of London into Tinerhir, and the strain this simultaneity set upon my imagination, put me in mind of Marshall McLuhan's dictum that all the world has become a tribal village. Simultaneity, confusion, randomness, I take him to be saying, are breath of life to the tribesman. I wonder what tribesmen he has been observing. The tribal mentality, if I understand it at all, is dedicated to imposing order on what might otherwise appear random, and excluding or reinterpreting any "message" that threatens that order. Claude Lévi-Strauss says that tribal institutions are apt devices *to congeal change,* and I believe he is right. It is when I try to arrest too rapid change around me that I am harking back to my tribal roots. And that is when I turn off the television set.

The sheep market was held next morning in a clay quarry the shape of an amphitheater. The town's last houses made the backdrop: walls of the same rich brown clay, and every small window outlined in whitewash. ("It keeps flies from entering," this common practice was explained to me—which it certainly does not.) Since the earliest morning light, people of the surrounding douars had been filing down the bed of the gorge that opens into Tinerhir. Robed and hooded figures drove their flocks beside the pale water and the lavender cliffs and waited at a shallow ford while muzzles were thrust into the stream. Beside the trail, a blind man and his wife sat against a rock, her eyes raised to every passer-by. Each dropped his alms at her feet—a horn of bananas from the pannier, a bunch of turnips, a few good chunks of firewood. All was done in silence.

We stood on the rim of the quarry and looked down: dark, brindled donkeys, gray and white fleece of sheep, and exactly similar tones of long homespun robes. The turbans, seen from above, are white rings around a dark center—the crown of the head. Strong, weather-hardened faces peer long at animals for sale; friends salute each other in the old style: after the handclasp, each carries his hand to his lips. From time to time, some mindless panic seizes a circle of sheep. All bleating at once, forelegs flailing, they climb upon each other's backs, only to be dragged off by the tail. A goat decides to make a break for it and scrambles part way up the quarry wall; caught by the hind leg, he is smacked back into the herd.

A quartet of figures stands around a fine fat ewe with a nuzzling lamb at her side. A "followed ewe" commands the highest sort of price. Both her owner and the potential buyer are attended by seconds, as in dueling, which indeed the bargaining resembles. Gestures are sharp as knives. The seller grabs the other's palm and chops it with the edge of his hand, then flings aside to consult with his second. He turns back only when the buyer, after like consultation, strikes him on the shoulder. After hearing the new offer, he shrugs hugely; then, kissing his hand as he swears by some saint, he barks his counteroffer. Next, he bends and thrusts his widespread fingers deep into the fleece and looks up fiercely at the buyer, as if to say, "Can you do without such wool as this?" The buyer leans down to tug at the animal's teats. A new offer, another round of palm-smiting to seal the bargain, and a sheaf of notes changes hands. A blotch of crimson dye daubed on the ewe's rump, a rope slipped round her neck, and off she goes, the chocolate-brown lamb teetering after her.

Marabouts

Tribalism, everyone agrees, has been decreasing for a long time, and three factors are cited for its decline: the loss of many tribal territories to private ownership, the urbanization trend throughout this century—accelerated now in the rural exodus—and, since Independence, the government's cautious effort to wean the tribes from their traditional separatism and integrate them into the new, centralized nation. Despite all these pressures, a great many countrymen still recognize loose tribal ties more clearly than any others. In the isolated regions of north, south, and east, the old system works very much as it always has—not efficiently, perhaps, but tolerably.

That friction between neighboring fractions does not exceed the tolerable is due in large measure to the marabouts, for one of their functions has been to keep the peace. In a society where the kasbah dwellers had to fear not only raiding nomads but also the covetous eyes of settled neighbors, some kind of arbitration had to be devised, or fighting and reprisals would never cease. Sensibly, the tribes assigned mediation to their marabouts. Dealing with their own caste across tribal lines, the marabouts negotiated intertribal peace. And at home they adjudicated the individual quarrels.

But arbitrating feuds is not the marabouts' only function. Their greatest value is a spiritual one—to soften the austerity of the faith and bridge the awful gap between man and the supernatural. Islam has no clergy, in our sense of ministers to the personal anxieties and private bewilderments of people everywhere. The Ulema expound doctrine, the cadis rule on all the intricate matters detailed in the Sacred Law, the Imam preaches at the Friday service and reads from the Koran, wherein all truth is contained. Allah, as every Muslim knows, has grace, divine blessing, and favor—all summed up in baraka—in abundance for every believer. But the believer has often felt himself at a frightening distance from the Godhead. The many forms of Islam have closed this gap variously, with a greater or lesser degree of mystical heterodoxy. The Moroccan—and his kindred of the Maghreb—has found the answer to his need in holy men close to his condition, whose wonder-working proves their holiness. The marabout is a lightning rod for baraka.

In death, he continues to be a benign influence. His tomb—the little mud-brick cube crouching close to earth, with a domed roof not much greater than a man's height—still radiates his baraka. Whenever possible, it is whitewashed, and stands out clear and comforting against the awesomeness of a Moroccan landscape. Usually, it is shaded by a tree that somehow flourishes mysteriously in the midst of stony wasteland. Thousands of these reassuring little presences are visited in time of personal trouble or mass pilgrimage.

Someone has made an apt comparison between the whitewash laid upon the mud-brick structure of the little wayside tombs and the gloss of Islamic doctrine that overlies the fundamental paganism of the Berber. It has always been the Berber way to convert rather readily to whatever faith was brought to them, and then adapt it to their needs. High Atlas villagers who were proselytized by Jewish missionaries in the first and second centuries have remained converts to this day; but, being Berbers, they have made adaptations that would scandalize any city rabbi. Similarly, when they accepted Islam, they brought into it a genial paganism that has survived every effort to efface it. There is something obstinately durable about the Berber strain. (The name "Berber" is a foreign import. Far more apt is the name by which they call themselves: *Imazighen*—"Free Men.") The North African native has never been truly assimilated into any of the invading cultures; rather, he has assimilated them. Perhaps it will be clear one day that he has managed to do the same even with the latest invasion by the West.

The trend toward saint-worship spread even to the cities. Marrakesh has nine patron saints, their tombs still lovingly tended. Even Fez, that stronghold of orthodoxy, has its sacred tomb of Moulay Idriss. Merchants' and craftsmen's guilds all over the country honored their individual saints with yearly pilgrimages. But maraboutism flourished best in regions remote from the disapprobation of the Ulema and the sultans' suspicion of any baraka but their own.

Saint-worship, it seems to me, is the religious dimension of tribalism: one needs, in addition to one's own people, a holy man of one's own. To become a marabout, a man must have persuasive religious fervor and a compelling presence. "Moral vividness" sums it up best.[3] This warmth and force of character will draw men about him for prayer and for catharsis in mystical rites under his direction.

In the past, some marabouts were so persuasive—and so ambitious—that they became founders of brotherhoods, with chapters throughout the country. Some of their rites included self-mutilation, glass swallowing, and dismembering live sheep at the climax of hysteria. But most were more restrained, aiming at exorcism of evil through dervish dancing to bring on trance, or simply hyperventilation and incantatory repetitions of Allah's name. Whatever the rite, the purpose was the same: ecstatic union with the Godhead. At the turn of this century there were more than five hundred active brotherhoods, some of them powerful enough to threaten the throne. (A couple of them played a pivotal role only fifteen years ago in the plot to depose Mohammed V.) The Moroccan is by nature an admirer of "strong man politics and holy man piety,"[4] and he loves to find both attributes focused in one man whose leadership he can espouse. Even now that all political activity of the brotherhoods has been suppressed—outwardly, at least—some of them continue to enjoy prestige, large revenues from dues, and a degree of loyalty that it would be hard to measure.

But relatively few marabouts founded brotherhoods; most have been content with a local adherence. How, then, is a marabout made? Since Berbers are a very practical people, more is expected of a holy man than just leading followers to mystical experience. Any claim to sainthood must stand the test of efficacy, and a marabout must constantly demonstrate his baraka to the advantage of the tribe. Uncanny things must flow from his presence—works of healing, rescue in time of disaster, drought brought to an end, or some supernatural insight that resolves bewilderment. A fever may abate where he has passed, or a stolen goat be located when he has studied the wrinkles in a bit of cloth crumpled in his fist. If he has inscribed an amulet with a verse from the Koran and great blessing befalls the wearer, is this not proof that through this man the Word becomes active in human affairs? Thus, step by step, the saint-in-the-making enlarges the range of his credibility; his claims must keep pace with the community's response. Above all, the marabout must honor his responsibilities—if a man has slaughtered a sheep on his threshold, that man has become his client. The marabout must take on that man's trouble and find some solution for it.

In life, he mediates quarrels, interprets signs and portents, and brings blessings. In death, he passes on his baraka to the men he has fathered. (How

3. Clifford Geertz, *Islam Observed* (New Haven and London: Yale University Press, 1968), p. 44.
4. *Ibid.,* p. 8.

absurd celibacy would be in saints, when baraka is heritable!) Again, his lineage must vindicate their claims with works; but now they enjoy the benefit of the doubt. Many a tiny douar set on the boundary between two fractions is a maraboutic settlement. They need not bear arms because they are holy; their presence there acts as a buffer. And because they are above all local pressures and frictions, this tiny community can take charge of affairs when the tribesmen must go far afield—on transhumant migration, or on the search for seasonal labor. The marabouts keep an eye on water rights, on the stored grain, and on the behavior of the women left behind. When one man or one group has injured another, they intervene to keep reprisals from escalating into feud; the penalties they set represent the most ancient form of justice—an eye for an eye, but never more than an eye.

To look about you in country where marabouts function is to see the need for men with a special gift for traffic with the supernatural. For here nature itself seems to know no laws but those of might and caprice. Rivers can bring life and plenty, or they can vanish underground. The desert encroaches, dunes shift or disappear. Oases spring out of a stony waste like miracles; or sometimes they recede before you, and finally disintegrate in mirage. Lightning dances on a distant hill, where later a new spring gushes from the rock and a new stream is born. If conditions were uniformly harsh, men would at least know where they stood. But here nature, like the very worst sort of parent, is alternately severe and seductive, raising hopes only to dash them.

Even the traveler along this road at the feet of the Atlas feels the capricious alternation of threat and promise. We, in our small car, are like playgoers before whom the scenes are shifted in a trice and a new mood presented to our startled eyes. The Dades Gorge, for instance, renowned as one of the most spectacular in Morocco, is wide and smiling at its mouth, the gently sloping banks planted in a brilliant mosaic of greens, and a little walled douar leaning back upon the amethyst cliff behind it. The road up the gorge is macadam, the season is May, the worst of the flood danger is over, and all damage has presumably been reported.

After a mile or so, the mood changes as the rock walls approach each other and the car, zigzagging upward, leaves behind it a long, tortuous thread of road. Looking back and dizzily down, I am reminded of a toiling spider and the fragile thread it spins behind it. The road is now so narrow I shudder to think of turning on it—let us hope it comes out somewhere. . . . Above my head, the sky is narrow and jagged; I have a fleeting impression that this gorge has been riven by a giant chisel in the hand of God. The road has dropped low again; it is only about thirty feet above the water. On the opposite canyon wall, I see with astonishment a line of silt *on a level with my eyes,* and am just about to speak when the brakes shriek. A yard or two in front of the car, an apron of macadam is hanging in a strange dimpled way above the void. The section of cliff that has subsided still juts out of the water, which snarls around it with white lips. Inch by hairbreadth inch, we swivel the little car around. And I know, down to the soles of my feet, I am not going to forget the Dades.

Route des Kasbahs

Once released from its rock walls, the river abruptly changes both character and direction. It veers west and nourishes a smiling valley between the Atlas foothills on the north and the final spurs of another range, the Anti Atlas, on the south. It is an old route, this natural passage, and even today affords the only east-west road behind the Atlas. From time out of mind, kasbahs have stood wherever route and river coincide; here, crops are plentiful enough to be stored up in tall fortified granaries within the village wall. But, between kasbahs, wherever the valley narrows and the Dades becomes treacherous again, the road must leave the river to struggle over arid hills. Thus the traveler is passing continuously from stark heights to gentle green reaches beside the water.

Gentle green—and the eyes of raiders roaming the hills above. Each kasbah crowns its heavy wall with a high lookout tower. And nature aids concealment, for each village is entirely of a piece with the surrounding earth. Wall, houses, granary, and tower—all are of the same rust red or ocher or rosy brown of the soil and rock from which they are built. So perfect is the camouflage that only by the tender green of its palm grove can you detect a village from a distance.

In May, one kasbah is pure enchantment—el Kelaa of the M'Gouna, completely engulfed in roses. All tales about the roses agree in one point only— they came from Isfahan in Persia; no two agree on who brought them to the spot where the M'Gouna valley joins the Dades. El Kelaa is an outburst of luxuriance. Grapevines, fruit orchards, and almond trees fight for space between the rose hedges. Women walk down the road with huge sacks on their heads, each sack compact with rose blossoms. Under an arch of acacias, even the road is strewn with escaped petals. The scent, of course, is overwhelming. This village is thriving—there are new houses, of earth nearly as crimson as the roses, and a new school, with fluttering Cherifian banners. Metal smokestacks of two rose-attar factories thrust up as high as the towers of the granary.

These women in procession along the road are of the Aït Atta tribe, famous for the beauty of its women and their robust fondness for exchanging male partners and remaining quite unreconstructed about it. They pile their black hair high, so intricately entwined with coins and woven bands and bangles that it is not worthwhile to dismantle the structure at night. They paint black triangles at the corners of their eyes and rouge their lips and chins, and the way they walk is token enough of how good they find life. Perhaps el Kelaa is not magic after all—perhaps some village industry like the rose-attar factories could touch each of her sister villages into the same plenitude of life. . . .

The scent of roses fades, el Kelaa falls behind, and all that opulence must have been a dream. In the next village, the air darkens suddenly; the palms tremble in what appears to be a breeze, and is not—it is a horde of locusts. The ground seethes with their bodies, ears of grain bend under their weight, even the walls of the fortress tower disappear behind the armature of their scaly backs. We spurt forward up an avenue of wings, desperate to outstrip them, grateful that the road will soon forsake the river and all succulent life and so leave the plague behind. Once more, we climb a sharp crest. All verdure is forgotten now; boulders and camelthorn are the landscape. In a small patch of shade, a woman is crouching on the ground while her mule waits behind her. Her head, wrapped in a dark cone of cloth, is turned to look down upon the afflicted village in the valley. Parting the folds of her shawl, she bares a heavy breast to an infant in her arm, but all the while she still looks woodenly down upon her home.

Skoura's gateway bestrides the road: two slender ocher towers and a connecting bridge, well furnished with musket slits. There is just barely room for a car to pass below. The towers, with the Berber gift for line and proportion, are made to taper subtly as they rise, to grow like living members out of the ocher soil. All Skoura is ocher, except the whitewashed mosque and several low white domes of marabout tombs almost hidden by clumps of flowering oleander. Perhaps because of the strange color experience, I was especially aware here of the organic nature of anything built out of mud-brick and faced with earth applied by hand. The texture and outlines both suggest living forms. All the surfaces are pleasing to look at because of their soft irregularities, the contours are gently off true, and what symmetry there is depends not on exact correspondence but on a balance between the parts. The earthen facing takes ornament as naturally as human features take on expression. I think part of my very personal feeling about Morocco may be a response to adobe, as well as to the people who work it so skillfully.

For a short distance beyond Skoura, the Dades still parallels the road. Then, deflected once for all by the Anti Atlas, it angles away to the south. With it goes the grateful shade of willows and fluffy tamarisks and the stately lines of palms. Despite all the grandeur of its gorge and the volume of its waters in season, the Dades suffers an extraordinary fate. It empties into Morocco's most astonishing river, the Draa, and for many miles the two create a long slender palm oasis thrusting down into the desert south. Here grow the finest dates Morocco produces; here, at Zagora, the tall, elusive Tuareg, their skins permanently blue from the indigo dye of the robes they habitually wear, bring their camel herds to market, and then are gone as mysteriously as they came. And here the Dades-Draa vanishes. Vanishes so completely that its underground course can be traced only brokenly, across hundreds of desert miles, by occasional oases. Then, five hundred miles away to the southwest, it reappears again on the surface, amid total desert—just in time to empty into the Atlantic. Need anything more be said about evidences of supernatural caprice?

All signs of luxuriance lost to us with the Dades, we entered again upon mountain immensities and emptiness. Somewhere ahead to the west lay Ouarzazate, our destination and the nearest thing in the South to a city. But now, among the buttes and astonishing jagged spurs of the Anti Atlas, I could see nothing moving but cloud shadows, nothing alive but a kite hovering on motionless wings high above.

Thus it was startling to come suddenly upon a series of arches thrown across the road, arches of interwoven palm fronds built to celebrate the passing of the King. This May of 1966, Hassan II had made his first royal progress through the South since his accession. His passing along the *Route des Kasbahs* was the reason for the scarlet banners and little clusters of flags we had been seeing everywhere as we came through, a few days behind him. Every school, every kasbah, every loyal household was supposed to hang out at least one flag; I even heard of fines being imposed where none was displayed. But flags, even small ones, cost money. So some of the little douars built triumphal arches of palm branches instead, wherever the royal route passed closest. But now that Moulay Hassan had passed and would not come again, the arches were being scavenged, and dwindling fast. For who in his senses would leave a good palm frond up there, useless, when it was sorely needed to complete a house roof?

Companies and platoons of clouds had been massing for some time, and now they all but filled the sky. A clear rim of green ran around the horizon, sky as green as shallow tropical water. Outlined black against it were the basalt mountain crests, all tilted parallel by the same convulsion of earth. They reared like the bows of a line of ships, all sinking at once by the stern. A shaft of sunlight piercing the clouds picked out a hill ahead, and on it, the town of Ouarzazate.

Ouarzazate

There must always have been some settlement on this town site, for several streams come together here into a respectable oued. But two modern events combined to raise Ouarzazate above the status of just another kasbah: the rise to feudal power of the House of Glaoui, and the need of the French for a supply base for their conquest of the South. Both the Glaoui and the French are gone today, but the town has not lapsed into insignificance; it is a provincial capital and the gateway to one of the most spectacular of the French-built Atlas passes. Furthermore, since reminders of Mahkzen power are never out of place in the Land of Insolence, there is a large royal army garrison. As for the Glaoui, two of their immense kasbahs on the outskirts of town will continue to make admirable film settings, until some other use is found for them.

When we arrived, the King had only recently departed, sweeping on to Marrakesh with everyone of any importance following in his train. A general morning-after mood prevailed, in which there was an element of relief after strain. Flags and banners drooped. At the hotel, houseboys padded about, barefoot at last; even unbuttoned uniforms went unchallenged. The electric pumps whined with exhaustion, water emerged from the tap in a reluctant trickle, and there wasn't a fresh towel to be had. The members of a *Club de Cinéastes,* who had moved out during the royal visit and had just returned, were jabbering in six European languages at a dazed staff.

But soon they found something to train their movie cameras on: a magnificent arch above the main doorway, whose red and green lights had brightened the gala days, was being dismantled. It proved to be a tacky little cardboard structure that threatened repeatedly to fall about the ears of the workmen; no two shouting, gesticulating figures could agree on how to bring the thing down without endangering life; nor did anyone seem willing to stand back out of range. Light bulbs were falling with a splattering crash on the gravel, while the *cinéastes,* delighted and sardonic, filmed the sleazy underside of royalist display.

We joined a group of them in the bar that night. "Tell us about the royal visit," we said.

"A veritable *kermesse!*" ... "Each member of the entourage tried to outrank the others by the size and prestige of his car." ... "I saw a Mercedes 220 stop on a pfennig to let a supercharged Ferrari glide across its bow."

One man, who was also a reporter, said thoughtfully, "But you have not really seen conspicuous consumption until you have been in Black Africa. While I was in Senegal, the President gave an interview about 'the disgrace of the Affluent African.' He called on his compatriots to rid themselves of the values and way of life that colonialism had taught them to admire, and he concluded: 'It is up to the new African man to bring about his own decolonization.' But the effect was a little spoiled when he drove off in a custom-built Alfa Romeo."

"But King Hassan—what was the popular reception here?" I asked. To preserve our own freedom of schedule, we had chosen to follow in his wake rather than become involved in the massive tangle of reservations wherever he was present.

"One saw very little of him, just a hand thrust out the window of a large black car, acknowledging the crowds and the cries of homage. The security regulations were very strict; but I felt there was devotion among the people—

I doubt if they had to be convoked. However, I fancy they will soon be asking each other how much longer they must wait before any tangible improvements in their lot will result from his visit. . . . He is certainly very hard-working: from morning to night, there was a line of officials waiting to be interviewed."

One result of our strategy of moving in the wake of the royal party was that, as we might have known, all the top officials had left with the King for the great review to be held shortly in Marrakesh.

But we set off anyhow to the caïdat the next day, if only so we could say in Rabat that we had tried. It was a Saturday. Moroccans, partial to any excuse that will limit working hours, are apt to tack the very un-Islamic concept of *le weekend* onto their Friday holiday, and so escape with a four-day work week. This Saturday, a spontaneous carnival was being held in the mosque square. The women and children had congregated under an immense olive tree, eating, giving suck, chattering like magpies, while they waited for the men, who were all inside a tent watching a male dancer. I caught a glimpse through the open flap. At the center of a circle of sitting men was the dancer, in just his everyday trousers and a sports shirt, and there was no drumming or even clapping. He danced in place, his eyes half closed, all his muscles rippling and quivering like the leaves of a quaking aspen.

Across the square, lottery prizes were being awarded, and over the loud-speaker came a wheezy recording of a Noel Coward tune of thirty years back. We climbed the steps under the crossed flags of the caïdat, and a plump, comfortably unbuttoned man detached himself from the crowd and hastened after us. Apologetically, he mustered us into the largest office and the most rump-sprung of chairs. Yes, the caïd and the khalifa were both gone to Marrakesh, alas. Of course we realized how the royal visit had instilled new hope in Ouarzazate! Soon, now, perhaps . . . the cement, the hydraulic engineers, the pay for the local workmen that had fallen in arrears, also the payments in grain, which somehow had not arrived. . . .

We did not press him further; it was apparent this recital had recently been poured into important ears. It was also apparent, I thought, that the "new hope" was a little guarded. Thanking him, we rose to go, and Bill mentioned that we had thought of driving out to see the great Kasbah of Taourirt. Our friend came to life at once and announced he would accompany us; he was so obviously delighted at the prospect that we could not demur.

In our car, he began pointing out things he wished us to admire. "Our splendid mosque," he said; but what drew my eye was a magnificent six-foot tribeswoman striding across the square, erect as a queen, apparently oblivious of the weight of two babies strapped one on each shoulder. "Notice over there our new civic laundry," he said; but what I shall always remember is a man standing fully clothed on the laundry-stone and singing lustily while he poured a jerry can of water over himself.

Just outside of town, we overtook a plodding line of camels. Our happy official launched into an account of how indispensable they were; and did we know the legend that the reason they look so august is that they alone know all the hundred names of Allah? Having heard that one innumerable times, I smiled politely. But why, I asked, if they were so indispensable, were there so few about? "I'm sure I've seen at least ten mules to every camel. And— here in the South—almost never a horse! Tell me, why is this?"

"Perhaps Madame does not know how much a camel costs! Several neighbors will own one camel jointly and arrange their plowing schedule accordingly. But the mule—ah, that animal is irreplaceable! He is stronger than a donkey, has more stamina than a horse, can go longer without water, and can subsist without grain—these are the reasons you see mules but no horses amongst us."

I wanted to say that this was all very well, but how could one escape the fact that for every mule, there must sometime, somewhere, have been a mare. . . . But just then a great mound of rock came into sight, an outcrop a third of a mile wide and rising high and sheer above the plain. On it stood Taourirt Kasbah. It looked entirely without plan, a hulking conglomerate of fortress walls and towers massed together within a forty-foot curtain wall, scowling down upon the plain. There was something more than forbidding about it, something very unpleasant. Perhaps it was that the whole thing, rock base and citadel alike, was an unseemly rose pink. Our companion watched our faces while we took it in.

"There it is—just one of a score or more of the Glaoui's kasbahs! You find it romantic, the story of the 'Fox of the Atlas'? Or do you know of him as the Black Eagle? No doubt his story makes exciting reading!"

"You remember him well, then?"

"Does one forget—in only ten years—the man who extorted more taxes than any sultan would dare to ask? Who took our women, and made gifts of any he did not wish for himself—who kept slaves by the thousand and bred more every year? Against the law of the land, he *owned* our villages, because he had the fighting men to make us acknowledge him. He would build a kasbah like this, entrust it to some relative, and order him to extract everything that could be wrung from nearby villages. The French looked the other way, for he was useful to them—ah! how useful! In my youth, there was a saying: 'Morocco is a cow; France holds her by the tail, while the Glaoui milks her.' He claimed more than half the water rights throughout his enormous domain, and woe to the fellah who stole some drops destined for the Glaoui's olive groves."

All this time we had been climbing the road to Taourirt, and now left the car and stood in an alley within the Kasbah. I did not know what to say in response to his account of the Glaoui's power and rapacity, for under the anger of his tone there lurked, unmistakably, a hint of pride. "He was a daring man! Perhaps even a great man, in his fearful way?" I ventured.

" 'Lord of the Atlas'. . . ." His voice was ambiguous. "It may be there is a time and a season for such men. Bism'illah. But one thing is certain: his time is done." He pointed to a section of wall from which all adobe facing was gone, and rubble between the stones was washing out. Wind and night frosts make short work of an exposed wall like this. "See here, where only cactus holds the stones together. Like all Glaoui property, Taourirt now belongs to the state. But, while there is no use for it, we do not inquire too closely who finds temporary shelter here."

The powdery dust we walked in was the same unhealthy pink as the Kasbah walls, and at each step it rose and settled on us. A pink dog sidled away at our approach, and a turkey, pink to his wattles, scuttled before us. Suddenly a small girl materialized in our path.

"*Argent, M'sie.*" It was neither a question nor quite a demand, but rather a statement of fact. We had it, she wanted it. As simple as that. Our companion looked hard at the dust-caked, pointed little face. It is always embarrassing to a Moroccan when foreigners with him see a child begging. In the city, they say only riffraff from the country fail to train their children; in the country, they say only city people have lost their pride. After a struggle with himself, our functionary reached for his purse. As we turned back to the car, he muttered, "It is a true saying—'An empty sack cannot stand upright.'"

CHAPTER SEVEN

MARRAKESH

Though there are no true cities behind the Atlas, the South has its capital, larger than any other city save Casablanca, and as important a trading center as Fez: Marrakesh.[1] It lies, not behind the mountains, but in *Maroc Utile,* and all the Atlas passes converge upon it. By the same token, major roads ray out from it to all the other cities. Its character is that of the South. Backed up against an august line of snowbound peaks, embedded in a hundred thousand palms whose branches roof the city, enclosed by miles of rust-red battlements, it is a man-made oasis. By order of its founders nine hundred years ago, underground conduits were laid, deep-dug and rock-lined, to bring Atlas waters to the city. Where there had been nothing but stony, sun-baked plain, the forest of palms grew up. And high above their roof of green, there rose a single, uniquely lovely minaret.

Marrakesh begs to be described in superlatives. It is at once the most alluring and the most raffish of Moroccan cities. It is the home of many of the most expert traders in the realm, and also of some of the finest con artists anywhere. Long before Winston Churchill made it famous, the Mamounia was one of the finest hotels in Africa, set in vast private gardens at the edge of the medina. The medina is the largest in the country—two and a half square miles of close-packed souks, palaces and hovels, and lanes tangled like eels in a sack. I could go on with the superlatives and contrasts: a winter climate of tropical luxuriance, less than an hour from ski slopes where Moroccans in burnous and turban shoulder their skis among the zippered Europeans. . . . But this is all somewhat beside the main point: Marrakesh is a prime commercial center. Long before there were roads, it was a vital

1. The common pronunciation gives the name three syllables, but Moroccans pronounce it *Marráksh,* with the stress on the last syllable. It means "Morocco City."

entrepôt on the caravan routes from sub-Saharan Africa, and so was bound to be a locus of political power.

A line of camel breeders founded the city, desert men who veiled their faces against sand and glare. Fanatic converts to Islam, these Almoravids became the first native dynasty of "warrior saints." (Their name derives from the root word for "holy.") After the line of Idriss had died out in Fez, the country had begun to slip back into its pre-Islamic condition: an agglomerate of small, pagan, Berber republics. The Almoravids were both zealous religious reformers and very capable fighters. Answering a call for help from the Muslim princes of Andalusia, they repulsed the Christian advance in Spain and spread their African domain to Algiers. But after only eighty years, their asceticism had so far succumbed to the sweet uses of luxury that they became targets for the next wave of warrior saints.

The new conquerors were led by an astonishing figure, a sort of Savonarola of the Atlas. Ibn Toumert went from his mountain tent first to Cordoba to study the pure faith, then to Damascus and Cairo.[2] He returned to the Atlas calling for jihad against the corrupt winebibbers in Marrakesh, and his followers poured down out of the mountains, razed the city, and set him upon the throne.

Under this dynasty, the faith was reformed once more, and the empire extended to Libya. A temporary peace descended; it was said then that "a woman or a Jew might safely travel from Castille to Tripoli"—which tells us something about more usual conditions. These Almohads were also great and distinctive builders. But—such is the nature of Moroccan history—nothing of their work has survived but three great minarets: the Giralda of Seville, the Tour Hassan in Rabat, and the exquisite Koutoubia of Marrakesh, the classic tower that welcomes you to the city from afar.

Medina

The city built by these two lines of warrior saints—the medina of today—is encircled by eleven miles of red battlements (as any Marrakshi will tell you, "the longest, and tallest, and thickest of any city") that run without break or interruption, save for eight arched gateways giving access to the teeming life within. Some of these, like Bab Aguenaou ("Gate of the Guineans") are very splendid; others are humbler, like the Thursday Market Gate, where the camel market takes place, a scene compounded of dust, noise, evil odors, and the vicious biting those animals indulge in when too closely crowded. Be-

2. This was the era of the greatest of Muslim philosophers, Al Ghazzali, called the Aquinas of Islam. The centers of theological study were all stressing the need to purge pagan accretions from the pure vision of Allah.

tween the gates on the outside, at almost any time of day or night, community life goes forward in rich variety.

The wall, sectioned off at regular intervals by great jutting square towers, is like a series of stages against the backdrop of rufous masonry. On any one stage, several actions unfold simultaneously: a bicycle repairman, all his equipment about him on the ground, is roused to fury by the flying feet of boys playing soccer; a vendor of patent medicines drifts uncertainly toward a knot of cardsharps beckoning to him; little girls playing hopscotch with babies strapped to their backs accidentally topple the pyramid of little oranges a man has just finished piling up with loving care. Donkeys cross and recross the scene continuously, their riders seated far back on the hips, where the spine is not so sharp, or sitting sideways and drumming rhythmically with both heels. From one pannier protrudes the quivering black nose of a very young kid. And in and out among them all, numberless urchins dart between men's legs, looking for cigarette butts or a carelessly held coin. All at once, the whole scene is obscured in a cloud of red dust as one of the great auto-buses roars along the road thirty feet away. On its roof, amid the bicycles, baggage, bundles of trussed hens, and bales of fodder, a bewildered ram, with all four legs tied to the rails, braces himself against the lurching. It looks unlikely that he will arrive at his destination in condition to sire any tooth-some young lambs for some time to come.

I don't know whether or not the darker skins of Marrakesh have anything to do with the fact that this city on the caravan routes from below the Sahara was always one of the prime slave markets. The range of skin color seemed to me fuller and richer here than anywhere else, a beautiful orchestration of tones, all the way from bronze to raisin brown and shining black. There is something else about the Marrakshi: their gift for concentrated, unabashed staring. It must be deeply satisfying to them, in spite of the number of tourists they see year in and year out, or they wouldn't put their hearts into it as they do. There's nothing hostile about it; it is simply their cheapest form of entertainment.

The medina is so large that we thought to get an over-all view of it first by car, which proved to be a fearful mistake. The streets became progressively narrower, until we were pinning pedestrians to the walls; and by then there was of course no faintest possibility of turning around. Anyway, we had lost all sense of direction and all hope of getting to a gate. Youths leaned in the window to get a better look at us, each more importunate than the last about guiding us; when we said we wanted nothing so much as to get out of there, they shook with delighted laughter and leaned affectionately on the fenders. Finally, it was a little boy who agreed to run ahead and clear a path until we were in sight of a gate. And run he did, even though from time to time Bill called to him not to burst his lungs, and to come back to retrieve a sandal that had flown off. His sense of importance seemed to keep him at full gallop—

or else he thought the faster he ran the more we'd pay him. The only trouble with parking outside the medina, which we always did thereafter, was that we had each time to run the gauntlet of touts in the outer rim of souks, where the art of importuning tourists has been raised to a fine pitch.

In time, we found a little-used gate giving directly on the souks where work was done for native entrepreneurs. Among the ironworkers, we came on a sooty trio. A child of about seven pumped an enormous bellows and a slightly older boy shaped incandescent lumps on his anvil and tossed them, with a deft flick of his wrist, to drop precisely at the master craftsman's feet. With four strokes of his hammer, the craftsman closed the still red-hot rod into a link in the fast-growing iron grille before him. It was all a smooth, swift, sure chain of judgments and movements. Boys and man alike bore themselves with a jocular grimness that suited their blackened faces and the fierce heat.

While we stood there, a wild-eyed disheveled man appeared, beating on a little drum and demanding contributions from each souk in turn—in all likelihood, a deranged fellow claiming to be a marabout. He jibbered at me and got no response but a startled stare. So he shrugged, and began picking over the discarded ends of iron lying about the artisan's feet. He must have made off with more than the market would bear, for the workman called him back good-naturedly, and subtracted half his take.

Not everyone is even-tempered. I saw trouble brewing between three boys making fine-tooth combs from an evil-smelling mound of hooves and horns on the ground between them. They worked fast, using their toes to steady the gouge or one end of the knife-like saw. Two of the boys were scowling. One tossed the little blade carelessly and cut a deep nick in the other's shin. The hurt boy's shaven head flew up, his eyes flaring wide. He grasped his chisel and took deliberate aim. On the instant, the third child stepped between them and, gazing steadily from one to the other, forced upon them an interval to come to their senses. Then, still without a word spoken, he swabbed a rag across the cut and stooped to hand the injured boy the delicate little saw.

A little farther on, Bill stood transfixed before a woodworker who, with a set of motions too rapid for me to understand, was turning out little carved handles for kebab skewers at the rate of a pair a minute. The wood was poplar—the poor-man's wood. The craftsman sat on the ground; in front of him, a slender bit of wood spun in place, braced by one set of toes. The other foot and one hand guided the chisel. All the while, the free hand swept what looked like a violin bow back and forth without a pause. Bill murmured to himself, "I never thought to see a bowstring-lathe in operation in my lifetime." The finished length of wood, rather like a spool-bedstead post, went up against the chisel; the wood snapped in two, and another pair of handles fell onto the pile.

It was the Friday morning scene that I liked best, the hour just before the weekly mosque service. Shutters came clattering down on most of the souks, and the usual din of hammers and shuttles and muleteers' shouts began to abate. As the noon hour approached, the crowds thinned out, even if few went to the mosque, and a mood of respite prevailed. Then a scribe, sitting quietly in a shady corner, would read a letter aloud to a woman who hung on every word, her eyes anxious above her veil. Once I saw a man sleeping beautifully within a large cardboard box he had mounted, like a howdah, on his donkey's back. His head lolled with each step of the little creature, but his face wore a look of peace. Clearly, the donkey could be trusted to get him home.

Friday morning was the time, too, for the free dispensary, where women waited with two or even three babies packed on their backs like nestlings. Across the way was a dentist's sign, and under it dozed the dentist himself, his bare black feet propped on the stool for his patients. Then I saw an official-looking man delivering what I took to be rent slips to the few souk-holders still about. Each recipient examined his slip with a few quiet ejaculations; some who weren't sure of their reading conferred with a neighbor. It was clearly bad news, but—I gathered from the resigned hunching of shoulders—there was little to be done about it.

Outside a medersa buried deep in the medina, we stood watching men gather before the mosque. The serenity of the empty, beautiful medersa we had just visited was still upon us when a smell of smoldering rubbish stung my nose, and I saw, across the square, an attendant whose business it appeared to be to rake the smoking pile until it was consumed. A cripple approached him and, when a coin had changed hands, was allowed to mount the pile and dig about within it, and pocket any useful detritus he could find.

Men were going into the mosque, and we prepared to move on. Bill crushed out a cigarette beneath his foot. Quick as a flash, an urchin shot forward, retrieved it from the cobbles and puffed hard on it to revive it. An august-looking fellow who was passing a few yards away turned and advanced upon the boy, who by now had hidden the cigarette end in his armpit. The personage shouted at the child; and the sly, cross-eyed little boy stared impudently back. I wondered how long he would have to hold his pose, blandly shaking his head while the live butt burned through his rags. The man raised his arm in a threatening gesture, and the imp jumped aside. Then, to restore his insouciance, he seized on an orange lying in the gutter and began dribbling it before him like a soccer ball. I was almost sure I saw a wisp of smoke curling from his armpit.

Necropolis

A way to keep Morocco's early history in mind is to picture a seesawing of power between the two Imperial Cities, Fez and Marrakesh. Allot the ninth and tenth centuries to Fez, with the first Islamic conquerors; then the next two centuries to Marrakesh, with the two lines of warrior saints. Return again to Fez for the great Merinid epoch, roughly the fourteenth and fifteenth centuries. Finally, swing back for the last time to Marrakesh with the Saadians. You can also sum it up in a series of physical images: the Tomb of Idriss and the Qarawiyin, at Fez; the red walls of Marrakesh, and the lovely Almohad minaret; the glorious Merinid medersas, and their tombs on the hillside above Fez. This sequence brings us to the sixteenth-century Saadian Tombs.

Like all western Muslim architecture, they give no hint on the outside of what lies within. The tradition is entirely different from that of Europe. No mosque is built to be admired, like a cathedral, from a distance. No beauty is discovered until you have stepped inside the courtyard; and even there, the decoration only prefigures the splendor of the prayer hall. So it is with these tombs. They appear to be merely three little green-roofed pavilions of brown stucco, set in a garden of oleanders and hibiscus.

But stand in one of the doorways looking in over the low barrier, and you are encompassed. This is the final peak of Moorish art, recalling the Alhambra in style, but on an appealing and intimate scale. The columns are pale marble; so are the simple slabs sunk in the floor to mark each grave, some of them infant-size. From carved alabaster capitals, the arches spring straight upward before their curve begins, which gives them the long-necked line characteristic of this period. The walls, above a dado of soft-colored tile, are carved plasterwork too rich and intricate to convey in words. Think, rather, of the complexities of snow crystals, or of a chiseled honeycomb, or of cell structures seen through a microscope. These walls are white or ivory or gold, depending on how much sunlight is at that moment bathing them, for high windows have been cunningly placed to bring each wall to a blaze of sunlit gold at some period of the day.

I could not take this rich diet for very long at a time. One pavilion was enough, and then I would withdraw to the garden to sit for a while under a rose tree, smelling the hedges of marjoram and watching a stork plane overhead and clamber into his untidy nest on some distant rooftop. Sometimes snatches of chanting drifted to me from a mosque nearby, and I thought how Gregorian it sounded. Once, a pair of women made a devout, tomb-kissing pilgrimage through one of the pavilions. Since they stepped over the low barrier without hesitation, I assumed they were—or believed they were—remote Saadian descendants. From my bench, I was watching them orient to Mecca and begin their prostrations, when a third woman appeared, unveiled and very brisk. She must have been a public-monuments official, for she hustled the worshipers unceremoniously to their feet and back behind the barrier.

Sitting there among princely tombs, the Preacher's theme filled my mind: All is vanity. The palace of Abou the Golden, who built this mausoleum to the glory of his line, lay in rubble a hundred yards away. Fifty years of civil war followed the last Saadian. They were good fighters, this last Marrakesh dynasty, and halted the Ottoman advance across North Africa. Sultan Abou conquered Timbuctoo, but all the gold of Guinea brought no peace, and for the usual reason: it went straight into the coffers of rulers and their viziers. Moroccan dynasts have shown more genius for building and for war than for governing.

No sultan more fully bore this out than the first great Alaouite, a contemporary of Louis XIV. Moulay Ismaïl was as mad and terrible a man as Caligula, but he was effective along the lines of his two obsessions: driving out the Europeans who had been colonizing both coasts, and building at Meknes a new Imperial City to outshine Fez and Marrakesh. He turned his hubris on Marrakesh and razed everything that might compete with his "Moorish Versailles." For this megalomaniac who so hated the Christian was nonetheless strangely fascinated by European rulers. He sent embassies to the French and British kings, urging them to convert to Islam. To the Sun King he offered a concubine from his harem of five hundred, and demanded in exchange the hand of Louis' daughter. (There is, unhappily, no record of the latter's reply.)

Romantic renegades from all over Europe were attracted to his glitter. He transformed Meknes, which had been a Berber village before he built his Mechaouar, into an insane grandeur of acres of lakes, miles of stables, granaries the size of any normal palace, an inner city for his 40,000 slaves and another entire city for his Black Guard.

He purged the country of intruding westerners, and he realized his great Mechaouar. If he had been equally effective at governing, he might have saved Morocco from the decline that lay ahead. But after fifty-five years of wars, building, and taxes, he died, returning his people to the civil chaos from which he had rescued them, and to renewed penetration by Europeans. And today his Moorish Versailles is a thousand acres of ruins. The cycles of Moroccan history are like a frieze of arabesques: themes of conquest are followed by relapse; superb effort tapers into passivity, brilliance into slow decline—the familiar motifs appear, submerge, recur, and close the cycle where it began.

Djemma

For many people, natives and foreigners alike, Marrakesh means one thing above all others—the notorious, the raffish, the highly entertaining Djemma el Fna. It is a very large open square in the medina where almost everything is going on at once, a circus of several dozen rings. It is also a good place to keep your wallet in your inside breast pocket and your wits about you. Always teeming with people in from the country to do business, it is their Sodom and Gomorrah and quite irresistible, even though they can be swindled there as promptly and thoroughly as any foreigner. There are conjurors and acrobats, soothsayers and storytellers, snake charmers, sword swallowers, and vendors of potions and philters guaranteed to work the will of jealous women or impotent men. It is said that there are no tastes too bizarre for the procurers of the Djemma to satisfy. The word *djemma* means "congregation" or "assembly"—a mosque is a djemma—and *Fna* means "dead." But there is disagreement on the significance of the whole name; it may mean "Place of Execution," "Assembly of Sinners," or of the "Spirits of the Dead." The interpretation I like best, which has little or no linguistic justification, was given by an Italian writer as "Place of the Nimble Get-Away."

On the edge of the square, where makeshift stalls sell all kinds of food and gimcracks and itinerant barbers ply their trade, we joined a rapt crowd about a storyteller. He was handsome and sly, and wore a beautiful saffron-yellow turban. So expressive was his miming, one did not need Arabic to be swept into his story. His fable had to do with grossness and the tricks that impudence can play upon it, and his characters were a fat, lopsided grapefruit and a squad of nimble walnuts and little tangerines. The dwarf nuts were sent ahead to prepare an ambush; the stealthy tangerines tormented the lumbering, pompous old grapefruit until our sympathies veered to the victim of so much impudence. (Here the storyteller held us suspended while his boy made the rounds to collect coins.) Then the saturnine face under the bright turban changed to pure buffoon; he ripped off some bawdy quip and made us laugh over the humiliation of that bloated victim, which, being overripe, burst with a satisyingly vulgar splatter on the cobblestones.

As we all broke up and moved away, a flock of tumbling, cartwheeling child acrobats encircled us. In shrimp-pink or livid-green baggy trousers, they blocked our way with their swaying pyramids. As soon as their act was done, their faces showed pitiful weariness, and every line of their small bodies sagged. We paid our way out of this congestion and joined another circle, where a man with wooden splints on both arms lay flat upon the ground, his head covered in a bag, thongs tight around his legs. Standing above him, a nasty-looking fellow was casting a spell; the crowd was noticeably disinclined to get very close, but watched with slack jaws as the body on the ground writhed. As we backed away, I felt something pulling at my skirt, and looked down into the gimlet eyes of a withered little monkey. In an instant, four more creatures jumped from their attendant's shoulders and joined the first in a wild little dance. Before we knew the dance was over, the monkeys were at our fingers, scratching gently for coins.

The water seller on the Djemma makes most of his take posing for photographs of his big hat and jingling harness of little brass cups. Since everyone gawking on the Djemma is by definition ripe for plunder, whether you want a drink or a picture or neither, you pay him to move out of your way. And now before you, sitting in voluminous black on a small stool, is a very dark woman with a face as wrinkled as a dried fig, her client of the moment a distressed middle-aged man. He hands her a big lump of amber; she gazes closely into it, presses it to her forehead. An assistant places the client's hands upon her shoulders. While the anxious man leans close to hear her mumbling, she passes the amber egg several times across the nape of her neck. When her mumbling ceases, the client's lips move, rehearsing her instructions. But when he reaches to take back the stone, he finds her fingers closed upon it and her eyes fixed ominously on his. Chin sinking to his breast, he shuffles off.

Wild drumming breaks out above all the other din as some black Gnaoua ("Guinean") dancers spring into the air, snap their jaws, roll the whites of their eyes, and rattle their iron castanets. But the Djemma can quickly become too much. At this point, our mood broke and we longed for quiet, restraint, and a place to sit down. Just beyond the square, the perfect lines of the Koutoubia minaret rose in classic elegance, presiding, as it has for centuries, over all the drama and chicanery of the Djemma—the sort of contrast that is of the very essence of Marrakesh.

Two hundred feet the slender tower rises above the teeming, reeking life of the city. Most of the tile facing has fallen away, leaving only touches here and there of soft greens and blues. But this only frees the eye to enjoy all the better the proportions and the fine alternation of carving and restful, undecorated stone. This is no culmination of Hispano-Moorish intricacy; this is the twelfth century, and a work of the same purity and simplicity that the Almohads meant to restore to the faith. Each side of the square tower allows a restrained crescendo of decoration as it rises: first, only a single blind arch and two narrow, fretted lancets; then, thirty feet of warm tan stone, texture its only ornament; above, a slightly more elaborate stage, carved in deeper relief and throwing bolder shadows. I found an orange tree to sit under in the garden at the Koutoubia's feet, and let my pleasure sweep upward to the triumphant openness of the muezzin's gallery, all interlacing arches and full-strength shadows. Resting lightly on it, the little cupola with its mast and balls of gold carried the eye finally to the empty sky.

The original Koutoubia mosque is nothing now, thanks to Moulay Ismaïl, but rows of column stumps. The foreigner is not welcome to wander there, for it is still sacred ground. I kept my distance from old men lecturing to dusty groups at their feet, and from a pair of evangelists who raked their listeners with accusing eyes. A little apart, against a broken column, a proto-typic figure rested: curved back against the stone, arms and hooded head resting on drawn-up knees. He was a Moroccan, waiting; for what, not even he could say.

Mellah

We had glanced once or twice into the old Jewish mellah; it was a dispiriting place, easier not to think about. But thoughts about the remaining Jewish population continued to trouble me, especially when I began to chafe under what I called the meretriciousness of Marrakesh—the souvenir sellers, the self-conscious restaurants with Moorish-Roxy decor, the night club called the Atlas, which advertised, *"Tous les Samedi soirs Les Bip-Bips,"* the artful exoticism of hotel gardens, where astonishing birds burst out of thickets of bamboo and cascades of bougainvillea. One might easily sink into a torpor beside the swimming pool, listening to the tinkle of glasses and smelling the scented suntan oil. I was beginning to understand quite well how those ascetic warrior saints had lost track of their mission once they had finished building their artificial oasis.

So one day we set forth for the mellah. The name is also the word for salt and is said to derive from one of the offices that Jews were compelled to carry out: pickling in brine the heads of the sultan's enemies. In Morocco, as in every Muslim country, Jews have lived under harassments and penalties, but there is also another side of the picture. The Koranic guarantee of freedom of religion to "People of the Book" has prevented any such long-term and sys-tematic persecutions as the Christian West devised. The Muslim record is not good; but it does not include an Inquisition, or a Holocaust.

Arab and Jew are blood brothers, which has much to do with the claim by the younger faith that it supersedes the older. Arabs trace their descent from Abraham's son Ishmael, banished, according to *Genesis,* to the Arabian desert. Other Biblical characters, from Solomon to Moses and Jesus, are honored as forebears and great teachers. (Hence the many Arab names drawn from the Old Testament—Brahim, Yacoub, Youssef, Suleiman.) Muslim doc-trine has borrowed freely from Judaism; both religions contain survivals from their similar origins in a tribal, desert society. Mohammed the Prophet is believed to have been transported by an angel to Jerusalem and to have re-ceived, on the Rock of Abraham's sacrifice, the message of the Koran. But when Mohammed claimed to be the promised Messiah, the Jews furiously rejected the idea; Mohammed insisted they had tampered with the Torah, removing passages that would establish his identity.

Thus the antagonism between the two peoples has very ancient roots, and many of the elements of a blood feud between relatives. What put the Jews at a dreadful disadvantage was that they had no asylum to flee to from persecution, and no state to retaliate on their behalf. Now that exactly the reverse is true, with a Jewish state in existence, the tragic consequences of the ancient tension are being acted out.

The early Arab conquerors found many Jewish communities in Morocco. While verbally honoring the Koranic guarantee, the conquerors immediately imposed strict segregation and numerous penalties: Jews must be in the mellah by sundown; they might not carry arms or ride a horse; they must wear distinctive clothing and pay a special tax; they were not to be allowed any part in government. The Law held that they were in Morocco on the sultan's sufferance—they were not true citizens, but protégés. And when the sultan was *not* well disposed, a number of spiteful limitations could be invoked: they must not raise a hand in self-defense, except in their own homes; they must go barefoot outside the mellah, could not use saddles on their mules, and must carry their dead to their cemetery at a run. At such times, religious toleration must have seemed a very empty phrase indeed. But there was also the other swing of the pendulum. The Sephardic refugees from Spain were accorded high respect, and the era from the fourteenth through the sixteenth centuries has been called the Golden Age of Moorish Jewry. They won recognition in banking and commerce, in intellectual life, and in the arts. Their reputation for good workmanship became proverbial, so that to this day every refined piece of gold- or silverwork is assumed to have come from the hand of a Jew.

The West's economic penetration of nineteenth-century Morocco deeply involved the Jews. Thousands of them rushed to embrace the security of a foreign nationality when the great powers' consuls in Tangier were selling protection. Moreover, as dealings with the West increased, Arab merchants found it wise to employ Jews, who were relatively more familiar with European ways, as their own agents. Thus a good many Jews became wealthy, and often expatriate as well.

The predictable backlash followed. But it was the mellahs that suffered, not the superficial crust of powerful Jews. Four hundred were massacred in the Tetouan mellah, their leaders dragged through the street at the tails of horses. Other mellahs were subjected to capricious visitations of savagery, plundering, and abduction of women.[3]

In 1863, Sir Moses Montefiore, having won permission to study the condi-

3. The desire of the Moorish male for the forbidden Jewish woman, like the attraction of white men for Negro women, seems a persistent one. Even today, stories of abductions continue to come out of the Casablanca mellah.

tions under which his Moroccan brethren lived, made a public plea on their behalf to the sultan. In replying to the distinguished foreigner, the sultan explained that any attempt by him to better the mellahs might only provoke neighboring Muslims to violence. But the Jews of Europe had been awakened, and help began to pour in for mellah schools and welfare agencies. By the end of the century, though the bulk of Jewry still lived precariously and in poverty, most of them were better-educated than all but a few Muslims. This was observed with rancor by the Muslim majority, and inevitably associated in their minds with European interference in their country.

Then came the interference par excellence: the Protectorate. While this was rapidly becoming a naked attempt to annex the country, Arabs everywhere were becoming disillusioned by what the West was doing. In the Near East, arbitrary and irrational boundaries were drawn, and Mandates set up— none of which the Arabs had been led to expect from the smooth promises of World War I years. And now, in Morocco, the French were protecting the Jews, advancing the educated to positions of responsibility, giving their children access to French private schools while denying it to Muslim children. Each mellah now became largely self-governing and, with its own taxes and welfare budget, achieved better living conditions than the Muslim poor enjoyed. More and more, the prosperous Jews embraced a western way of life, moved into the Villes Nouvelles, and took part in the Protectorate administration. All this looked, to the average Moroccan, like one more case of manipulation by the perfidious West.

Then came the *coup de grâce*. Palestine, the home of Arabs for thirteen centuries, became the state of Israel, with clear support from the West. Even Moroccans, never very strong pan-Arabists, saw here an insult to all Arabs. And at home, in the ensuing struggle for independence, Jews collaborated with the French. (Why, indeed, would they not?) The Istiqlal now took an openly anti-Semitic position. A young Moroccan told me, "When we were called on by our cell to take part in some sabotage plan, we would slip through the streets looking for Jews on the way. Just for good measure, we would lob a few grenades into the mellah as we ran. . . . The worst insult we knew was to call a man a Jew." Two serious pogroms took place. There was good reason to anticipate massacre on a huge scale as soon as the French were driven out.

It never occurred, thanks in good part to the firmness of Mohammed V. He appealed for sanity, pointing out that a mass flight of the best-educated segment of the population would seriously endanger the country. Mehdi ben Barka supported him: "To let the Jews go is to cut our veins and drain out the lifeblood." The King pleaded with "his loyal Jewish subjects" not to succumb to panic and reminded them that, even when the country had been nominally under the Vichy regime, he had refused to apply the Nazi racist decrees. He awarded Cabinet and National Assembly posts to Jews. But the exodus got under way—after all, who knew how long Mohammed could control el Istiqlal? When, in 1959, political pressures obliged the King to join the militantly anti-Zionist Arab League, the Jews' fears seemed justified. Thousands sought escape but found exit permits held up on flimsy excuses. Hazardous and clandestine escape routes began operating, and there was a stampede of Jews to the ports. A ship lying to at night off the rocky cliffs near Casa sank with a full complement of passengers. But, despite all the obstacles and tragedies, the exodus accelerated.[4]

Morocco has been one of the very few Arab lands whose official policy is peaceful coexistence with its Jews. The King sends royal delegates to the High Holydays, and frequently receives leaders of Casa's Jewish community. Hassan was the only head of an Arab state to move decisively and effectively to suppress violence in the wake of the June War of 1967.[5] He put a stop to an Istiqlal boycott of Jewish businesses and imprisoned the secretary-general of the labor movement for talk about "Zionist domination of the nerve centers of the Moroccan state." I grant that the King may also have been motivated by the need to prevent a *rapprochement* between two wings of the opposition —it is the first time I know of when labor and the Istiqlal have made common cause. But he spoke with a realist's conviction, I believe, when he said soon thereafter that "Moroccans must learn to distinguish between real problems and artificial ones. The real ones are dams, ports, and schools; the artificial ones are those that cause us to lose time."

But, within ten years after the French withdrawal, the Jewish population had dropped from one-third million (the largest in any Arab country) to 65,000. Given the precarious state of politics, the steady emigration is not surprising; nor is the continued effort of all who wish to remain to secure French passports, Three-quarters of them all are now concentrated in Casa, poised, as it were, at the very edge of the country.

In the Marrakesh mellah, only a few hundred Jews remain, mingling with the poorest of the Muslim poor. Necessity has broken down segregation as nothing else could. On Saturday mornings, a few old men in black kaftans and yarmulkes still make their way to the synagogue. Few of the young remain, and those who do have lost touch with their elders. They are not happy, and complain that they have been overeducated for the only jobs open to them, and list instances where they have been passed over in favor of a Muslim.

This mellah is a grim place of dark passageways and crumbling houses,

4. Many of the well-to-do who escaped went, not to Israel, but to France. Despite the claims of the Istiqlal, much of Moroccan Jewry is not Zionist.
5. Though, as a member of the Arab League, he was in duty bound to furnish troops at this time, somehow or other, none of them ever reached the scene of those six days' chaotic action. In any case, Hassan had designated only a few thousand troops to fight Israel; the bulk of his army he kept at home to *protect* his Jews.

where families of eight or ten are jammed into a single room. The only home of one old woman is a wooden box, four feet by two. One souk's entire display is six eggs, three cakes of soap, and some withered fruit. A cross-legged cobbler, working in the middle of an alley, wears a torn old garment whose original color can no longer be distinguished. A Jewish pharmacy consists of an old man squatting beside a pile of herbs under a sign in French: "Guaranteed to cure." But most of these sad people are not Jews. For the first time, there is an alternative for Moroccan Jewry.[6]

"Picasso Berbère"

Like most visitors who become devoted to Morocco, we wanted a Berber rug, and preferred an old one for the sake of its bolder colors and more primitive designs. Old rugs are scarce now, and all the more likely to be overpriced. But then, anything a tourist wants is going to be overpriced to begin with, and will probably remain so, unless he has developed a capacity to engage in a long matching of wits and wills. We doubted very much that we would do well in the necessary ritual of retreats and renewed engagements; at the same time, we knew that nothing so confounds the Moroccan's sense of the seemly as the American's constraint and ineptness in the performance of this ritual. I think even an Arab rug merchant doesn't really enjoy taking a foreigner as much as he enjoys the fencing that in time culminates in a good sale. We had no hope of being good at it, but we did know a few things: we must take our time; we must have no money on our persons when we began any dickering, to ensure that we would have to retire and think it over; and we must show no interest at first in any rug that appealed to us.

Plunging again into the souks, we entered a street lined with banners. Or so it seemed. They were, in fact, coils of vivid wool hanging from poles across the lane, scarlet and saffron and black, deep blue and white and green. Bars of shadow fell across them from a rush lattice above and striped all the figures moving from stall to stall and the merchants squatting beside their scales.

On our way to the fonduk we had been told was reliable, we passed a weaver and his apprentice, one on each side of their wide loom. A typical Berber blanket was growing there—bands of strong primary colors across the warp, and a little tufted geometric pattern knotted in at intervals. The master weaver moved from center to edge with effortless speed, drawing lengths of black or white yarn for the design from a fluffy mass in his left

6. I have drawn much of my information from issues, too numerous to cite, of *The Jewish Chronicle* (London: The Jewish Chronicle, Ltd., *passim*), and *The American Jewish Year Book* (New York: The American Jewish Committee, *passim*).

hand. A light brush of his fingertips told him how many strands of warp to draw up. His movements were fluid as a dancer's, and as perfectly synchronized: he worked the treadles, caught the shuttle, banged the woof with mighty strokes, knotted in his design, and sent the shuttle flying back. But then would come a painful pause while the apprentice peered and struggled with his bits of yarn. Watching closely, I saw that the boy was nearly blind.

The Jew with whom we began operations in the fonduk was wonderfully plausible. He justified his preposterous prices with nice interpretations of the symbols woven into the rugs: "See, here you have the ancestors of the woman who wove this beauty—you note these small black stick figures? She is out to remind her bridegroom-to-be that her lineage includes these several members of the sultan's Black Guard. . . ." That little rug interested us immediately, so we shook our heads at it. But he must have detected some gleam in our eyes, for he did not have that rug carried off; it lay tossed a little to the side. I tried my best to keep my eyes from straying back to it, and asked to see a large one with barbaric colors. I turned back the tufts, pointing out how badly the colors had faded, and then pushed it away. Soon we sat among piles of discards, and it was time for him to offer us tea.

Berber rugs have long been a specialty of the Atlas tribes living on the slopes above Marrakesh, and all but the biggest modern ones still come from looms built onto the supporting poles of tents or huts. The art of knotting in the designs is taught to little girls while their fingers are still small and deft enough to outpace larger hands. The woman in charge of a loom will have as many as six children working all at once on one rug. She is so expert that she carries the pattern in her head, while the children work from little paper sketches. Each tribe follows its own distinctive mode and, until recently, made its own dyes as well. I wish someone knowledgeable would study the affinity between American Indian and Berber weaving. The best Indian work is more sophisticated; these Berber rugs are primitive in both color and design, and shaggier because of the tufting. But the same symbols are common to both, the same skill and charm with asymmetry, the same intuitive flair.

On this first visit to the fonduk, we refused a third glass of tea and rose, saying we had seen nothing we wished to buy. The Jew knew the last impression our eyes must take with us and reached quickly for the little rug we had both liked: "Now you must look once more at this little *'Picasso Berbère.'* Forty thousand francs is a pure giveaway for such a work of art." (This was about $80.) I noticed he had already lopped off 5,000 francs since he had first displayed the rug, but the figure was still far from credible. Now he insisted on showing us the firm's receipt book, to establish their reliability. And there, large as life, was the signature that was expected to make us putty in his hands: El Laurans again, alias Peter O'Toole. . . .

Two days later, the Jew saw us—ostensibly passing his doorway en route elsewhere. Quickly, he accosted us, "Today will be the day, M'sieur, Madame!

Business is so bad now, you will find yourselves my first clients of the day!"
We indicated that we would not object to looking at another rug or two. This
time, Bill had traveler's checks in his pocket. And this time, as soon as we had
settled on the divan and the heaps of rugs had begun to pile up at our feet, the
Arab shop owner joined us and the Jew silently retreated into the background.
On our previous visit, the owner had observed us from an inner room but
addressed us only in greeting and farewell. His taking over now indicated
that the climax of our ritual was in sight.

When we had discussed the poorness of the tourist season, the lamentable
state of trade, and the high level of discrimination that his favorite clients
enjoyed, the small *"Picasso Berbère"* was unfolded before us. The Arab
mentioned 30,000 francs. We offered half. He shrugged and twitched the
little rug out of sight. We began to be sure we would never get it for the
20,000 we had determined not to exceed. His next move was to introduce a
little rug we had never seen before. It was beguilingly gay: eight geometric
improvisations ran in a band around the edges and converged in the center
in a harmonious blaze of color. The Arab, quite correctly, counted on our
surprise to confuse us into bidding on two rugs instead of one. He ordered
the two boys standing by to hold up both rugs together.

"Now, you see what is really right for you! Note how this little *'Couche-
Soleil Mauresque'* complements the other! Agree, M'sieur, Madame, they will
not be happy apart." He was right, we agreed, conferring in English—the
"Moorish Sunset" did enhance the other, and the two together would look
much better. The merchant leaned toward us conspiratorially and whispered
that both were ours for 50,000. Bill promptly countered with 40,000, with the
cost of shipping thrown in. The Arab rolled his eyes upward and breathed
Allah's name. Then, sighing pleasurably, he signed to the boys to stitch cloth
tags onto both rugs and ink in our address. It was all over but the tea, and the
expressions of mutual esteem.

Promotion Nationale

At the time of the King's visit in May of 1966, the city was more than usually
brilliant. When we sat on our balcony at night, the floodlit ramparts cut
across the deep black of the sky, and high above the swaying tips of palms,
the Koutoubia rose in a shaft of light, its cupola glowing like a domed crown
on a black velvet pillow. Up from the streets came the clopping of hoofs as
carriages bore visitors to the casino and the night clubs. Frogs kept up a
ceaseless bawdy croaking from the irrigation ditches. Once, waking very
early, I went out to sit in the freshened air and watch the dawn touch the
incredible snow peaks to opal. The stridor of the frogs was beginning to

falter, and now a dozen different bird songs came in snatches from the hearts of the palms, like a chamber orchestra tuning up. The cloud of smoky blue along the avenue was a line of jacaranda trees in flower. The street sweepers were at work already; I heard the hiss of straw brooms as they began to gather up cartloads of papery bougainvillea blossoms. A sound of coughing came from the car park at the feet of the palms, and the hulking night watchman appeared, stretching himself from sleep in his small thatched hut in the midst of the cars.

A great triumphal arch had been erected across the Avenue Mohammed V, in preparation for that review we had heard about in Ouarzazate. For reasons I never saw explained, the review had been postponed. The King had left the city after a few days, and was now on a tour of hydraulic and agricultural projects nearby.

We repaired to the regional office of the *Promotion Nationale* to pay our respects and inquire about a glimpse into some of the local projects. As it does in the country, the *Promotion* starts things in the city that the poor can put their backs into because they will profit soon and directly—schoolrooms, low-cost housing, clinics. As the *de facto* Berber capital and hence more than once also the capital of the Land of Insolence, Marrakesh is a good place for the *Promotion* to be hard at work. The official we had been talking with for some time was informed, enthusiastic, and said he meant to accompany us: "We will go tomorrow. To an urban project, then to a new village coming into being. If time permits, I will send you also to the caïd of an Atlas commune—a fine fellow, and a friend of mine."

"But," Bill said to this man we were liking so much, "you can't do these things with us tomorrow. Or perhaps you had forgotten that His Majesty the King is expected back in the city tomorrow?"

The official slapped his forehead, remembering. Then he said: "Never mind. His Majesty does not need *me*." I demurred again, saying we would wait. Then, looking at a spot somewhere over my left shoulder, he spoke very rapidly but with emphasis, "*Moi, je ne m'occupe pas des* rois, *je m'occupe des choses!*" ("Things, not kings, are my business.") I thought it discreet to show no sign of having heard this, and replied only that we would be honored to have his company. Bill fixed the time and the place, and we left. Only when we were some yards down the street did we dare compare notes; we had both heard it.

But, at eight o'clock the next morning, we found him in a spanking-fresh dress uniform and an impressively close shave—something rather rare among Moroccans of undistinguished rank. Not bothering with any explanations, he simply handed us over smoothly to a young man who would accompany us. "I find I am not able to be gone today," was all he said.

Though there was still no announcement of the King's return, fresh palm branches were being applied to the triumphal arch above Avenue Mohammed V. Strings of colored lights were being hung about all the public buildings, and floodlights set up around each fountain that the traffic circled. I wondered if uncertainty about the day of the review was for security reasons, or simply to keep officialdom on its toes and let fervor build up among the populace. Or perhaps the King's return was not really being postponed, but only the misinformation that is standard in Morocco made it appear so. Today soldiers were being moved into the city in large numbers. The youth with us looked at them with brooding eyes. As we drew away from the heart of the *ville nouvelle,* expensive red bunting was replaced by five-pointed stars chalked on the walls. The poor streets rang with mules' hoofs, and people ran out to buy little flags from the carts they drew.

When the streets could get no poorer, we came to the housing project. Cement-block units, stretching out of sight in stark uniformity . . . a door opened to us . . . a courtyard, and a kettle above dead embers . . . five children squatting round it, fishing up gobbets, the older making way for the younger. "The woman wants you to know the two eldest are in school every afternoon!" says our young man to us. I nod to her, acknowledging that I am impressed. She holds my eyes on her and goes to an empty windowframe. "She tells you there will soon be a pane there," says the youth, and she draws her hand with pride across imaginary glass.

"Her husband works for a builder, whenever he can. The rent here is twelve dirhams a month." ($2.50.) She goes back to the court and pulls open a shed door, releasing a scuttling hen. We peer in: scraps of scavenged lumber, and many dried palm branches. "When they were moved here, only one room was complete, and outer walls for two more. Bit by bit, they will complete the inner walls and make a roof."

Nearby was a Center for Illiterates. More exactly, for that half of the young population who never had a chance at schooling, and for all those who were out of phase through failing more than the one allowable year. A big room, bare of desks, and youths of assorted ages taking turns at the blackboard, painfully forming the difficult Arabic characters . . . the library: many shelves, only a few books in use . . . students running their fingers, right to left, across the line of script, their lips moving, their faces knotted with determination.

Upstairs was a demonstration kitchen, full of young women. "They have *la manie folle* for the gas stove!" the teacher said. She was young herself and had one of those faces to be found the world over: warm with commitment, sad under the brisk smile. "I tell them, 'One day you will cook for a splendid household!'" The women were very gay indeed. It was a shock to look from them to the face of our young guide, who leaned against the wall and looked loftily about him.

We headed out of town then, past a car dump with red flags stretched from roof to roof. All removable car parts had been stripped, and thatch annexes were built onto the gutted bodies. Even here, each family contrived its own courtyard, with walls of camelthorn and cactus. The city had installed a few hand pumps, and beside each a laundry stone and a watering trough for the goats.

A troop truck rattled past us, packed with raw young Berbers, some of whom looked strong enough to crunch an ox's jaw. In their midst huddled a few hollow-chested young city boys in baggy uniforms.

"Draftees?" I asked. The question opened a floodgate. This young guide of ours was laboring under fear of the new draft law, by which all able-bodied men between eighteen and thirty must serve for eighteen months—a brief basic-training period first, the rest of the time given to some form of service to the state.

"See for yourself the two types—the savage young oafs from the Bled who join up voluntarily—just for the sake of being able to rattle about the country in a truck from Tangier to Agadir! And then the others—you saw them! Probably students who joined some demonstration. Do them good to discover life is more than shouting slogans and going on strike when their scholarship money isn't forthcoming. I know, I was enrolled in the University ben Youssef for a while."[7]

"And when the money was cut off, you got this job instead?" He nodded.

"But since you are already working for the state, why should you be drafted?"

"That is what I ask! I have already started my application for exemption through the mill. It will be six months before I hear anything. Rabat is already flooded with applications—the whole country will be a sea of paper! It is not reasonable to take people like me and make them strut about with rifles for six months and then be transferred to some course for hotel employees or assigned to some bridge-building job."

"It seems more rational to you that disaffected students should be taken? Do you think what I've heard is true, that even a married man above thirty may be drafted if he gets out of line?"

He looked sharply at me, and then, without answering, turned to gaze out the window. Moroccans have a number of ways to deal with untactful questions, one of them being simply not to hear.

At a rural crossroad we stopped, facing the most striking of contrasts. To one side, a douar of smoke-blackened huts and courts hedged with Barbary fig cactus. Beside it their market: lopsided stalls with oil-drum roofs, rangy dogs who looked part jackal, and some children who kicked them away from a clump of rabbits hanging head down and looking suffocated. The men and older boys were all across the road, working on the new village of the *Promotion,* all crisp new whitewash against the brown plain. A line of willows showed where a stream ran by; backed up to it, a row of houses was

7. This old, traditional university of very few students is affiliated with the Qarawiyin.

rising, some of them finished even to the traditional blue doors. We walked over. But our escort said he must stay with the Simca—locking it meant nothing in these parts. Though we had left it unguarded a hundred times and never found it tampered with, we said nothing. He had little stomach for the things we had come to see, and would be happier reading his newspaper.

The project's superintendent was a big countryman. Though he had little French, he understood our questions and expressed himself partly by gesture. Men were shoveling concrete dexterously into little individual brick molds with thumbscrews, while a cement mixer stood by idle. Oh, yes—the superintendent grinned and mimed—it had broken down again. Better so. By hand, the men could *feel* with their shovels when the mix was ready. And what foundations, we asked, were these out in front of the new houses? Why, the new souk, of course! (He outlined a street of stalls and acted out brisk trading.) Once it was operating, and once the douar across the road was settled in, three more douars from the neighboring region would follow here.

Just then I saw something glint on the outer wall of a finished house. To my immense surprise, it proved to be a brand-new shower-head. A power pump someday, then? Oh, but certainly . . . as soon as the electricity came out this far. All down the hopeful row, every house had one, and also a new concrete ditch, dry as yet, leading from the stream to a small growing plot.

He was eager to draw us back to the focus of his pride: the communal hall, which he called the *Salon d'Enthousiasme*. On the way over, two men jumped up from their bricks and came to pull Bill's sleeve, gaps showing between their teeth as they smiled and pointed back to the whitewashed row. Each tapped his chest, and then pointed to the house his hands had built. Every head of household, our companion said, received free materials and two dirhams' worth of U.S. wheat a day for his family—but only while the building was in progress. After that, they must return to making their own living.

We came to the half-built hall. "Why '*Salon d'Enthousiasme*'?" I asked, delighted with the name.

"Because look what will be here! Over there—Moorish café, you know? Tea, one must drink tea! Here—the space for speeches, storytelling, dancing." He mimed opening and shutting a door. "Latrines. Over there, a big radio. Perhaps, some day, TV—and the soccer matches in Casablanca!" He paused to search out words carefully. "Only so can village life hold more . . . and people will not need to drift."

Across the monotonous brown plain and up savagely eroded foothills, we came at length to the caïd who was to show us the *Promotion's* largest demonstration project in the region: 6,000 acres of new tree plantations on former grazing land. I had expected a caïd to be self-important, the image of the successful bureaucrat; but this young man, like his friend in the regional office, was forthright and stood on no ceremony at all. He seemed relieved that we would not delay to drink tea and, after one glance at the Simca, backed out his Jeep.

It was a ride I thought at times we would not survive. The hillside was innocent of even a level track between the young trees. Each grew in a carefully banked saucer, the rows staggered to prevent runoff of a single drop of rain. "Three years ago, only goat tracks and thistles here," he said, taking both hands off the wheel to show us. "The land was veined and withered like an old man's skin." It had been two fractions' grazing land—fractions of different tribes, cantankerous with each other. More or less to embarrass the others, he thought, one fraction had agreed rather readily to the state scheme: in exchange for removing their flocks from a large acreage and ceding all rights to the land for six years, they would be given thousands of young fruit and nut and olive trees. They must contribute labor to plant them and agree to continuous supervision during the six years.

"But the scheme could not begin until the other tribe came in also. Meetings with their tribal council dragged on and on while they changed their minds from month to month. It was God who brought them at length to their senses. The day after an earthslide carried a hectare of their pasturage to the bottom of a ravine, they accepted partnership in the project."

A hooded man came pumping his bicycle along between the rows, his body canted sharply sideways to stay upright. They saluted each other, and looked up to see if a few precious drops of rain could be expected. Then the old fellow went off about his ceaseless inspection tour of 100,000 trees.

"All the first year, while the roots were shallow, we had to carry water *every day* for miles on muleback. . . . Now, look around you! In three more years, 'nch Allah, this commune will repossess its land, restored and healthy —and with it, the promise of a good yield from the mature trees. It is so we implement the government's most cherished aims: reducing pastoralism, creating a new crop for the region, and rehabilitating the soil."

But what of their flocks, we asked; had they given them up altogether? He laughed shortly. "That day has not come yet—not while the mythic tie with the sons of Abraham dwells in their blood. But on a reduced pasturage, the flocks are smaller, and I can engage their interest in stock *breeding,* that is, breeding for quality rather than quantity. 'Where is the security,' I ask them, 'in many lean sheep who succumb easily in a bad year, and in ewes who become sterile?'"

Wasn't the religious tie to pastoralism a brake on modern ideas? I asked, thinking of the climactic Feast of the year, Aid el Kebir, when the head of every family slaughters his best sheep. The King, as the father of the whole realm, slaughters ritually at the same time, in a great pageant outside the palace walls. "If a man slaughters his most valuable breeding ram for the Feast of the Sacrifice," the caïd retorted severely, "it is not piety that moves him—it is merely the desire to show off!"

As we drove home, I thought of the one item on the government program we had not touched upon: the need to make the tribes accept the commune system. Then it dawned on me that the caïd's hidden agenda here was detribalization. By such an ingenious scheme as this, the government was trying to efface tribal thinking and replace it with a gradual understanding that the *region* was the reality, not fragmented tribal holdings scattered over great distances. The new commune boundaries are rational geographic units, with fairly uniform physical and economic necessities. What this caïd was doing was even more important than effecting a change in land use; he was engaging two stubborn, particularist rivals in the rewards of a long-term plan and supra-tribal cooperation.

How many campaigns to be waged at once, I thought—the battle for the Bled, to restore it, to keep the people on it; the subtle work of detribalization, which must be accomplished without alienation; and the battle of the slums, where dissidence makes headway. The King's royal progress was part of the same campaign—providing a pageant, and a dramatic focus for loyalty.

Fête Folklorique

The city still awaited Moulay Hassan. He was now addressing the tribes of the plain just to the north and making some land distributions. Each night in Marrakesh there was a dance festival, with deputations of dancers sent by many of the tribes. The setting was a palace built in the 1890s by the famous Black Chamberlain of Hassan I, who later became virtually regent—one of the rare and conspicuous cases of blackness wielding power. The plan of the palace, if plan there ever was, is lost in a succession of battlemented courts, covered passages, and stairways descending to secluded gardens.

Torches flaring from brackets in the masonry lighted our way, as attendants stationed at each corner beckoned us on. At length we arrived in a huge courtyard almost entirely filled by a rectangular pool across which three platforms had been built for the dancers, so that the black bands of water in between would reflect the dancing figures. At the far end of the pool rose an arched portal flanked by crenelated towers; under the arch was heaped an enormous pile of brushwood. Just as we took our seats, frogs in the water below began their ribald chorus. We watched with concern the efforts of television cameramen to find a secure footing on their flimsy scaffold. There were as yet no floodlights, only rows of little oil lamps bordering the pool, their reflections flickering in the water. Women around us settled their gorgeous kaftans and set aside their veils.

Except for the frogs, we waited in silence. From an adjacent courtyard came the sound of rhythmic clapping as the dancers warmed up. There were a few shouts, a few bursts of song, and the sibilance of many bare feet. There must have been a big fire in there with them, for their shadows, leaping and cartwheeling and stamping, raced along the rufous walls high above them. Then they came on stage in a burst, running, shouting, and clapping, the drums and pipes going at full pitch. Even though the cameras were grinding and the floodlights blazed down, they danced as if alone in their isolate world. Berber dances are rituals, leaving no room for improvisation. The aim is corporate expression and release, wherein individuals lose themselves in a larger unity.

The mood changed, quiet fell, and most of the dancers withdrew. The formal, stately lines of the Middle Atlas Ahidous were redoubled in the black water. Two lines of white-robed figures faced each other. The men, with leather powder bags over one shoulder and glittering curved scabbards at the other armpit, swayed in unison, bent their white turbans to one side and the other as they chanted and beat their tambours. Facing them, the line of women clapped a counter-rhythm and sang antiphonal refrains. Melody is uncomplicated in these tribal songs; it is a reiterated outpouring of a single theme—now rising, now falling, now hoarse, now poignant. The complexity is in the rhythms and syncopations. Castanets hang from the women's wrists; half the chorus punctuates the clapping with an intricate counterpoint. The songs invoke Allah's clemency on crops and flock, others are prayers for rain, for fertility, for deliverance from flood.

There is one song about the spring on which the tribe's life depends, which lightning has struck and sealed dry. The tribe implores Allah to show them how to appease the spirits who drew the lightning down in that dire place. The same refrain recurs over and over: "Who will bring back life to our fields?" Another song invokes "Lord Solomon, King of Djinns, Master of mountain, snow, and water."

They offer a sacrifice:

> See our young virgins pour out water . . .
> Virgin water calls forth virgin water, for the recovery of our spring.
> Pity, O Allah, upon your slaves!
> Return to us our water, fecund mother of all plenty. . . .

The Guedra, the dance of the desert region in the far southwest, can easily be mistaken for a dance concerned only with human sexuality. I think it is that, and more—addressed equally to the potency of mankind and of nature. This is the Guedra: on her knees, at the center of a circle of men, a woman sways blindly. A blue robe is thrown over her head and the upper part of her body; a string of enormous beads hangs to the waist, below the blank face. She leans to the rhythm the men clap out, undulating from side to side, her arms thrown wide and her taut slender fingers speaking, like a Thai dancer's, a ritual language. She arches backward, then throws herself forward, almost prostrate. The rhythm accelerates. She inches forward on her knees, swaying now in a wide circle, the outstretched fingers intricately weaving their pattern. She is herself the unfathomable symbol of fecundity, and at the same time she implores the fertilizing force that can release that fecundity. She is woman, and she is the earth.

Here is another song, about a thunderstorm, that shows the same fusion in the tribal mind of forces of nature and forces of human nature:

> Gold of lightning tears the sky
> Thunder roars in the clouds,
> Roar resounding in echo!
> Lightning is the blade of a plow—
> It falls upon the earth, and enters.
> Lightning flash and clap of thunder—
> Desire leaps from eye to eye,
> Roars in the heart like thunder
> And hears in another heart its echo.
> Desire strikes, sets thought afire.
> This love is lightning flash and thunderclap;
> Aïsha! You are the echo in the valley.
> Aïsha! You are the benign rain.
> You alone can appease me,
> If Allah will permit.

Groups of dancers came and went, were followed by acrobats and more dancers. Their inverted doubles, dancing in the water, heightened the colors of women's brilliant striped shawls, the many necklaces each wore, of silver and turquoise and coral and amber, and the bracelets as wide as manacles. Not only the water but also the battlement walls redoubled the volume of sound. Suddenly, quiet fell. All the men filed off the platforms and lined up along one side of the pool; the little oil lamps played on their faces, bearded, dark, and intent. The women in their turn filed off on the opposite side. All singing and all movement stopped.

Then, racing out from the wings with a din of shouts, came the Gnaoua, the black Guinean dancers, whirling and stamping and rattling their iron castanets. Drummers poured out with them, pounding the guttural rawhide with hooked sticks and spinning as they drummed. Their white tunics furled and unfurled around the furious legs as they reversed direction. These men are not Berbers, they are African demon-exorcisors, who for centuries have lived among Moroccans. They rolled their eyes up in the sockets and drew back their lips, gold teeth glinting, and spun their heads until the black tassels on their caps stood out straight like pinwheels.

Drummers threw themselves to the ground and, catching their drums between their knees, continued to flail out the rhythm. They leapt up with hoarse cries and drew together in a circle, facing inward. This was the test of exorcism. The drums questioned . . . the Gnaoua listened. Unsatisfied, they flung out their arms, spidery fingers widespread, and poured again into the dance. With castanets and drums throbbing to a climax, they stamped and whirled and grimaced, their heads thrown back in frenzy. Sweat streamed down the coal-black faces and the puckered scars of tattoos. The peak came. The drums stopped dead, the dancers froze in place, and then, as one man, they folded limply to the ground. The silence was enormous.

It was past midnight when the grand finale began. Here an alien touch intruded, no doubt the finger of the Ministry of Fine Arts—something contrived about a procession carrying a bride in her jeweled box on the shoulders of six men. When the floodlights dimmed and went out, the audience supposed the show was all over. Women groped for their handbags or adjusted their veils. Suddenly, there was fire at the far end, under the arch. Flames licked viciously up the twenty-foot pile of brushwood and shed a raw glare over the darkened courtyard and the shimmering water. Then fifty rifles went off at once, as the hidden men surged out from under the arcade. Bill flung himself upon me, whether to protect me or himself it was hard to say. As the roar of guns echoed and re-echoed from wall to wall, I thought I heard him mutter, "Holy Mother of God!"

High Atlas

The day of the review dawned hot. Not sorry we were unable to get tickets—for the parade would last all day, and watchers would be pinned to the stands —we drove up into the Atlas. While Hassan II stood under the royal awning in Marrakesh, we found something appropriate in looking down on the city from those mountains that have so often set the limits of the Dar el Mahkzen, the House of Government.

To make pacification of the South possible, the French built two great passes: the Tizi n' Test, giving access to the southwest, and the Tizi n' Tichka, to Ouarzazate and the southeast. In so doing, they outflanked the natural passes that tribesmen had long controlled. Demnate, astride one of the old passes, once throve on the tolls levied on struggling caravans; now, only a line of donkeys carrying water jars from the spring pass through that formidable gate, and the mosque square is empty save for some turkeys pecking at a carpet of blue fallen from a great jacaranda. To whichever side I looked, the bastion of the Atlas rose sharply. It was a very warm day, even here, yet fingers of cloud stroked the peaks, laying down a new mantle of snow. Demnate, a forgotten village near the roof of the world, lives alone with its legends.

A certain Dr. Gunning, who had worked up there among the local tribes, wrote an article I found in an old copy of *Maroc Tourisme*[8] about the pre-historic paintings he had found in a cave. He questioned the tent dwellers nearby:

"Who painted those?"

"The Portuguese."

"Who are the Portuguese?"

"Wild men who used to live in these caves before the Chleuh [Berbers] came. They went naked, dwelt in caves, and lived by hunting."

Of another grotto, hung with dripping stalactites, he was told that a monster had lived there and terrorized the region, until all the warriors banded together and killed it. But the carcass was transformed into crows, and became a worse plague than the monster. So, one spring night every year, all the men still gather in the grotto by torchlight, to exorcise the transmuted monster that devours their crops.

The doctor often had to leave his Jeep where the track had faded and walk the rest of the way to the tent where someone lay ill. More than once, he was pelted with stones by monkeys living in the caves. On one occasion, snow prevented him from regaining his Jeep the same night, so he stayed on in the tent. It was there, as the November dark was falling and the tribesmen gathered around their transistor, that they heard the news: one half-hour before, John Kennedy had died in Dallas.

On another expedition, the doctor came upon what he identified as a dinosaur footprint, where once there had been a lake. The illustration with the article looked convincing enough, and I wanted to see it for myself; this rooftop world, where all things past and present fuse, had me in thrall. But Bill said, if I didn't mind, I could look for it alone, while he smoked a pipe in the car. (I had strained his patience enough while we looked for the grotto of the spring exorcism. Guided by cairns and rags fluttering from bushes, we found it easily enough, and wished we hadn't. Hundreds of birds issued from the cathedral vaults of the roof each time our feet sent a slippery stone rolling away, and only some of what dropped on our heads was water from the stalactites.)

So now, alone, I searched and searched, coming reluctantly to the conclusion that Dr. Gunning's *patte de dinosaur* was most unlikely to show up while the grass was so high. Then I saw a shepherd at a little distance and thought perhaps he would know about it. I was making for him diligently when a lark plummeted out of the sky, trailing its song behind it as larks do the world over. For some reason, this familiar sight brought me to my senses and released me from the idiocy of this pursuit. I began running back to the car, wondering at the spell that had possessed me, and imagining the

8. Dr. K. F. Gunning, *"Demnate, la plus ancienne ville Marocaine,"* in *Maroc Tourisme,* No. 26 (November 1964), p. 18.

look on that shepherd's face if I had asked him to direct me to a *patte de dinosaur*.

Another caravan route across the High Atlas, the now disused Tizi n' Telouet, passed not very far away from Demnate, through the domain of the Glaoua clan. The caravans came here because of vast deposits of a precious commodity: salt. With the wealth that accrued from mining it, the Glaoui built their enormous Kasbah Telouet in a valley between towering peaks. A mid-nineteenth-century caïd el Glaoui fathered two sons by the same Ethiopian concubine—two very dark and very clever men who ruled the clan in succession and built a great feudal barony. Their story is a tortuous one of intrigue and nice calculation, of rapacity and bluff and cunning.[9] By the ethic of the time and place, there is nothing singular about it but its scope and its success. Everyone played the power game the same way, from the sultans and their viziers down to the rival Great Caïds of the Atlas—and, in their turn, the occupying French. Three episodes in the Glaoua story involved great gambler's risks.

The first gamble was taken in 1893, when Hassan I was returning from a *harka* (a pacifying and tax-collecting expedition) in the Tafilelt. The Sultan's army had been decimated by disease and hunger, and Hassan himself was severely ill. As the ragged train struggled up the mountainside toward Telouet, a great blizzard engulfed it, and hundreds more corpses lay in the wake of the royal passage. Madani el Glaoui, the older brother, was tribal caïd and of course owed his sovereign assistance and hospitality. But, on the more practical level, Madani had to decide if he should just let the Sultan and his feeble force die there in the snow, and then put his own candidate on the throne—a course that might bring rich rewards. He calculated quickly and decided to honor his sacred obligation. Madani was rewarded by being made khalifa of the region, and in addition was given the caïdat of the Tafilelt and a large amount of modern arms and ammunition. Though Hassan died a few weeks later, while still on harka, his heir confirmed the appointments. Madani turned the bronze Krupp cannon that the Sultan had given him on his rival Great Caïds, and the House of Glaoua seemed certain of pre-eminence in the South.

In the next gamble, Madani played kingmaker. He helped the new Sultan's brother-rival to overturn the throne and capture it for himself. Again, Madani was rewarded; he was appointed Grand Vizier, and his brother, Thami, was made pasha of Marrakesh. But the gratitude of a sultan in those days was apt to be short-lived. The Sultan became jealous of the power his Vizier was accumulating, and in a sudden stroke removed both brothers from public office. Retiring to Telouet, the Glaoui brooded vengeance on the Alaouite dynasty.

9. For a detailed and colorful account of the Glaoui, see Gavin Maxwell, *Lords of the Atlas* (New York: E. P. Dutton and Co., 1966).

Though this gamble seemed to have failed, they used their period of relative eclipse to extend their power over the tribes of the South. By pillage, intrigue, and extortion, they amassed great wealth and turned Telouet into an impregnable fortress without and a luxurious palace within. You have only to stand in that high, narrow Atlas valley and look up at the great curtain wall and the massed towers and turrets behind it to feel the arrogance and might of the Glaoui. Bill, standing before it, recalled that very qualified oath of fealty that the Aragonese nobles pledged to the Spanish kings: "We (who are as good as you), swear to you (who are no better than we) to accept you as our King, provided you respect all our liberties and rights—and if not, not!"

The advent of the French gave the lords of Telouet a new set of risks to assess and new gambles to take. Publicly, they rallied demonstrations against the Sultan on the ground that, by calling in foreign troops to rescue him and thus opening the door to the Protectorate, he had "sold the Cherifian realm to the infidel." Privately, the Glaoui explored the rewards of collaboration with the occupiers. Before long, most of the male members of the huge clan —sons, nephews, sons-in-law, and a host of minor relatives—held all the positions of power in the Atlas and the South. There was in effect a second reigning dynasty; and this one was hand-in-glove with the French. After the Second World War, nationalist sentiment grew strong enough to alarm the French. At the same time, the young Mohammed V was proving troublesome: with dignity, and with an unshakable belief in his divine right to rule, he would bow to French pressure only under duress; and then quietly, blandly, stubbornly, he would repudiate the concessions wrung from him, and reassert his sovereignty. As he lent his support more openly to the Istiqlal, the French saw the direction they must take: Mohammed would have to go. The tribes could be brought to revolt against him on grounds that he aligned himself with city-bred secularism and modernism and was not fit to be the Commander of the Faithful. The tool for this strategy lay ready to hand: the Glaoui.

Madani had died. Thami el Glaoui was, if possible, even greedier and more cunning than his brother. And he had broken with the palace in 1950, after a violent quarrel with Mohammed, who had questioned him about his extortions from the poor. The French had seen to it that he was again pasha of Marrakesh. Some 3,500 minor pashas, caïds, and sheiks owed their appointments to Thami and functioned as his henchmen. Fabulously wealthy, he presided over the palatial halls of Telouet, where he entertained foreign notables with Oriental feasts, music by Negro concubines, slaves by the hundreds, and delicious Chleuh dancing girls with tinted-ivory skins. No mention was made at these feasts of the underground dungeons, and the cells below the dungeons, where his enemies rotted. His foreign visitors were apt to be dazzled by his exotic grace, his sunken, dreamy eyes, his exquisite politeness and lavish gifts. Winston Churchill was so enthusiastic a guest at his Marrakesh palace that the pasha considered himself in line for a cordial reception at the coronation of Elizabeth II. He sent his gift in advance of himself: a gold crown encrusted with emeralds as big as walnuts. What must have been his rage when the gift was returned to him with a polite note, and without any invitation to the coronation ceremonies? In Paris, was he not received with all the honors usually reserved for heads of state?

Tête-à-tête with the French, el Glaoui developed his strategy for the plot against Mohammed. In 1951, he formed an alliance with several of the secret brotherhoods (who were naturally opposed to any strong, interfering sultanate), and together they spread the doctrine that Mohammed had deserted Islam and the tribes, and had sold out to the irreligious urban modernists. (Had he not imported a French midwife for his wife's confinement, and strange, damnable things like bottles and sterilizers?)

At a signal from the *résident général* in Rabat that the time was ripe, the Glaoui coalition sent out word that tribesmen were to report to the capital for vaccinations, and to receive at the same time extra rations of tea and sugar. Since Berber chieftains never went anywhere without their horses and their muskets, the first hundreds to arrive and encamp in the Mechaouar could be seen very clearly from the palace enjoying their favorite sport of charging in phalanx with upraised guns. The *résident* had just flung his ultimatum at Mohammed: the Sultan would sign the decrees he had been resisting or be deposed. When he again refused to sign, the *résident* led him to the window, from which he could see what appeared to be a tribal revolt. He gave in, for the moment, and signed.

But the nationalists saw through the ruse. They redoubled their proselytizing and their agitation, until all the cities were seething. It was clear that the Protectorate was in serious danger. Many colons, many French businessmen, bankers, and investors supported the Glaoui plot. Though Paris strictly forbade the Sultan's deposition, Rabat gave the plotters their signal. In May 1953, el Glaoui and the head of a powerful brotherhood convoked a gathering of two hundred and seventy rebellious caïds and pashas around the tomb of Moulay Idriss; after sacrificing two black bulls, they took an oath to drive Mohammed from the throne. In Rabat, more constraints were laid upon the Sultan; finally, in August, the *résident* demanded that he abdicate. Mohammed replied that it was not possible for the Imam of the Faithful to abdicate. He was told that a new sultan was at that very moment being proclaimed in Marrakesh and civil war threatened if he refused. While he went to his midday rest, el Glaoui set out from Marrakesh with the feeble old Ben Arafa, the puppet candidate. French tanks surrounded the palace; the Sultan and his son were aroused and hurried, still in pajamas, to a small waiting airplane, and exile.

The reaction was immediate, spontaneous, and far-reaching. The Ulema denounced el Glaoui as treasonable; in the Tetouan mosque, civil disobedience was proclaimed the only course of piety. General Franco, delighted with a new chance to embarrass France, refused to recognize Ben Arafa. The Spanish Zone and Tangier became headquarters for exiled Istiqlal leaders. Women tore off their veils in disrespect of Ben Arafa, and refused their husbands conjugal rights, lest a child be conceived during the ignominious reign. People deserted the mosques rather than hear the Friday prayer offered for the country in Ben Arafa's name. An impromptu boycott went into effect on the French monopolies of tea, sugar, and tobacco—and the voluntary mass sacrifice of these cherished pleasures proved as nothing else could have that the people, not just the city intellectuals, were in revolt. In the Bled, the word went out: "Ifna [our Lord] is on the moon—his face is there." For the first time, country and city were unified. In the exiled Sultan, they found their focus and their hero.

Two frightful years of terrorism and counterterrorism followed. The cabal of colons, French companies, and Casablanca businessmen pushed successive *résidents* into ever greater defiance of orders from Paris, where intellectuals and Cabinet ministers joined in impotent condemnation. Finally, a moderate and reforming *résident* was imposed on Rabat. But it was too late—only independence would do now. Mohammed was flown to Paris from Madagascar, and discussions began about the terms and timing of French withdrawal. El Glaoui, disowned by the French and his countrymen alike, was turned out of office with all who had supported him. Hastily, he flew to Paris. Thousands saw him on television—now a broken old man who prostrated himself and crawled painfully forward to embrace the feet of the Sultan he had betrayed.

On November 16, 1955, a small plane circled over Rabat and set down its passenger, King Mohammed V of a free Morocco. In the general rejoicing, his charisma and his saintliness seemed to guarantee a future without problems. He pardoned the Old Fox of the Atlas, for this was the part of a saint. Others saw to it that all Glaoui property was confiscated. The palace of the pasha in Marrakesh, splendid with three carved cedar porticoes giving onto the street, now bears a sign: *Club de la Jeunesse Ouvrière*. Telouet is sinking quietly into elegant decay; rain seeping through the coffered roof stains the lovely stucco lattices, and the fifteen-foot doors are beginning to sag on their bronze hinges.

Whether the *condottiere* type has vanished from Morocco for good, whether the Land of Insolence has truly been gathered up in the House of Government, remains to be seen. The *guardien* unlocked the last gate for us and stood rattling his ten-inch keys while we assembled an ample tip. Glancing at it quickly, he shed all his obsequiousness and pushed it away with a face full of sullen anger. We proffered it again, and he snatched it just as the door clanged shut. No matter, we said, this can happen anywhere, and we drove down the narrow valley while the clouds boiled like surf around the peaks.

Slowing for a sharp rock in the road, I saw three youths converging on the car, little puffs of dust rising from their flying feet. I had to negotiate the rock outcropping carefully and was hardly aware of a fourth youth at the open window beside me. He leaned in the opening and demanded a tip. "Shut your window," Bill said, but the boy's shoulder blocked it. Clearing the rock, I pressed down on the accelerator, and felt fingers graze my cheek sharply and saw my sunglasses disappear in his grasp as the car jumped forward. A second later, a rock thudded against the rear fender.

CHAPTER EIGHT

THE ATLANTIC COAST

Tizi n' Test

Of all the great Atlas passes that connect Marrakesh with the South, the steepest and most dramatic is the Tizi n' Test, giving on the southwest. It was January when we crossed it, after waiting several days in the city before hearing it was safe. Then—"The plows have come through. But hurry, before the next snowfall." January is the height of winter on the northern slopes of the Tizi, but the beginning of spring on the southern side, where oueds rampage and cause earthslides.

It is a sobering prospect. Drawing away from Marrakesh's sleek oasis, we begin the climb. The car seems very small for the enterprise, no more than an automated donkey. The gradient increases sharply, and the switchback road begins to gleam here and there with an ooze of water from the rock wall that turns the roadbed to lavender clay. But no time to worry about that, for the breathtaking curves are succeeding each other without pause. Dizzyingly high above, snow is smoking off the peaks. As the road snatches us inexorably from one tight curve into the next, we wonder about the wisdom of attempting this Tizi. Only the Simca's heart never misses a beat. In any case, it would be vain to change our minds, for there was no room to turn. If we should meet a car descending, what would we do? Thankfully, we remember that the climbing car has the right of way—the other must back until there is room to pass. Our turn will come later to worry about that; meantime, keep moving, don't lose traction. The signs announcing hairpin bends and rockslides are interspersed with the warning ACCOTEMENTS IMPRATICABLES! This seems a rather academic way to describe the road's treacherous shoulder. There are no guard rails.

Bill is driving. There is only one way to keep my anxiety at bay—I tell myself to concentrate on the small details flashing by. It is a landscape composed entirely of rock surfaces in variegated colors. Slit your eyes for an instant, focus only on the rich, rough textures of this rock tapestry. . . . It is somewhat reassuring to meet road-mending teams. Only ceaseless vigilance can maintain these miles of vulnerable road. The embankments are always dry-wall work, no mortar—it would be madness not to let the water drain through. One dare not try to restrain it here; the best one can do is diffuse it. It is all well and good to call the Atlas Morocco's great reservoir, but that makes everything sound simpler than it is. In reality, there are few places where even the utmost ingenuity will permit man to harness these waters. Somewhere far below us now is the great Cavagnac dam, in a valley so contoured by nature as to permit hundreds of tons of concrete to restrain thousands of tons of water. I know of only one other major dam high in the Atlas.

Ice, patches of ice across the road, dispelled my attempt at reverie. Then one more spiral, and snow lay all about, and an astonishing green brocade of leaves on a field of white. Brilliant sunshine, and the peaks above us glowing rose against the sky. The snowbanks leaned in upon the narrow lane; for a time, the red tips of the meter-high markers showed above, until they too were swallowed up. An icy wind snatched at the little car. And then at last we were upon the saddle of the Tizi, and the snow was swirling against a bronze plaque commemorating the work of the French Army Engineer Corps. Only by building these great Atlas roads could the French successfully exploit Morocco's mineral resources. They found lead, cobalt, asbestos, and, not far away, on the other great Tizi that leads to Ouarzazate, uniquely pure deposits of manganese. There, it was startling to look up, in the great emptiness at the top of the world, and see, through a tear in the mist, giant buckets traveling high overhead on an aerial line. Once again, you were forced to remember the legacies of the Protectorate that belong on the credit side.

We began the descent, and now had to listen sharply for the sound of an ascending motor. In this cold silence, it would be possible to hear one miles away. Below us, the road laced across the mountainside, a narrow scar appearing and disappearing in the depths of blue distance. How did we dare—but there was no time to think. Each moment, each spiral twist, was a complete preoccupation. At last there was a turnout space. Only as we stepped out of the car and fetched up deep gulps of the thin crystal air did we realize the snow had vanished. We had entered the rain-shadow world again. It was astonishingly hot. "Morocco," Marshal Lyautey said, "is a cold country with a hot sun." For the first time, we could see a line of peaks floating above the cloud rack far to the south—the Anti Atlas. Between them and us lay one of the most delicious valleys in Morocco, the Sous.

It was just then that I smelled smoke and felt the feather stroke of panic across my skin. I saw only one image: squeezing around a hairpin bend, we are confronted with a wall of fire across this narrow road, this tenuous life-line to the world below. I scraped my feet against the palmettos growing like overlapping scales of armor along the ground. They were tinder. I insisted upon staying where we were—where we could turn the car around and race for the snowdrifts—until we had located the fire. Bill swept the binoculars around and around, while I walked along the road with all my hackles raised, stepping gingerly, like an animal who scents fire. Then Bill shouted. Something like a half mile below us, on a slope far from the road, men were tending a large blaze, beating out tongues of flame on the edge of their clearing. In the center was a pile of wood reduced to charcoal.

To burn anything, even scrub juniper, whose roots might help to hold the soil, clearly spells future disaster on steep slopes like this. I supposed that somewhere along the great Atlas barrier there must be a rock slide every few minutes. Looking up at an apron of scree above the road, I marveled at the "angle of repose" that held it there, temporarily inert until—what? Could the slight vibration of a passing motor loosen it? Or an ooze of water? Rocks resembling prehistoric mammoths rested on this unstable field; plenty of them had already bounded and crashed across the road, and lay below us, momentarily arrested. I imagined that I saw a line of fine print dancing before my eyes: "The management will not be responsible for any sudden changes in the angle of repose."

The Sous

Relief tingled along every nerve when at last we debouched onto a plain, where a little oued wandered beside us in search of the River Sous. Crossing the Tizi n' Test now seemed to have been a joyful adventure. Laughter seized us, and a line of willows hanging over the stream looked like a line of green girls washing their hair together. We came upon a shepherd urging his flock across the brook. The sheep, all dappled with shade, made the crossing just as slowly as they could, and then turned around to try to recross again before he could snatch them back. He was tall, dark, bearded, and most improbably beautiful. He wore a white turban and carried a small lamb in his bosom. As soon as he saw Bill's camera, he saluted us, mentioning his price. Then he chose a site and struck a magnificent pose for us: behind him, the flood of sheep scrambling from rock to rock across the gentle water, the sunlight filtering through loose folds of his burnous, the lamb against his breast, supported by one brown hand. With his free hand he thrust out his crook and drove it into the ground at arm's length, and looked at once quite Biblical and wonderfully self-satisfied.

The world sings with an original gaiety along the River Sous. All is lush.

Sugar-cane plantations alternate with date-palm and citrus groves; the dates are the best in Morocco, and the oranges even better. The people of the valley, Chleuh Berbers, are renowned for sorcery and for their mastery of the smiling arts, poetry and love. In fact, their dialect has but one word for both. Nowhere but among the Chleuh could so many female saints have prospered; many managed to confer sanctity upon their husbands while sharing with them the delights of love. The Lady Tiznit, patron saint of a town near the coast, only abandoned a prostitute's career for the sweeter pleasures of mysticism. From the Sous orange trees there is distilled an orange-blossom water of the most exquisite fragrance. It must be hard to tell whether it is her silky perfumed skin that brings a Chleuh woman the lover she desires, or the sorcery taught by the village wise-women. Girls from this region have enhanced the richest hareems from time out of mind, and the delicate dancing boys have supplied palaces from Tangier to Marrakesh.

Here is an anonymous Chleuh song:

> Until the day when the crow turns white—
> Until we hear men saying "The salt marsh lies fallow
> And they are gathering honey from the oleander"—
> Until the day the acacia grows without thorns,
> And the serpent is without venom—
> Until cannon balls or the powder that flames
> Have lost their power to harm—
> Until that day, my love, I shall not leave you.

Taroudannt, capital of the Sous, was too rich a prize for greedy sultans to forgo, but also very hard to hold in subjection. The prize meant more than just the valley's opulence, for Taroudannt was also a prime slave and gold market, supplied by those caravanners of the desert, the tall, indigo-stained Tuareg. The lords of Taroudannt were only too pleased to trade with the Portuguese on the coast and ignore the demands of the exigent rulers of Marrakesh. So at least once a century, the flow of taxes from the Sous would dry up and another harka would be organized to plunge across the perilous Tizi and punish the region. Then the valley people, gathered behind Taroudannt's formidable battlements, could only be reduced to submission when the sugar cane growing right up to the walls had been set afire and the city was encircled with flame.

That same bisque wall, so many times rebuilt, and those same deep-chested defense towers seem pure theater today—perhaps it is because of the neat white ibises sitting primly, one to each crenelation. The flavor of Taroudannt is serene indolence; climate and cash crops have softened life's sharp edges. In these souks, you can still buy—for a prince's ransom—the famous Taroudannt jewelry: daggers with silver hilts and carved ivory sheaths, jeweled swords, lumps of amber and turquoise the size of peach stones, and wide-mouthed muskets banded with silver. Even the olives of the Sous gleam like jewels, sleek and glistening mounds of midnight blue and gold and topaze.

A Frenchman who felt he had the soul of an Arab succumbed to the seductions of the Sous and built, a few miles out of Taroudannt, an astonishing bit of *maroquinerie*—the Gazelle d'Or, the smallest, most expensive and exotic little inn in the country. Ten small bungalows smothered in bougainvillea and screened from one another by walls of hibiscus . . . walks hedged with rosemary leading to the central pavilion, where the dining room is a matter of ten tables for two, each at a discreet distance apart. The food and wines were the best we found in Morocco, and the lounge an extravaganza of all the excesses of Moorish décor: forests of clipped velour arabesques and brocaded sunbursts, and cacti trailing from a concrete Moorish chimney breast. As I stared uneasily at a bizarre design in inlaid marble on the floor, the maître d'hôtel whispered that it was the creation of the Frenchman's daughter. This information was followed by a religious silence, which was broken only when muffled Andalusian music began to issue from a loudspeaker concealed somewhere in the cacti.

Still bemused the next morning, we were met by a breakfast tray piled high with croissants and the establishment's own pink honey, the whole crowned by an assortment of those wide, cabbagey roses I associate with the dowager queen of England. In the field outside our bungalow grazed a milk-white camel. The servant, withdrawing, remarked that horses awaited us, should we wish to ride. Fine animals they were, too, we discovered, with the Arab strain's velvet mouths and manners to match. "Don't you think," I asked Bill, "that a ride *tout-inclus* makes all this seem *much* less extravagant?"

Despite the deceptive air of indolence, the Soussi are an industrious and highly independent people who have not taken kindly to regulation by the central government. The commune idea does not sit well with them. Ordinarily, a caïd will win cooperation in time by passing benefits to those who cooperate. Gradually, the commune council he has appointed to consult with him fades into a rubber-stamp committee, and before long the commune is the reality instead of the tribes who compose it.

But the Soussi, compliant and graceful, have a stubborn core. They may say a pleasant Yes to the caïd, and go home to instruct their own tribal council to work at cross purposes with him. This they can afford to do because their valley, fertile and almost tropical in climate, can produce delicacies for the European market earlier than any Mediterranean grower. Nowadays, these *primeurs*—the very first peaches and almonds and oranges and apricots to ripen anywhere each year—are bringing a sizable amount of cash to the valley. Furthermore, the Soussi have another string to their bow—they are Morocco's grocers. Every year, most of the active males go off to the big cities to run profitable groceries. Meanwhile, their women and their marabouts run affairs at home, and the men return just in time to help with the harvest. You hear other Moroccans say bitterly, "Never trust a Soussi—he's only a grocer at heart. And he'll charge more than any just man would."

To visit such a village run by the grocers' women, we crossed the River Sous and began to climb into the Anti Atlas, which rise sharply on the southern side. We were still climbing the foothills, with Tafraoute somewhere high above us, when dusk began to fall, the velvety African dusk that deepens so quickly. Just before the mountains closed in we stopped at a gas pump and were served by a one-eyed boy who, knowing no French, filled our tank in silence. Our own voices dropped to whispers as we flung ourselves at the violent contours ahead. Night was upon us. We traveled up the funnel of our headlights, speaking little. I saw an animal, too high in the hind quarters to be a dog, slide quickly across the road.

Several times, as we twisted along a ridge, I caught sight of a brilliant beacon just before it disappeared behind a rocky shoulder. Finally I broke the silence: "It *must* be a plane! But . . . here? Where would it be heading, and how would it dare to fly so low?" Bill shook his head and said nothing. It came in sight again, long enough for a good look—it was a star, so large, so low, and so bright that it seemed to lean in upon our smallness.

Each time we swung past a dark hut, I thought I saw from the corner of my eye a flashlight beamed upon us from within. But that was nonsense—why should anyone awake and peer after us? It must be starlight glowing on a white interior. There went another jackal, vanishing into the roadside shadows. And Bill was frowning, and tapping the glass over the gas gauge. Finally he got out to look in the tank. The cap had been left off, and there seemed to be very little gas left. So we had to coast whenever we could, switching the engine off and slipping soundlessly down each slope and into each blind curve. Each time the engine came back to life again for a new climb, we regretted the noise as much as having to use the gas. The mechanical sound seemed a profanation of this emptiness, tempting fate by drawing attention to us. And then a full moon lifted from behind the ridge and blinded us, its light like a blow in the face. It was impossible to look into it. We bent our heads and continued. I have never felt closer to fatalistic resignation, bound interminably to this road that had long ago forgotten to lead anywhere; and never closer to understanding why the infinite has so overwhelmed the minds of men of the desert.

We came at last to a small miracle in the midst of a numbing chaos of peaks and volcanic rock: a mountain oasis, stream-fed, ringed by hillsides of blossoming terraces—Tafraoute. Whenever I think back on it, colors spring to mind—sun-dappled russet and tawny red, blue shadows, warm rose of earth and rock, deepening to purple. The house roofs come down the steep slopes like steppingstones; in fact, you can walk off the path onto a roof, and down an outside ladder to the lane below.

The women are lovely, and the children plentiful. The girls still marry at thirteen or fourteen, and when you see them walk, swaying under a great bronze pitcher on one shoulder, you think this is probably just as well. And their husbands? Gone to the cities, to their groceries. They will come back, in time to sire the next generation of grocers. Meanwhile, the women tend the crops and the orchards foaming with blossom. A stone olive press waits in the square for the crop that is ripening. The sacred eels in a spring-fed pool up the road are consulted on all matters of importance. On a slope above the village, the cemetery is bounded by stones set upright in the ground—slender, sharp-pointed stones selected because they look like snakes' heads raised to strike, and thus will protect the dead against malicious djinns. And perhaps against jackals.

Such men as we saw in Tafraoute were over forty. Having made their pile in Casa or Rabat, they had come back—not as played-out old codgers to a retirement village, but as men who had earned their leisure, and now were ready to enjoy living and the wives they'd had so little time for. But Ibrahim was different. With a gentle, candid, wistfulness quite unlike the complacency of the other men, he presented himself to us as "the official guide." The first time I took the steering wheel when he was with us, I saw panic on his face in the rear-view mirror. Though I drove very circumspectly, he perched on the edge of the back seat and seemed to hold his breath for several minutes, until at last he released it with a long sigh. "Now I see it is true what I have heard—abroad, the women are taught to do *everything!*" he marveled guile-lessly, and allowed himself to lean back.

One day, Bill asked him about the campaign ribbons pinned to his burnous. Shining with pride, Ibrahim tapped one of them. "This one," he said, "this one was for the battle of the Kasserine Pass—a good sixty kilometers from here, at least!" Bill looked at him thoughtfully. "That is—you mean—six thousand kilometers—?" "Exactly, exactly . . . not too far from here, after all. Ah, yes, without doubt, that was the grand epoch, was it not? When you and we were colleagues!"

He was a devout man, mindful of all the prayer hours, and obsessed with a desire to make the pilgrimage to Mecca. But it cost so much. . . . Oh, certainly, there were men like himself who were able to get jobs as cooks on the steamers plying out of Casa. But to be chosen for such a job, you had to know somebody high up. . . . Perhaps he could make enough money for the hajj if he could get a job in the United States. Would we tell him, please, shouldn't he be able to earn a good living? After all (and he spoke with dignity), he was master of three trades: he was a fine cook and an excellent *valet de chambre,* and could prove a most reliable porter and night watchman. Gravely, we promised to bear him in mind.

We took care to make the return trip out of the mountains by daylight. When we came again to that village gas pump, a big, raw Berber was in attendance this time. We told him about the boy who had left off the tank cap and nearly stranded us on the mountain. The Berber ruminated and spat in the dust. Pointing with his chin toward a hut down the road, he said with scorn, "*Aaah! ti sais . . . cet Arabe—!*"

Two Towns

Crossing the River Sous again, we began our trek northward up the Atlantic coast. From Agadir to Casa, the shore is studded with cities that began as Portuguese trading colonies, each well fortified with citadel and garrison because the Moors, after giving trading rights, were prone to turn about and push the infidel into the sea. Even when the foreigner was allowed, for the sake of revenues, to go unmolested on Moroccan soil, he was given no guarantee against the corsairs. They preyed at will on the frigates passing within easy range on their way home, heavy-laden, from both the East and West Indies. Piracy was, in effect, the Moors' covert retort to the foreign penetration going on ashore. But piracy was not enough to stop the West. Except during the isolated epoch of that bone crusher, Moulay Ismaïl, the penetration continued. Soon after that warrior had purged the coast of foreign enclaves, the Europeans returned. If they built no more garrisons and stationed no more troops, it was because the Mahkzen was now too weak to resist their increasingly powerful economic strangle hold.[1]

It is customary, today, to see this process as a sin committed by Europe on the helpless body of Morocco. It would be fairer not to ignore the part played in the transactions by Moroccan greed and self-interest. If sultans had refused the high profits they were offered, if Berber tribesmen had supported the Mahkzen instead of using any period of threat from without as an opportunity to advance their separatism—if, in short, Morocco had been ready for nationhood, she might very well have repelled the European. There is a parallel here worth noting with the anti-western attitude of some of the new black African states today, who prefer to overlook the part played by their forebears, the chieftains who purveyed slaves for the European slave traders.

Morocco's entire Atlantic coast affords not a single good natural harbor or a navigable river. The old ports have succumbed either to the silting-up of their river mouths or to the furies of the westerly gales in winter. On February

1. While piracy did not eliminate the infiltration, it did at least continue lucrative for a long time. By the late eighteenth century, the maritime powers were paying the sultans very substantial tribute for protection from corsairs. When the brand-new American republic first began to think of a foreign trade, its Minister in Paris, Thomas Jefferson, was outraged: "When this idea [of tribute] comes across my mind," he wrote to Congress, "my faculties are absolutely suspended between indignation and impotence."

29, 1960, Agadir, at the mouth of the Sous, was like many another coastal town, with its Portuguese citadel and mediocre harbor. A big sardine fleet was readying—this was the eve of departure for the spring catch. Then came the earthquake. In a matter of seconds, 20,000 lives were snuffed out and Agadir was rubble.

Five years later, a new city was rising, phoenix-like, from the ashes. Since virtually everything was destroyed in that apocalypse, Agadir has afforded Moroccan architects a first opportunity for rational city planning. They have done an interesting job that shows a nice balance of convenience and quiet authenticity. Nothing is grandiose, but nothing is trivial, either. Until trees have had a chance to grow up in the open spaces, the expanses of reinforced concrete are hard on the eyes. But there are many signs of an imaginative search for a really national architecture—one that relies neither on traditional horseshoe arches, green-tiled pyramid roofs, and fretted stucco, nor on the sterile modernism that makes some of Israel's new cities so disastrously ugly.

Northward along the coast from Agadir, spurs of the High Atlas spring out of the sea. This is magnificent hunting country; and here also is a tree population that must be seen to be believed: goats. The argan tree, an ancient species extinct almost everywhere but in this part of Morocco, exerts an attraction entirely irresistible to goats. This argan forest is alive with them—standing on their hind legs to browse the lowest branches, climbing on each others' backs to begin their ascent to the top of the tree, swinging aloft and out on the topmost limbs with perfect aplomb, for all the world like two-horned, black-and-white apes without tails. Meanwhile, on the ground, the herdsman and his children flail the tree with long sticks, trying to bring down all the hard little bitter fruits that have eluded the goats; the pits, when pressed, yield a passable cooking oil. All in all, a grove of argan trees is a precious bit of property, carrying with it the most bizarre grazing rights I know of.

The sharpest contrast with Agadir is not far away. A hundred miles up the coast, on a rock peninsula jutting into the sea, with surf crashing on its sea wall and spume flying upward from grottoes, sits a little town called, quite simply, the Picture—Essaouira.[2] The citadel and fortifications are the warm tan of sandstone; the city within—Kasbah, Grand Mosque, houses, impeccable little inn—is glistering white in the salt air, and a wide esplanade is planted with the most beautiful trees in the world, Auracaria Excelsa, fifty feet tall and shaped like Cherifian stars layered upon a spindle. Behind a long mole, where a painted fishing fleet is drawn up on the beach, men are busy with pitch and drying nets. One sixty-foot hull is a tuna boat that plies far out to sea.

One might suppose the fortifications, so picturesque and so wholly intact as to be almost unconvincing, to be Portuguese. They are not. Moulay Ismaïl's

2. The old name is Mogador, still found on some maps.

grandson, with a touch of his ancestor's mania, imported a disciple of Vauban and ordered him to build this fantasy fortress-harbor, which, since there has never been a Moroccan navy, none but corsairs would ever use. On one of a dozen rocky offshore islets, a fort commands the approaches; inshore, the sea wall is lined with gunports and the snouts of forty bronze cannon. A high tide, whipped by the westerlies, fumes up the citadel wall, and even at low tide the earth shudders under the surf's impact. Essaouira is a tableau, a city caught outside time. Orson Welles saw it and knew he had found the set for his film *Othello*.

Safi

Safi is a city in more than name only. Here, for the first time on our northward progress, we felt the pace and vigor of a true port. Though not at the mouth of any river, and though its hinterland is the bleak bush-steppe west of Marrakesh, the air rang with the clangor of harbor noises, huge trucks congested the traffic, and the city was ringed with new high-rise *cités ouvrières* to house the large working population. There was an overpowering smell of fish—"Sardine Capital of the World" is no empty boast. From April to September each year, the fishing fleet brings in a vast harvest, and the canneries operate on double shifts. (Each April, polygamy takes a sharp upswing. An extra wife then can bring in a good wage; in the fall she can be divorced by the simple Muslim act of repudiation.) But even here catastrophe can strike. In February of 1966, a hurricane lashed the coast, building up a series of tidal waves that swept over the mole and dashed half the fleet to pieces.

It is not the sardine industry, however, that makes every Moroccan businessman and government official straighten up with pride and hope whenever Safi is mentioned; nor is it sardines that caused a railway line to be run out to the coast from the main line to Marrakesh. It is phosphates, in an abundance and of a quality to make Morocco the second producer in the world. This has wide implications for the future; how this budding industry fares may determine, more than any other single factor, whether Morocco will be able to develop a self-sustaining economy.

Early in this century, a French geologist explored the steppe behind Safi and found at Youssoufia, in the midst of an ashen landscape of gray sand and buttes rising abruptly against a featureless landscape, very extensive phosphate beds, which the French lost no time in exploiting. Since a colonial philosophy does not run to capitalizing a country, the phosphates were exported raw, as were all the other minerals the French discovered. Immediately after independence, Morocco nationalized the mines, began to discover more beds, all of exceptionally high quality, and set herself the goal of processing the new product.

The mines at Khouribga have proved to be the most important single source of phosphates known in the world. They afford an astonishing sight. After miles of bleached steppe relieved only by racing cloud shadows and the stark buttes, a thousand smokestacks come suddenly into view. Earth dug from new mine galleries is being carried on conveyor belts and dumped in mountainous dunes; a 7,000,000-ton treatment plant is already outgrown, and a second is being built. Raying out from Khouribga are *cités* for the 80,000 souls who live by the mines—wide avenues, rows of whitewashed houses rapidly turning gray, little green parks that stand out in the dust like priceless jewels, hospitals, clinics, shops—and schools, schools, schools. In the midst of a wilderness of camelthorn, a cinema and milk bar . . . behind a hedge of Barbary fig, between the communal bake oven and the Moorish bath, a supermarket and a swimming pool. Around each new *cité* a secondary service population has sprung up. I imagine that there may be more cash in circulation under the pall of Khouribga's smoke than in all the rest of the Bled put together.

In the ten years under native management, Youssoufia and Khouribga have doubled their production. Together, they yield the state $120,000,000 annually, and another $2,500,000 in taxes—heady figures indeed for a hard-pressed new state. But most of the millions have to be budgeted back to the works for expansion and improvements. For the story of OCP (Office of Cherifian Phosphates) is the story of Morocco's first and crucial entry into the world market with a processed product. By no means has it proved a quick or easy story.

In the first place, even her abundant supply of cheap labor is of no advantage while 81 per cent of it is illiterate, the more so since complex machinery and techniques are involved. So school is compulsory for all workers. The more capable have a little physics and mechanics thrust down their throats, and the ambitious can continue with a second cycle of technical education. All this means, of course, a considerable time lag before maximum productivity can be reached. The OCP's related goal of Moroccanization—superseding all foreign technicians, right up to the top echelons, with Moroccans—will not be realized quickly either, with only a trickle of engineers and scientists emerging each year from University Mohammed V. And there have been many setbacks; the rule, in any developing country, seems to be one step forward and at least half a step back.

It was easier to decide that Morocco must process her phosphates than it was to find a loan for the necessary plant, particularly when the first years of the OCP were shaken by a graft scandal gaudy enough to deter any investor. Finally, a few years ago, the U.S. was satisfied with the prospects, and the Chemical Complex began to rise on the shore beside Safi—the most important capitalization of the country since Independence. With appropriate fanfare, the Complexe Chimique was opened by the King in June 1965. Beguiled by all the oratory and forgetting the scale of enterprises in newly developed countries, I came to it expecting a young Pittsburgh.

It was hardly that. It was the sort of agglomeration of tanks, pipelines, generators, and large anonymous structures that Americans pass without a second glance beside any of their main highways. But it looked different if I tried to imagine it through the eyes of the women trudging single file beside the railroad track, with untidy loads like stork's nests on their heads and short knives hanging from their hands. They had been out in some field cutting palmetto, and now bore home enough branches to thatch a roof or run up a wall. They had to scatter when the train from Khouribga came by, the sort of small chuffing train we westerners now see only in children's books. The women screened their eyes against the rain of cinders and watched it pass. There was a shrill whistle, a gate flew up, and the train clanked into the yard of the Pride of Morocco.

The Complexe got off to a modest start, but two things about the operation were encouraging: quantities of fertilizer, at a subsidized price, were distributed through the discouraged Bled; and in this newest plant in the country, two-thirds of the engineers and all but a handful of other employees were Moroccans. But most important of all is the hope that this industry will provide that sharp rap necessary to knock the whole economy off dead center. No matter how urgently needed the OCP's revenues and employment rolls may be, they still will not be enough if the Complexe fails to trigger a new set of industries and end the economic stagnation of the past ten years.

Once the pump is primed, the theory goes, dozens of other industries should proliferate, and foreign capital should be attracted. The new venture in sugar beets waits only for more refineries to be built. (Will Frenchmen be likely to invest in them when French sugar is one of Morocco's large imports?) Then there are the new cotton plantations at the foot of the Middle Atlas, where that finest, long-staple variety Egypt is famous for has been grown recently. But again, the mills are few—for lack of capital. Foreign investors wait for two things: for the political situation to give more promise of stability (which in turn waits on the economic situation), and for Moroccans to prove that they can run an industry without graft (which is difficult to prove until there is scope to prove it). Even if these conditions were met tomorrow, Morocco would face hard going at best. For the Haves of international commerce extend no cordial welcome to the Have-Nots. No sooner was the Safi Complexe ready with the first year's processed phosphates than the already established manufacturers—most of them American—undercut the going market price, and Morocco could find only one buyer. Several times we were told, "Safi is in trouble. . . ."

It seems sometimes that a developing country is hemmed in beyond the possibility of growth. Everything rests on everything else; progress in any direction depends on prior progress elsewhere. Someone once summed it up neatly: "The road to economic development is paved with vicious circles."

The Complexe is not all there is to Safi. Indeed, it might have been in the opposite corner of Morocco, for all its impact on the lives of quiet, conservative families long established in the city. One of the most delightful of these lived up above the city, where a cape thrusts out into the sea and a marabout's tomb sits, low and white against the blue horizon. Mahjoub Jilali was that rare person, a moderate conservative: a devout man who yet felt no need to condemn the less devout; a man in government employ, but little concerned with the scrabble for influence and power; erstwhile deeply involved in politics, but now detached and unusually tolerant. Once, when someone criticised the King in his hearing, he said in a mild aside to me, "Our King is a little young and headstrong, and does not always recognize poor advice."

We met Mr. Jilali first in an American household, where cocktails were being served to Muslims and foreigners alike. Sipping his tomato juice, he passed among us in great good spirits and showing not the least consternation. He had been assigned at one time to the New York Consulate, spoke rapid English with just a touch of Bronx accent, and felt protective toward Americans. His wife he treated generally with unusual consideration, but when an enthusiasm swept over him, he could invite twelve people to dine the following night, and only afterward remember to ask her if she could manage it.

Comfortable of build, quite short, and with an ingenuous friendliness, he did not look like a resistance fighter. But it came out in conversation once that he had been in prison when his first son was born. When I inquired further, he smiled in deprecation and spoke only of the long journey to his internment. Packed upright in a cattle truck with a load of prisoners all blindfolded like himself, he had tried to guess where they were being taken. The truck ground up mountainsides, and he smelled forest; later, when heat blazed up from the ground, he knew they were in desert. But his blindfold was only removed when he was thrown into a little round hut of thatch.

"How fortunate I felt," he said, "that they thought me dangerous enough to put in solitary confinement—at least there was room to lie down! But I worried about my wife. I was not allowed to write. I became very weak and hungry—would you believe it, I even tried to make myself eat the worms that dropped all around me from the thatch! It was so dark, I thought I could eat a handful without seeing them. One day, my guards took pity on me and cut a little window in the hut. They were good fellows really, Goums—you know?—Moroccans co-opted into the French army. Through my little window I could see pure desert, and now and then a passing Tuareg. Then I guessed: it was Tarfaya, down near the border with Mauritania. At last one of the Goums smuggled out a letter for me, and in another two or three months—it was hard to keep track of time—I got the message back that my son had been born!"

I looked at Latifa Jilali. Her face, a broad oval, hardly ever showed emotion; she looked more Oriental than Moroccan—light-skinned, with a very full mouth and almond-shaped eyes that were usually downcast. She looked like one of those demure, enameled ladies in an old Persian miniature. But now she raised her eyes and looked full at her husband. I heard her say, almost in a whisper, "I could not have endured it without the help of my God." She spoke little when men were present. Her life seemed to satisfy her fully; much of it was taken up with supervising a few servants, whom she scolded affectionately. No dish left the kitchen before her scrutiny. She would watch over the roasting of a young lamb for the tajin and make the grape and almond sauce herself. Her braised fennel with saffron was a marvelous dish. There were only two children, both boys, the three-year-old still greatly indulged and petted.

Though her husband in no way wished seclusion upon her, Latifa went out only rarely without him. Her home was her domain and her fulfillment. One afternoon, having exhausted my patience trying to reach her by phone (Safi's system was only slightly worse than other cities', but that is saying a great deal), I rang her doorbell to deliver a message in person. It was she herself who opened the door, her face moist from exertion and her skirts tucked up above flowered trousers. A broom and bucket stood in the background. She led me to a sitting room, twitching her skirts down as we went, and I learned that the young girl who took care of the cleaning was ill. She was six months pregnant, and Latifa, finding her bent over with cramps, had put her to bed and watched over her all morning until she fell asleep. The girl was twenty, Latifa told me, a Chleuh from the Sous, who had come to them three months before asking for work, her husband having just divorced her and taken a six-year-old son with him. They gave her work, but had recently sent her back to her village to try to find another husband. When she reappeared, a young cousin was with her, willing to marry her if they could both be absorbed into the Jilali household. Mahjoub agreed of course— Latifa said it as though this was not an unusual occurrence.

A scooter spluttered to silence at the front door, and the sixteen-year-old Mehdi came in, raised his mother's hand to his lips in greeting, and withdrew as soon as possible. "He has forgotten all his English," she said, "and is embarrassed. Now it is the new vogue for karate that occupies him after school."

This woman and her husband belong to what I believe is the most stable part of Moroccan society, that group which alone keeps alive the spirit of "all things in moderation, nothing in excess," which is one of the classic goals of Islam. They are not tradition-bound, neither are they lashed to the banners of modernity; not inwardly threatened by change, they borrow from the West the things that enhance their comfort and pleasure, but they have no intention of reshaping their philosophy of life. It is Morocco's loss that this group is not a large one, and that few young people are likely to replenish it.

The Jilali house resembled its owners. As you entered, your first impression was of tiled floors, archways, a shady inner courtyard, fine wrought ironwork, and a great deal of cool, uncluttered space. A grandfather clock, probably bought sixty or seventy years ago, when it was very fashionable to import one, stood in the place of honor. There were European lounge chairs in the first sitting room, and the inevitable large and ugly radio. But the inner sitting room was entirely traditional: no furniture except divans around three sides of the room, and brass trays on stands set before the divans at regular intervals. The carpet was old, of that deep and dreadful red made famous by Rabat weavers. Thick walls kept the room cool; the windows were narrow and high above eye level. Embroidered panels called *haïties* hung on the walls, of patterned velour with mother-of-pearl sequins. There was a brass brazier, probably still used for warmth on winter evenings.

One evening, as we sat there chatting before dinner, I noticed that all the women present had seated themselves in a row along one wall, facing the row of men opposite. Though Bill and I were the only foreigners, everyone wore western clothing except Latifa, who must have been hot in a velvet kaftan with an overdress of embroidered silk tissue. The young Chleuh girl, quite recovered but now relieved of any heavy work, brought in the little son. Having delivered him, chic in a French suit and high-laced shoes, to his mother, she proceeded to shake hands with each of the guests in turn. The painted face that looked into mine was richly tattooed, her fingernails brilliantly enameled. I couldn't tell if she had been instructed to greet us or if it was her own idea. She didn't speak a word, but moved with the cumbersome grace of an animal heavy with young. After this ritual, she presented us with glasses of warm Coca-Cola, careful to step out of her slippers each time before she crossed the carpet.

Not so the child. His feet were everywhere—on the divan, on the cushions, in his father's lap. He rolled across the floor and climbed to his mother's arms. When he became wriggly, she called the girl to take him to bed; but he bawled immediately, and so hard that he was brought back. From then on, he sat still beside her, his eyes more and more glazed with fatigue until at last he slipped sideways and slept profoundly at her side. I always wondered at the sharp change a Moroccan child must undergo when he reaches the age for circumcision, at six or seven, and passes abruptly from his mother's indulgences to the discipline of the all-male world that will be his until marriage. The sharpness of the change reminded me of the weaning of kids in the herd—one harsh day, every she-goat's milk bag is wrapped in cloth. Pointed sticks secure the cloth and serve the further purpose of deterring any nuzzling.

Mr. Jilali had invited for our benefit a boyhood friend who had only recently returned to live in Safi after having been pasha of some minor town; he was supposed to be a fount of information for me on politics and cultural change. In his own way, he was. He was exceedingly opinionated, and all his views turned on the central point that the times were out of joint. The young were hopeless, a disgrace. No discipline, confused by too many changes: "Our people need *authority*. There is no other answer to their unruliness, their irresponsibility. . . . Worst of all, they are being overeducated. The country needs more mechanics, more skilled laborers, a sound lower class. Morocco simply hasn't the advanced jobs for all the cockerels being turned out by the lycées! Perhaps in each town there might be three or four boys who should have that sort of education—the rest should be taught the needed trades in grade school, and fewer frills. Tell me, what need has a mason for *belles-lettres*? Take my stonemason, now—there is the good old type! My house has been damp, part of one of my outer walls is a couscous ball—a stone over here, some bricks over there; in between, nothing but rubble. I call my friend the mason, who doesn't know one end of a pencil from the other. He rocks back on his heels, he squints up at my wall, thinks for a few minutes—then he comes up with a sensible estimate, and the job will be done right, and on time. But these half-educated, insolent ne'er-do-wells—! Their one idea is to lord it over people less fortunate than themselves. . . ." Then he said something quite uncalculated; I think he was surprised as he heard himself say it. "The only Moroccans I know who are at home with themselves now are the uneducated!"

Whenever the pasha's monologue grew oppressive, a few quiet conversations would open up in English, which he did not understand. Once, to recapture the center of the stage, he slid off the divan to the floor. Cross-legged, with a rigid back, he demonstrated how he had to sit, four hours at a stretch, listening or reciting in his Koranic school. "This was how we learned discipline. The young people today can't stick to their tasks—they are weak and lazy!" When our attention threatened to wander again, he pulled four or five cushions down from the divan and leaned against them, lying on one hip and one elbow, announcing that "only the Oriental style was really comfortable." (He looked, in his tight European clothes, thoroughly uncomfortable.) Then he was off again, discoursing on the virtues of a fat wife—"When you lean against her—so—she doesn't fall over."

His wife, looking down on him from the divan, let her face show no expression. She was a regal person, lithe and tall, her skin a lustrous black, her features pure African. She was an Alaoui, of the "dark strain" in the King's family. Jeweled earrings swung beside the long column of her neck, and her fingers were heavy with rings. Perhaps her husband bored her; or perhaps she saw, beneath the exhibitionism, the distress of a man not "at home with himself," confused by a world whose former certainties were crumbling.

I listened to the women talking among themselves about the Chleuh girl's divorce. Like Latifa, they were more annoyed about it than surprised—they felt the young husband shouldn't have been allowed to get away with it. The newly reformed divorce laws call for a period of consultation with a cadi before a man may repudiate his wife; further, they require him to provide for her for three months after the divorce—a grace period to allow her to get back to her father or some other male relative. Apparently, this girl's husband slipped through the loophole—the reforms can be enforced only when they have been recognized in the marriage contract. Since basic social change can never be accomplished by passing laws alone, in all this area of women's rights there is often a great disparity between the law and common practice. The "Code of Personal Status" passed in 1959 fixes the minimum marriage age at sixteen and stipulates that no girl shall be forced to marry against her will. She can, moreover, insist that her marriage contract forbid a second wife. But I imagine only a very few of the untutored of the Bled have ever heard of such a code, and even fewer are disposed to fall in with it.

When I asked the pasha's wife about polygamy in this region, she replied with a pronouncement: it existed only among the poor—no educated person now would think of it. This left me wondering how she would explain polygamy at the top, in the palace for instance? But I did not ask; one does not speak of the King's personal affairs. Not only is there no queen of Morocco, but no announcement is ever made of the mother of any child born to the King. As if she sensed the direction of my thoughts, the pasha's wife went on, "Ever since our King Mohammed unveiled his daughter, wishing all women to be free, we have understood that by free he did *not* mean having to share a husband's affection with other wives. It is unthinkable." Then she went off onto that favorite topic, the Lalla Aïsha, daughter of Mohammed V —her important diplomatic post, her exemplary family life, her Dior dresses, her significance as a model for all Moroccan women. . . .

But the pasha had heard the word polygamy, which he could understand even in English. Now, as he cornered our attention again, his buffoonery gave way to a simple nostalgia for "the good world of his childhood." People nowadays, he averred, dwelt only on the *evils* of polygamy. To be sure, when women were petty or mean, there were always outlets for their vulgarity— jealousies and rivalries, bullying by the senior wife, all the worst side of women's nature. And of course there was the other side of the coin, too: by banding together, they could win their own way—how often he had seen uncouth wives of the Bled gang up on their husband and beat him into sub- mission! But, among decent women, there could be great security in a plural marriage—no child would ever be orphaned or go untended while its mother was ill. The women divided the labor sensibly, according to their skills. There was plenty of time for leisure, for music, cards, storytelling; no need to go out for entertainment—the roofs were theirs, and their friends could step across the parapets and join them. Oh, there was never lack of conversation on the rooftops!

In his father's household, there were four wives and nineteen children. But that was not the whole of it; there was always at least one grandmother as well, a widowed aunt, always a relative or two by adoption, the servants, some nephews being trained for the business—probably forty people at any one time. The old and the poor always had a home in those days. . . . There was warmth, there was affection, there was stability. And divorce was much less frequent. Wasn't easy divorce just a matter of successive polygamy, after all? Wouldn't we Americans concede him a point there? Certainly it was true that there was segregation; at the age of circumcision, he and his brothers passed from the care of women to the companionship of older males. His sisters remained with the women; they ate together, after they had served the men, and no one found it a hardship. The two worlds came together for evening prayer, and of course on feast days and for marriages. It was a mistake to talk of the tyranny of men—his father never forgot the obligations that his authority entailed. Since every decision was his alone, he always took thought; he could not forget his responsibility before God. In those days, there were certainties. . . .

It was an idealized picture that he painted of course, and I'm sure by then he remembered nothing else—none of the autocrat's caprices, none of the intrigues and ruses that dictatorship inspires. But I was impressed by the tenor of his account. I only wondered a little why such a halcyon childhood had produced such a tedious man. . . . A day or two later, I met Mahjoub Jilali on the street. For once, there was mischief in his ingenuous eyes. "Never again," he said, "never again shall I trust my boyhood recollections of a friend! Why, our pasha has become a blabbermouth!" It was the only unkind thing I ever heard that serene man say.

Evangelist

The whole Atlantic coast is much broken up by forbidding cliffs and shores of tumbled black rock. Only the old Mazagan of Portuguese days enjoyed a fairly safe natural harbor. But soon after the Portuguese had been driven from their immense citadel, built above an eerie underground world of dungeons, guardrooms, and cisterns, the harbor silted over. So Mazagan, now El Jadida ("The New"), today aims to become the "Moroccan Deauville." Perhaps it is inevitable that a country that must have tourist revenues should ape those same European resorts it hopes to supersede. But I feel very glum about the enterprise. Tourism of this sort is fickle, as a host of villages on the European coast have learned. Where Morocco need never fail is in preserving that distinctiveness that does not go out of vogue.

Not only the cash investment is irrecoverable. There is the human factor, the impact on Moroccan self-respect of an invasion by the unregarding affluent. Before the Ministry of Tourism attracts more Holiday Inns and Clubs Mediterranés along its relatively few good beaches, it might be wise to listen to the President of a tiny Caribbean island a few years ago. In an interview for the New York *Times,* he pleaded for economic help, he pleaded for visitors, but only in such numbers as the island could handle without being transformed. "Help me," he said, "keep my people from becoming a nation of busboys and waiters!"

Just north of El Jadida, the great slow River Oumer Rbia opens into the Atlantic, and the ramparts of another town rise sheer from the riverbank. In Azemmour lived a man Mahjoub Jilali had directed us to—"an Islamic evangelist, a man to show you better than I can the strength of our faith." He had been until lately the préviseur, or principal, of an important lycée, and then had retired "for reasons of health" (often the euphemism for rustication).

It was an awkward meeting at first; it seemed we might never get off the subject of Azemmour's Carthaginian past. When at length I asked directly if he would tell us about his religious movement, he was vague, said it had arisen in connection with Scouting—and would we not agree Moroccan boys could profit from that sort of thing? Refusing to be fobbed off with Boy Scouts, I told him our interest was not casual; in fact, we had for some time followed very closely movements for renewal in the European church, with which there might be some interesting parallels. This elicited nothing more than a perfunctory politeness; we all endured a long pause, while I realized that parallels with other religions are not always a welcome subject to evangelists. I sought another opening. "I have wondered, as we talked with Moroccans, what has become of the great Muslim awakening that stirred the Maghreb in the early part of this century, and infused the several nationalist movements with the promise of a revitalized Islam. But now, all I hear from young people is, 'As soon as the old generation is gone, there will be an end of religion.' Tell me, how has this come about?"

Now, at last, the préviseur had been provoked to talk. "Generalities like that have been uttered before this by the young—it is an idea that seems quite possible, before young minds have had time to learn the perennial nature of the thirst of the spirit." He looked down at the big hands on his knees, bent and unbent the fingers. "You ask, 'What has become of the renewal?' To answer you would take many days, but I will give you some clues, in case you should wish to reflect on the matter. First, can a religion be yoked to a secular creed like nationalism without suffering severe distortions? All Muslims who came under the heel of colonialism made this mistake, natural enough perhaps in a time of oppression, but a mistake nonetheless . . . and the price is now being paid all over the world of Islam.

"Secondly, in a time of social upheaval there are always those who would turn the clock back. In their attempt to do this foolish thing, they corrupt both themselves and the faith they wish to preserve. Will not all men of conscience then turn against so debased a religion?" He looked from Bill to me and back again. I thought the aversion to speaking of religious matters with foreigners was making this very difficult for him.

Fixing my eyes on a pattern in the carpet, I asked if religion was not still very vital in the lives of the poor, and those whom change had passed by. (Pictures came into my mind: a man in the souks, disregarded by his fellows, pressing his sooty forehead to the earthen floor . . . an isolated figure beside a waterhole in the South, scrubbing his arms and head, then turning to face Mecca across the horizon . . . under the wall of Marrakesh, while hawkers drowned out the muezzin's cry, a lone figure, stock-still in the hurrying crowd, filling his lungs and breathing rhythmically as his arms rose and fell and his lips moved in recital.)

The préviseur spoke in Arabic with a cadence that suggested the Koran. After an instant's pause, he translated: "And We have watched over the weak and the oppressed, and found in them models for you. We have made them Our inheritors."

He seldom looked directly at us after that. As he talked his brooding eyes fastened on some bars of light and shadow on the wall. The painful things he must say were not for us; they were an act of contrition performed by a man accountable before God for his country's loss of faith:

"In the days of the resistance, belief united men of all walks of life, the belief that when the French had been expelled Morocco would become once more a community of the faithful. Patriotism and religion were as inseparable as the two handles of one pitcher. But when freedom was won, the leaders let self-interest take over their lives. Anyone can see the outcome today— venality on all sides. It would have been well at an earlier time to take to heart the Koran's warning: 'What you are will become what you wish for.'"

He paused, his breathing harsh, and seemed to struggle for breath. I pondered the likeness between the verse he had quoted and 'Where your heart is, there shall your treasure be also'—a statement so profound it is usually put the wrong way around, and thus reduced to banality.

The voice resumed. "The men who spoke for religion were as bad as any —groping for power, they talked as if the great issues were still the same as in the days of the Prophet, when life was organized around survival in the desert. They made a charade of religion! And so the educated came to believe that Morocco must evolve along western lines into a modern secular state. The cleavage with the religious became wider every day, morality drained out of politics, and all sincere men came to a crisis of conscience: their choice seemed to lie between a narrow, meaningless piety and a loose humanism. . . . What followed was a wave of suicides among those who had fought in the resistance—each week brought news of one more old friend who had surrendered to despair. As for the young, they withdrew into a deep inner malaise, where all meaning was lost, and all sense of identity. Kif became an escape for some, hedonism for others. The longer this meaninglessness persists among us, the more dangerous our times become! For it is when men have lost belief in God that they will look for a dictator to believe in."

The préviseur was seized by coughing; he choked until his eyes watered.

We watched in anxious silence while he went to the window and looked out over the slow brown river. When the coughing had subsided, he faced us again: "A touch of asthma. . . . They tell me it is psychogenic!" We half rose to go, but he shook his head. Going to the phone, he spoke briefly in Arabic, then returned to his chair.

"Two young men who are with me in the Movement will be joining us in a few minutes. Then I will not talk so much!" We spoke little while we waited, and my mind went back to a time when Morocco was threatened on two fronts. In the seventeenth century, the religion of the medersas had withered into a faith with no meaning for the masses; and at the same time, the Portuguese were infiltrating the country from footholds all along this coast. Then it was the marabouts who launched a revival. Preaching a faith accessible to all and warm with humanity, they unified the country around a common purpose of expelling the intruder. . . . Why hadn't the renewal succeeded in the twentieth century? Was it because, this time, a terrible doubt had been planted? How had it come about that the French, though unbelievers, had achieved such obvious material and technical superiority over the People of God? Progress, western civilization seemed to teach, is best defined in secular terms.

The two young men came in quietly. I thought I read distrust of us in their faces; they turned opaque eyes on us while the préviseur introduced them. "Abdul and Hakim are my spiritual sons. When I left my lycée they followed me here. For a time, Abdul was a disciple of pan-Arabism. I had to wrestle with him to show him his error. Muslims must not make the mistake the Jews have made—identifying their religion with one of the races of man. . . ."

He sat back in his chair, smothering a cough. There was silence. Both young men avoided our eyes. I ruminated on what the préviseur had just said, thinking of that great Islamic scholar Louis Massignon, who entered so deeply into Muslim thought that some said he had converted. Toward the end of his life, he gathered around him a small colony of Christians and Muslims, all dedicated to a common search for ecumenical harmony. Tirelessly, the great man wrote and taught that "Islam must not be Arabism—it is supranational."

Abdul still sat looking at his feet. Hakim defended him: "But there was some reason in our looking to Arab solidarity for a solution. We were all disgusted by the fascination we saw all about us with Europe, with western ways. We knew democracy is decadent in the West—altogether decadent. Our hope is in socialism.[3] This is why I used to believe that the monarchy must go, and the Ulema must go also. But now I am no longer concerned with revolution, or with abstractions of political theory. . . . What is moribund

3. It is well to remember that socialism, in developing countries, is not seen as the arch enemy of capitalism, but is, rather, a pragmatic philosophy: what the private sector will not or can not do, the state must.

will wither and drop away when the time is ripe. In the Movement, we live in the existential moment."

Abdul looked up. "Has the Sidi explained our work to you?" Shaking his head, the préviseur replied, "It is you who have the right to speak of it."

"Well then, it is this: we start with the study of the Moroccan nature—there is no better place to begin. We enter into all the *milieux* of the poor, the disinherited, the uneducated—but we come to learn, not to teach! While we listen and watch, we are trying to submerge our identity in theirs, so we may understand their *being*. And what we have learned is a great admiration for this Moroccan nature—"

Softly, Hakim interpolated "—the people we used to think of as primitive, bound by superstition, ignorant . . . Ignorant! No, they are not ignorant; it is, rather, that they insist on putting into practice those things they know. Sometimes I have had to think twice about their 'superstitions'—I cannot be sure many of these are not ways of summoning up a deep, unconscious vitality. . . . It may not be the amulet that does the trick, but the tapping of an inner force we 'educated' ones have lost touch with."

I said: "Please tell me about the workers in your Movement—who is your 'we'?"

"Young people between twenty and thirty, most of us lycée or university students."

"Some of us are married, and our wives take part in the Movement." They were absorbed now, so intent on describing their work that they came in on each others' heels:

"This spring, three hundred and sixty of us met for a seminar in the Forest of Marmora, near Rabat. After that, we were assigned to our 'caravans' for the coming summer. Soon, some of us will gather up children from the *bidonvilles* and take them to a vacation colony—not so much the little children as those who are already beginning to think, to wonder. . . . We will not indoctrinate them—"

"No, we would rather try to stimulate the growth of a new, and very likely painful, hope. Sometimes it is our job to replace passivity with malaise. . . ."

"Other teams will fan out, camping among the mountain people and the fellahin. We do not hurry—it is better that we learn to know one group over a longer period. Again, I must remind you: our purpose is not propaganda. It may take any team a long time to establish the rapport that is necessary if anything is to come of all this. We often use spontaneous drama, without a prearranged script, as a means of getting at the problems that are real in their lives."

Hakim laughed, thinking back on his experience. "And if you think the problems we spend our summers on are metaphysical ones, I would assure you they are more likely to be about sewage!" He stopped as I caught my breath sharply. I found I was sitting on the edge of my chair, so startling had been my sense of *déjà vu* for the past few minutes. How long ago was it that I had listened to these same ideas, almost the same words and phrases, pouring from the lips of young worker-priests in France? Hakim waited a moment, but I decided to say nothing, fearing that these young Muslims might be unhappy with any reference to a European movement like theirs.

He went on. "Each team member finds one special friend in the tribe—one 'uncle' for whom he will work his hands to blisters. Here is the important thing to understand: we are not political manipulators, *telling* the people what they lack, what they must want. We are enablers. Being with them, almost *in* them, we spur them to think for themselves—to reach, as only they can reach, profound insights into what is needed to give their lives meaning. (Who could do that for them?) When they have found their convictions, they will not be put aside. They will be irresistible. Even the power elite cannot long block the deep will of the masses."

I felt sadly let down, and couldn't hide my disappointment. "You rely then, in the end, on moral suasion?" In my own country, I reflected sadly, Negroes had been forced to conclude that moral suasion was not enough. . . .

"What is better?" the préviseur asked. "Demagoguery? Organizing the masses into believing what you believe? Every demagogue's movement in history has ended up by substituting one repression for another!" He paused, then added gently, "I suppose it is natural for you, who are the child of a secular culture, to believe mankind must arrive at its own solutions. We are Muslims. We cannot agree to that. The issue must rest with God."

"Oh . . ." I said, on a long exhalation of breath.

Abdul looked at me bluntly. "You will label that fatalism—the Muslim fatalism you have probably heard much about . . . and perhaps understand poorly. What we do, in fact, believe is so simple: *Islam* means *submission*. But submission is not resignation to evil! No! It is the Ulema who preach passivity—they are fanatic on this, because they are committed to the status quo."

"And fanaticism," the préviseur murmured, "is a poor way to arrive at any truth. The Ulema have not understood Islam. It has flown over their heads. . . . Here is the core of our faith: a Muslim believes it impossible that God's will shall not be accomplished. But we men have been given a part to play. It is our business to bring clearly to the fore the illness of our society, to make us all confront the plain choice between good and evil. Then, and only then, is our part done. Then, and only then, is the time for submission—not at the beginning, but at the end! You see, our hope lies in the paradox within human nature: there is cunning in God's gift of identity! No man accepts his higher nature readily; he will turn this way and that, trying to escape it. But, like the fish on the hook, the harder he fights God, the more surely the hook bites deep! Now, perhaps you see why our fatalism is, in fact, a great optimism."

✿

Moved by their passionate sincerity and conviction that only a profound moral commitment would lead Morocco out of her present confusion, we resumed our route to Casablanca. No sooner had we crossed the mouth of the Oum er Rbia, that great mother of waters that so liberally nourishes this region before it seeps like a slow brown stain into the sea, than the road swung slightly inland. Now we were skirting a district called the Chaouia, one of the "Verdant Three" and a showcase of modern techniques—commercial truck gardens, impeccably tended orchards, and wide rich acreages planted to the finest wheat. A region like this presents a sharp outline of one of Morocco's dilemmas. Nowhere is the contrast between her two agricultures more glaring. Here were the great mechanized *domaines,* which yield, acre for acre, six times more than any traditional farm can grow; and here also, in little pockets between their boundaries, a few miserable smallholdings of the fellahin.

Government economists urge the conversion of more land into *domaines,* arguing not only for higher productivity but also for the greater revenues that would accrue for all the state's humane purposes. In sharp debate with the economists, the King's political advisers press for any and all means of allaying the fellah's restlessness and anchoring him to his small farm. Was it because I was "the child of a secular culture" that it seemed to me impossible to discern a moral dimension in this debate? Would the *préviseur* see here an opportunity to "confront the ruling elite with a clear choice between good and evil"? I thought it likely that only hindsight would in the end demonstrate which policy was the more essential.

On an impulse, I turned the car down a dirt track that ran along between a vineyard drinking up the sun and a new citrus grove. Where the irrigation channels ended and the ground became too uneven for machinery, a fellah was cutting new mud bricks and laying them in rows to dry beside his tumbledown hut, with one wall gone. His field, marked off by a hedge of dead gray branches of camelthorn, had never known irrigation or fertilizer, and was studded with rocks. Was it indolence, stupidity, or the low energy of the ill-nourished that allowed the rocks to remain there, and the palmetto that was strangling his barley? Soon he would have nothing to eat but the palmetto "cabbage," the little bud at the center. If the state should decide to give him priority, and lease out to him and thousands like him small parcels of irrigated land, how good a risk would he prove? I looked again at the two neighboring properties and thought that the will of God concerning the allocation of Morocco's resources seemed tragically inscrutable.

Casablanca

Surely there was nothing to indicate a brilliant future for the ill-favored little harbor between jagged black cliffs after Moulay Ismaïl had dislodged the Spaniards from it. They left nothing behind them but the name: Casablanca. Thereafter, only treacherous seas disturbed the lives of the fisher folk, until in 1906 the sultan gave some French engineers permission to begin construction of an artificial port. Soon afterward, the natives fell upon the new installations and looted everything movable; some workmen were killed; a rumor flew that a Muslim woman had been raped, and a serious uprising developed—the first Casablanca riot. The soldiers assigned to the port quelled the disorder—the first operation of French troops on Moroccan soil.

Twenty years later: Marshal Lyautey has completed construction of the first safe all-weather port on either of Morocco's coasts. The fishing village has become merely the old medina of a mushrooming city of banks, insurance companies, and shipping offices. An elegant Place Administrative has been built, in that style supposed to suggest that a harmony could exist between Moorish tradition and French domination—the Palais de Justice is arcaded and crowned with a green-tiled roof; and the Hôtel de Ville is surmounted by a clock tower meant to look like a minaret. By now a new medina is filling up rapidly with a new kind of Moroccan, a lower middle class of clerks and foremen on whose backs the commercial edifice must stand.

After World War II, the growth accelerates hugely. Casa has become the greatest port of the Maghreb, larger than Oran and Tunis. The population is thirty times what it was in 1906, and growing by 50,000 a year. The thronged streets of the *Centre* are now lined with steel and concrete office buildings, the port with warehouses and railway spurs. Casa is the heart and soul of France's going concern in Morocco, the size of her investment in the city the strongest argument for converting the Protectorate into a permanent arrangement. An intimate working relationship has developed between the French bankers, businessmen, and colons on the one hand, and the bureaucrats of the Place Administrative on the other. French capital pours in, and profits pour out. Allal el Fassi's voice cries out, on behalf of all nationalists, against "this monstrosity of a city the foreigner has erected on our soil." And, every year, more of the Bled drains into the *bidonvilles.*

It was during the brutal years of the fight for independence that Casa's dangerous significance was revealed. It was—as it still is—a trouble spot, a natural center of agitation, with its teeming slums and vulnerable installations. And it was—as it still is—the most vital center of investment in the country, to be protected at all costs. In 1952, it was French police who machine-gunned the crowd; in 1965, it was the native government that

opened fire. Labor had called a general strike. But it was disgruntled students, not labor, who sparked the serious riot that followed. Then the army
and the police needed all their murderous efficiency.

Contrary to some expectations, the riots did not prove to be the signal for a
vast conflagration—for one thing, the *bidonvilles* did not rise en masse. This
for two reasons: they are poorly organized as yet; furthermore, to the people
who live in them, the *bidonvilles* are no worse than the circumstances they
left behind them in the country, except for the gross congestion. These are
not surly people, ripe for riot—*yet*. They are bewildered not to find the city
the golden place they thought it, with jobs growing on trees and television
sets going begging. But their shanty life is often more interesting than their
douar was, if only because the tribal elders are not breathing down their
necks. As soon as a man has a few centimes to rub together, he is apt to go
and buy an empty oil drum or two, scrounge a plank here and a carton there,
and run up another shanty to rent to the next comer. He will stint himself on
food to buy a radio or go to a sports match. He would not move into the dank
old medina even if he had the chance. There is considerable liveliness in the
bidonvilles; to some extent, they act as a melting pot for all the old regional
and tribal differences. There is wretchedness, too, on a frightening scale. The
riots brought out enough of the shanty dwellers to indicate mounting discontent. If all these people were ever to be organized for a concerted protest,
that conflagration could indeed come to pass.

Meanwhile, the shipping offices and new companies have proliferated; the
clock tower is dwarfed by a twenty-one-story skyscraper. In the new industrial center on the north fringe the growth is random. Any space left
between cement works and textile factories is taken up at once by *cités
ouvrières*—grim, gray housing blocks, where the only color note is lent by
bright Berber blankets hanging down from the windowsills. To take the
pressure off the *bidonvilles,* more *cités* spring up every year. As early as 1960,
Casa was twice as big as Rabat and Marrakesh combined, and still growing;
even then it accounted for three-quarters of all the industrial investment in
the entire country.

The early sixties were a time of fear and uncertainty, which to some extent
continues into the present. The French, whose investments had not lived up
to expectations, began withdrawing both their trained managerial skills and
their capital. In 1961, Mohammed V, who had been holding the country
together with his charisma and his gift for astute compromise, died suddenly,
leaving an heir known to be hostile to labor and the Left. The new King has
faced an impossible situation: if Casa stalls, the economy stalls. By a cruel
twist, this is *not* because her industries have a beneficent, reciprocal effect on
the rest of the country—quite the reverse is true—but because a dangerously
large proportion of state revenues comes from her export trade. The other
cities and the rest of the economy do not benefit, in much the same way that

traditional agriculture receives no impetus from the modern farms. Indeed, Fez, Marrakesh, and Meknes often feel Casa is a detriment to them and point resentfully to the fact that it consumes every day a full half of all the electric power the country can generate. They question if it is healthy for this one city to so dwarf the others. With more than a million inhabitants, Casa requires a separate governor for the city alone. Indeed, the prefecture buildings are so august that one is inclined to look back on Rabat as on a provincial town.

Not all the foreignness of Casa—and it surely does not feel in any way like a Moroccan city—is due to actual foreigners. No one can boast a more European outlook, no one can cultivate a more foreign way of life, than some of the wealthy Moroccans who make their home there. The Corniche, stretching along the coast southward to the fashionable suburbs, is lined with exclusive beach clubs with names like "Acapulco," "Miami," and "Tahiti," each with its cunningly devised sea-water swimming pool, Polynesian restaurants, psychedelic night clubs and discothèques. Then come the magnificent villas, most of them very modern, some good architecture and some bad, but all exceedingly expensive. It is here that the newly rich Moroccan lives, or longs to live; and he may well appear more French than the French, even to the disparaging way he speaks of the backwardness of the country and the primitiveness of Moroccans in general. (Could anyone have guessed, back in the days of the resistance, that France, expelled, would leave behind so deep an impress on native hearts and minds?)

I found it hard to imagine that Tangier could ever have been more an International City than Casa is today—at least while I remained in the *Centre*. Standing in a bank where I could hear five languages, I looked out down the wide avenue: sprinkled between the immense, blatant hotels, the offices of Ford, Volkswagen, Frigidaire, Volvo, ENI (the great Italian corporation that built Morocco's first oil refinery just up the coast). Gleaming plate-glass windows on both sides of the street bore the names of every shipping company under heaven. Each time the bank's doors opened, all the clangor of a modern western metropolis burst in. I thought: I must seek out, in this city of foreigners, some of the people whose concern is with and for Moroccans.

Just as we left the bank, I saw an American uniform, an officer engaged with a taxi driver in some frustrating kind of non-conversation. The driver's voice was raised, he was gesticulating and pointing with his chin at the other taxis lined up in the rank. The American backed away slightly and looked at a loss. We came up and asked if we could be of any help. The driver grabbed Bill's sleeve: "Just let him ask any of the other drivers—the fare will be the same!" The officer, who had no French, had just arrived in Morocco, and wanted to get to the Nouasseur airfield, where a big new international airport was being built with U.S. assistance. We helped the American sort out his strange new currency, explained that the distance was considerable and that the fare asked was probably standard. Only after we were a hundred yards down the street did the realization break upon me: the compatriot we had been talking with was a Negro. Because we had for months been meeting people of every shade of skin color and giving it no thought, I had perceived only that this man was American and needed help. When, oh, when, I asked myself, will it be possible in my own country to be so un-self-consciously color blind?

An appointment had been made for us at Averroës Hospital, Morocco's largest and most diversified. Our interview with one of the directors was constantly interrupted by staff confronting yet one more emergency; he dealt with each with a kind of contained nervous irritability and then, pausing only to light another cigarette, resumed his headlong recital to us: "You would get no idea of the extent of our work just by looking at all our treatment facilities here. Many people who need us would never come to a hospital. So we go to them, with our mobile teams, our X-ray trucks and traveling laboratories and clinics. Our technicians we must train in accelerated courses—and then straight out into the field with them. The same with pharmacists, who are the closest thing to a doctor many of the poor will see. To supplement our scarcity of nurses we take women with only a primary-school education and give them a four-year practical course. Students come to us from the medical school in Rabat for their final two years' training—and I can assure you we find plenty of work for them. We have one French midwife, *one*. So the midwives' school in Rabat sends us all their trainees as well."

While he paused to search for his packet of Gauloises amid the litter on his desk, I got in a question about the perennial doctor shortage. He frowned. "When you hear we have one doctor per 35,000, do you understand why this is? For the answer, one has only to think back ten years and recall how few Moroccans the French gave any form of professional training. When we achieved independence, those few educated men were desperately needed for a score of functions. (Did you know that most of our first ambassadors were *doctors?*) Now finally, this year, we shall have our first graduates of the medical school, and they will give the next two years exclusively to the public service. Even after that, they will be obligated for several years to give seven hours a day. But we cannot retain them indefinitely, in face of the fact that they could earn twenty times as much on their own as the state can pay. . . . There is the same problem with those modern midwives—so far, the government has held all their diplomas in escrow, to keep them from going into private practice. But sooner or later, we will have to stop restricting their freedom."

The telephone jangled. Whatever question it was that was put to him caused the muscles to bunch along his jawline while he debated. Then, his decision reached, he barked his order and put the instrument down roughly.

"Always it is this hideous question of priorities!" he said. "How much of our effort should be spent on restoring health, and how much on preventing disease? (Never, *never* think in terms of European budgets when you hear about the choices we must make in Morocco!) Just now—" and he gestured at the telephone—"I have to cut back on services to paraplegic children in favor of a new prenatal clinic. You know the bait we use to attract women to such clinics? Free tea, and a few grams of sugar to take home!" The sudden smile made him look ten years younger.

"And so the women come back just for the tea?"

"Oh, we have many forms of propaganda—films, wherever we can capture an audience. We're not above frightening them, if necessary, with pictures of the effects of malnutrition, or syphilis. . . . We will make headway against tuberculosis only by dwelling on two cardinal points: prevention, and early detection."

The next interruption was by an American consular official come to arrange the transport home of a recently deceased patient. During these formalities, we waited outside in the hall, where everyone in sight was moving at a smart jog, and doctors carried on their consultations at a trot. Snatches of high-pitched conversation drifted to us; the atmosphere was of purposeful, controlled frenzy. When we returned to the office, the doctor was standing by the window, rubbing his thumb along the dark stubble on his cheek. I wondered again if he was forty-five or thirty. Feeling compunction about taking up his time, I suggested we take our leave of him now. For reply, he pointed to our chairs and flung himself into his own.

"I have not finished until you have heard some of the things that keep us going, why we do not throw up our hands and say, 'It is impossible!' First, there are the successes: we have all but wiped out leprosy; we are very close to control of malaria; and every year to date we have lowered the infant and maternal death rate. Second, there is hope. Take tuberculosis, our number-one scourge. Everyone knows the only real attack there lies in clearing out the slums. Have you seen Ain Chok *bidonville?* And the *Carrières Centrales?* Well, you should have seen them five years ago! Now the prefecture is building 4,500 new housing units each year. The authorities guarantee to have wiped out all *bidonvilles* in another five years. . . . Well, if one wishes to be skeptical, let us say ten. *If,* that is . . ." and he threw down the pencil he had been toying with and stood up. Accompanying us to the door, he finished soberly, "*if* we can stop the influx . . . and cut the birth rate . . . *and* find work for the unemployed."

Employment . . . work skills . . . an opening into the closed circle of poverty. It is in Casa that the most impressive effort is being made. The Organization of Rehabilitation through Training is a Jewish effort, and on behalf of Moroccan Jews. But, like the French schools for French children under the Protectorate, it could be a model—a frustrating model, to be sure, for while world Jewry can muster half a million dollars a year to train a few thousand young Moroccan Jews, the Cherifian government has not many times that amount to spend on several million children of the poor. But, though you do not hear Moroccan Muslims speak of ORT, they—being not at all stupid— must be watching it, just as they watched the French. ORT is not oriented toward or against emigration; its job in Morocco is to give native Jews the means to do productive work within their own context. Its schools are primarily for those who will work with their hands, and who must work as soon as possible—for young people, in short, facing much the same future that the great bulk of Moroccan youngsters face. ORT's success in streamlining basic education and dovetailing it with occupational skills is very much to the point for the sort of modern labor force Morocco needs. As far as I could discover, though, the only schools in the country where manual training (other than traditional arts and crafts) was being taught were some Jewish primary schools served by ORT. I was reminded more than once of the tedious pasha's rather sensible remark about masons and *belles-lettres*.

Since most of the 60,000 remaining Jews are congregated in Casa, this is where the most ambitious ORT programs are under way. Though the electronics laboratory was not big enough—or appropriate—for all the boys who longed to work in it, its very existence served to awaken aspirations; and those who could qualify did not have to struggle through a long curriculum first. Though most of the girls were following the ordinary kinds of vocational training, no one here saw anything strange about encouraging a gifted *girl* to become an industrial chemist. As for the young illiterates who, through no fault of their own, had missed schooling, they were not chiseling stucco or preparing for domestic service; they were getting a little literacy, and the skills that could lead them promptly into some good apprenticeship. Lest anyone drop out on account of family need, there was a work-study program that allowed for six months of wage earning and six of school. Thus a boy from a squalid mellah—whose father soldered scraps of tin cans into reusable shapes, all day, every day—found himself in the advanced auto-mechanics class, reassembling a six-cylinder engine.

Some of this bold and pragmatic approach must be adapted into the regular state system. In view of the critical need in the Bled for enlightened farm methods and the shortage of skilled labor in the cities, even a few agricultural and polytechnic schools could do wonders; I think they would profit the country as a whole more than twice their number of the sort of unimaginative and discouraged schools that the poor now attend. Only something innovative and very practical can begin to close the gap between Morocco's two non-reciprocating worlds, the modern and the traditional.

It is a rare thing anywhere, and particularly exciting in Morocco, to find an individual trying an experiment of his own devising to meet a spiritual or emotional need that he sees all about him. The préviseur's small band of disciples was one case in point. A man of Casa called Taïeb Saddiki was another. He is a playwright, actor, and director who has been trying for ten years to encourage the growth of indigenous theater. He translated Gogol's *Diary of a Madman* into Arabic dialect, adapted it for television, and won a showing for it. But then he wasn't satisfied—too many of the people he wanted to reach do not see TV. So one day, he moved onto an empty lot between factories in the industrial quarter and, in among the random rubble there, set his stage against the backdrop of the high, anonymous walls. While cyclists swirled past to the Simca plant and the idle stopped to stare, he dragged a cot out onto the bare earth. On crumbling mud-brick walls, all that remained of an abandoned house, he painted primitive African symbols. The casual crowd increased; in Casa, a crowd always draws a greater crowd. Saddiki began his one-man performance. He mimed and spoke the story of Auxence Ivanovitch and his progressive drift into madness.

Why that piece? he was asked later. "Because it is the drama of the little man—just any man, ordinary, untalented, but all the same a creature with a dream and a spirit. He feels alone, finds no communication with his kind. So he escapes into his diary. He ends by going mad because he is alone. And because he is mad, they lock him up—alone! It is the story of our own little man. He comes up against a wall, shouts, hears not even an echo. . . . He is destroyed."

Saddiki was able to draw attention; he was interviewed for one of those precarious journals published by the Left: Did he think Moroccan intellectuals are alone? "If they feel alone, it is their own fault. Everything awaits them; everything has yet to be created. It is they who must reach the little man." But are they not caught between two worlds and two generations, the unfortunate intelligentsia of today? Saddiki has little patience with self-pity: "Moroccans have *always* been under multiple strains and pressures! One does not fly from this; one learns to profit from it. Of course people suffer—isn't that universal? They give up too soon on Morocco. Giving up is an easy, an individual solution. Should combat be abandoned because of the scarcity of combatants? I am shocked by Driss Chaïbi—he writes one brilliant work in Arabic, then goes into voluntary exile and writes in French. . . . They are traitors, the intellectuals who give up. One may not abdicate! The essential is to be present, and to work. There is theater to be performed everywhere—marionettes, roving troupes. . . . We must go to the mass of the people and provoke them! There are many avenues. There is *everything to do!*"

CHAPTER NINE

RABAT

Maghreb

The sun throbs powerfully over the Maghreb in summer. Even now, in June, it was hot enough at midday to make us ask ourselves why we weren't in England, as planned, instead of driving across North Africa. It was 1965. After our first visit to Morocco, and further months in the Near East, we came to rest in Rome. There, the zest that months of travel had depleted began to flow back, and we realized that what we most wanted was not England but Morocco again, to be seen through the prism of the Near East. So we made our way to Sicily in a new little Karmann Ghia, and across that island, propelled less by our own motive power than by insane car horns behind us. Sandwiched between kamikaze drivers, we reached Palermo, only to ask ourselves there whether it was more dangerous to cross a street at the point where there *was* a policeman or where there was none to challenge the machismo of Sicilian males.

In Tunis, Bill nudged me. "Look at that!" he said, indicating a policeman who didn't even need the safety of an island to stand on—he merely extended an arm, and moving cars came to a stop. We had forgotten that order reigns in Tunisia. It is a tiny country, and President Bourghiba "runs it like a family business." His Neo-Destour Party brooks no rivals; but a single-party state has proven time and again to be the developing country's most practical form of government for the transition into modernism. The regime is called socialist, for that is a magic word among the recently de-colonized. Actually, Tunisa's striking progress in her twelve years since independence has been due to a gradualist, Fabian sort of polity that has been so visibly successful as to leave little grounds for opposition.

Habib Bourghiba has courage, too: he openly takes a drink of orange juice on a midday in Ramadan and exhorts, "Eat or fast, as you will. But let nothing impair your work. We are building a country!" A 6 per cent rate of economic growth has allowed him to contradict Nasser frequently and imperturbably; more than once, he has pointed out that Arabs can blame their own weaknesses for Israel's superior progress. He launched a government birth-control program before the Ulema had finished researching doctrine on the matter. "Tunisia is the best friend the U.S. has in Africa," he asserts, and receives the highest per-capita aid of any Arab country.

Our last night on the delicious seacoast, with the wind blowing warm and sweet off the gulf of Monastir and ruffling the palms like the skirts of can-can dancers, I recognized that I was dreading the drive across Algeria. Tunisian bookstores could supply no maps of that country: "One has few dealings with our neighbor on the west. . . . No one has asked for a map before." My lurking anxieties seemed somewhat eased when I had bought from the surprised management a talisman for the trip—one of their goose-down bed pillows.

Across high, windswept barrens, with the sun sinking through a fine grist of sand in the air, and ruined Roman temples rearing suddenly among the oleanders, we sped for the border. Bill talked, I remember, of Timgad and Tebessa, and of how he had finally evened the score with his older siblings the year he was an undergraduate at Cambridge. During the Christmas vacation, he and a friend had hiked from the railhead in Tunisia. "We crossed into Algeria as dark was falling. Being eighteen, we only then wondered where we would sleep. Light was streaming from a ruin, which proved to be one of Justinian's fortresses. French troops stationed there loaned us blankets, and we spent Christmas Eve on the ground beside them. Next morning, we struck out for Tebessa. Often, the only way to keep on the track was to feel through the sand for the old Roman paving stones. For hours, there was no sign of man. Except once: a plaque let into a rock, commemorating some Foreign Legionnaires murdered in a native uprising."

When he paused, there was nothing but the steady cicada hum of the Ghia's motor. "Go on, please," I said.

"After a long time, we saw a group of men ahead, and I felt the new automatic in my pocket thumping against my leg at every step. They turned out to be Legionnaires, of every nationality under the sun, young, homesick and desert-weary. We ate our Christmas dinner with them—mostly bread and sand."

Many years and three wars of independence later, a red-and-white-striped frontier barrier lay across our road. Soldiers scrutinized our visa (the only one required of us on this long journey through the Near East), the barrier slanted upward, and we were in Algeria.

It is a country of magnificence, five times bigger than Morocco, a wild land, honey-colored, with leonine mountains cutting across the southern horizon.

Behind them, the desert sweeps away for 1,300 miles, an ocean of sand out of which rise fantastic towers and wind-sculptured ziggurats. There was to be no Timgad or Tebessa for us this time. Hugging the coast as soon as we could reach it, we experienced only breadth, not depth. Though the coastal strip is far and away the most populous part of the country, it seemed strangely empty. The towns were still visibly war-ravaged—rehabilitation had hardly begun in 1965. From every wall slogans proclaimed: LONG IS THE ROAD OF SOCIALISM, BUT VICTORY IS CERTAIN AND SOCIALISM IS THE END OF EXPLOITATION! I thought the people looked stunned and confused. VOTEZ OUI! the placards shouted. But when the people obeyed, they found Ben Bella had banned the right to strike.

I pondered, as we drove, on the fact that all three Maghrebi countries have come, since winning independence, under more and more autocratic rule. Two of them were blessed with great leaders at the start: Bourghiba and Mohammed V. Hassan II has found that it is not easy to play the heir to George Washington. Bourghiba is old and ailing, and has designated no successor. And now Algeria: in spite of massive French aid, and not inconsiderable sums from Russia, in spite of sweeping nationalizations and fervent socialism, the country just was not moving.

We left each town behind as soon as possible, for the heat was bad whenever the wind of our passage slackened. We paused only to change drivers. While I rested, I fed Bill wedges of bread steeped in the wine we had stowed in the back of the Ghia, and I peeled many oranges. (Since no Maghrebi currency is negotiable beyond the country of its origin, before crossing a border we converted what dinars remained into petrol, wine, and oranges.) The 1,500 kilometers of our trajectory were beginning to feel more like 1,500 miles. Between the towns, the emptiness was striking. Vast Algeria has a population smaller than Morocco's—only one-sixth as many people per square mile.

Kabylia, a region just east of Algiers, is a place of primitive splendor, of virgin forests of cork oak, all aisles and columns of silence. One early morning, we drove along a ledge bordered by these low "holly oaks," whose leaves Caesar once chose to wreathe his imperial brow. Trees grew thick and dark on our left; on the right, only their top branches reached the level of the road. I felt rather than saw movement on my left. The next instant, a troupe of twenty or thirty apes burst onto the road. I stamped on the brake; they bunched together, eying us, then in a leaping squadron sprang into the leaves across the road.

Along the Kabylia Corniche, mountain spines clothed in gold-flowering broom plunged steeply into a sea still drowsing in morning mist; offshore, more crests rose out of the water in chains of rocky islets. Scent of thyme drenched the air, and the mist rose slowly, languid as sleep, from narrow, fawn-colored beaches. The road tunneled through rock, spanned gorges, and once traversed a vast, echoing cave. A railroad line paralleled the road, still unrepaired since the rebellion. Now and then, its steel rails rose up against the sky, twisted and frozen in place by a dynamite blast. For months now, we had been skirting the hem of war—ruin in the cities of Cyprus, where sandbags separated Greek and Turk, searchlights trained at night on walls pocked with shell-holes in Jordan, and derelict armored cars rusting beside an Israeli road. The plague, it seemed, was everywhere abroad.

The Berbers of Kabylia have long been a tight-knit, fiercely independent group, who resisted first the Turks and then the French. Now they had been in revolt against the socialist government. When I read in the newspaper that "peace has settled upon our brothers of Kabylia," I surmised that quite the reverse must be true. In countries where the press is a propaganda arm, one gets the news mainly by inversion. Most of the traffic we were meeting now was motorcycle columns of soldiers and truck convoys. The natives turned their backs and trudged out to harvest their wheat.

A dozen miles short of Algiers, we began to see observation towers manned by guards. Placards bloomed everywhere: BE A LOYAL CITIZEN—PAY YOUR RENT! . . . TO DO MILITARY SERVICE IS TO CONFORM ACTIONS TO BELIEFS! Was conscription hard to enforce, then, even under Big Brother? It seemed strange that the slogans were in French; I suppose most of those who could read at all were French-speaking. Now there were frequent road checks: Where were we bound? Why? At our response that we were en route to Morocco, I sometimes thought I saw a flicker of curiosity in the soldiers' eyes, before they stood back to let us pass. It was, indeed, remarkable how many of the Algerians we talked casually with pressed us for information—could we perhaps give them an *aperçu* on Morocco? Was life comfortable there? The wistfulness was unmistakable.

I was eager to get to Algiers, and fresh newspapers. The last news from Morocco had been worrying. The King, castigating all politicians alike for "obstructionism," had suspended the Constitution, dissolved Parliament, and declared a "State of Exception." *Jeune Afrique,* the most widely read French-language newspaper in North Africa, had editorialized cautiously: it was all to the good that Moroccans should face up to the caricature Parliament had become. But, even had this body done its best to function effectively, were not certain provisions of the Constitution sure to paralyze legislative action? (And the editor permitted himself to wonder if the King had perhaps designed it so?) However, we should now watch what will follow— very likely a new war on corruption, a new effort in education, where so much discontent lies, and a new emphasis on the *Promotion Nationale.* But, the editorial concluded, will His Majesty change anything but appearances? Will he utilize men of the Left? "Once more, everyone waits, believing time has been gained. . . . But the problems remain."

The problems, it is only fair to recall, were not of Hassan's making. In good part they arise from the discrepancy between ideal goals and practical possibilities. Mohammed V seems to have been genuinely attracted to the principles of democracy. "Let Morocco become the showcase of Africa!" he exhorted, and set the prince to supervising the drafting of a constitution to provide for a Premier, a Cabinet, and an elected legislature. At the same time, he knew the country was not ready for parliamentary government, and that he must rule as well as reign. Moreover, he was a religious man and a cherif, and did not mean to see his country secularized.

No one disbelieved the basic honesty and wisdom of Mohammed's compromises. (While declaring the emancipation of women, he practiced polygamy; while encouraging modernism, he symbolized in his person the obedience due the old tradition.) Though the Constitution was long in coming, a provisional Consultative Assembly was set up to foster the formation of parties and the open discussion of political principles. In successive Cabinets, he managed to keep the Istiqlal in check by including members of smaller and more liberal parties. (While holding talks with native Communists, he did not lift the ban on the party imposed by the French. The Communists in their turn avowed loyalty to the monarchy, at least for the immediate future.)

But from the beginning there has been something insubstantial about Moroccan parties, for the throne has been the only true focus of unity and national identity. As Charles Gallagher says, "To some extent the power and prestige of the throne and the veneration accorded its occupant . . . have restrained political forces in Morocco from their fullest play."[1]

Cracks had long been showing in the conservative Istiqlal. In 1959, Mehdi ben Barka, a leader of great stature, split the party and took most of the younger men with him to found the other major party, the UNFP (National Union of Popular Forces), modeled on classic socialist lines and with close ties to labor. Much went wrong in the kingdom within the next few years: there were the tribal revolts, the economic crisis precipitated by French withdrawals of capital, and at the height of this, King Mohammed's death on the operating table. Moulay Hassan came to the throne at the age of thirty-one; the border war with Algeria broke out; and Ben Barka was implicated in a plot on Hassan's life and escaped into exile.

Then, in the spring of 1965, came the Casablanca riots, beginning as a demonstration by schoolchildren against the new age restrictions, which threatened to end their education, and escalating into riots that were echoed across the country. This tarnish on his regime seems to have been the last straw for the King. He went on the air to tell his subjects, in pungent Maghrebi dialect instead of the pure classical Arabic he normally uses, that the time had come to put an end to "negative thinking and obstructionism," in parliament and

1. Charles Gallagher, *The United States and North Africa* (Cambridge: Harvard University Press, 1963), p. 99.

out. He scolded everyone roundly, whether for allowing their children to pillage and riot, or for trying to sidestep the bitter reality of hard work. "And to you, members of Parliament, I say: Enough of your hollow speeches and vain words. Stop brandishing slogans about this or that reform, for most of you are totally ignorant of what you're talking about. The essential for each of you has been flattery, not a concern for the general welfare. I myself believe firmly in democracy, but I doubt your faith in it."[2] Two months later, he invoked the right he had written into the Constitution to suspend it and dismiss Parliament.

As we pushed on toward Algiers, I turned over and over in my mind two remarks made by the King: he once said he had designed the Constitution "to bring forth a parliament that will walk with me." And at another time, when the Count of Paris warned him, "Do not go far down the path of democracy," the King replied, "Do not worry, we take only from you that which is reconcilable with our character and our traditions."[3] There is more than one way to understand these words. . . .

The stately St. George Hotel crowns one of the most beautiful hills of Algiers. Under its mood of benign and frowsy elegance—nothing had changed there in forty years—ran a current of apprehension. The much-publicized, often-postponed Second Afro-Asian Conference was to open the day after we arrived. We could not stay more than one day, the hotel having been commandeered after that. Bidding the conference to Algiers had been Ben Bella's most grandiose gesture to date, and now the organizers were fearful that foreign delegates would fail at the last minute to show up. Quite a few minor dignitaries of the Third World had arrived to report back on the lay of the land before their chiefs should leave home, and were now looking about them with discreet curiosity, noting among other things the tragic squalor of the war-ravaged Kasbah, still housing thousands, and still unrepaired; the long, wide cracks in the main avenue, which the traffic had been skirting ever since part of the cliff it ran along had subsided nine months ago; the shouting posters, and the general air of a capital in the hands of men ill-fitted to run a country.

I got a strong impression that what the advance diplomats were there to ascertain was whether the Chinese delegation, with help from Ben Bella, was going to be able to swamp the scheduled proceedings with an agenda of their own. But we had to leave without seeing the denouement.

The great Algerian Tell was richly magnificent this June, heavy with wheat and grapes. But west of Oran the road skirted that terrible salt plain that no engineering has yet been able to redeem, then climbed through the

2. As quoted by Claire Sterling in "Morocco's Troubled Young King," *The Reporter,* June 17, 1965, p. 23.
3. William I. Zartman, *Morocco: Problems of New Power* (New York: Atherton Press, 1964), p. 196.

driest part of the Tell toward the mountains of Tlemcen. I saw a pipeline humping over the exhausted brown hills like the coils of a great python, one of the conduits through which the Saharan oil—12,000,000 tons a year— flows out to France.

At last, just before dark, we came to Tlemcen, an old city redolent of Andalusia, elegant with fountains and Moorish arcades, and high enough to promise coolness after nightfall. "We've made it!" I said, and rubbed the small of my back. More than three hundred miles is a very creditable distance in Algeria, and now the border was almost at hand. Morocco beckoned like home, but I knew it was purely romantic to pretend that Oujda and the "invasion corridor" through Taza would be any more comfortable than the last scorched region we had traversed. There is no natural boundary—it is all one ecological unit, one skeleton of mountains and sparse slopes where a few olives trace the meandering course of oueds. But Tlemcen, once a capital of the Almohads, is urbane and lovely.

"Shall we go on?" asked Bill, whose face was tired and powdered with dust.

"Oh." I hesitated, punching the Tunisian pillow that had proved a hot companion at my back. "Don't you ache a little? Wouldn't you like to spend the night here?" And so the decision was made that we would not quickly forget.

Tlemcen

Up on a ledge above town we found room for the night in a small inn with geraniums sprawling over a terrace, and a view in the dusk of an exquisite minaret. At seven the next morning, we set out for the frontier. The town was still asleep—or was it? All doors were closed, but at each intersection a soldier and a policeman stood on opposite corners, eying each other. "Funny," said Bill, "the police aren't wearing their holsters."

In Mahnia, a border village, a soldier flagged us down. "Border closed," he repeated over and over, answering no questions. I lied quickly. "But we are *expected* at the American Embassy in Rabat—we must get on without delay." The soldier, tiring of us, stepped back: "Well, go on then, and find out."

A half-mile beyond, there was no question about it. The red-and-white-striped pole was lowered across the road, and soldiers stood about it in the shade of their trucks. We argued, of course to no avail, and could get no explanation. Across the narrow no man's land, Morocco's striped pole hung slanting skyward above the open frontier. There were a number of cars about on our side. A Frenchman was haranguing the ranking border guard: "Now let us be reasonable! I am a captain in your own *gendarmerie,* teaching at the police school in Beni Abbès—my papers show it. I wish only to cross

Morocco. Understand me, please, it is no pleasure trip—my brother has been killed in an accident in France." He entered into frightful detail, but the official strode away. One by one, the cars turned and went back, and we followed.

By ten o'clock Mahnia was impacted with halted travelers, all French but the two of us. Since it was Saturday, the banks were closed; and most people, like ourselves, had disposed of their last dinars. There was one telephone, and a long line. "And what would I use for cash, if I stood in line?" Bill asked. Silently, I drew from a concealed flap in the passport case a ten-dollar bill. All these months it had lain there, as we wrote at border after border: "Foreign currency, *nil*."

"Keep a little bit of Green always about you," someone had said a long time ago, before we left the United States. Bill winced. "This may get me in trouble, you know." But it worked miracles. Pretending not to notice the exchange rate we had been given, we were ushered into an office where there was a second phone. Lines to the embassy in Algiers were choked, and there would be a long wait for the consulate in Oran.

"Can't you at least tell us what is going on?" Bill asked again. The Algerian who had changed the money smiled. "Some things one is not free to discuss. Now think—if I were a member of your FBI, would you be expecting many answers from me?" Out in the street, someone had a car radio. A family feeling had developed among us; we pooled all our small change, and someone bought coffee and rolls; those who knew Arabic translated the newscasts. "It's all muffled in propaganda and exhortations to stay calmly at one's post. That means it's a *coup d'état*." Idiotically, I said, "But how can they do that when the Afro-Asian Conference is just convening?" Bill's elbow was tugged, and he went to the phone. A few minutes later, he told us that the consul had confirmed our guess: a Colonel Boumedienne had taken over, after Ben Bella had been arrested in his bed at 3:00 A.M. There was not much fighting so far. The consul urged us all to stay as near the border as possible, and asked Bill to ride herd on a number of young Americans he knew would soon be piling up. "Poor young guy, he sounded pretty confused" Bill said. "He's only been at this new job a week or two. He says he won't know any more than we do from here on out."

A number of us turned back to the little Beau Rivage above Tlemcen— Babin, the captain of *gendarmerie,* his wife, and an older couple with a timid maiden daughter of thirty-five and a heavily pregnant Boxer bitch who so preoccupied them that I thought of them as the Chienne family, and tried to remember not to use the name to their faces. We all gathered on the terrace, passing warm wine from hand to hand, and listened to a radio that poured forth quarter-hour doses of "Forward with revolutionary socialism! Our directions have not changed, nor shall your loyalties. All is quiet—stick by your duty!" The only reference to Ben Bella was veiled: the party command, disturbed by a cult of personality that had been growing on the country, and by a leaning toward "irresponsible foreign adventuring," had decided to place power in more stable hands. Now I could appreciate as never before that the radio has done more than break down rural isolation; by reaching into the smallest hamlets, it can effectively manipulate the minds of a whole people.

The little inn had taken on the look of a caravansary: heavily loaded cars gathered in a circle below the wall, their noses pointing inward. Two people ran the inn—Fauzia, with stumps of teeth and hennaed hair, and her son, who darted from desk to kitchen to telephone and back to serve in the dining room. Fauzia's was the only woman's face I saw in Tlemcen, for, being at home, she did not shroud all but one eye with the white Halloween sheet Algerian women wear.

I offered my condolences to Captain Babin for his brother's death. After an instant's bewilderment, he burst out laughing, and I felt better about my own unsuccessful lie. He told us about Boumedienne: a silent, pinched-faced man anxious to avoid the spotlight, he had been chief of the army under Ben Bella, and continued to be. One knew little more about him. Perhaps the radio was right, that he did mean to restore the Revolutionary Council's primacy. If so, that would probably mean a great deal of factionalism and inefficiency . . . until finally Boumedienne would be forced into the role of dictator.

We went into Tlemcen to cash traveler's checks. The town looked normal, except that men were not gathered in knots but stood about singly, looking speculatively from face to face. The wineshop was open, the merchant very ready to cash checks if business would follow. Bill liked the fellow; they talked long about wines and the business situation and kept well away from politics. Looking out on the street, I saw a Halloween spook of a woman gesturing to me. After trying not to see her for a minute—I was taking my anxiety out on these women, hating them for their acquiescence in this outrageous shrouding—I went out to her. Though she had no French, she somehow made me understand she wanted to use the wine merchant's phone. Evidently, she could not bring herself to speak to a man and ask to have the phone connected. Like a ghost, she scudded in behind me and slipped into the booth, even her one exposed eye almost covered.

According to Fauzia, the women of the region loved Ben Bella. A native of Mahnia, he had come only a few weeks before to open a new bridge. After snipping the ribbon, he stood up in the open car, his sulky handsome face sweeping the crowd, and made a short speech in which he reiterated the familiar promises that he would effect the liberation of women. (If they wished to be liberated, then why did they skulk so? I muttered to myself.)

That evening, the Babins told us they had paid a visit to an old friend, the French consul of Tlemcen, and had taken the liberty of suggesting that they should bring us along for a Sunday *apéritif* the next day. The captain had also made contact with the local *gendarmerie* command and felt sure he could tip us off when the border would be open. We went, comforted, to sit on our balcony in the dark for a few minutes before going to bed. Though a curfew was in effect, there seemed still to be movement in the town—we could hear the swish of many feet on cobbles, and then a pulsing chant that I dimly associated with the FLN during the revolt against France. There must have been women abroad tonight, too, for a thin ululation rose above the darkened houses. Then there were two shots, and a third—and absolute silence. My transient comfort left me.

But the consul and his wife were quite unruffled—studiedly, I thought. The takeover in Algiers had been almost bloodless, the consul said, planned to the last detail, executed with precision. "Perhaps this is truly the golden age of the *coup d'état*—in Africa in the sixties it has become a fine art. Here, it has been accomplished with only a few skirmishes in Algiers and Oran. As for the little fracas here in Tlemcen last night, I'm not sure yet what version to believe—that two students were killed, or that some women were hurt, or that the shots were fired in air to enforce the curfew." His wife, urbanely sipping vermouth, asked if we Americans felt uneasy. "It is one thing for us, who have been long accustomed to these alarums; but perhaps for you it is unsettling?" This was tonic, for she put me on my mettle to appear as composed as she. Annoyance can accomplish what discipline cannot.

She was also kind, and pressed pills upon me for back pains brought on by tension. And, though she spoke of the Algerians as children, it was doubtless true that no foreigners understand Algeria as the French do. It was clear that the consul and she meant to stick with their job, helping all who applied (he was called several times to the phone, and they were Algerians who were asking for assistance). It seemed farfetched to view them as agents of a crafty neo-imperialism. Like many French of this class in Morocco, they felt a commitment to see Algeria through its transition to modernism. What France had set its hand to they would not abandon in mid-passage. (There is, to be sure, a myopia wherever a matter of real economic independence arises— but a myopia exists also on the other side. As far as I know, Algeria does not protest the fact that France must subsidize the price of Algerian oil to keep it competitive on the French market.)

I did not like what I heard Babin telling Bill about a "School of Insurgency" that Ben Bella had established at Mahnia, where commandos were trained for subversion abroad—one good reason why Algeria was so unpopular with its neighbors. Then the consul discussed our situation. He thought Algeria might soon open its frontier, if only to demonstrate that everything was normal again. But Morocco might then promptly close *its own*. A purely reflexive response? No—more than that. Ben Bellistes would surely try to slip across into Morocco, where they would hardly be welcome guests. Then there was another possibility: Boumedienne, commander of the army when

Morocco roundly trounced Algeria in 1963, might seek a foreign diversion in this moment of wavering support for his coup, and march on the neighbor who, by defeating him, had stained his military honor. Even if the idea did not occur to Boumedienne, was it not sure to occur to the King of Morocco?

Late that night, Babin tapped at our door: "Be ready at seven o'clock tomorrow; we shall go in convoy to the border. I am told it will open for two hours only." So, while mist still clung to the nut-brown mountains, we set out, somehow dragging the Chiennes with us, after a maddening delay over the Boxer's condition. Along the road, we picked up three gleaming American station wagons with USAF license plates. "Ah!" said Bill. "The Americans I was supposed to chaperone." Except for a lone male, they were all young women. As we drew up at the frontier, trucks there ahead of us disgorged their load of dust-caked Moroccan laborers, who promptly crawled under the trucks for shade.

The Americans, Bill discovered, were schoolteachers from Wheelus Base in Libya, bent on a summer vacation in Morocco. "They appear very self-contained," he said. "I'm glad I don't have to chaperone them."

"What makes you think this is the end of our togetherness?" I asked sourly.

"Get in line," he said. "Clear the car through customs. I'll attend to the passports."

I got in line, still clutching the Tunisian pillow. At eight o'clock exactly, the line stirred. I saw Algeria's red-striped pole go slanting up and hang suspended, like an arm raised in salute. The border was open. In ten more minutes, our car was officially out of Algeria. Looking out the window, I saw the Moroccan laborers cross no man's land, singing. I watched them reach home; and I watched the barrier swing down behind them. Morocco had closed its frontier. Slowly, the facts came in upon me. We would be here indefinitely. . . . but the Ghia was technically *out* of Algeria. Now it would be illegal to drive it.

But no one protested our heading back to Tlemcen with the others. With all, that is, except the young Americans. On the way back, Bill released some of his frustrations about Dan: "He's persuaded the girls to follow him down to the coast for a swim—they think it a lark to thread their way through a minefield. If they don't blow up, maybe they'll find a spot where they can slip through the border. He told me to forget about them; I think I shall, happily!"

The ensuing hot days melted together in a blur of rumors, anxieties, and attempts at distraction. We were a group of about fifteen by now, as business-men and engineers from various parts of the country piled up with us. We all pinned our faith on Babin to get us through. Once, Bill and I visited the lovely Almohad mosque, as close as one can come today to knowing the inside of a Moroccan mosque. The pillars rose high, as in an airy forest with much light. Rush mats tied around their bases made the stone kinder to lean against; in the aisles between their tall trunks, prayer rugs were scattered here and there, vibrant with color. Cross-legged on the floor, men sat around an elder who read from a Koran laid upon a most beautifully carved Koran rest in the shape of a wide X. Other men prayed; some simply rested and talked quietly. There is no sanctimoniousness in a mosque. It is a place of relief and release, where the individual does what he sees fit to do.

As we were leaving, I saw in a corner by the portal an aged woman wrestling with grief. Her hair was disheveled, and the headcloth had slipped away from the seamed face. Eyes closed in prayer, she carried both hands to her breast and face, then held them cupped before her in the immemorial gesture of supplication.

When we had decided in Rome to return to Morocco, we had written our younger daughter to meet us there, at the end of her college year. Now the day was almost at hand—she would arrive in Casa this very Thursday night, when it seemed likely we might still be captive here. So I sent wire after wire, with a "receipt requested" form attached, to a friend in the embassy in Rabat. He must surely know the frontier situation, and might, in addition to making some arrangement for Molly, be able to start some wheels turning that would release us. When no receipt arrived, I went to the Red Crescent. The agent's mournful eyes expressed little confidence, even while his lips assured me that he could reach her with a message. My feeling of impotence redoubled my urgings, until I realized with some surprise that I was representing Molly, who was twenty and quite sound of limb and mind, as very young and helpless, if not in fact rather dim-witted.

I cornered our innkeeper that evening. "Tell me how long *you* think the border will remain closed?" I asked. He responded at first, as Arabs will, with assurances that all would soon be cleared up, and then, with no change of intonation at all, gave tongue to a vast skepticism that the border would *ever* reopen: "*Une fois que ça déclenche, Madame ...*" and he hoisted his shoulders most eloquently.

Something, I felt, was wrong with Bill. His calm had subtly hardened into fatalism. So I became the more frightened, and aggressive. "I insist," I shouted, "on going to the border one last time tomorrow!"

"All right, all right"—with that exasperating patience—"but what do you propose to do if that doesn't work?"

"Your initiative is paralyzed! You're just like Monsieur Chienne. I saw your face when the daughter came and pleaded with you to do something to get her father's mind off the dog and make some plan. You looked back at her like the worst sort of Muslim—like a man who will embrace any fate to find peace!"

On Wednesday morning, some kind of gale swept us all up, even the Chiennes, and we took off as birds do at some invisible signal. The barrier was still down on the Other Side. More truckloads of laborers were there, some with wives, and hens tethered to their knapsacks. The men crawled under the trucks for shade, the women munched carob beans and gave suck to two-year-old children. There was no water. I sat on the steel counter of the customs shed until my tormented back sent me out again to the stone steps.

A persistent rumor circulated that a Moroccan commissioner of police would appear shortly—at ten . . . at noon . . . at three. . . . Each time any figure stirred over there beyond no man's land, a herd movement sent us all up to the line of Algerian soldiers at parade rest beneath their raised barrier, and there would ensue a babel of argument, protest, and even a few meaningless threats of reprisal, before we all drifted back to the shed again. To keep his mind off the panting Boxer, I engaged M. Chienne in helping me draft another message to Rabat. This time, I meant to get the Moroccan commissioner to telephone it. M. Chienne was indulgent, and completely skeptical.

It was five o'clock before another ripple swept over us—a uniformed figure had been sighted Over There. Our deputation surged forward, and while the protests were warming up, I shouted across the void, "*Monsieur le Commissaire de Police!*" At the third shout, a figure stepped into sight, gazing toward us. I gathered my resolution about me, looked down on the carbine barring my way, then, fixing my eyes on the young soldier's, I seized the barrel and pushed it up. As I walked alone across those hundred yards, I had so thoroughly convinced myself by my own histrionics that tears were running down my face. I beat passionately on the striped pole, calling on the commissioner. He came, he listened, and he promised.

We went back to Tlemcen. At ten o'clock that night, he somehow got word throught to the Beau Rivage that he had delivered my message. Long live that man! Long live humanity! I thought, and sank into sleep.

Next morning came the shock: the Babins had left early and gone back to their home in Beni Abbès. And then another: the young painter I used to chat with looked up from his pails of whitewash and said very simply, "You ought to leave Tlemcen today." I found Bill. "Please don't wait to phone Oran, *please* don't. We'll find out soon enough whether planes are flying. Just get the suitcases."

I sought out the Chiennes. The daughter opened the door, her eyes red with crying. "It's too late—it's no use now . . . nothing you say. . . . The accouchement is in progress."

On the way to Oran, the stiffness between Bill and me began to melt. We could see a pattern now: during the first days in Tlemcen, Bill had borne all the responsibility, taken all decisions, while I suffered fits of panic and was of no use. Then, as often happens subtly in a long-established relationship, the balance had shifted. . . . We agreed that playing my hunch meant problems ahead. Even if the air frontier proved to be open, what shipper would take on a car that did not legally exist? And even if the port were open, whose ships came to Oran, and bound where?

The streets of Oran were full of glass, and iron grilles covered the shattered windows. In the airline office, we found that the air frontier had never been closed.... There was a plane that evening. But then, while the Algerian contemplated with disbelief what remained of our round-trip tickets from the U.S., and began examining the carbons of our stages through the Near East, I remembered something: the last stub would be stamped *Tel Aviv*. That would prove us Zionist sympathizers, traitors. While he went wonderingly through one ticket, I withdrew the other and wandered off. With a wet finger, I rubbed until the stamp became a blur. Then I substituted my ticket for the other while he was on the phone, and repeated my performance. He returned, smiling. There were two seats for us on the plane.

It took all the rest of that day—seven hours, if I remember—to arrange for the car. Everything began discouragingly—the port empty, all schedules suspended. But everyone was sanguine—it was just a matter of time before normal business would resume. We had not time? Now, that was a pity.... A Spanish line had several ships due in. Since we were to fly home shortly from Madrid, this seemed the best bet. But, they said charmingly, if we could not wait a week or two for a ship to come in, well—perhaps we should find an agent.

It is one of the great strengths of the Mediterranean culture that if you wish to do something out of the ordinary, in due course a man will be found to undertake your business for you. Arabs are especially good at this; but it is well to choose the right Arab. The line was helpful, and produced our man. The consul was able to authenticate him. Tirelessly, he led us through formalities that should have been sufficient for the safe-conduct of the Kohinoor. Traveler's checks drifted down like leaves in the fall, and we accumulated a thick sheaf of papers. It may seem strange, but our confidence grew that we would see the Ghia again.

With a very few minutes to spare, we came at last, exhausted and hungry, to wait for the airport bus we'd been told to take. Familiar voices fell on our ears. There, in a café, sat Dan and the station-wagon girls, calling for Coca-Cola. Bill looked relieved in spite of himself and went over to ask if they'd had a good swim. But he came back glowering. "Oh, sure! They've got everything under control. Do you know what they've done with their cars? Just dumped them on the consul—left them in the street outside his door, and sent word to him they're flying out to Lisbon tonight...."

All we could find to eat at the airport was a kilo of oranges. We had breakfasted at 6:00 A.M. Just as I began peeling, the loudspeaker crackled, and in an instant we were sprinting for our plane, which had decided to leave a half-hour early. I fell into a seat, entirely disenchanted for the moment with all countries *"en pleine voie de développement."* My seat companion leaned toward me, offering his hand, and I recognized an Indian gentleman from the St. George in Algiers. In a minute, my curiosity reawakened: What *had* happened to the Afro-Asian Conference? Saturnine, he smiled. "What would you expect? But, believe me, even if Ben Bella had not been spirited away in the night, it was doomed."

"Why?"

"For lack of substance." When I still looked puzzled, he gave me what is probably the definitive answer: "Tell me—have you ever met an Afro-Asian?"

While we hurtled into the setting sun, I heard him only by fits and starts: "In Africa, 'socialism' and the 'politics of the Left' are as popular as they are poorly defined. . . . Governments calling themselves socialist are really following the politics of the Right, while they make spectacular declarations and talk of 'revolutionary principles.' . . . Some sincerely believe they have achieved socialism because they have nationalized everything and lined everybody up under a paralyzing bureaucracy. Socialism is too serious a concept to be thus played with. It is also a long-range achievement, a goal, not something to be realized in an instant, like winning membership in a club."

That seemed to sum up a great deal. Whereas, in the monarchy that lay ahead of us. . . . But I was too tired to think about Morocco now, and I dozed, only to wake in a few minutes as the first sight of Casa sprang up in a starburst of lights. My companion's voice went on as though there had been no break: "And how long do you think the Moroccan stalemate can last? I was here in Casa in March, saw the pavement ripped up for barricades in the medina, saw cars overturned and set afire before the occupants could escape. . . . We in India have known rioting, but what I had not seen before was high-school lads drenching a policeman in petrol and setting him alight."[4]

✿

Like so many over-rehearsed arrangements, my efforts on Molly's behalf proved ludicrous. Our friend Josh had been told of our message to the embassy, and had met a succession of planes from the West earlier that night; she was on none of them. We found a cable at the Balima: she was waiting in London, having been told that all Moroccan airports were closed. . . . The final touch of fantasy came in our de-briefing at the embassy. The Secretary who had received our message found it difficult to believe our story: "Now let's go back again and get the facts straight. Now, it was not the *Moroccan* border that was closed, was it? I am assured it has remained open throughout."

The *état d'exception* did not make itself felt on the surface, which appeared as usual. When at length Molly joined us, we had no time left for investiga-

4. To suggest how far our horizons of horror have widened: I thought then, in 1965, "How near the surface the old Moorish savagery lurks!" little dreaming that within three years I would read in the Berkeley student newspaper the words of a girl leading activists down Telegraph Avenue: "Now let's see who has the balls to set a Pig on fire!"

tion—the Ghia had arrived in Spain. From Madrid, we went our several ways, we back to the U.S. and she northward across Europe. Weeks later, as she tramped up a Norwegian fjord, rucksack on her back and tied on above it the great cartwheel hat she had bought in Chaouen, she heard a voice calling from a hotel above the road. *"Ma'mselle! Ma'mselle! Toi, qui vient du Maroc—"* and she turned. A thin brown lad in a busboy's jacket pounded up to her. "You have been in the Rif—I see it on your back! Speak with me, speak with me a little of my country. . . ."

Rabat, 1966

Less than a year later, we were back, for the summer visit that has already entered into this account at many points. A year of reflection and study had given rise to questions I could not have entertained before. Those contacts that we had prepared in the interval were now open to us, and many of them have been described. I shall be speaking now of Rabat as we saw it that early summer.

The white city rimmed by sea seemed more beautiful than ever. Bougainvillea rustled in orange and magenta against pale walls, and canopies of jacaranda shaded the streets. Changes were noticeable in the city since we had first known it eighteen months before—several boldly designed new buildings that, to my mind, are more successful than the modern architecture of many western cities. They are a blessed relief from the Protectorate era's hydrocephalic banks, and from that fussy French cathedral, rising above the flower market, whose many pinnacles and Islamized spire suggest asparagus fern rendered in concrete.

There were subtler changes, too—I thought the miniskirted office girls laughed more freely in the streets; unchaperoned young couples appeared in our favorite restaurant, openly courting. The French owner was gone, and the new man was a Moroccan; we were welcomed as though our return guaranteed success to the house. There were several luxurious new hotels, and more snack bars had blossomed. Outside a place calling itself Dolce Vita, the brigades of international drifters formed and re-formed—androgynous young figures, their faces quite uniform in expressing amused superiority. (It was the year the word had gone out: youth must travel East. "Man—haven't you heard? This year it's Katmandu for Christmas!") Rabat had made it on The Scene.

On the surface, the city seemed as confidently brisk as ever and, like all capitals, preoccupied with its own importance. Though there was no Parliament, and all political life was supposedly in abeyance, party positions were still aired publicly—the conservatism of the Istiqlal, the moderate socialism of the UNFP, and the indecisive driftings of the rural Popular Movement. I thought that there were two main attitudes about the *état d'exception*: those who thought it a necessary first step toward rooting out incompetence and corruption ("Now foreign investment will be encouraged, and will save the economy"); and the others, party men of all persuasions, lumped uneasily together as "the opposition," who saw the King's act as autocratic, and were dismayed. This was too ill-assorted a group to concert any action—when word got about that a leader of one party had been summoned to the palace for "talks," all the old rivalries opened up again.

I believe that there are both internal and external reasons for the political immaturity that plagues the country and provides a rationale for the *état d'exception*. An internal reason is that no one has political experience or an organized power base. When would-be leaders must seek support from unsophisticated masses, they have recourse to slogans, because nothing subtler will be understood.[5] Then, inevitably, slogans harden into policy, and policy becomes the prisoner of its own shallowness.

There is no better illustration of this than the story of the United States air bases in Morocco, which we acquired by secret negotiation with France in 1950 for the purpose of protecting NATO's flank. Though it was Paris that insisted on secrecy, when the facts became known it appeared that the U.S., conniving behind Mohammed V's back, had illegally seized five slices of Moroccan territory. So the renegotiations—with a free Morocco—began in a climate of hurt and suspicion.

Several times during a trying two and a half years, negotiations broke down amid cries of Moroccan politicians, bedeviled by the need of popular support, for "sovereignty" and "immediate evacuation." The United States held the view that it was enlisting a partner in the defense of the free world, and that military and economic aid would enter into this partnership, the amount and conditions to be arrived at after refined bargaining. Mohammed V, while genuinely trying to preside over the growth of a multi-party system, was determined to preserve U.S. friendship while a solution was worked out. The U.S. maneuvered for time (for the Strategic Air Command's days were numbered anyway), made handsome grants-in-aid, and waited for realistic demands. It was no thanks to the politicians that a phased withdrawal was finally agreed upon and U.S.-Moroccan relations salvaged.

The great *external* handicap on the growth of responsible politics is that Morocco, through no fault of her own, has had to begin to define herself as a state at a time when world politics have been obsessive—the period of Cold War paranoia. She has watched two superpowers try to polarize the world into rival power blocs. At such a time, it is not just hysteria that makes small countries see them both as imperialist. What other word describes great

5. Professor Zartman's book (*Morocco: Problems of New Power*) discusses these problems helpfully.

powers that insist on policing the world? (When I was a child, we played a nightmare game called Get-Behind-Me. The two biggest children raised their arms in an arch under which each of us must pass. To each in turn came the inescapable moment of choice: the arms locked around your shoulders, and one of the leaders whispered, "Will you have chocolate or vanilla?" Having made your blind choice, you heard one of them say, "Then get behind ME!", and you went stumbling off to the end of the line for the dreadful, inevitable tug-of-war.)

When Morocco takes exception to what the U.S. is doing or wants to do, that does not mean she is taking a pro-Soviet position. (She is, of course, quite able to accept offers of financial and technical aid from Russia, not because of Marxist leanings—Morocco is too Muslim for that—but just to stimulate the U.S. into counteroffers. She would be imbecile not to exploit the rivalry the superpowers have ordained.) As early as 1965, U.S. actions in Vietnam were anathema to Moroccans, who could not fail to see us as simply prolonging French policy there. We even use the same word the French used in Morocco—"pacification" of tribes and villages. It is our persistent and not not very subtle support of the current Moroccan regime that may in the long run endanger our relations with her people. U.S. wheat was used (probably without our foreknowledge, but we made no attempt to stop it) to swing local elections in 1963. The Voice of America's wave length has on occasion been used by the government for an intemperate attack on the opposition. It is said, and widely believed, that some of our "technicians" are training Moroccan sûreté police in counterinsurgency, and that the palace leans heavily on our CIA.

So even in our most cordial contacts with Moroccans, we felt that, purely as Americans, we waked in their minds the question: What does the steadily growing American involvement in their country signify? Does U.S. help offer a way to neutralize dependence on France, a chance to get something from both without being swallowed by either? Is the U.S. a safer friend than France, or merely bigger, but with the same tendency to look on Morocco as a satellite? It may well be in our short-term interest to back the status quo, and it may be that we can find no other way to extend help to a friendly and beset country. The test of our disinterestedness will come when a viable alternative to this monarchy begins to emerge. If it does not appear immediately to be a "friendly" alternative, then it will be seen how much we have learned since we landed Marines in the Lebanon in 1958.

What the *état d'exception* amounted to in 1966 was this: the King, now also Premier, maintained a direct, personal rule with the aid of a hand-picked Cabinet. Army men had gained ground; scarcely a Ministry was without one or two representatives. General Oufkir was both army Chief of Staff and Minister of the Interior, a man known for his barbarous handling of rebels during the Rif revolt. The previous winter had seen the kidnaping and probable murder in Paris of the still popular Ben Barka; and the initial hearings had implicated several Moroccan officers, if not their chief himself. When De Gaulle, enraged as much by the shadow cast on some of his police as by the crime, demanded that Oufkir be turned out of office, Hassan allowed a long pause before making his reply. And Oufkir remained.

The newspapers reflected a general restiveness. When the Istiqlal's paper warned that "affairs were tending toward anarchy and business was suffering," it was suspended for several days. Then another solid businessman's paper, *Maroc Informations,* disappeared from the stands. That particular day, I talked with M. Zenined, the vice-premier's *chef de cabinet.* He told me to be sure to read the papers assiduously to learn what was going on. "We have a free press, you know." I told him of my visit to the newsstands that morning. "Ah, but that is because of an infraction! *Maroc Informations* printed an interview with the exiled head of the Communist Party." Two days later, the paper reappeared, carrying on its front page an apology to its readers for "its involuntary suspension." For this gallant gesture of defiance, it was punished with three more days' suspension. But there was something in what Zenined said—the press continued to be far from docile.[6]

University Mohammed V

The 1965 riots had been evidence of grave discontents throughout the country—grave enough to warrant the King's extensive tour of inspection in the spring of 1966 inspiring loyalty, jacking up lagging projects, and making a few land distributions. (There was even talk of a new three-year plan to reclaim all *domaines* still in French hands.) But the clearest focus of discontent was with schooling at all levels. So it was natural for us to gravitate to the University Mohammed V, where a few weeks earlier there had been demonstrations to mark the anniversary of the Casa riot. Even those to whom we had no introduction received us with no appearance of distrust; it seemed to be enough that we were of *"le monde universitaire."*

Mohammed V, the only modern institution of its kind in Morocco, is a bewildering congeries of faculties and related institutes.[7] One gets an idea of

6. While it is true that almost all governments of developing countries, whether radical or rightist, are hostile to freedom of the press, I believe that Morocco's is freer than most. There is no restriction on news leaving the country, and correspondents may go anywhere they wish.

7. Outside Tangier, a new University of North Africa is being built, a joint Moroccan-American undertaking, with emphasis at the start on business training. While some Moroccans fear it might become, if not a tool of American foreign policy, then at least imbued with an American frame of reference, the Moroccan government is strongly supporting it with both money and manpower. The goal is to turn it over eventually to Moroccan hands.

the cultural complexities it faces, and the diversity of the country's needs, from the variety of diplomas that can be earned. The law faculty, for instance, offers five different kinds of degrees, in French or in Arabic. The next largest is the arts and letters faculty, its 2,000 students cramped into outdated buildings passed on from the Protectorate.

In the seclusion of our roof-terrace, we listened to a group of these liberal-arts students. At first, we heard only of their hardships and repressions. Their side of the story was not pleasant: they had all come to the university on full scholarship, with the understanding that they would teach for the state for eight years after completing their course. But living allowances had been cut repeatedly (they did not say in response to what strikes and boycotts), and finally eliminated altogether. Scrounging for whatever hand-to-mouth jobs they could get, they clung on, while most of their friends had to drop out.

The grumbling grew. Defying the prohibition on Student Union meetings, they congregated on the anniversary of the riots. Soldiers were sent in, chased students upstairs; boys fell from third-floor windows. Five were killed, scores injured. (In 1966, stories like this did not have the dismal familiarity they have all across the world today. We were deeply shocked.) Demonstrations spread to the lycées. We were told of two sixteen-year-olds of Fez who, having refused to buy their Throne Day flags, were taken by truck and dumped in the desert without food or water.

There can be little doubt that repressions were severe. What disturbed us even more, however, was the prevailing attitude among these students: they owed the government nothing. They would go to any lengths to avoid their *service à l'état*. I could see little likelihood that the repressions would not intensify.

As they talked further, another and deeper source of their discontent began to emerge: the spectre of unemployment. Students of law, engineering, science, and medicine would be snapped up for well-paid, prestige jobs before they could close their books. But for these young liberal-arts students, trained in the French tradition and thus subtly encouraged to see themselves as an elite, there were no openings except the schoolroom door. One out of every two twenty- to thirty-year-olds in the country was out of work.

Of necessity, the only faculty members we knew were professors in the modern subjects taught in French. The others, who taught in Arabic, seemed to be a quite separate and smaller community not highly regarded by the European-minded. There was no lack of complaints among the men who talked with us, though they were not all radicals by any means. There had been no salary increases for ten years; inflation was pinching severely. "But with the Teachers' Union banned, what recourse have we?" With a grim pride, they worked under back-bending schedules.

In the university precincts, where soldiers guarding a nearby entrance to the

Mechaouar seemed oppressively close at hand, and were usually staring in our direction, they were discreet. But in their own homes or walking in the streets, they spoke very freely. Because much the students told us had reminded me of a period when I had lived in Fascist Italy, I half expected to find here the same apathy among intellectuals and the same brooding fear. These Moroccans were not apathetic. There was pessimism, black humor, some cynicism, and a great deal of determination. The university was expanding rapidly. A new sociology institute was to be followed soon by another for political studies; the latter provoked some sardonic conjectures about how it would be circumscribed.

"Perhaps it will be enough just to *talk* about political studies—and let it die there," a chemist said, and he told us about a technical institute funded by the IBRD: "The building rose, the doors opened—and then it was found the money for staff and equipment had mysteriously evaporated."

"But see how much harder UNESCO makes it for us now!" another man joked. "This time, the funds are supervised every step of the way—which no doubt means one or two bureaucrats have had to go on short rations. . . ."

As is often the way, it was an out-and-out radical who dominated the group's conversation as we sat one evening in his house. I shall call him Tawfik, though he looked like Van Gogh. He used his voice as smoothly as the slither of a knife. The talk had been about the stringency of the university budget—"I will explain it to you," he said, and fastened his eyes on Bill. "It is doled out, one year at a time, at the King's whim, with what remains after the army and the Sûreté have been satisfied. Promotions come only to the docile, you understand. . . . 'No money remains,' we are told blandly. Or, it can happen to any of us who steps out of line that his dossier will quite simply be 'lost.' Then quietly off to the Frigidaire with him, where there is always room for more. Yet, no matter who goes short, there are always millions for prestige spending. For example, the very splendid new Alaouite mausoleum. . . ."

Here, I thought Tawfik was talking nonsense. One did not have to approve Hassan II to grant the appropriateness of his building a monument to enshrine the tomb of Mohammed V, a great king, the hero of Independence, and the symbol of national unity. The site is well chosen. On a serene height of land above the Bou Regreg rises a blunt, impressive minaret called the Tour Hassan, a sister monument of the Koutoubia. Here the King was building a mosque and mausoleum for his father's tomb and his own. To call this merely "prestige spending" is to overlook entirely the native tradition of princely magnificence, which sees in palaces, great mosques, and splendid tombs not an unnecessary display but the very epiphany of greatness. Even if one could sever Morocco overnight from this heritage—an absurd idea— national pride would still require a pre-eminent monument to Mohammed V. At times I thought Leftists like Tawfik had lost all touch with their Moroccanness.

A great many Moroccans, and virtually all intellectuals, agree that the nepotism so long embedded in their culture and now called corruption is the largest single obstacle to progress. No one defends it; some are only a little more patient than others in understanding its persistence. (I sometimes thought that the breast-beating about "ingrained corruption" only siphoned off some of the feeling that could have promoted reform.) Our friends that night dwelt on it unhappily, speaking of nest feathering in high places, and the consequent shuffling and reshuffling of positions of power. Tawfik knifed into the discussion:

"It is not enough that we have musical chairs at the top—that is only the beginning. Each turnover reaches down as far as the level of the caïds, so that even local administration is paralyzed. I ask you to consider what this tells us about the range of patronage?"

"Then the 'war on corruption' is slow to make itself felt?" Bill asked.

There was an uncomfortable silence; then someone told a story: "This happened in an African country we won't name, where it is being whispered from ear to ear—the 'Arab telephone,' you know? The Minister of Finance is receiving a delegation, and there have just been strong words about the need to fight corruption. 'Here is a draft of a decree, Monsieur le Ministre, that imposes heavy penalties on any official caught receiving favors. We believe you can get it adopted.' 'Splendid!' says the Minister. 'What praiseworthy citizens you are. Now let us have tea,' and he sends all the underlings out to fetch it. The door closed, the Minister resumes, 'Good. Now we talk business. If I get your decree adopted, what will there be in it for me?'"

The laughter was not merry. Tawfik sliced elegantly through it: "There can be no war on corruption while a despot uses the slogan to get rid only of the men he distrusts. The whole system must change, all those devices aimed at keeping the people docile—the distribution of flour to the poor . . . all the foreign monies that support the status quo. We do not need aid from abroad, which always means foreign leading strings. We have, in fact, the second highest per-capita income in Africa! What is needed is confiscation of private wealth. Until then, we shall be kept in subjection with handouts. Change will come only when there is further deterioration in the Bled and the *bidonvilles,* when there is real starvation. Then, and only then, will the revolution come!" (Can this man, I asked myself, ever have looked on the faces of famine?)

For once, Tawfik had gone too far. A disheveled physicist, whose introspective look I had mistaken for a poet's, spoke slowly and painfully. "Talk of revolution is easy. The young do it every day, because it is easier than preparing ourselves for an alternative to the monarchy. I have been abroad, and have heard a truth spoken about us: 'The Arab thinks words and ideas will translate automatically into facts, without strenuous effort.' It is our failing to talk big and do little. Which of us believes revolution will automatically bring a better system?"

A man near me said softly, "It goes like this—the more unrest, the more danger to the throne, the more the King must accede to pressure to move army men into strategic positions. If we listen carefully, we can hear him say, 'Push me too far, try my patience too greatly, and I will retire to the Riviera and leave you to—Oufkir!' "

Midnight

I tossed wearily from dream to dream that night, dreams whose symbolism was all too clear when I woke briefly, only to be sucked back again into the next. Flocks of children wheeled like angry birds around me, the nearest clawing at me with little stumps of arms, while I tried to protect myself by scattering birdseed, which turned into flour and drifted back into my eyes. . . . A wall of mud brick bulged like an abscess and then opened, to pour a bilious liquid over my feet. And all the time, a strong melodious voice was calling me in Arabic (which in the dream I could understand) to return, to believe, to return. . . . I managed to wake, pull myself out of bed, and go to the window facing toward the medina. The voice was real enough, and it came, amplified, from a great distance. It rose or fell at the end of each phrase, as in plainsong. Not hortatory like the call to prayer, this was a voice to sustain and comfort. Somewhere in the medina, a man stood in a minaret and, in obedience to some habous bequest, released upon the night a prayer on behalf of the wakeful.

Beautiful as it was, as soon as the voice fell silent my comfort ebbed. I found no answer there to my question: Was Tawfik right that only revolution could bring change? (Change it undoubtedly would bring, and—unless there is an unseen Bourghiba waiting in the wings—probably a dictatorship more restrictive than this monarchy.) Social science teaches that revolutions come about when two conditions are fulfilled: when the proletariat recognizes that it has nothing to lose, and when the middle class realizes it *is* losing under the status quo. These conditions were on the way to fulfillment here. Businessmen were losing confidence; the poor were gaining it. Doctrinaire radicals say that the only answer is socialist democracy, and will not acknowledge that the country is not ready for it. Standing there by the window, I recalled these words of the King: "Democracy is a state of mind, and requires that one conduct a patient, thankless, permanent struggle against one's impulses and instincts." I might doubt the fervor with which he is waging this struggle, but I could point to no leaders who have learned the truth of his words.

There are many things in Morocco's favor, chief among them a great deal of native intelligence. There are courageous and honest intellectuals, and at least some conservatives who are wise and not merely threatened. There are devoted professionals, workers like the young evangelists, writers and thinkers like Taïeb Saddiki, and sober, hard-working, and determined men among the bureaucrats. The unhappy and volatile young could, with leadership, become catalysts for reform—and God knows there are plenty of them. The question is only: How much time is there for these forces to mature? For while democracy is a slow-growing thing, Morocco's exigencies grow at an explosive rate.

Birth Control

"When the King declared an *état d'exception*," a prominent journalist said, "he laid but one charge on his new team of ministers: 'Succeed!'" It was clear to them all that there could be no success while an uncontrolled population increase aggravated every problem and canceled every gain. Neither industry nor agriculture nor education could pull sufficiently ahead of the growth rate to make any improvement felt.

Two Ministries responded promptly. The Health Ministry pointed out that the average standard of living was actually declining under the population pressure; and the Ministry of Education, estimating the population at 14,000,000 and *one-third of it under the age of ten,* publicly declared that schooling for all would be out of the question if the increase rate continued.

But everyone knew that the psychological resistance, which was inevitable at best, would be insuperable if the government moved too abruptly. Though two neighbors, Egypt and Tunisia, had already taken steps to limit births, Morocco is less secularized than either of these. Like the Old Testament, the Koran exhorts: Be fruitful and multiply. In an institution as all-embracing as Islam, it is useless to try to discriminate between religious scruples and cultural values, so long have they been intertwined. The old, deep-lying attitudes are *felt* to be religious, particularly by the uneducated.

Among these primal feelings is the desire of a new wife to bear children promptly and in close succession, to content a husband who might otherwise threaten divorce or a second wife. Fecundity is both her protection and her justification. Even today, a woman will still sometimes plead that she has a child "asleep in the womb" if she has been infertile for several years. Her husband, too, sees his manhood confirmed in many children. Then there is an old idea that is being used insidiously today by those who would play on ignorance. In the old days, a man served his tribe by procreating abundantly; a dwindling tribe would be helpless before its neighbors. This idea reappears today in a new guise: "Birth control is an imperialist plot!"

These many forms of reluctance are likely to be articulated as religious scruples. In the spring of 1966, the Grand Mufti of Jerusalem pronounced that "doctrine would not be violated" by family planning. But weeks after several Ministries had publicized this pronouncement, even so educated and reasonable a man as my Safi friend, Mahjoub Jilali, could say, in answer to my question, "Birth control? Well . . . a Muslim would have to say that *self-control* is better." If he felt this, even after the Grand Mufti's verdict, how much less susceptible to argument would the pious and unsophisticated Moroccan be?

The Ulema of Morocco remained silent on so sensitive an issue. The King, too, said nothing, beyond a passing reference in a minor speech. ("His Majesty," an Under Secretary of Health told me, "has given us his encouragement in the *most delicate manner.* . . .") But he did order a national survey to test the attitudes to family planning of both women and their husbands. The preliminary reports showed just what one would expect: the response was least favorable among the rural population, and the greatest degree of approval came from those city dwellers who inclined to a modern style of life and hoped to educate such children as they bore. In short, the emergency was least clear to those on whom the greatest burden of it would fall.

The Health Ministry did all within its power. Restrictions were lifted on the sale of contraceptive pills, and clinics and dispensaries throughout the country gave free information. Only hospitals could offer loop insertion, and then only after medical examination. This meant unavoidable bottlenecks wherever the response was favorable. At first, husbands were required to appear at the hospital to signify their consent, but this stipulation was soon relaxed. That first summer, there seemed to be grounds for great optimism when the hospitals were swamped by unanticipated numbers of women applying. Pilot projects launched simultaneously in four leading cities were followed by requests from more cities and towns than the Ministry could satisfy on their stringent budget. The chief medical officer of the kingdom gave two lectures in Meknes. The first night, he faced sixty silent people; the next night, several hundred.

But that initial optimism has been hard to sustain as the battle has proved to be far from won. Even since the government has come out with an official endorsement of family planning, the program has been handicapped by lack of money and sometimes inept administration. Psychological opposition, feeding on rumors that the IUD can cause permanent sterility, and on every story of bleeding that races from mouth to mouth, lies too deep to be reached by argument. And fears are reinforced by pathetic ignorance. One cannot tell whether to laugh or cry over the woman heard saying to her neighbor, "And if they did persuade me to try, how could I manage to swallow that coil?"

Messaoudi

Something had gone wrong with our interview at the Ministry of the Interior. We had been sitting for two hours outside the office of the *directeur de cabinet,* helpless as mutes because only Arabic was spoken here. At seven that morning, the phone had jarred us awake, and when I picked it up a woman's voice drenched me in Arabic. In time, another voice came on the line, limping in French: Monsieur Messaoudi wished to change our appointment, since he was summoned to the palace at nine. Would we be at the Ministry at ten? Confused, I said the appointment had been for ten; was there a change? The long ensuing pause suggested that I had not been understood. Then the voice merely reiterated: please, promptly at ten.

The Ministry might have been under siege, so well was it guarded. General Oufkir's establishment did not look kindly on visitors—soldiers stopped us to examine our appointment slip at the heavy gates, then in each courtyard, stairway, and corridor. During the long wait, secretaries looked in on us from time to time and clearly wanted to tell us something but could not. It was not unusual for us to wait some minutes for an interview, for these were very busy men and subject to unexpected summons from above. (And when we did see them, they were liable to constant trivial interruptions, since their secretaries are not trained to any form of screening. Even Ministers seemed to delegate nothing.) But this two-hour wait constituted more than a delay.

By twelve o'clock we knew the name of every commune on the great wall map, and I had gone over and over what I hoped to learn from M. Messaoudi. I could put it quite simply: When two-thirds of the population lives by a primitive agriculture that barely keeps them at subsistence level, and when unemployment is dangerously high, what can be done about it? I could not ask directly: Is the *Promotion* solving any problems, or is it merely an effort to tranquilize the Bled and forestall more radical change? But I hoped this man, who was said to hold original opinions and to be unusually outspoken, might tell me a good deal.

The King himself appeared to feel that the *Promotion* was not enough, for he had recently responded to rural grumbling with a few more token distributions of lands, and had again said that land reform was "under study." One of those radical journals that somehow manage to slip past the censorship had just published an angry article that concluded pungently: "There have been studies *ad nauseam.* But, like the chorus of an opera which declaims in unison, 'Come, Come, Let us set forth!,' no foot takes a step forward."

We took heart when one of the office girls, holding a phone in one hand, looked around the doorway to see if we were still there. A few minutes later, a soldier appeared, led us to his bicycle, which was equipped with a splendid sort of outboard motor, and bade us follow him in the Simca. Whenever, unlike him, we paused cautiously at an intersection, he would roar back, Cherifian pennants streaming from his handle bars, and circle the car like an anxious shepherd dog. Finally, he stopped us before a modern villa, and managed to stand at attention, salute with one hand, and hold the garden gate open with the other. Down the path between fiery cannas came Messaoudi, his face very grave with reserve.

"I sent a message. You were not able to come to my office at nine o'clock?" We explained, so happy to be released from our dumbness that we tripped over our words. I think it took him a few minutes to believe us, and constraint lingered as he led us to an airy room with light washing down the walls from high windows. From the next room came rapid Parisian French, the chatter of children, and the smell of a good meal.

"We are keeping you from your lunch!" I said. "If we had known, we could so easily have been at your office when you expected us."

"Arabization of government offices cannot go forward without some inconveniences, perhaps?" The rather heavy face smiled for the first time. "So let us dispense with apologies on both sides."

He saw Bill standing before two magnificent ebony masks on the pale wall. "From Senegal," he said. "If you have a taste for African art, you should visit there." He brought *apéritifs* from a well-stocked Danish cabinet. This man, I thought, seems to have the western idea of time. Perhaps we can come straight to the point.

"And there are questions you wish to ask me?" he said, as though reading my thought.

I plunged right in. "We have been much impressed by the *Promotion Nationale* and, wherever we have gone, have looked for the local projects—whose rationale, as I understand it, is to instill hope by demonstrating that the countryman can help himself. Do you believe this approach will be sufficient to renew the vitality of the Bled?"

He considered me. "It is a very long time since the fellah has known hope. By now he has forgotten where to look—into himself. I drive past a field where a huge rock stands in the middle, and the man is driving his mule around it. I ask him, 'Why is that rock there?' 'I cannot move it,' he whines, 'so I am waiting until They come to take it away.' 'Go on the instant, get your pick, and split that rock in half. Then you and your neighbor together can carry away the pieces.' 'Yes, Sidi, yes—I will do it directly,' he says. But when I pass again, the rock is still there. This nerveless humanity is our bane—our fatal inheritance from the French, who killed our self-reliance. Morocco cannot come to life until we have changed this nature!"

(Never mind the routine blame-passing to the French, I told myself; he probably doesn't believe it very deeply. Something else was more striking.

The intensity of his tone evoked the young apostles of Azemmour: "*We have taken as our starting point the Moroccan nature. . . . And we have come to admire it very deeply.*" The tone was so similar, the convictions so opposite. Here, I thought, I am listening to what is called the completely *évolué* Moroccan, a man at the utmost possible distance from the common creature, whom he desires to help with a fervor quite as great as the préviseur's. . . .)

"And if that fellah were himself the owner of that field, do you think he would have removed that rock?"

He looked me squarely in the eye. "You raise the issue of land reform. Very well, I will try to answer you. No one doubts that something must be done for the fellah—the *Promotion* is but an emergency measure, not a permanent solution. But when it comes to distribution of lands, I must ask *you* a question: Have you any notion of the number of hectares that would have to be distributed to make any appreciable difference? No? Well, neither have the proponents of theories. Madame, so great is the yearly increase of our rural manpower that we should have to distribute tens of thousands of hectares annually, with no end in sight! And there is not that much arable land in all Morocco."

I must have looked properly taken aback, for in a moment he continued less astringently.

"The theorists are fine fellows, but they confuse means and ends. The man who is beguiled by means will forget his destination—like the little artisan who, wishing to go to Casa, leaps upon the train. Soon he forgets all in the novelty of the occasion—the noise, the smoke, the speed. And he is so entranced he lets himself be carried on to Marrakesh!"

He was a splendid mime. While he spoke of the artisan, his hands and shoulders took on the yokel's awkwardness, his face the wonderful, exuberant witlessness.

"Well, then," I asked, smiling back, "what will do the trick? Cooperatives?"

"Madame, before we have cooperatives, we must have cooperators! Take the poor fellow with only one arm: when others about him clap, he too wishes to clap, but he is ashamed. . . . But look! There, in the crowd, is another amputee like himself. Sunk in his misery, he fails to see that if he would but go to join his comrade, *together* they could clap!"

Bill, who had been looking into his glass at a jewel of light winking in the garnet liquid, raised his head, and the other man turned to him. "I remember," Bill said, "that when the great struggle for the unification of Italy was won, Cavour said, 'Now we have an Italy—but we have not yet our Italians.'" Messaoudi looked long at him and slowly nodded.

There was a sob from the doorway, and a small blond child hurtled in, his French little-boy's suit rumpled and stained down the front with gravy. Messaoudi opened his arms, and the child rushed to him, wailing that he had been made fun of. "My son has called you dirty? Now, shame upon him—in his own house, too!" It was always a surprise to realize how young these men were who stood at the top of their government, until I remembered that only a decade ago, no Moroccans were being trained. Messaoudi kissed the child, tucked in his blouse, and said, "Go to your cousin and say (may God forgive me, a Muslim, for this!), 'Chouki, you are a *pig!*'"

As he looked after the child's hurrying little bottom, his smile faded. "You will be right to ask me, 'Then where does hope lie for the Bled?' Here is my answer: I do not believe in keeping men on the land, but in taking them off it. My colleagues are scandalized when I argue we should liberate one-half of our agricultural workers, and set tractors on all the good land."

"And displace the fellah—!"

"Madame, he is already displaced—by sheer numbers. As things are now, he can find work for less than half the year. No, it is not ownership the fellah needs, but *usefulness!* What we must have is small rural industries that will bring new vigor to the Bled. For every one of the village industries we have now, we must have a hundred more. Canneries—we can use twenty times as many. But we have not stopped with agriculture; already we have built *petites usines* for textiles and tanneries, for fiber products and glass works— our people, remember, are skilled craftsmen. So far, we have hardly begun with our mineral wealth—our lead, our cobalt, the very highest grade of manganese. We shall learn to process these, as we have learned with phosphates. No longer need any of our minerals leave Casa in the raw state—"

He saw he was outrunning himself, and stopped with a laugh. "Of course this means more capital than we have. We shall need your help! But always I add this: too much of our native wealth is now devoted to the old style of commerce. We have more habits of mind to change than the fellah's. We go to a rich man for risk capital, but—conservative fellow that he is—he backs away: 'Grain,' he says, 'grain is surer than your *petites usines!*'"

Messaoudi slumped in his chair, miming dejection. Then he sat forward, the Arab shrewdness creeping into every line of face and shoulder. "Watch, now, how we shall break down his resistance: 'What, you do not wish to build a mill? Have you not heard that our new cotton and sugar-beet plantations have increased their yield by between 20 per cent and 30 per cent every year to date?' Smelling a good thing, but still suspicious, he asks what profit our mills are showing, and he is frightened when he hears what we must pay off first—the cost of all that British machinery. Oh, he is slow to learn, our businessman—but what he cannot long resist is the sight of success! And succeed we *shall*. Even now, we have something more important than immediate profits, far more important in its wider effect: around our mills there at the foot of the Middle Atlas, three new towns have already sprung up. Thirty thousand people have work where there was none before. Is this not the beginning of an outline for the future of the Bled?"

May Day—Achoura

A day rich in contradictions, ambiguous, and therefore thoroughly Moroccan, was just coming to a close. We had returned to our room; I stood now at the same window where I had listened to the muezzin's midnight voice offer a comfort that held no answers. If there had been answers today, I could not discern them. Looking down at the crowd along Boulevard Mohammed V, I mused on the double meaning that attached to this day. By coincidence, the Muslim feast of Achoura fell on May first this year—the May Day of European labor movements and of the Moroccan Left. The meaning of May Day is specific enough; Achoura's religious meaning is diffused in a popular and strongly traditional festival.

In Casa, May Day had swallowed up Achoura. The UMT—the largest labor movement in Africa and often the most aggressive—held the stage exclusively. Rumors were in the air of a tentative rapprochement between the Istiqlal and labor's political arm, the UNFP. The two outstanding leaders of the Left, Ben Seddiq of the UMT, and Abdullah Ibrahim of the UNFP, had brought together a selected group to sit with them on the reviewing stand— important foreign guests, Moroccan bankers, businessmen, and government officials. While 100,000 men in blue serge trousers and bad shoes paraded past under banners reading AN END TO POLITICAL TRICKERY! and ONLY IN SOCIALISM LIES OUR HOPE, the guests were left to their own conjectures: What exactly did the Istiqlal mean by this morning's editorial in the party newspaper, titled "Under the Sign of Unity"? They heard Ben Seddiq reply to it with a call to "all old comrades in the struggle to work together for renewal of the country"—a telling reference to the unity of the resistance period.

There was no mistaking the fact that this year May Day was politicized as never before. Wild acclaim met Ibrahim when he rose to speak. This onetime President of Council under Mohammed V, this man whose mistrust of the present King was matched only by Hassan's mistrust of him, presented himself to the crowd as a man of the working class and as the single person who "could preside over a government having the confidence of workers and the people." The carefully selected guests observed, calculated, and considered. Was the wind of change stirring at last?

A new and untested constituency appeared in the parade: "The National Federation of Workers of the Soil" marched past in old trench coats and mud-stained trousers, at their head a lean old gray horse and a rider in burnous and turban, a tribesman's musket slung over his shoulder. For the first time, men of the Bled were marching in Casa. . . . Just over a year ago, the UMT had showed its muscle with restraint: it had called a general strike, but for a half-day only. When the spontaneous March riot followed on the heels of the strike, the UMT remained conspicuously disengaged. The radical Left had then charged it with "selling out to the palace." What was the UMT prepared to do from now on?

But a quite different mood pervaded the capital fifty miles away. In Rabat, the marchers had carried no hortatory placards, and there were no political speeches. In fact, the only evidence of politics was the presence of two separate groups in the parade, the UMT and the Istiqlal's rival labor wing. By midmorning, the two groups were still lining up in their separate streets, from which came sporadic bursts of music, and then no more. By now the halted traffic had backed up to the ancient keyhole gateway that straddles an arterial road. A century plant, springing like a giant candelabrum from the weathered brown stone of the arch, had chosen this day to open into flower. Behind the gate lay the university, silent and empty. Neither the Teachers' nor the Students' Union would be allowed to march today.

Achoura is a day for the devout to visit honored graves, a day for all to give gifts to children, and to eat a meal out of doors. The crowd waiting for the parade was in a festival mood. Drifting from one newly set-up food stall to the next, they munched sesame cakes or tore with their teeth at roasted ears of what I would have called cattle corn. Children carried new cap pistols or garish celluloid dolls, and boys thrummed on little jug-shaped pottery Achoura drums while the girls clapped in syncopation.

A determined sound of band music, and the crowd surged toward Boulevard Mohammed V. Floats smothered in bunting and flowers were moving at last. The Textile Workers' Union . . . miners, stripped to the waist and sinewy . . . dispensary workers, professionally white and crisp under a six-foot papier-mâché hypodermic needle. But then, a delay . . . the forward band drew ahead, the next one behind lost touch with it and faltered, out of time. From every intersection car horns began belting out the lost beat, and the crowd stamped and clapped. Finally, the construction workers appeared, having once more secured to its moorings the half of a bridge precariously loaded on their truck. Hard-hatted and muscular, they postured bravely.

Between the floats marched other workers, jigging in time to the nearest band. They danced with long colored scarves hanging from each hand—a jog step, a swirl of scarf across the leg, then a step to the other side, and another bright flash of color. One man in a red sweater stood still and shivered with the belly dancer's undulations. He was very good. Then slowly he arched backward, still swirling his scarves, until his head touched the ground. The paraders parted admiringly on both sides of him, and onlookers whistled and cheered. Just before the next float was on top of him, he sprang into the air and leaped after his companions. A group of women somewhere burst out in ululation, and the Union of Pesticide Sprayers swept off their rubber hats to wave to them.

Midday heat descended. The parade over, workers rejoined their families and headed home to rest. By late afternoon, May Day had merged quietly into Achoura. It was then that I went to our window above the Boulevard and stood watching the crowd drift lazily by, each with a gaseous fruit drink in one hand, and in the other a few sprigs of lily of the valley, the Achoura flower. The day was cooling rapidly as dusk gathered. I felt the sea wind and saw it catch a flag above the Boulevard and slowly open out the Cherifian star at its center.

The government would have been watching this day closely—here and in Casa; in the old cities, where conservatism was still strong; in the drained and discouraged countryside; in the new douars of the *Promotion,* and in those new villages where perhaps "an outline of the future" could be traced. The King would ponder everything reported to him and once more face his question: How much self-determination dare he give these people? Or, put another way: If he did not move to meet their desire for change, would their discontents combine with the frustrations of their leaders and flow together into a tumultuous flood?

Bill called from the terrace, and I went to join him as the lemon sky of evening silhouetted the city's tallest trees. An Atlas cedar rose like a monument above the roofless little ruin of a medersa, and off to the west a monarch Auracaria, black now against the sunset, tapered to its star-shaped peak. A million swallows began their aerial acrobatics. I listened for the sound that had become part of this hour—the call of the scissors-grinder, and the little Panpipe he played while waiting below a customer's window, a pipe such as the shepherd children play from hill to hill.

It was as well he did not come, for householders were on their roofs tonight, spreading carpets around the charcoal fires where mutton or a hen was roasting for Achoura. The plonking of drums came from each roof, and somewhere a wavering gimbri played an Andalusian air. The sea behind the medina paled into mist, the sun sank, and the prayer flags fluttered out. After the muezzin's call, there was an interval of silence. By now, it was too dark to see who rose and turned to Mecca, and who did not.

Glossary

Bibliography

Index

Glossary

Baraka	holiness, grace, blessing
Bled	the countryside
Burnous	countryman's heavy, circular overgarment
Cadi	a religious judge
Caïd	literally, agent of the central government; formerly often a feudal lord, now a middle-echelon civil servant
Cherif	descendant of Mohammed the Prophet
Couscous	stew of semolina, meat, and vegetables
Dirham	twenty cents, or 100 old French francs
Djellaba	hooded overgarment worn by both men and women
Douar	country hamlet
Fellah	settled countryman, half pastoralist, half farmer
Fez	brimless red felt cap about four inches high
Fonduk	merchant's warehouse or place of business
Gimbri	two-stringed instrument
Haïk	long, wide shawl in which some countrywomen still wrap themselves
Hajj	the pilgrimage to Mecca
Hajji	title earned by a man who has made the pilgrimage; often shortened to Hajj
Hammam	public steam bath ("Moorish bath")
Harka	punitive expedition by the sultan's troops
Harira	thick, rich soup
Igherm	fortified granary
Imam	leader of a congregation
Istiqlal	the Moroccan nationalist party
Jihad	holy war
Kaftan	overgarment, often elaborately braided, with small buttons from neck to hem
Kasbah	fortified compound, often including a citadel
Khalifa	deputy

285

Kif	Moroccan hemp plant: also its chopped leaf product, similar to marijuana
Mahkzen	central government
Marabout	saint, holy man: also his tomb
Mechaouar	palace complex
Medersa	religious high school
Medina	literally, city; in modern parlance, the old city
Mellah	Jewish quarter
Moulay	title of highest respect, reserved for sultans
Muezzin	man who cries the call to prayer from a minaret
'nch Allah	"If God wills it"
Oued	stream or stream bed
Pasha	roughly, mayor
Sidi	title of respect ("Your Honor")
Souk	bazaar; also, stall in the bazaar
Tizi	high mountain pass
Ulema	religious authorities, members of the national Council of Ulema

Bibliography

The literature on Morocco is extensive. I list here only those works
cited directly in the text.

American Jewish Year Book: New York: The American Jewish Committee, *passim.*

Epton, Nina: *Saints and Sorcerers.* London: Cassell, 1958.

Forbes, Rosita: *El Raisuli, Sultan of the Mountains.* London: T. Butterworth, 1924.

Gallagher, Charles: *The United States and North Africa.* Cambridge: Harvard
University Press, 1963.

Geertz, Clifford: *Islam Observed.* New Haven and London: Yale University Press,
1968.

Gunning, Dr. K. F.: *"Demnate, la plus ancienne ville Marocaine." Maroc Tourisme,*
No. 26 (November 1964).

Harris, Walter B.: *France, Spain, and the Rif.* New York: Longmans Green, 1927.

————: *Land of an African Sultan.* London: S. Low, Marston, Seale and Rivington,
1889.

Huxley, Elspeth: *Forks and Hope.* London: Chatto and Windus, 1964.

Jewish Chronicle: London: The Jewish Chronicle, Ltd., *passim.*

Lacouture, J. and S.: *Le Maroc à l'Épreuve.* Paris: Editions du Seuil, 1958.

McNeill, William H.: *The Rise of the West.* Chicago: University of Chicago Press,
1963.

Maxwell, Gavin: *Lords of the Atlas.* New York: E. P. Dutton and Co., 1966.

Roosevelt, Elliott: *As He Saw It.* New York: Duell, Sloan and Pearce, 1946.

Royaume du Maroc: *Annual Reports of the Ministry of Education.* La Promotion
Nationale.

Stevens, Edmund: *North African Powder Keg.* New York: Coward-McCann, 1955.

Sterling, Claire: "Morocco's Troubled Young King." *The Reporter,* June 17, 1965

Zartman, William I.: *Morocco: Problems of New Power.* New York: Atherton
Press, 1964.

Index